# Russia's Youth and its Culture

The political whirlwind that struck Russia in the mid-1980s has fascinated the Western media, but how much do we really know about the dramatic changes that have gripped Russian society and culture?

In this book, Hilary Pilkington applies the methods of cultural studies research to the study of Russian youth. She does this by 'deconstructing' the social discourses within which youth has been constructed and by providing an alternative reading of youth cultural activity, based on an ethnographic study of Moscow youth culture at the end of the 1980s. The book also aims to chart the passage of Western youth cultural studies in the twentieth century and suggests some new ways forward in the light of the study of the Russian experience. To this end, the author traces the changing approaches to the study of youth culture in the Anglo-American tradition and within the Soviet Union, before examining the impact of glasnost on the discussion of youth. Against this background the latter half of the book comprises a study of Moscow's youth cultural groups based on field work and interviews in the city.

The author provides the first ethnographic study of Russian youth culture by a Western academic and places it in the wider field of youth cultural experience. This book will be of great value to students of Russian studies, sociology and cultural studies.

**Hilary Pilkington** is a lecturer in Russian Politics and Society at the Centre for Russian and East European Studies, University of Birmingham.

D0221985

## Related titles

**Moscow Graffiti**
Language and subculture
*John Bushnell*

**Russian Politics and Society**
*Richard Sakwa*

**Soviet Society under Perestroika**
*David Lane*

# Russia's Youth and its Culture

## A nation's constructors and constructed

Hilary Pilkington

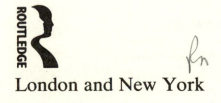

London and New York

First published 1994
by Routledge
11 New Fetter Lane, London EC4P 4EE

Simultaneously published in the USA and Canada
by Routledge
29 West 35th Street, New York, NY 10001

© 1994 Hilary Pilkington

Typeset in Times by Florencetype Limited, Kewstoke,
Avon
Printed and bound in Great Britain by T.J. Press (Padstow)
Ltd, Padstow, Cornwall
Printed on acid free paper

*British Library Cataloguing in Publication Data*

A catalogue record for this book is available from the
British Library

*Library of Congress Cataloging in Publication Data has been
applied for*

ISBN 0-415-09043-1   ISBN 0-415-09044-X (pbk)

For Katya,
without whom this work
would never have begun

# Contents

# Figures and tables

**FIGURES**

**TABLES**

# Acknowledgements

I would like to register my thanks to colleagues at the Centre for Russian and East European Studies, University of Birmingham for their support and advice during the researching and writing of this book. In particular I would like to thank Dr Nick Lampert for his encouragement throughout my time at the Centre, Mr Mike Berry for generously passing on relevant press articles and Dr Linda Edmondson for her support. I would also like to thank Marea Arries, Tricia Carr and Nancy Moore for their patient – and good-humoured – technical help.

Professor Julian Cooper, Dr Richard Johnson, Dr Nick Lampert, Professor Richard Stites and Professor Paul Willis were all kind enough to offer their comments on earlier drafts of this book. I am grateful to them for this, although I take full responsibility myself for the failings of the text as it finally appears.

Much of the research for the book was done in Moscow and would not have been possible without the financial support of the British Council and the academic and moral support of Russian colleagues. In particular I would like to thank Marina Malysheva, Mikhail Topalov, Mikhailina Shibaeva and Valentina Konstantinova for the interest they showed in my work and for being such stimulating interlocutors. Most importantly, the project would have never got off the ground without the help of the young people I interviewed in Moscow, and I thank them for their tolerance of my presence and questions. A special thanks must go to Natasha, Ira and Nadia for their help and encouragement during the Spring and Summer of 1991 and to Katya, Olya, Ira, Zhanna and Valerii for their constant friendship and support. Thanks also to Ira and Natasha for their help in transcribing the tapes and to Susie Reid, Sally Dalton-Brown and Birgitta Yansson for 'being there'.

I would like to thank my family – Malcolm, Mavis, Rachel and Louise – for putting up with my long absences, and my friends – Gill Cooke, Janet Dalton, Janet Handley, Clare Madge and Paul Tann – for being such good ones. Finally, my thanks to Tony for all his help and support, and for keeping me in touch with a reality beyond the *tusovka*.

Hilary Pilkington
Birmingham, January 1993.

# Glossary of abbreviations and terms

Words cited in the text in Russian are transliterated according to the Library of Congress system except where names of individuals or places have become widely known in a different form (e.g. Yeltsin). In order to preserve consistency, where name changes have occurred new names (e.g. St Petersburg not Leningrad, Russian Federation not RSFSR) are used only when a period is referred to after the name change has occurred.

| | |
|---|---|
| *Afgantsy* | Returnees from military service in Afghanistan |
| *apparat* | administrative apparatus (of CPSU, Komsomol etc) |
| BAM | Baikal-Amur Railway |
| *besprizornik* | orphan, waif |
| CPSU | Communist Party of the Soviet Union |
| *dedovshchina* | 'hazing' or bullying in armed services |
| DOSAAF | Voluntary Society for Collaboration with the Army, Air Force and Navy |
| *druzhinniki* | voluntary police |
| *dvor* | courtyard |
| *fartsovshchik* | speculator |
| GAI | traffic police |
| GKChP | State Emergency Committee |
| *khorovod* | round-dance |
| *khozraschet* | cost-accounting or self-financing |
| *kommunalka* | communal flat |
| *Komsomol* | see VLKSM |
| *lichnost'* | personality, individual |
| *limitchik* | Gastarbeiter |
| MZhK | Youth Housing Project |
| *Narkompros* | Commissariat for Education |
| *narod* | the people |
| *neformaly* | informal (non-state) groups |
| NEP | New Economic Policy (1921–8) |
| NTTM | youth scientific-technical production unit |
| *ottepel'* | cultural thaw (under Khrushchev) |

| | |
|---|---|
| *podrostok* | teenager |
| *podval* | basement, cellar |
| *pod"ezd* | entrance-way (to block of flats) |
| *pokolenie* | generation |
| *poshlost'* | banality of everyday life |
| *posidelka* | evening party or working bee |
| *proletkult* | movement for the formation of a proletarian culture |
| *propiska* | residence permit |
| RSDLP | Russian Social Democratic Labour Party |
| RSFSR | Russian Soviet Federal Socialist Republic |
| SNUM | Union of Ukrainian Independent Youth |
| *sotsial'nii zakaz* | demand dictated by socialist development |
| SPTU | vocational technical school |
| *Sputnik* | 'Companion' – name of youth travel agency |
| *subbotnik* | voluntary labour day |
| *uskorenie* | 'acceleration' (economic programme launched by Gorbachev) |
| VKSh | Higher Komsomol School |
| VLKSM | All-Union Leninist Communist Union of Youth, usually shortened to 'Komsomol' |
| VOOPIK | All-Russian Society for the Preservation of Historical and Cultural Monuments |
| *vospitanie* | moral education, upbringing |
| *zastoi* | 'stagnation' |

# Introduction

The research project of which this book is the result was conceived with two goals. First, it aimed to explore how youth (*molodezh'*) had been viewed in Russian society, and the impact of the wider perestroika of society on the theories, institutions and popular beliefs which shaped the youth debate through the Soviet period. The second aim was a more general one of bringing the study of Russian society into the mainstream of cultural studies by utilizing the new opportunities for conducting research in and on Russia. To this end an ethnographic study of the Moscow youth cultural scene was conducted in order to begin to develop an understanding of how Russian youth constructs its own cultural worlds. In the field of Russian studies, this kind of empirical study, aimed at uncovering the experience of the subjects of Russian society, should complement existing political systems approaches and policy-orientated studies. It was also hoped that the study of Russian youth culture might add to contemporary debates in cultural studies; whilst the work of the ethnographer is highly specific, the wider study of European societies, whose experience both compares and contrasts with that of Anglo-North American societies, can only enhance the understanding of systems of cultural production and reproduction.

For many readers, these two aims will sit unhappily together since they are achieved via a peculiar mixture of textual deconstruction and ethnographic 'reconstruction'. Chapter 6 outlines some of the author's own misgivings about this, but also her conviction that, whilst telling us much about how the dominant culture conceives of youth, deconstruction work alone would leave the cultural practice of young people largely unexplained. The lack of methodological purity, it is hoped, will in the final instance facilitate rather than hinder understanding.

Since the book has two such disparate aims, it also has diverse audiences and for this reason has been structured in such a way as to allow readers to use the book as their own interests dictate. Chapter 1 provides a concise outline of the development of youth cultural theory in the West – its primary purpose is to provide readers unfamiliar with Western cultural studies with the background necessary to render comprehensible the analysis undertaken in Part III. As such it may be used purely as reference or read in its entirety. For those whose interest is comparative youth cultural studies, the chapter should provide a useful summary of the genesis and development of the study of youth culture as well as raising some of the problems of comparative study which will be encountered later in the book. Chapter 2 traces the chief paradigms in which youth and its culture have been framed in Soviet society. This will set the cultural context for those readers with a minimal knowledge of Russian/Soviet society by indicating its key institutional forces as well as giving a sense of continuity and change over time. The chapter will also address the issue of the interaction of ideology and reality by questioning how monolithic these paradigms were. The chapter is thus essential background to the more detailed study of the impact of perestroika on the paradigms framing the understanding of youth culture in the former Soviet Union set out in Part II of the book.

The second part of the study begins with Chapter 3 whose focus is the impact of glasnost and party self-criticism on the breadth of discussion of youth cultural activity. The 1985–6 period, it is argued, marked only a partial break with past paradigms through its self-limiting exposé of the 'real conditions' of Soviet society which were thought to be rectifiable by means of an improvement in the ideological work of the existing institutions and the more effective control of youth. Chapter 4 considers the period of democratization (1987–9) and the turning point this marked in the discussion of youth culture. In this period the youth debate became politicized around the issue of the 'informal groups' (*neformaly*) whose activity was at one and the same time encouraged, as evidence of vital independent initiative, but also perceived as potentially threatening to the pre-defined goals of perestroika and to social unity itself. The 'differentiated approach' which emerged to deal with this contradiction inherent in the Gorbachevian notion of democratization is discussed with particular reference to the emergence of an important new input into the youth debate: that of the criminologists. Chapter 5 follows through the paradigm switch which had begun in the previous period by charting the collapse of the Young Communist League and with it the youth paradigms of the Soviet period. The emergence of new institutional and ideological frameworks to house the youth debate is outlined to show how the vision of youth as the vanguard of the construction of communism was finally laid to rest and replaced by the use of youth as a social metaphor for a collapsing society and an object of a paternal social policy. Attention is also paid to the new divergence in academic studies as socio-psychological and criminological studies of youth groups began to challenge the more traditional sociological, classificatory studies.

Part III of the book aims to balance the macro approach of Parts I and II by considering the cultural practices of Moscow youth cultural groups over the period 1988–91. Chapter 6 outlines the conception of the research project as a cross-cultural, urban ethnography and the problems encountered in its realization, while Chapter 7 paints the broader picture of the Moscow youth cultural world at this point in time. The latter includes a brief description of the chief youth cultural trends and their interrelationship. The map is essentially that of the informants themselves (a brief profile of whom is given in the Appendix), although some background information is drawn from Soviet academic literature. Chapter 8 offers an analysis of the youth cultural practices of young people in Moscow based on ethnographic data collected over two periods of study in Moscow (September 1988 to June 1989 and March to September 1991). The empirical material gathered is analysed: synchronically (how the youth cultural world is structured); diachronically (by following the life history of a particular group); and from a gender perspective. By guiding the reader around the cultural symbols and practices of the Moscow youth cultural world, key themes are pinpointed in the experience of Moscow youth that may be compared to the experience of youth elsewhere in Russia, and the world. A glossary of youth cultural slang is included at the end of the book in order to facilitate the reading process.

Despite its broad scope, the book of course remains partial. It makes no claims to explain the experience of 'normal' (i.e. non subcultural) youth and, in this sense, is open to the same criticism to which it subjects past youth cultural studies. Moreover, the in-depth study which is the subject of Part III of the book focuses on Moscow – the most unrepresentative of all cities – and a particular subcultural group characterized by an unusual gender balance and an upward orientation not typical of Russian provincial youth culture. This very abnormality, however, was integral to the project. As is explained in Chapter 6, since this kind of ethnographic study is as much about researching the researcher as the 'objects' of interest, the cultural overlap which existed was an important facilitator of the research. Furthermore, for practical reasons, it was impossible to attempt a study of provincial youth culture. When the first period of field work was undertaken in 1988–9, the future of reform was still highly uncertain and the ethnographic work was done whilst officially engaged in a study of press representations of the *neformaly*. Applications to visit the city of Kazan' (where provincial gang fighting was at its height) were twice refused and a private visit that had been arranged was blocked by 'visa problems'. Times have, of course, changed and cooperation with Russian academics in this area would probably now be welcomed, although, arguably, such work would be best left to them.

The partiality of the case study, however, need not mean that no conclusions can be drawn other than for those few people at that particular time. The relations of gender, class (centre–periphery) and race, which were shown to be central to the structuring of the Moscow youth cultural world provide important markers for future studies in different times and places. As market reform continues to penetrate newly independent

Russia in an uneven way, these relations are likely to become even more important and to require significantly greater attention than they have received here. In particular the importance of consumption, changing regional and national identities and the interaction with global youth cultures need urgent study.

The fact that the combined impact of the policies of glasnost, democratization and economic reform gradually whittled away the foundations of the youth discourse that heralded Soviet young people as the constructors of the new society, however, does not mean that young people in Russia today are a lost generation caught between the past and the future. As the constructors of Brezhnev's road to nowhere, young people were at best the pseudo-subjects of social relations. The spaces they created for themselves in the mid- to late-1980s allowed them to regain a sense of movement and creation, of belonging and identity. Although these spaces were never free or separate from the structures of the dominant culture, they did allow different interpretations to flourish. As the new economic and political system becomes rooted, these spaces are rapidly closing. In Moscow, the peculiar forms of youth culture have already lost much of their distinctiveness as they have been increasingly infiltrated by global drug and music cultures. This renders the present study of a tiny part of that culture all the more timely, whilst simultaneously indicating the need to move on, from what is now the past of Russian youth, to look at its present and possible futures.

# Part I

# Youth and youth culture: theoretical paradigms

# 1 On the road to nowhere?

## Understanding youth culture in the West

It is not the aim of this first chapter to provide an exhaustive critique of studies of youth culture in the West – for this the reader shall be directed elsewhere.[1] What is attempted is an outline of the main discourses on youth and its cultures, indicating their academic and institutional origins, their paths of development and their common themes. For many readers this will be very familiar ground, but it is essential to map out the territory anew before stepping out into a less familiar cultural context. The theoretical debates raised in this chapter will be dealt with briefly and will be confined to those issues which re-emerge as key themes in the youth culture debate in the former Soviet Union or which frame the analysis of the empirical material in Part III of the book. For readers who are unfamiliar with the Western academic debate around youth and its culture, the chapter will act as a basic introduction to Western theories providing a framework for further reading.

The simplest and clearest way of mapping the field, would be to present a chronological review of academic study of youth culture, indicating the way in which such studies have reflected the concerns of contemporary society. Whilst this approach might provide the most authentic historical account of the development of Anglo-American studies of youth, it would not readily facilitate the exploration of cross-cultural themes. At the risk of de-contextualization, therefore, the chapter is structured according to key themes in the discussion of youth and its culture. The focus is the academic discourse on youth, but attention is also paid to the influence of other discourses, such as medicine, law and order, economics and politics. These themes are not always concurrent, however, and the discussion aims to incorporate a sense of change over time by rooting the discourses in the material conditions of changing social relations and their institutional representations (prisons, psychiatric hospitals, schools, training colleges and schemes, youth magazines and fashion commodities). The chapter concludes with an evaluation of the debate on contemporary youth culture and asks whether the path that has been traced through the theoretical minefield of contemporary cultural studies has opened up new horizons for research and understanding, or left the academic community stranded on the 'road to nowhere'.

## YOUTH IN THE CITY: SUBCULTURES AND DELINQUENCY

The discussion of youth culture began with the discovery of 'youth' as an independent socio-demographic category with its own distinct ways of life. The material conditions for this lay in the displacement of youth from the controlled environment of rural communities to newly developed urban spaces. In England the process of rapid urbanization had begun with the enclosures[2], which gradually transformed peasants into wage-labourers, disrupted the traditional pattern of inheritance and pushed young labourers into the new towns and cities (Gillis 1974: 41). The first recognition of youth as a peculiar social group, therefore, was in a period of social upheaval with accompanying moral uncertainty. This manifested itself in a fear that, in the absence of the peer and elder guidance to which they had been subjected in the villages, society would lose control of its new urban youth. The Elizabethan Poor Laws constituted an early attempt to limit and manage the social dislocation caused by heavy rural–urban migration, and as early as 1555, London's Bridewell had been constructed in order to control the vagrant bands of young people who begged, stole and prostituted themselves on the city streets. This was England's first institution designed exclusively to control and contain destitute, handicapped, vagrant and orphaned youth (Brake 1985: 30).

According to Gillis, however, it was in the period 1770–1870 that urban, working-class youth gangs – based on neighbourhood affiliation and vying for supremacy and control of territory and courtship – emerged as the basic unit of youth culture (Gillis 1974: 62). Some of these gangs bore the characteristics of modern urban subcultures – the London costermongers of the mid-nineteenth century for example, and, in the latter part of the century, the Birmingham 'peaky blinders' and 'sloggers' and the Manchester 'scuttlers' and 'Ikey lads' (Blanch 1979: 103–4). Another of these early subcultures – the 'hooligans' – were to remain embedded in popular consciousness as a symbol of the English culture that was not spoken: working-classness, loss of control, riotousness and youthful defiance of authority. The hooligans[3] became widely known following the arrest of large numbers of people for drunkenness, disorderly conduct, brawling, assaults on police officers and street robberies during the August Bank Holiday festivities in 1898 (Pearson 1983: 74). Subsequently, the hooligan gangs came to be associated with street battles between themselves (street against street) and assaults on outsiders including cafe and bar staff, the police and innocent passers-by (76). According to Pearson, the original 'hooligans' were not just a disparate mob of bored teenagers, but a distinctive youth culture who had adopted a uniform dress-style: bell-bottom trousers narrowing at the knee and with a buttoned vent in the leg, colourful neck-scarves, caps, heavy boots (with steel toe-caps), studded leather belts, and a characteristic 'donkey fringe' haircut (92–6). This is borne out by Roberts writing from his own childhood memories of the Manchester scuttlers. According to Roberts, although the initial brutality of gang fighting of the late nineteenth century diminished, nevertheless, street battles between gangs named after their street continued until the First World War. Certain streets, where fighting was notoriously bad, had to be avoided at night for fear of attack (Roberts 1971: 123). But the establishment of territory was not the only purpose of the street gang – it also constituted a communal gathering which had great social, cultural and economic importance, providing a space for working-class lads to discuss wages, work, politics and sex (124).

The concern registered about the hooligans, and other urban, youth subcultures, was clearly a concern for law and order. But the prevention of crime was not the only reason for the articulation of the hooligan subculture through the law and order discourse. Although increased delinquency was recorded in crime statistics, Gillis argues that this was to be explained by the widening of the definition of delinquency (to include many peer-group street activities) rather than an actual rise in violence and crime (Gillis 1974: 176). In fact, the street pick-pocketing and other petty crime practised by peer-group gangs like the hooligans was only one part of their distinct way of life which appeared threatening to the social and moral order. The real issue concerned the social control of a potentially rebellious and dissolute working-class youth. As had been made clear by the Bank Holiday disorder of 1898, which made notorious the hooligans, the existing agents of social control in the city – the police (or 'rozzers') – often incited rather than prevented disturbances since they aroused much hostility from the urban, working population (Pearson 1983: 74; Roberts 1971: 129). A second central theme of the law and order discourse on youth, therefore, was the promotion of new urban-based organizations of social control, which, it was hoped, would take the place of the traditional, rural mechanisms. Between 1890 and 1914, a whole host of such organizations emerged in Britain, including the Church Lads' Brigade, the Boys' Brigade, Army and Naval Cadets, the Young Men's Christian Association, the Street Children's Union, the Manchester Lads' Clubs and the Scout and Guide movement (Blanch 1979: 105).

One final issue raised by the discussion of these early delinquent subcultures is the question of cause and effect, i.e. whether delinquent behaviour was a socio-psychological characteristic of the young urban working class which elicited a controlling response from the state, or whether pressures to conform to state-preferred patterns of behaviour resulted in a collective opposition or resistance from working-class youth. Gillis, for example, argues that juvenile delinquency itself was evidence of the *resistance* of working-class youth to a middle-class image of the model adolescent which was being foisted upon them and which included attempts to redefine their leisure spaces away from the street (Gillis 1974: 137). The themes of subcultures as units of adolescent problem-solving and as forms of working-class resistance were to become recurrent themes of sociological understandings of youth subcultures.

### Slums, street corners and gangs: the city as living organism

In the inter-war years a series of studies of the internal structure and the cultural practices of urban gangs were undertaken in the United States. This research was conducted as part of the development of a new school of thought in urban sociology known as the Chicago School. The Chicago School approach (or social ecology model) was based on applying the principles of ecological stability in the natural world to the urban environment; it suggested that there was a pattern to urban development which mirrored that in the plant world. Urban districts grew up not arbitrarily but around important resources (natural or man-made) and, as the city grew, the natural location of populations around their places of work became threatened by the competition resulting from population growth. As a result, central locations became affordable only for business and industry and the affluent population moved out to the suburban areas leaving the less well off and new urban immigrants to compete for increasingly run-down and inadequate housing in the central area (the inner city). Since such urban in-migration was related to wider patterns of immigration into the United States, the internal community organization of different ethnic groups became an important element of these studies of ghettoes and slums and their distinct ways of life.

The social ecology model was premised on the notion that the pattern of urban development described had significant social implications: the equilibrium of the community was disturbed as neighbourhoods were 'invaded' by new immigrants leading to the loss of the norms of social control. This 'social disorganization' was manifest in the activity of delinquent gangs, and empirical studies of such gangs were conducted in order to describe how the delinquent tradition or subculture was passed through generations of young people in the slum areas of American cities (Downes 1966: 25).

Delinquent activity was not the only activity of the gang, however. The social ecology model was also adopted by those who were interested in the 'street corner groups'. Thrasher's 1927 study of gangs in Chicago, for example, indicated that although fighting and conflict (both between gangs and with the police) was an important element of gang activity, it was only one of many. His description of the 'Dirty Dozen' gang showed that they participated in various sporting activities such as football, swimming and athletics, in peripheral economic activities (dealing in alcohol and junk) and simply gathered at the pool hall either to play or to chat (Thrasher 1963: 37–40). The structure and traditions of the gang are not developed solely in order to facilitate effective gang-fighting, therefore, but also express the 'spirit of the group'. From his study of street corner groups in 'Cornerville', William Foot Whyte concluded that it was not so much that the slum district of Cornerville was a 'disorganized community' but that its own social organization failed to mesh with the structure of the society around it (Whyte 1955: 272–3). His description of the workings of the gang he observed suggests a high degree of internal stability based on commitment to the peer group from childhood, a system of mutual obligation and a strong leader (256). The problem, as he saw it, was that the notoriety of the district as disordered, lawless and *Italian* prevented the lads of Cornerville getting onto even the first rung of the social mobility ladder that American society so valued (273).

The second input into theories of delinquent youth stems from the functionalist sociological approach, which will be dealt with in a more integrated fashion below. This model also associated delinquent or deviant behaviour with the loss of norms or social control resulting from a disruption of social stability. The difference lies in the explanation of the origins of social disruption, which depends not on models of the natural world but is borrowed from Durkheim's concept of anomie.

In its basic formulation anomie describes an environment or situation in which social norms have lost their hold over individuals' actions, and Durkheim argued that this disorientation of the individual was an important element of modern society. Robert Merton took up Durkheim's notion to explain deviant or delinquent behaviour, which, he argued, was the result of anomie arising from the gap between aspirations in modern, consumer society and actual possibilities or opportunities for their realization. However, anomie, and thus delinquent behaviour, was clearly not universal in modern society, it took root amongst those who had the least opportunity to realize their internalized achievement orientations – those from deprived areas, ghettoes or slums. The reasons for this, according to Sutherland, were to be found in 'differential association'. In other words, it was the group of people with whom one associated which determined whether or not one adopted a career in crime (Downes 1966: 97). Glaser adapted the notion of differential association in a way which emphasized not the determining role of the environment but the choice of the individual actor. He argued that the individual interacts with both criminals and non-criminals – thus it is the level of identification that the individual has with real or imaginary persons in the criminal world which is important. In this way, a delinquent or criminal subculture can provide an alternative, and positive, identity for the adolescent (Brake 1985: 47).

The notion that young people opted for deviant behaviour rather than being inherently delinquent (as a result of certain psychological factors) or conditioned into delinquency (as a result of social deprivation) was largely a product of ethnographic studies of delinquent gangs, which emphasized the activities rather than the motivations of such gangs. One example of this was Albert Cohen's study of gang culture. Cohen rejected explanations of delinquency based on the break-down of social norms on the grounds that: slum or ghetto areas are not 'jungles' where community organization and control had broken down; and that even if community controls had failed to restrain delinquent behaviour, the question of the origin of this behaviour remained unexplained except by psychological predisposition (Cohen, A. 1955: 33). For Cohen the essence of the juvenile delinquent subculture was the collective definition of a cultural solution to a shared problem; the problem was 'status' (66). Cohen explained the higher rates of delinquency among lower socio-economic status adolescents by their internalization of middle-class status values combined with their disadvantaged starting point in gaining that status (119). Richard Cloward and Lloyd Ohlin's study of delinquent gangs also saw young people as seeking to fulfil aspirations not realized through the usual channels such as the education system. Such people often sought 'legitimate' alternatives, by aspiring to become sports or entertainment stars, for example, but when pressures from blocked opportunity became sufficiently intense, many adopted illegitimate alternatives (Cloward and Ohlin 1960: 104–5).

Cohen's view that dominant middle-class norms were internalized by working-class adolescents was given some support by the work of Matza and Sykes, but also subjected to revision. Matza's focus on delinquents' own explanations of their actions led him to suggest that juvenile delinquents did not invert or reject conventional morality, but 'neutralized' their deviations from it through learnt techniques of justification and denial of responsibility for deviant acts (Matza and Sykes 1957: 664–7). As Brake notes in his discussion of Matza's later work, this suggested that juvenile delinquents were not rejecting dominant values but taking up sub-themes (such as hedonism, disdain for work, aggression, violence and masculinity) which were present throughout society, but not part of the official value system (Brake 1985: 55). Furthermore, the delinquent was not predisposed towards deviancy, nor driven into it by social circumstance, but consciously chose this behavioural pattern as the most attractive available (56).

A second challenge to Cohen's theorization of the delinquent subculture came from the findings of ethnographic work conducted in slum areas of Britain by David Downes. His studies of two areas of London refuted Cohen's hypothesis that juvenile delinquency was related to the prior existence of a delinquent subculture, and suggested that criminal behaviour resulted less from 'status frustration' than from 'a process of dissociation from middle-class dominated contexts of school, work and recreation' (Downes 1966: 257). The relative absence in British society of the 'illegitimate opportunity structure' described by Cloward and Ohlin had prevented the emergence of criminal subcultures (134) and thus, Downes argued, the failure to reach middle-class standards by the English 'corner boy' led not to frustration or alienation but to a reaffirmation of working-class values (258). As will become clear from the discussion below, the primacy of class over urban space in the theorization of youth subcultures marks a major divergence between British and American subculturalists.

This difference of emphasis can be seen in the later work of American sociologist Claude Fischer who, although dropping the focus on delinquency, retained the notion of a direct relationship between urbanization and 'unconventionality' (often labelled as deviant behaviour) over and above the differences attributable to those of age, ethnicity, life cycle and social class (Fischer 1975: 1321). Fischer maintained that as population size increased, so did subcultural variation among its groups, and as urbanization intensified, so did subcultural activity. Although the intensification of subcultures (fostered and consolidated by the emergence of institutions and services such as dress-styles, newspapers, associations) took place alongside a cultural diffusion, Fischer argued that the processes of consolidation and diffusion did not simply act to negate each other. This was because the core values of the subculture were shored up by the process of intensification, whilst modification and change occurred at the periphery through the process of diffusion (1326–34). Hence, higher rates of deviance and disorganization were found in cities, but these should not be accounted for by alienation, anonymity and impersonality, but by the congregation of 'critical masses' sufficient to maintain viable unconventional subcultures (1320). This kind of relationship between urbanization and subcultural activity was an important development since it provided for a more positive notion of subculture, as indicative not of the breakdown of community, but of the creation of smaller communities for those whose integration into mainstream society was only partial. In other words the city could be liberating as well as alienating since it might provide spaces for gay, Bohemian, radical political and other subcultures.

Fischer's questioning of the natural relationship between subculture and deviancy indicates the growing influence of a new school of thought in the debate about deviant and delinquent behaviour – that of transactionalism or labelling theory. Although such approaches – which suggested that deviance was not a psychological predisposition but a learnt behaviour pattern induced by societal labelling of the individual as deviant – were generally employed in the study of more mundane manifestations of juvenile delinquency, they occasionally also appeared in the study of spectacular youth cultures. The clearest example of this is to be found in Stanley Cohen's classic study of society's reaction to the clashes between mods and rockers in 1960s Britain, *Folk Devils and Moral Panics*. Cohen's examination of the reaction of the mass media, the public and the agencies of social control showed how initially scattered and unspectacular incidences of fighting between youths shaped a social phenomenon – a 'moral panic' – of national proportions. Moreover, this societal reaction actually encouraged deviance and violence as well as giving much greater structural cohesion to the mods and the rockers and succeeded in bringing the arch enemies together against the community. It did this through: the mass media's publicizing of a deviant role model (the creation of mods and rockers as 'folk devils' necessitated detailed descriptions of the kind of behaviour in which they indulged as well as the symbols by which they could be recognized); raising social tension by creating an expectation of trouble and an audience for deviance; and by the arbitrary and discriminatory treatment meted out to mods and rockers by agencies of social control (Cohen, S. 1987: 175–6). Although (in the second edition of the book) Cohen criticized himself for having originally concentrated too much on the 'reaction' at the expense of the 'action' (on the moral panic rather than the folk devil), his work remains a classic study of the interaction between the means of mass communication and the formation of youth subcultures. For this reason, in Chapter 4, some of Cohen's methods and conclusions will be taken up in an analysis of the role of the mass media, the *Komsomol* (Communist Youth League), the police and academia in the emergence of one particular subcultural form in the former Soviet Union.

## 'THE GENERATION GAME': YOUTH AND THE STRUCTURAL FUNCTIONALISTS

The 'delinquent' behaviour of young people was capable of unleashing such popular moral panics because of the symbolic importance youth held; the future health of society depended upon the moral health of its youth. This symbolic importance had its roots in biology since youth was seen as a distinct social category because of the physical and psychological characteristics it displayed. Youth marked the transition from the irresponsibility of childhood to the responsibility of adulthood, involving the passing through puberty to sexual maturity, adjustment from child to adult roles and the transition from emotional dependence to independence. The sociological recognition of youth as a distinct category was also determined by the growth of the discourses of psychology and pedagogy. In these discourses youth (or, more usually, in this context adolescence) might be experienced by young people as a period of 'storm and stress' resulting in rebellion or resistance to the adult world for which they were being prepared. Consequently, it became a common-sense notion that this period of the life cycle was a difficult one and that, for its duration, young people required adult guidance (parental, school, medical, or state institutional) to keep them on track.

For social scientists, however, 'youth' was not only an individual, psychological experience but a social one and this gave rise to a second important sociological category, that of 'generation'. A generation was a social group created as a result of the common experience of this period of the life cycle and, in a rapidly modernizing society, each generation was seen to be distinct from that before and after it. The concept of the generation helped to explain key social processes, especially those of continuity and rupture. Modern industrial societies were seen as far more complex than traditional ones, in which the end of childhood was marked simply by ritual or celebration when the new member took up her/his ascribed place in adult society. In contrast, in modern industrial societies, the roles performed within the family were no longer harmonious with the wider social system and thus identification with members of the family did not ensure the attainment of full social maturity and status in the social system. Consequently, age-homogeneous groups arose to satisfy the needs of individuals for role performance based on ascriptive, diffuse, universalistic and solidary criteria (Eisenstadt 1956: 54). Thus age groups might facilitate the continuity and stability of the social system, acting as one of the main channels for the transmission of social heritage, since they constituted an interlinking sphere between the family and other institutionalized spheres of society (political, economic, etc). But alongside this integrative function they might have a 'disintegrative function' manifest in deviant peer groups (Eisenstadt 1956: 270–1).

The role of generations in history is associated with the work of Karl Mannheim. Mannheim saw generation not as a mechanical product of biology (being born at a certain time), but as a social construct formed by historical conjuncture and, consequently, generational consciousness was taken to be more prevalent in periods of rapid social change or instability. Mannheim's notion of generational consciousness indicated his belief that change was not only reflected but also effected by youth and he explicitly rejected any kind of social Darwinism which envisaged generations as simply stepping-stones down the road of progress. On the contrary, certain generations could act in a reactionary manner, while others could throw up revolutionary or utopian movements. Moreover, according to Mannheim, segments of a generation (generation units) often experienced the same concrete historical problems in very different ways and the potential of generational location was far from always realized (Mannheim 1927: 304, 309). Nevertheless, the generational dimension of society remained an important factor 'impinging upon the social process' (320).

It is in the degree of agency accorded to the social category of generation that Mannheim diverged from the notion of generation employed by structural functionalists such as Parsons and Eisenstadt. Eisenstadt, for example, explicitly stated that, 'It is not the relations between ages which explain change or stability in societies, but change in societies which explains relations between different ages' (Eisenstadt cited in Allen 1968: 321). This divergence becomes still clearer when the notion of youth culture is considered. Mannheim, basing his understanding on the student unrest after the First World War and the counter-culture that emerged and rejected the Old Germany, saw ideas and symbols being used in the formulation of distinct generational identities which were in conflict with others (Cohen, P. 1986: 25). In contrast, Parsons saw youth culture as a key aspect of the socialization process and thus as a mechanism of *maintaining social stability* rather than bringing about social change.

This notion of youth culture as a mechanism of acculturation or socialization must be viewed within the context of Parsons' work as a whole, the aim of which was to explain how society functioned as a social system. His explanation pointed to subsystems in society which develop in order to meet the requirements of the system if it is to survive. These functional prerequisites were adaptation, goal attainment, integration and pattern maintenance. Thus Parsons' approach was termed 'structural-functionalist' since it envisaged society as a system whose component parts could be analysed (structuralism), whilst at the same time seeing those parts as functioning to readjust, reintegrate and restore balance in a way similar to an organic or biological system (functionalism). Youth and youth culture is significant in the grand theory of Parsons in that it reveals some of the structural tensions in the transition from traditional to modern society. Youth is seen to be located at the maximum point of tension between the two value systems of traditional and modern society since the roles the child learns in the family no longer match the adult roles which she/he must adopt in wider society. Youth subcultures, according to Parsons may simply express a rejection of traditional values, but more usually they have 'important positive functions in easing the transition from the security of childhood to that of full adult in marriage and occupational status' (Parsons 1942: 101). In providing this bridge to adulthood, however, these subcultures may also transform the traditional value system where it has become outdated. Thus they not only allowed the socialization into the existing adult world but secured the future of that world through adaptation.

It was Eisenstadt, however, who most consistently developed the functionalist approach to youth and its cultures. Eisenstadt argued that youth culture played a major role in the preparation (or socialization) of young people for the world beyond the family. It did so because it created a set of values, attitudes and behavioural norms that engendered a sense of power lost by young people because of their marginal socio-economic and cultural position in modern society (Frith, 1984: 20). Young people were thus seen to be seeking a collective cultural solution to a socio-economic status problem, and the form that solution took was viewed as more or less irrelevant. Hence, an important implication of the functionalist approach is that it leads to an undifferentiated notion of youth culture. For structural functionalists, there is no need to talk of youth cultures, only youth culture, for whether skin or punk, mod or rocker, participation in youth culture is essentially a psychological not an economic or political act.

This socio-psychological (rooted in the biological) reading of youth cultural activity is evident in another key concept of the functionalist interpretation of youth culture; the 'peer group'. Peer groups were seen as important to young people not because they gave access to the creation or adoption of new values but because they offered a new way of *placing oneself in the world* and, once the transition to adult status had been achieved, they became redundant. The peer group was simply a facilitator which helped smooth the transition from particularistic to universalistic values, from a social world in which decisions were made by reference to parental authority and family tradition to a social world in which decisions must be referred to universally agreed, rational principles (22).

For Parsons, Eisenstadt and other structural functionalists, therefore, no matter how bizarre or deviant the youth cultural activity might appear, its function was essentially adaptive (Cohen, P. 1986: 10). Society was seen as a set of interrelated subsystems which worked as a functioning whole; school prepared the young person for the world of work, her/his positioning in the latter determined the stratification system which in turn influenced the political system. It is this tendency to interpret all action as functional – as working towards the achievement of the stability and goals of the social whole – which has been the major source of criticism of Parsons and other structural functionalists (Craib 1984: 50). However, the specific case of youth culture reveals how functionalists were also looking at the tensions and strains in the functioning of the social whole and at the importance of the cultural sphere in providing a means of limiting those strains (as in making the transition from child to adult roles). That functional explanations can show *dys*function as well as function was evident in Merton's contribution to subcultural theory and was taken up by his fellow anthropologist Margaret Mead, who saw a deep dysfunction in contemporary socialization practices. Mead argued that the extraordinary developments which had taken place in the mid-twentieth century (including the splitting of the atom, massive population growth, environmental devastation and the forging of a single global community through communications developments) had brought about 'a drastic, irreversible division between the generations' (Mead 1972: 87–8). For Mead not even new forms of peer-group socialization were adequate for this new society in which the knowledge and experience of parents was no longer relevant as a role model for the young.

Mead's universalization of cultural processes reveals traces of a second important criticism levelled at the structural-functionalist approach; the replacement of class by generation as the primary social category. This tendency led to a vision of youth culture as undifferentiated, involving, as it did for Parsons, the temporary rejection of adult responsibilities and work ethic in a period of pre-adult hedonism. Working-class youth cultures were not examined by Parsons at all and, from the 1950s, even middle-class youth was seen to be moving towards greater acceptance of the achievement and performance values of the middle-class, dominant culture. Hence, Brake argues, by 1962 Parsons had moved from his original view of youth culture as 'a compulsive independence of, and antagonism to, adult expectations and authority' combined with 'a compulsive conformity' to the peer group, to a notion of youth culture where peer group loyalty remained strong, but youth had become more responsive to conservative adult control, and hence more integrated into adult mainstream culture (Brake 1985: 40).

## FROM JUKE-BOX TO KARAOKE: YOUTH AS CONSUMER

The structural functionalists were not alone in their portrayal of post-war youth as a more or less passive receiver of the dominant culture. Parsons' picture of youth culture reflected the new social climate of the post-war period characterized by notions of the affluent society, the right to leisure as well as labour, and the expression of self through consumption. One of the key players in this affluent society was the 'teenager'. The teenager was a new social phenomenon and seen as a direct product of the new society characterized by: a greater disposable income; a reduction in working hours (and concomitant increase in leisure time); rapidly expanding leisure and entertainments industries, and an elongation of the period of youth due to the extension of compulsory schooling and increase in the opportunities for further education. Thus the teenager – or rather the teenage consumer – came to be seen as a key economic actor, developing particularly teenage patterns of consumption. Using general consumer surveys, Mark Abrams argued that teenage consumption was peculiarly highly concentrated in the areas of clothing and footwear, alcohol and tobacco, sweets, snacks and eating out, and entertainment products such as tickets for cinema and dance halls, magazines, paperbacks and records (Abrams 1959: 10).

Perhaps the most important implication of the teenage consumer was that she/he was seen to be consuming not only the products of the rapidly expanding service industries, but culture itself. According to Abrams, the teenage market was also characterized by its patronage of the mass media – especially the cinema (14),[4] and this, coupled with the biologically essentialist notions of youth discussed above, led to a belief that young people not only consumed goods but were consumed by the goods. Abrams also suggested that because young people were intensely preoccupied with discovering their identities and establishing new relations with peers and members of the opposite sex, the teenage market was highly volatile and teenagers were looking for consumer goods which were 'emotionally charged' (19). The implication of those who were critical of the new society was that young people were not rational consumers of products for pleasure, but manipulated consumers of image.

The mindless consumption by youth of mass media products and images was particularly associated with the arrival of rock 'n' roll and the youth cultures which developed around it. Prior to this there were fan cultures around individual film stars but rock 'n' roll was the first cultural form to be transmitted through all the new means of mass communication and the films, magazines and memorabilia of its stars marked a new stage in cultural production and consumption. The packaging of individual singers which began with Elvis Presley produced an unending stream of consumer goods to collect, swop, talk about and otherwise consume. Of course teenagers were not the only members of the new affluent society involved in the consuming process – but they were seen to be most at danger from it. Since they were still forming their own moral codes, teenagers could be more easily influenced by those embedded in the media images they were busily consuming. Consequently an important part of the teenager discourse on youth was its association with hooliganism, delinquent behaviour and amorality. Key in this association was the teddy boy youth culture which was the outward manifestation of youth's adoption of rock 'n' roll. According to Richard Bradley, it was the teds who made the crucial link in the public mind between rock 'n' roll, gang fighting, promiscuity and general delinquent behaviour following the riots at cinemas showing the film *Rock Around The Clock* (Bradley 1992: 86).

For Europeans the cultural consumption associated with the arrival of rock 'n' roll (films, records, juke-box cafes and milk bars, brilliantine and bobby sox) had a second association: that of America and Americanization. Even ted style – generally traced to the adoption of Edwardian dress – took a good deal of inspiration from the American western 'city slicker villain' (Frith 1983: 184). The importance of this association should not be underestimated in considering how the notion of the teenager was used in the theorization of youth in the post-war period. The globalization of culture which had arrived on the back of developments in media technology led to the loss of a sense of differentiation, a 'massification' of culture, which was resented by those who retained a notion of high culture, but also by those who were at the forefront of the project of creating new and wider understandings of what constituted culture, such as Richard Hoggart.[5] Hoggart portrayed the young people who frequented the new juke-box cafes as a worrying portent of the new 'machine-minding' working class whose average representative was a 'hedonistic but passive barbarian who rides in a fifty-horse-power bus for threepence, to see a five-million-dollar film for one-and-eightpence' (Hoggart 1957: 250). But for Hoggart, this 'barbarianism' was not the pre-cultural one of an unenlightened underclass, but a post-cultural one of a youth dazzled by the neon lights of America. His description of the new youth culture was of teenage lads sporting 'drape-suits, picture ties and an American slouch' centring their lives around the juke-box in the local milk bars which reeked of a 'spiritual dry-rot amid the odour of boiled milk' (248).

Hoggart's vivid portrayal of the changes in culture among the working class of the industrial towns of Northern England brought to life elements of mass culture or mass society theories being developed by Marxist thinkers on the continent. The key concept for critical theorists of the Frankfurt School concerned with the critique of culture in developed capitalist societies was that of the 'culture industry'. The culture industry was used by Horkheimer and Adorno to describe the way in which cultural products had been turned into commodities for the extraction of profit and were used by those holding property and power to control individual consciousness and thus defend the status quo (Held 1980: 90). Mass culture in modern society (television, film, radio, newspapers and magazines, best-sellers and popular music) was not a culture *of* the masses (i.e. a popular culture), but *for* the masses since the culture industry did not respond to cultural demands but manufactured those demands. Moreover, the cultural forms created – which were standardized, unoriginal, conventional, undemanding and even soporific – acted to produce set responses, recognition and affirmation and thus reduce criticism and resistance (101–4).

The work of the critical theorists on mass culture must be seen within the context of their wider concern with new social and cultural forms developing in the transition period from early to late capitalism. Central to this theorization was that the fashion, music and entertainments industries were founded on new narcissistic pleasure principles which allied self-gratification with particular commodity forms and which – following the breakdown of the traditional patriarchal structuring of the family as portrayed by Freud – were centred on pre-oedipal subjectivities (Cohen, P. 1986: 43–5). Not all critical theorists were so damning of popular cultural forms, however. Walter Benjamin saw the new technologies of cultural production as the raw materials with which each new generation (through fantasy, play and imaginary vision) envisages and creates its own future out of its own past (50). Hence, far from ensnaring the masses, the culture industry had a radical potential.

In contrast to the structural-functionalist discourse on youth culture, therefore, the mass culture debates were very closely concerned with the category of class. The teenager debate evoked a general concern with the moral implications of the growth of consumption – not least because, as Abrams put it, 'not far short of 90 per cent of all teenage spending is conditioned by working-class taste and values' (Abrams 1959: 13). From the other side of the fence, Hoggart's pessimistic view of the changing nature of working-class culture in the post-war period suggested the whittling away of authentic working-class culture as the tabloid press and other forms of mass communication began to bind the working class not only physically, but mentally to their subordinate social position.[6]

Critiques of mass culture, then, have not been forgotten, but their focus has moved from its production to its consumption – especially issues of by whom and how it is consumed. An early example of this new focus can be seen in Simon Frith's study of the production and *consumption* of rock music. Frith's study of music listening amongst teenagers in the early 1970s revealed important class (as well as age) differences. Music listening of sixth-form (predominantly middle-class) pupils centred around albums, lyrics, concerts and folk clubs and a rejection of 'commercial rubbish' (Frith 1983: 205). In contrast, fifth-form pupils who intended to leave school as soon as they could were much more likely to consume non-music products of the rock industry (magazines, television and radio programmes, posters), prefer music for its sound and beat, listen to music in a social setting such as the youth club or disco and identify with a particular youth style (206). Murdock also found a significant class difference in the consumption of culture among teenagers, although somewhat different from that indicated by Frith. Murdock's study suggested two major types of leisure practice: a 'street culture' of mainly working-class males involving soccer, cafes, pubs, dancing and hanging about with mates; and a 'pop media culture' based on values, activities and roles sponsored by the mass media for adolescent consumption, involving music, fashion, magazines, television and movies used by middle-class pupils who had no access to street culture (Brake 1985: 66).

Without dwelling upon its theoretical development and heritage, a recent trend towards a revival of the notion of 'popular culture' in the study of leisure and consumption should be mentioned here. The use of the term popular culture contrasts with that of mass culture in its movement away from a sense of manipulation and control by the producers of cultural commodities and its emphasis on the *use* of those products by their consumers.

An important influence in this development has been feminism and feminist theory, which has attempted to show that women are not simply the victims of patriarchal relations but invest their own meanings in, and create their own identities from their positioning in this social structure. A crucial area of study has been fashion. Whilst early feminist analyses of the fashion industry stressed the manipulation of the female image to force women to conform or aspire to super-feminine and glamorous images, to put themselves on display to men, and to identify with the appreciative male gaze, later work has stressed that women have not simply been duped or objectified by a male-controlled fashion and advertising industry but have used fashion to their own ends. Erica Carter, in her study of female consumer culture in post-war Germany, argues that the almost universal adoption by young women of nylon stockings was evidence neither of 'girls' blind submission to the dictates of the market, nor . . . female capitulation to fetishistic "male" fantasy' (Carter 1984: 208). By looking at the ways in which stockings were worn she argues that their wearing can symbolize very different things: an aspiration to freedom, democracy and the American way of life (since in the popular mind they were associated with America); or an expression of luxury, excess and resistance to parental moderation (since they were designed not to last, to wear out and be torn quickly) (208–12). Spelling this out, Elizabeth Wilson argues that contemporary fashions have liberating potential (whether or not this is realized) since they denaturalize the body and evade essentialist ideologies. The transgressing of gender boundaries through fashion and style reveals the fixing of gender positions for what they are, i.e., at most, temporary (Wilson 1990: 233).

These kinds of approaches share the starting point of the critical theorists in their recognition of a shift in the primary sites of social and ideological control of the working class from the place of work to places of leisure. They differ very significantly however in their vision of the consumer – whereas the Frankfurt School saw her/him as a passive receiver of the new mass culture, the new cultural theorists see her/him as an active user of the meanings embodied in the cultural commodities they consume. This kind of thinking is exemplified currently by John Fiske, who emphasizes the persistent attempts made by the bourgeoisie to control the leisure and pleasure of the working class by turning popular festivities (fairs, festivals, day-trips, popular sports) into official or national holidays granted as rewards for hard work and designed for the recuperation of energy before the return to work (Fiske 1989: 76). In looking at contemporary leisure activities, Fiske discusses the watching of soap operas and game shows and concludes that far from dulling the brain in order to prevent resistance to the oppressive structures of the real world, the meanings issuing from the shows were used by the watchers in their everyday forms of resistance. An example of how this occurs is given in his study of the enjoyment by women of a game show called 'The Newlywed Game' in which points are scored for agreement of wife and husband on the intimate details of their married life. Fiske found that feminist women gained no pleasure from the programme since it clearly reinforced dominant patriarchal messages. Nevertheless, he argues, non-feminist women who did regularly watch and enjoy the show were not simply accepting the dominant truths it reinforced, but were actively using their watching in their everyday practice of the resistance of patriarchy. They did this by: being part of a collective of women (the show is watched predominantly by women); making direct connections between the show and their everyday lives by building it in to their daily routine or using it as a reward for having finished a domestic chore; using the show to articulate and understand their own sexual relationships; and by relating to the subversive elements of the show. Thus, while points in the game might be scored for the agreement of the woman (representing her confirmation of the dominant group's ideological values), for the audience pleasure is derived from, and therefore popular support lent to, the woman who *disagrees* and thereby reveals the contradiction between those values and the everyday values of the subordinate (62–5).

The notion of *active* rather than passive consumerism is also central to Paul Willis' discussion of what he terms 'symbolic creativity' (Willis 1990: 18). Rejecting the pessimistic outlook of mass culture theorists, he sees not the manipulation of 'the masses' but a society constituted of 'creative consumers' born of a real and productive tension between market rationality and cultural consumption. This lies in the fact that 'whereas . . . work relations and the drive for efficiency now hinge upon *the suppression* of informal symbolic work in most workers, the logic of the cultural and leisure industries hinges on the opposite tendency: a form of *their enablement and release*' (19). In other words, in contemporary capitalist societies there is more 'symbolic work' and creativity in consumption than in production. Willis' point is also a political one: to locate the creative element of popular (or 'common') culture as opposed to the high culture of the arts establishment. But this position has not gone uncriticized – not least from those on the same side of the fence – for finding resistance or subversion where there is only tired escapism or relaxation (Williamson 1986: 14). It is this kind of romanticization of symbolically expressed resistance to the dominant culture that has been the chief criticism of the school of thought from which Willis emerged, and to which attention is now turned.

## RITUALIZING RESISTANCE: YOUTH CULTURE IN THE WAKE OF 1968

Class was not new to the youth cultural debate – as has already been seen, delinquency had been conceived of as a street cultural solution to the status problems of working-class urban teenagers. The heightening of class politics in the late 1960s combined with the economic slump of the mid-1970s, however, resulted in the issue of social class coming to dominate the study of youth and its culture. The first signs of this shift were to be found in refutations of the 'affluent society' theories on which those such as Abrams had premised their work. Refuting both contemporary 'youth as consumer' and 'youth as delinquent' theories, David Downes concluded from his study of delinquent subcultures in London, that the average delinquent was neither a bored teenager with too much money, time and leisure nor a child of the ghetto born into a criminal subculture. Instead, he argued that the 'leisure problem' was really a work and education problem, for:

> were it not for our educational system's failure to engage the interests and energies of the average and below-average working-class boy, with its subsequent corollaries of dissociation from areas of work and school, his leisure problem would be far less acute

> (Downes 1966: 260)

The attention paid to the meaninglessness of school for a large section of working-class youth and the cultural solutions it found was indicative of a new trend in British youth studies which diverged significantly from its American counterpart. The seminal work in this area was Paul Willis' study of oppositional working-class culture in a boys' secondary modern school (Hammertown). The study suggested that a culture (and style) of 'dossing', 'wagging' and 'having a laff' was developed amongst a section of working-class pupils allowing them to create a space away from the formal institution (school) which acted to socialize them into their, subordinated, place in the adult world. The culture of 'the lads', according to Willis, was an 'expressive opposition' directly counterposed not only to those in authority (the teachers) but also those who passively received their message, or conformed (the 'ear 'oles') (Willis 1977: 12–14). But, Willis argued, by adopting this strategy, 'the lads' actually *ensured* their subordination since they ended up ill-equipped for anything but work in the least skilled sector of employment. Consequently, as disillusionment with the adult working world set in, a return to education eventually began to be seen rather romantically as the only way out. Willis argued further that the counter-school culture of 'the lads' acted as a training ground for adult working-class or shopfloor culture into which they inevitably passed after school. On the factory floor, just as in the classroom, masculinity, toughness, attempts to gain and control time and space from the bosses and 'having a laff' at the bosses' expense were the rules of the game (108).

In the analytical section of his ethnography, Willis pointed to the key theme framing the new youth culture debate: the interaction of the reproduction of social relations in an ailing capitalist economy and the cultural forms of resistance to it. He argued that the indifference of 'the lads' to the particular job they took up after school revealed a level of awareness of the commodity form of labour power. This gave them the necessary capacity to resist or subvert the system to their own ends (136). This potential subversion was not fully realized (partly) because of deep divisions among the working class (on the basis of gender, race and mental/manual labour), and emerged as a 'particular subjective affirmation and "free" giving of manual labour power' (145). He also pointed to the role of the state, whose institutions (in this instance school) worked to encourage the reproduction of existing social relations.[7]

The reproduction of social relations in late capitalist society was central to developments in contemporary social theorizing – and it is not surprising that the study of youth should be heavily influenced by this, since young people were the key agents of the reproduction or subversion of these relations. Spearheading this research was the Centre for Contemporary Cultural Studies (CCCS) at the University of Birmingham, founded by Richard Hoggart in 1964. Initially inspired by a desire to cross the boundaries of literary and social science disciplines and reinstate the importance of popular culture, the work of its staff and students on youth culture in the 1970s and early 1980s reflected a distinctive blend of Marxist (especially Gramscian) theory, social and cultural history and structuralism. The work of the CCCS must be viewed within the context of the development of the discipline of cultural studies. The theoretical make-up of British cultural studies is vast and complex, and cannot be done justice here.[8] Neverthe-less, in order to understand the current state of the debate on youth cultural studies – which has largely taken up or taken on the work of CCCS – a very brief foray into the theoretical climate in which it was developed is essential.

### Culturalism vs structuralism: the origins of cultural theory

Underpinning the web of this new thinking was the continuing debate over structure and agency.

Culturalism – a term which came to signify an alternative to the method-ology of structuralism in social analysis (Williams 1988: 93) – first emerged as an important challenge (from within) to Marxist social analysis. In its most mechanistic form, Marxism theorized culture as part of the 'super-structure' of society which was simply determined by the social relations inscribed in its base, i.e. the economic mode of production. In classic Marxism this position is most vividly represented by Marx and Engels' anti-idealist declaration that the 'the ideas of the ruling class are in every epoch the ruling ideas' (Marx 1977: 176), while in the twentieth century more sophisticated attempts to theorize the relationship between economic and cultural production were explored by the critical theorists of the Frankfurt School and subsequently by the structuralist Marxist Louis Althusser.

Culturalists, from the start, envisaged a much more fluid interaction between culture, politics and economy. They sought a more fruitful defi-nition of culture than current ones which tended to envisage culture either as the body of intellectual and imaginative work in which human thought and experience are recorded, or in a purely social sense as a way of life which expresses certain meanings and values, not only in art and learning but also in institutions and behaviour (Williams 1981: 41–2). Their alterna-tive lay in the notion of *cultural practice*, or rather practice*s*, which constitute the ways of life and activities of human beings, and which not only reflect but also shape social relations. Crucially, these practices in-volved both the production and the reproduction of cultural forms (201). Alongside the emphasis on agency, therefore, an important element of this proto-cultural studies was the rejection of the definition of culture as high culture – or the end products of elitist cultural activity and aesthetic norms. Taking up the work of social and cultural historians such as Richard Hoggart and E.P Thompson, the sphere of popular culture became central to those working at the CCCS in their analyses of society and change (Hoggart 1957; Thompson, E.P. 1968).

The importance of Gramsci to the entire cultural studies project will become clearer when the new youth cultural studies are considered in more detail below; here only two very general points will be made. First, the taking up of Gramscian theory provided a link back to the Marxist debates about culture and the reproduction of social relations, whilst the idealist roots of Gramsci (especially the influence of Croce) ensured a clear distance was retained from the kind of vulgar materialist and economically determinist Marxism which the culturalists were keen to critique. Gramsci saw ideology as working not as 'false consciousness', but as having a *material* form. This meant that he saw the superstructural sphere as a key area of struggle and envisaged the seizure of the state (and its forces of coercion) to be necessary only in the final instance, once civil society had been captured in the long 'war of position'. By civil society, was meant everything outside the state. Consequently, the family, the church, schools, trade unions and any other sites of social interaction and formation of collectivities were important areas of struggle, for it was through these institutions that consent was won (hegemony was secured or counter-hegemony constructed).

Herein lay the second importance of Gramscian theory for the new subculturalists – it posited cultural institutions and the relations of cultural production as being central to political struggle. Gramsci was arguing that within both the dominant and the subordinate culture, pockets of resistance (or subcultures) could exist and that the dominant class must struggle constantly to retain its hegemony. In discussing the modern 'crisis of authority' (explained by the loss of hegemony by the ruling classes and their consequent resort to coercion), Gramsci directly referred to the 'problem of the younger generation' which he saw as a product of the inability of the older generations to 'lead' and the mechanical prevention of the emergence of new hegemonic forces to take up their position (Gramsci 1971: 275–6). This provided the new subculturalists with the basis for a political reading of youth cultural forms in the bleak period of post-1968 politics. The emergence and form of youth subcultures could be read as evidence of a breakdown of post-war hegemony being expressed not in street demonstrations, but symbolically, through style.

The second key strand in the new cultural studies stemmed from structuralist thinking. Structuralism took as its starting point not the agent, whose experience shaped cultural practice, but the *structures* of society which shaped and expressed that experience. These structures could be those of language (Saussure, Peirce, Chomsky, Voloshinov), literature (Bakhtin, Barthes), the unconscious (Lacan) or social relations (Levi-Strauss, Althusser). The origins of structuralism are generally taken to be in Saussure's *Course in General Linguistics* (based on lectures given between 1907 and 1911), for it was the idea that society was constructed out of systems which could be analysed in a similar way to language which constituted the common thread in structuralist thinking. The importance of structuralism for cultural studies was that it challenged any simple notion of 'meaning'. In other words structuralism denied any simple or natural relation between a sound or image (the 'signifier') and what was meant by that sign (the 'signified'). On the contrary, it was premised on the idea that signs were not naturally saturated with meaning, but meaning arose out of the *relation* of the sign to other signs; meaning was *produced*. Hence, to relate this to the subject matter of this text, there was nothing natural or given about 'youth' which had to be reflected in language – 'youth' existed only because of its relation to other categories of language such as 'adulthood' or 'childhood'. With reference to the sign system of language, this rendered actual words (*parole*) uninteresting to Saussure – since they were simply arbitrary signs. He chose instead to study the underlying *structure* of language (*langue*), which had its concrete expression in these words.

It was Levi-Strauss, however, who was first to use the notion of the existence of an underlying structure to sign systems in an analysis of society, and indeed to coin the term structuralism. In his anthropological work, Levi-Strauss analysed the universal structures of culture (such as the relations between man and nature, the spiritual and the material, the incest taboo) which were expressed in symbolic systems such as myth, magical thought and totemism. The latter are systems because myths, for example, cannot be understood singly but only as a body of differences and oppositions (Coward and Ellis 1977: 18). This conception of the structural system being a continual process of difference and transformation suggests that human beings do not stand above or outside the system and control it, but that the human subject is defined in and by the transformations of the system. But Levi-Strauss stopped short of negating the transcendant subject by positing the source of the myths in the human mind (20), and it is only with the taking up of structuralism by psychoanalysis (especially in the work of Lacan, see below) that an alternative solution is found to the question of where the structure itself originates.

Structuralism was also taken up within Marxism, most notably in the work of Louis Althusser. In this context the debate was focused on the concept of ideology rather than culture, but the root implication was the same; the crude Marxist base:superstructure divide was untenable. Through his notion of 'interpellation', Althusser argued that the structures of ideology (referred to as *ideological state apparatuses* and consisting of the family, the church, the education system, the political and legal systems, cultural and media institutions) shaped, and indeed constituted, the experiences of individuals. These ideological apparatuses are the material forms of ideology which represent the 'imaginary relations' which worked to *place* the individual in society through the category of the subject (Althusser 1971: 162–77). According to Althusser, the fixing of the subject was necessary for the reproduction of the social formation and acted to reproduce existing relations of domination and subordination. Althusser's claim that the individual's role in history is that of the *embodiment* of the process not as its *subject* (based on a re-reading of Marx which posited a fundamental 'epistemological break' between his early and his later work), constituted an important critique of culturalist and humanist-Marxist analyses of society since it 'de-centred' the subject making her/his own history, albeit in conditions not of their own making (Althusser 1970).

Althusser was not the first to employ the methods of structuralism to explain the workings of ideology in modern capitalist society. In a series of articles published between 1952 and 1956, Roland Barthes had already set about a semiological analysis of contemporary representations (including photographic images, advertisements, holiday brochures, sporting spectacles, the press, the theatre and the cinema). His aim was to reveal the process of the 'mystification which transforms petit-bourgeois culture into a universal nature' (Barthes 1989: 9), in other words, how society as a whole comes to accept meanings peculiar to a particular group as 'common sense'. Barthes adopted Saussure's division of the sign into signifier and signified, but saw this as only the first level of meaning – that of denotation (where the relationship between signifier and signified was arbitrary, but fixed). The second level of language posited by Barthes was referred to as 'myth' and here denotation was replaced by connotation. It is this development of Saussure which allowed for the *construction* of meaning. The most vivid example used by Barthes to illustrate this process was that of a photograph published in the popular French magazine *Paris Match* of a black soldier saluting the French flag. This image, Barthes argued, has two levels of meaning: the first is that the salute and implied flag signify loyalty and the link between nation and the military; the second level is that:

> France is a great empire, that all her sons, without any colour discrimination, faithfully serve under her flag, and that there is no better answer to the detractors of an alleged colonialism than the zeal shown by this Negro in serving his so-called oppressors.
>
> (Barthes 1989: 125)

Later Barthes rejected fixity between signifier and signified even at the first level of language and argued that notation itself was an effect of connotation, i.e. the relationship between signifier and signified was itself a constructed relationship. In applying this to literary criticism, Barthes argued that meaning was constructed through the text and that there were always plural meanings of any text. This made language and textual representations of experience crucial in the formation or construction of subjectivities and identities since they were seen not as fixed and unified, but socially produced and constantly reconstituted. Barthes illustrated this in his critique of the realist genre, which he saw as demanding of the reader that she/he regard the discourse of narration as the discourse of the unfolding of truth (Coward and Ellis 1977: 50). This, he argued, falsely fixed both the subject and the meaning of the text, and as such must be contrasted to avant-garde writers such as Brecht whose plays constantly disrupted the norms and forms of realist theatre (36).

## Desire, power and discourse: the post-structuralist critique

For culturalists, therefore, culture is created (produced in time) by human beings interacting with their social reality, whereas for structuralists (although many of those most associated with structuralism such as Althusser, Derrida and Foucault reject the structuralist label attached to them), culture is composed of symbolic systems (such as language, ideology, religion, art) through which these individuals are constructed, or 'interpellated'. To speak of the construction of the subject, however, is to cross into the territory of post-structuralism.

For post-structuralists, the human agent is not bound by the limits of the structures which express her/his experience, and (unlike Saussure) they see the relationship between signifier and signified as not only arbitrary but *unfixed*. In order to explain this, two crucial concepts of post-structuralist theory must be employed – the concepts of discourse and power. Discourse is the key to understanding the non-fixity of signs. Derrida argues that not only do signifiers (sound or image) exist as separate entities only in relation to other signifiers, but that there can be no 'transcendental signified' since meaning is created only by the play of difference (*différance*) in the process of signification (Giddens 1979: 30). For Derrida, signifier and signified are fused, meaning is produced within the discourse in which the signifier is located and texts must be deconstructed to reveal that discursive context (Weedon 1989: 25). But these texts are produced by and within social institutions and relations, and the dominance of one discourse over another depends upon the social and political *power* accruing to it. It has been the work of the French philosopher Michel Foucault, which traces changing discourse through history, that has been crucial here. Foucault saw the unfolding of discourse in society as taking place within the context of external restraints on who may speak and what may be spoken and this is developed in particular in relation to the discourses of sexuality, madness and criminality (White 1979: 89–91). His approach might equally be applied to the discourse of youth, however, to determine the constraints and restraints within which differing notions of youth (hooligan, teenage consumer, ghetto delinquent) have become dominant.

There are two important points about the concept of non-fixed subjectivity. First, if subjectivity is not fixed, but socially produced in language and discourse, then language and discourse become important sites of political activity – the struggle is a struggle for meaning. For feminists, for example, the battle is to replace patriarchal discourses on 'woman' with feminist ones (Weedon 1989: 36–41). Second, if subjectivities are not fixed – and can be developed in a liberating way – it is important to know how gendered subjectivities are acquired. This demands the evocation of the concept of desire and a discussion of a fourth important theoretical input into cultural theory – psychoanalysis.

The starting point in psychoanalytic theory must, of course, be Freud, for it was he who first argued that gender identity (femininity and masculinity) was not given at birth, but acquired through psycho-sexual processes in the first five years of life. For Freud gender identity was intrinsically linked to anatomical difference, since the former was acquired through a process of recognition of possession or non-possession of the penis. In boys, Freud argued, this recognition leads to a fear of castration and identification with the father, while for girls it leads to penis envy. In the resolution of the Oedipus complex, those traits and desires not compatible with the gender identity acquired, are repressed (in the subconscious) and may reappear and disrupt conscious life in the adult (45–51). Indeed, it was in trying to explain psychic disorders, primarily among women, that Freud originally discovered the subconscious. Although Freud's vision of a world structured by universal psycho-sexual processes retained much that was biologically determinist, it also made two important breaks with such theories. First, it posited the initial bisexuality ('polymorphous perversity') of the child which in turn suggested the social construction (within the heterosexual nuclear family) rather than the biologically-given nature of subjectivity. Second, if Freud is taken to be describing the processes of gender identity acquisition in modern, capitalist, patriarchal society and not universally, then his theory can be read as showing how the power of the father and symbol of phallus are reflective of a particular society rather than being the universal structure of social relations.

It is Lacan's interpretation and development of Freud that has been most influential in the understandings of the disunified subject which are so central to post-structuralist thinking. Lacan sees the unconscious as linguistically structured and suggests that gendered subjectivity is acquired through a process of misrecognition of self as Other (the Other being the position of control of desire, power and meaning). This is the 'mirror phase' of the development of the infant, and just as the infant 'misrecognizes itself as unified and in physical control of itself, so the speaking subject in the symbolic order (i.e. the social and cultural order in which we live our conscious lives) misrecognizes itself and its utterance as one and assumes that it is the author of meaning' (52). The patriarchal structure of the symbolic order is guaranteed, according to Lacan, by the phallus since desire is the motivating principle of life and the phallus signifies control of the satisfaction of desire.

French feminist psychoanalytic theorists have built on the Lacanian link between the acquisition of language and desire. They suggest, however, a separate and different female libido and thus also a separate and distinct female language. According to Luce Irigaray, just as female sexuality is plural and autoerotic, so female language is non-linear and not focused on reason – and both (feminine libido and feminine language) are suppressed by patriarchal definitions of sexuality (63–5). Cixous takes the link between feminine libido and feminine language further to suggest that masculine sexuality and language are phallocentric and logocentric and may be challenged by feminine writing. It is through writing that, on an individual level, women will reclaim their bodies which have been confiscated from them, and, on a social level, they will reclaim their space in the symbolic system (Cixous 1981: 250–1).

Both Irigaray and Cixous retain an essentialist link between feminine libido and female anatomy. Kristeva, on the other hand, argues that the feminine mode of language is open to male and female writers; the feminine is that which is repressed by the phallocentric and logocentric discourse which posits a transcendental, fixed subject (the thetic subject). The feminine (or semiotic) mode of signification according to Kristeva is seen in the pre-Oedipal infant before repression and in non-rational discourses which are marginal to the symbolic order and which show the subject in process (being fixed and refixed in language within the symbolic order) (Weedon 1989: 69–71). The 'repressed feminine' can be seen in some avant-garde writing, but also in feminine discourses of mysticism, magic, poetry and art that reject the rationalist norms of the symbolic order (72).

This tangential path through cultural theory has been a long but important one, for the questioning of the unified, transcendental subject is crucial to moving forward youth cultural studies. All the discussions of youth cultural activity which have been considered so far – whether Marxist, functionalist or historicist – have been based on such a notion of subjectivity. The subject is seen as being the author of meaning (articulated through language), and the expresser of experience whose social activity is characterized by acceptance or resistance. Questionings of the assumed, unified and transcendental subject, however, raise important methodological and political questions for youth cultural studies.

## Cultural studies of youth

The fundamental propositions of both structuralism (that society is composed of structures (language, ideology) which express our experience and position us as subjects) and culturalism (that culture is a more or less autonomous sphere of society in which people can act and change society) are evident in the body of youth cultural work which emerged – primarily from CCCS – in the 1970s and early 1980s.

The key text in the elaboration of a new youth cultural studies was the collaborative *Resistance Through Rituals*. The theoretical starting point of the work was a rejection of the 'youth-as-cultural-consumer' paradigm (outlined above) and thus also of the unity of youth culture. The authors rejected this discourse's underlying premise that society was experiencing the gradual disappearance of class (a process led by a leisure-orientated affluent youth). In this sense, the new youth subculturalists were closer to more class-aware interpretations of the delinquent subcultural theorists such as Albert Cohen. The difference between them lay in their conceptualization of the relationship between working-class youth and the dominant culture. Whereas the delinquent subculturalists identified subcultures as the resolution of a status problem for working-class youth faced with middle-class aspirations but not opportunities, the new subculturalists saw them as pockets of symbolic resistance. This interpretation rested on the Gramscian notion of a primary distinction between the hegemonic 'domi- nant culture' and a working-class subordinate culture which was employed in the development of the notion of the 'parent culture'. By this was meant not a generational culture but the class culture from which young people stemmed, and it was changes within and between classes which was not the only, but (à la Althusser) the 'determining' factor in the formation of subcultures (Clarke, Hall, Jefferson and Roberts 1976: 35).

Although subcultural forms might be *symbolic* for the CCCS, they were not *arbitrary* as they had been for the functionalists. Phil Cohen's 1972 study of youth subcultures in the East End of London suggested that the forms (styles) youth subcultures took reflected important changes in the social and economic situation of the parent culture. Post-war economic reconstruction and reorientation had seriously damaged the central pillars of the working-class community: the occupational structure, housing and neighbourhood structure, the family and leisure patterns. Consequently the 'respectable' working class was caught between two opposing pressures of social mobility; they could move upwards into the new suburban working-class elite or downwards into the lumpenproletariat (Clarke, Hall, Jefferson and Roberts 1976: 31–2). For young people this caused a serious dislocation as the old extended family was replaced by the less stable nuclear family grouped together on new housing estates, as automation undermined traditional craft skills and replaced them with the 'machine- minding' working class Hoggart referred to, and as the values of working- class puritanism were threatened by affluence and the sensation-seeking mass media (Clarke and Jefferson 1976: 141–2).

In line with other theorists of subculture, those around CCCS saw youth as seeking some kind of 'solution' to this dislocation. They differed from earlier subculturalists, however, in their rejection of the naturalized intern- alization by working-class youth of middle-class values. For the CCCS subculturalists, it was the role of ideology that was crucial in explaining how the subculture functioned. It was Phil Cohen who first raised this when he talked of subcultural groups such as the mods attempting 'to real-ize, *but in an imaginary relation* the conditions of existence of the socially mobile white collar worker' (Cohen, P. 1972: 24). Taking this up, Hall and Jefferson argued that the 1950s had been a period of real hegemonic domination, when the ideology of affluence (or 'never had it so good' thinking)[9] sought to dismantle working-class resistance to the authority of the dominant classes. But the 1960s and 1970s had seen an undermin- ing of this hegemony as working-class culture won space away from the dominant culture and the ruling class increasingly resorted to mechanisms of coercion rather than consent to retain its dominant position (Clarke, Hall, Jefferson and Roberts 1976: 40–1). Working-class subcultures were seen to be part of this working-class resistance – not simply living 'imaginary' relations but winning space and constituting 'a strategy for negotiating their collective existence' in an attempt to restore the lost community of the parent culture (47). What was illusory or 'imaginary' was that the real problems being negotiated by the subculture could be solved in this way.

It is when subcultural styles themselves are discussed that the influence of structuralism and semiology becomes evident in the work of the CCCS. Rather than interpreting style as simply the manifestation of affluent teenage consumption, commodities were seen as 'cultural signs' pre-assigned a certain meaning by the dominant culture, but, since meaning is not fixed, it could be appropriated or even subverted by subcultural use (55). John Clarke analysed the style adopted by different subcultural groups by applying Levi-Strauss' concept of 'bricolage' (in analysing the formation and transformation of myth) to the discourse of fashion. In this way he argued that objects (in this case fashion commodities) which already had an ascribed meaning (i.e. had been produced for a specific market) could be reassembled to create a new style generating new meanings (Clarke 1976: 177–8). Perhaps the clearest example of how this worked in practice can be seen in the style of the teds. The CCCS reading of ted style was as an appropriation of upper-class style, since the Edwardian suit (whence 'teddy boy') had been originally revived in 1950 by a group of Savile Row tailors and marketed to young, upper-class, city men and was subsequently taken over by working-class youths sometime in 1953 (Jefferson 1973: 9). The significance of this appropriation was the symbolic expression of the real material conditions of their own lives – i.e. the new lumpenproletariat could achieve the possibilities for social climbing in post-war Britain only on a symbolic level (Clarke, Hall, Jefferson and Roberts 1976: 48).

The 1960s equivalent of the teds were the mods. Like the teds, the mods symbolically moved out of their working-classness by adopting a super-smart style (suits, narrow trousers and pointed shoes), and taking up the leisure and enjoyment principle of the affluent by focusing their activity around discos and weekend revelling. Like the teds, who originated in South London (Fyvel 1961: 48), they came out of working-class areas in the poorer districts of London (such as the East End) but like them too, they adopted West End London fashion and lifestyles.

As can be seen from these two examples, for the CCCS, style consisted not only of fashion commodities or objects (the drape-suit, the parka, the winkle-pickers) since signs consisted of object plus meaning. In other words, in subcultural style, 'the object in question must have the "objective possibility" of reflecting the particular values and concerns of the group in question' (Clarke 1976: 179). The relationship between the object and the group was seen as 'homological', i.e. the constructed style of the group reflected its central values. The importance of homology between style and group identity was first explored by Willis in his study of bikers for whom the motorbike was not only their common interest but reflected and generated many of the central meanings of the bike culture (Willis 1978: 52). Examining this in more detail Willis wrote:

> The roughness and intimidation of the motor-bike, the surprise of its fierce acceleration, the aggressive thumping of the exhaust, matches and symbolized the masculine assertiveness, the rough camaraderie, the muscularity of language, of their style of social interaction.
>
> (Willis 1978: 53)

This relationship was taken up by other CCCS members; a homology was suggested, for example, between the bootlace tie adopted by the teds from American western films featuring the slick city gambler and the ted strategy of social climbing achieved by using 'ability and wits' whilst remaining on the outside of traditional working-class society due to their hedonistic rather than puritanical orientation (Jefferson 1973: 10).

Perhaps the clearest example of homologous style, however, was that of the skinheads. The skins' heavy industrial boots, work clothes (jeans and braces) and shaven heads were seen to reflect a tough masculinism, chauvinism (anti-gay and anti-black), puritanism and working-class communalism central to their strategy and, importantly, counterposed to the 'upward orientations' of other working-class subcultures such as the mods (Cohen, P. 1972: 24–5).

Looking at the subcultural scene as a whole, Cohen saw the problems of the parent culture (the retreat downwards into the lumpen proletariat or the upward social movement into the suburban elite working-class) being played out by the younger generation. Taking up this proposition, John Clarke offered a more detailed account of skinhead style in relation to changes in the material conditions of life of the British working class. According to Clarke, skinhead style was an attempt to recreate the traditional working-class community which was perceived to be under attack. Thus there was a strong sense of territory (skinhead gangs being linked to specific areas and marking and defending their boundaries against invasions from other groups) and a scapegoating of outsiders (especially immigrants) who were held responsible for the break up of the traditional working-class neighbourhoods through their social and cultural dissipation (Clarke 1973: 15–16). Skins also showed an overtly strong masculine identity, epitomized by the cult of football (especially the violence articulated around it), the 'bovver boots', standing up for oneself and attacks on those who did not (expressed most brutally in the campaigns of 'Paki-' and 'queer-bashing'). Clarke argued that the material conditions for the emergence of the skins lay in a relative worsening of the situation of the working class through the second half of the 1960s – especially acute for the lower working class and the young – coupled with the young's sense of exclusion from the exciting youth subculture (dominated in the public arena by the music and styles derived from the 'underground'). This produced a return to an intensified 'Us–Them' consciousness among lower working-class youth (13–14). Their solution to these problems, however, remained imaginary since skinhead style could not revive the community in a real sense – they had to use an *image* of what that community was as the basis of their style (Clarke 1976: 189–90).

The arrival of punk, shortly after the publication of *Resistance Through Rituals* must have seemed like a festival of bricolage for subculturalists and it is this element that came to dominate the work of Dick Hebdige in his analysis of subcultural style and youth discourse. The reading of style for 'hidden meanings' begun by the CCCS collective, was taken up by Hebdige who saw subcultural styles as 'gestures, movements towards a speech which offends the "silent majority", which challenges the principle of unity and cohesion, which contradicts the myth of consensus' (Hebdige 1979: 18).

Hebdige also took up the concepts employed by Levi-Strauss of 'bricolage' and 'homology', to read punk style. He saw 'a homological relation between the trashy cut-up clothes and spiky hair, the pogo and amphetamines, the spitting, the vomiting, the format of the fanzines, the insurrectionary poses and the "soulless", frantically driven music' (114). Not only was their style a reflection of the central values of the group, but also of the material existence of its members. 'The safety pins and bin liners signified a relative material poverty which was either directly experienced and exaggerated or sympathetically assumed, and which in turn was made to stand for the spiritual paucity of everyday life.' (115). But even Hebdige was forced to recognize the problem of reading punk signs – for the objects used to signify were not sacred, but chosen to be discarded (ibid.). Thus, when analysing the punk use of the swastika, alongside support of 'Rock against Racism' and the taking up of West Indian culture, Hebdige admitted that, with traditional semiotics, he could offer only 'the most obvious of explanations – that the swastika was worn because it was guaranteed to shock' (116).

In order to come to a better understanding of punk, then, Hebdige turned to post-structuralist thinking, and specifically the work of Julia Kristeva and her dual notion of the creation of subordinate groups through positioning in language, and the disruption of the process through which such positioning is achieved (120). Hence, Hebdige argued, the signifying practices of punk style differed significantly from the skinheads; whereas the latter fetishized their class position in order to effect a 'magical' return to an imagined past community, the punks' working-classness was always a disembodied and abstract one (120–1). The unity of form and content of the skinheads was replaced by a unity expressed through rupture (122) necessitating a reading of punk style as in a constant state of assemblage and flux (126).

**Critiques of CCCS from within and without**

The work of the CCCS had begun with a commitment to relocating youth culture in the material existence and structures of society rather than in generation gaps and anomie or images of affluent but bored teenagers. It ended, according to one of its initiators – Phil Cohen – by replacing the study of teenage behaviour with 'the reading of texts in which youth functioned as the "signifier" or "signified" ' (Cohen, P. 1986: 20). The structuralist influence had meant that style had taken on a separate meaning from life and the youth question had become radically disconnected from young people themselves, or in Cohen's words, 'it [the youth question] became simply the site of a multiplicity of conflicting discourses; youth had no reality outside its representation, no history other than the discontinuities which govern the present' (ibid.).

Perhaps the best example of the trend Cohen had already discerned came with the publication of Hebdige's *Hiding in the Light* in which Hebdige described the activity of spectacular youth cultures as a creative transformation of the discourses in which they were constructed – that of social policy and juvenile delinquency (the 'youth-as-trouble' paradigm); and that of post-war market research, marketing and advertising (the 'youth-as-fun' paradigm). Thus, Hebdige argued, 'spectacular youth cultures convert the fact of being under surveillance into the pleasure of being watched' (Hebdige 1988: 8). Another criticism of the primacy accorded to the reading of style was voiced by Stanley Cohen in his introduction to the new edition of *Folk Devils and Moral Panics*. He saw a confusion in the work of the new subculturalists on the question of consciousness and intent in subcultural groups' use of signs. Pointing to Hebdige's own lack of clarity on the subject of the punk adornment of the swastika, Cohen suggested that there was a deeper confusion in the argument that, on the one hand, signification need not be intentional (as argued by semioticians), whilst, on the other, subculture was seen to be an intentional communication, requiring – as John Clarke indicated in his reading of skinhead style – a degree of group self-consciousness (Cohen, S. 1987: xviii).

The degree of intentionality in the use of signs is also crucial to a second criticism of the approach set out in *Resistance Through Rituals* – the tendency to read style only for resistance. This, it is argued, either ignores any affirmation of dominant, commercial culture or chooses to re-read it as concealing a covert meaning (Cohen, S. 1987: xii; Williamson 1986: 14). Finally, both Phil Cohen and Stanley Cohen voiced a third problem emerging from the CCCS subculturalists' seminal work – the focus on the spectacular had acted to obscure the more mundane, but more common, experience of the majority of young people which was rooted in the worlds of family, school and work. For both of them, this also 'colluded' with the commercial entrepreneurs and American cultural imperialists and underplayed their importance in shaping the ideas and aspirations of young people (Cohen, S. 1987: xix, xii; Cohen, P. 1986: 24).

Phil Cohen's criticism of the CCCS's loss from sight of its original aim of rooting youth cultural studies in their real material circumstances was not a new one. The experiences of youth explored in the CCCS studies had been largely confined to those of working-class male subcultures, and the authors of *Resistance Through Rituals* came under sharp criticism for their lack of attention to the issues of gender and race in both their ethnographic work and their theorizing. McRobbie and Garber, writing in the same volume, asked whether the apparent absence of girls in youth subcultural writing was due to: their marginality to the concerns of the researchers; their marginality in subcultures as a result of male dominance; or their marginality in subcultures because of their centrality in a separate sphere of subcultural activity (McRobbie and Garber 1976: 211).

Their conclusion was that it was for all three reasons, but it was the third which came to dominate early feminist critiques of the work of the new subculturalists. The concern by both researchers and media with the spectacular and the violent concentrated attention on male-dominated forms of subcultural activity (212). At the same time, the greater control of girls' leisure time and the greater censure of their 'delinquent' behaviour meant that boys, and codes of masculinity, did dominate most subcultures (the mods being an important exception) (213). Most importantly, however, McRobbie and Garber located a separate sphere of subcultural activity which could be called girls' own. What was referred to as the 'teeny-bopper' or 'bedroom' culture was sited on female territory (the home) where girls acted out future relationships with men through obsessions and fantasized relationships with pop stars, fuelled by the consumption of pop and rock commodities (219–21).

This critique was later elaborated upon by McRobbie in her gendered reading of two of the classic texts of youth cultural studies: Willis's *Learning to Labour* and Hebdige's *Subculture – The Meaning of Style* (McRobbie 1980). Although Willis was not blind to the 'macho' nature of the anti-school culture he described, McRobbie argued that he failed to integrate his observations on masculinity and patriarchal culture into the context of the working-class family. This failure to take seriously the family as a key site of youth activity meant that the aggressive masculinity of the lads was seen as directed against school and 'the bosses', but never directly against women (mothers, girlfriends, wives), when in fact it was here that it often had its most brutal expression (McRobbie 1980: 41). Hebdige's work on style was unusual in the attention it devoted to the importance of black youth culture in shaping youth subcultures, which were themselves often racist. Nevertheless, McRobbie argued, Hebdige remained blind to the questions of gender raised. First, he saw style as exclusively male style; it was the suits of the teds, the bovver boots of the skins and the pornography-rooted rubber and pvc of the punks (44). Second, although recognizing the plays on gender-stereotyped dressing found in glamrock, he failed to explore the implications of the opportunity for escape from the prescriptions of heterosexuality (gender-bending) for men but the absence of it for women (44–5). Finally, in his criticism of the 'moral panic' explanations of media treatment of subcultures, he failed to address its gendered nature – if the Sex Pistols had been an all-female band spitting and swearing their way into the limelight, McRobbie noted, the condemnation would have been less tempered by indulgence (45).

This last point was taken up by Barbara Hudson in her discussion of the gendered nature of the discourse of adolescence. She argued that the growth of pedagogy, paediatrics and psychiatry as professions along with the extension of compulsory schooling beyond puberty (thus extending the period in which young people are subject to the discipline of teachers and parents on whom they are financially dependent) had led to a popular mythology of adolescence which associated it with storm and stress, tension, rebellion, dependency conflicts, peer-group conformity and black leather jackets (Hudson 1984: 34). Hudson maintained that this notion of adolescence was deeply masculine; the assumption was that in an attempt to emancipate himself from his parents, the adolescent resists their attempts to control him and transfers his dependency to the peer group whose values are typically in conflict with those of his parents. Consequently, adolescence is littered with essentially masculine images (of restless, searching youth, the Hamlet figure, the sower of wild oats, the tester of growing powers) and thus fits very uneasily with the discourse of femininity (35). When girls show signs of 'adolescent behaviour' – aggression, rebellion, adventurism – they disrupt not only parental authority, but the codes of femininity and are subject to much greater censure than boys, who, it is assumed, will 'grow out of' this phase. Hudson's argument effectively resists the notion of resistance employed in *Resistance Through Rituals* since it is itself constructed through expressions of gender and race oppression.

A second crucial dimension of the gender and subculture issue is that not only are girls invisible in the work of subculturalists, but that when they appear, they do so not as behaviourial 'deviants' but as sexual deviants, as breakers not of criminal codes, but of moral codes. Albert Cohen, for example, had noted a qualitative difference between male and female delinquency; male delinquency was the 'hell-raising' of the delinquent subculture, while female delinquency was 'mostly sex delinquency' (Cohen, A. 1955: 45). Indeed, this was seen as natural by Cohen, since women were located in the class structure of society only via their fathers and husbands, hence the male delinquent response to an imposed middle-class value system (the transformation of the middle-class disciplined and work-orientated achievement, aggressiveness, pursuit and active mastery into short-run hedonism, violence and predation) would be a wholly unsuitable delinquent solution for girls (139). In Cohen's theorization, the 'status problem' faced only working-class boys, for girls the problem was in treading the narrow line between enhancing their sexual attractiveness (in order to make a good marriage) while controlling actual access to their bodies (which would ruin their reputation and thus their position in the marriage market). Hence, the natural female delinquent solution was not hedonism or violence but sexual delinquency (146–7).

One of the crucial implications of the feminist critique of subcultural studies, was that the recognition of the absence of girls signalled the need for new ethnographic work and a return to questions of the activity of young people – including a diversification of the sites of that activity beyond the street environment. McRobbie, for example, undertook her own study of girls at a Birmingham youth club and their cultural activity (focused around school, youth club and home). She concluded that the material restrictions imposed on the girls were determined by both their class position and their sex, but took on specifically cultural dimensions in a femininity of exclusion, 'best friends' and 'pop culture fantasies'. In this sense, relations between girls were as important as relations between girls and boys.

The same conclusion was reached by Sue Lees in her study of sexuality and adolescent girls. What Lees found was that the labelling of 'slut' or 'slag' functioned independently of both the behaviour of the girl in question and of overt male censure; it was rather 'a general mechanism of control of girls' sexuality' (Lees 1986: 139). In this sense, she argued, it functioned in a similar way to subjective (as opposed to institutionalized) racism which often finds its expression in statements such as 'some of my best friends are black/Jewish but . . .' (ibid.). As Dave Hill shows in his study of racism and the football crowd, blackness may also be suspended by the colour of your football shirt whilst remaining an essential category of exclusion and abuse. This explains why a Liverpool fan, seeing John Barnes being brought down by an opposing black defender, may scream indignantly at the latter, 'You black bastard' and why Barnes' own success is attributed, above all, to the fact that he played 'out of his skin' (Hill 1989: 148–9).

At this subjective level, race and racism had always been recognized by the new subculturalists of the CCCS as an important issue in the exploration of working-class culture as is evident from their work on the skinhead subculture, for example. It was only later, however, that race and ethnicity began to be seen not only in terms of absences or categories of exclusion in youth culture but as constitutive of British culture in general and British youth culture in particular. Paul Gilroy argues that race and class cannot be separated and analyses the forms of 'black expressive culture' which spring up at the point of their intersection, as the cultural forms of the black diaspora are related to the individual's experience within British social relations (Gilroy 1987: 154). Gilroy's work effectively represents the flip side of Hebdige's understanding of post-war British youth culture as a 'succession of differential responses to the black immigrant presence in Britain from the 1950s onwards' (Hebdige 1979: 29). A powerful example of the creative re-representation of themselves undertaken by young black people is the play on the collectivities and exclusions of the white London working class and London's young blacks in the Smiley Culture hit song 'Cockney Translation'. As Gilroy notes:

> The patois into which the record translates white working-class dialect is shown to be more than a merely defensive argot . . . it is the oppositional core of a black culture based no longer in a wholehearted rejection of Englishness that answered the exclusionary effects of racism, but on an idea of its overcoming and redefinition in the association of black and white urban sub-cultures and their characteristically encoded communications which the toast makes mutually intelligible.
>
> (Gilroy 1987: 195)

## CONCLUSION

This sprint through academic and popular conceptions of youth and its culture over the last century has left little room for the subtleties of the issues they raise, let alone the arguments within which each are situated. The aim has been simply to show how the theoretical ground has already been staked out and thus indicate the frameworks from which the analysis of Moscow youth cultural activity in Part III begins.

This starting point is most cogently expressed by Phil Cohen: having moved from classical models of unitary subjects in unified social systems (the biologistic/historicist reading), through models of unitary subjects in divided societies (the critical Marxist or feminist sociology) and divided subjects in unitary societies (psychoanalysis), we must now construct a model of multiply divided subjects in a multiply divided society (Cohen, P. 1986: 52). But this need not mean that we are left suspended at the 'end of history' and the beginning of the 'road to nowhere'. The onward march of 'history' (whether driven by the laws of capitalist progress or the class struggle) may have been thwarted by the conditions of post-industrial, post-modern society, but history (as movement through time) has not (Clarke 1991: 31). Moreover, the basis of the human conception of movement through time – the individual and collective life history – remains intact. This movement remains em-bodied and our bodies – which are solid – have not yet turned into air.

This is not to deny the value of post-structuralist thinking in challenging notions of the unified subject, of a single reading position and the realist narrative which privileges experience. Nevertheless, if we are to explore and understand youth cultural activities, we must be able to see not only the shifting subject positions constructed in the codes of cultural reproduction, but also their grounded expression (and this means not only on the street but at school, at work and in the home). This need not restrain youth cultural activities in the classificatory strait-jackets of class, gender or race but, as Roman argues, may facilitate just the opposite. The combination of an ethnographic method of data collection with a semiotic reading strategy – which sees the codes of social relations not as stable but as historically determined by balances or asymmetries in sets of power relations – allows for the non-correspondences between one's objective location by class, gender or race and the discursive position articulated by the subject (Roman 1988: 150). Ethnographic work, which often reveals shifts and changes in the subjects' relation to specific elements of youth cultural practice (dance, dress, fighting, etc.), is thus crucial to the project of understanding how dominant codes are ruptured and new, previously subordinate codes may become dominant.

The study of Moscow youth cultural activity outlined in Part III builds on this dual approach. The very different material locations of Moscow youth, however, mean that not only do codes differ in their capacity to gain dominant positions, but new or different codes are central to the structuring of subject positions. The methodological issues involved in the negotiation of this cultural gap will be dealt with in Chapter 6, while the analytical implications drawn from the ethnographic work will be discussed at length in Chapter 8. At this point, therefore, the reader's attention will be drawn to just some of the general problems that will arise in any attempt to apply the principles of the Western theories outlined above in the context of contemporary Russian society.

First, working-classness is not a dominant code of youth cultural activity in Moscow. This is not to say that class itself is not an important category structuring relations of domination and subordination in contemporary Russia, nor that young people feel themselves to be part of a classless society – these would be 'imaginary relations' at their most imaginary. What is suggested, rather, is that the cultural reproduction of class is mediated (discursively fixed) in other subject positions such as ethnicity, provincialism, urban–rural divides and forms of political and economic patronage. Class identity must be seen within the context of late industrialization – induced largely by state and foreign capital – followed by rapid state-led industrialization in the 1920s and 1930s. The Stalinist modernization programme was accompanied by rapid and long-range social mobility and replaced by a solidification of the social structure in the wake of the economic stagnation of the 1970s and early 1980s. In addition, the importance of the political factor in the determination of privilege, access and needs must not be forgotten. Together these raise a number of serious questions in relation to the role of consumption and the commodity in youth cultural activity, all too easily assumed to be copied, adopted or aspired to by Eastern European and Eurasian youth cultures.

Codes of masculinity and femininity must also be explored in all their complexity. The question of whether housewives passively or *actively* consume soap operas, glossy women's magazines or the delights of shopping malls begs contextualization. The 'Russian housewife', for example, is still largely a figment of Western news reporters' textual accompaniment to pictures of queues in empty shops and Russian politicians' vision of a socially stable future for the country. Furthermore, despite the vicious commercialization of women's bodies and identities since the beginning of the glasnost era, women's femininity can, as yet, only be located in the consumption of commodities indirectly – by means of MTV and advertising boards in Red Square enticing them to unattainable (for most) holidays in the Canary Islands. A second problem in determining the codes adhered to in youth cultural activity is that the dominant codes of masculinity and femininity in society at large are under major reconstruction. The reduction of femininity to the combination of the social roles of mother and worker as well as the degradation of the 'male' public sphere to one of ritual and collective subordination in the Soviet period has led to the popular appeal of 'traditional' (i.e. pre-revolutionary) gender roles and identities associated with notions of the 'strong man' and the strong mother figure but the 'weak woman'.

Finally, there is the question of the social and political content of youth cultural activity. If youth discourses in the West have tended towards viewing youth subcultures as expressions of resistance (be it delinquent resistance as a result of unfulfilled aspirations or more or less conscious forms of class resistance), then the tendency towards politicized readings of Soviet youth cultures has been even greater. Much of the discussion has focused upon the location of young people's activity. The 'non-formal' nature of youth cultural activity positioned it outside the official structures of state and social and voluntary organizations and thus its very existence was read as a resistance to their universalistic claims. The extra-private but non-state space that youth cultures in the Soviet Union colonized was, however, less significant for any direct political *effect* it may have had in challenging the existing political structure than in the fact that it forced the acknowledgement of the existence of that space. The growth of non-formal activity revealed the overestimation by observers of the extent to which Soviet society had been politicized: the claims of totalitarian theorists that social bonds mediating between state and individual remained absent in Soviet society were shown to be untenable.

Neither this, nor the fact that the vast majority of members of such groups would resent the ascription of any overt political meaning to their activity, means that youth cultural activity does not have a political meaning, however. The non-formal sphere in former Soviet society is perhaps the clearest example possible of the site of the contestation of meaning. The forms of activity that take place in this space – described in Chapter 8 as 'embodied communication' – reveal the non-fixity of subjectivities as individuals and collectives are released from their 'formal' discursive positions (discussed in Chapter 2) and create their own. The acts of 'getting together' described in Part III, therefore, must be analysed at three levels: the significance of the activities themselves within the group; the structural context of these activities; and the relationship between the two. Only after such an analysis will the implications of the study of Russian youth cultural activity for youth cultural studies in general become apparent.

# 2 Building the road to nowhere
## Youth in the Soviet-Russian tradition

In Chapter 1 the main themes which have structured the debate on youth culture in the West were outlined. Traces of all of these can be found in the Soviet-Russian debate but their articulation is quite different. This difference would appear to lie in the political overdetermination of the Soviet debate. This does not mean that the nature of the political system in the Soviet Union necessitated a closed rather than open debate on youth and its culture, but that the socio-historical circumstances of the emergence of this debate have lent it a culturally specific tone. The key aspects of these circumstances are:

- The absence of a capitalist mode of production which, in the West, consigned youth to the secondary labour market and fostered a market-led youth culture.
- The historical conjunction of urbanization with the emergence of the *Komsomol* (Young Communist League) as a single, unified and ideologically motivated youth organization. As a result the dominant discourse in the Soviet Union linked urbanization to progress and social harmony, rather than vagrant youth on the streets, whilst the *Komsomol* acted as a youth-led (and thus relatively authentic) organ of social control of urban youth.
- The usually distinct areas of the youth press, the sociology of youth and the social control of youth were infiltrated – even co-ordinated – by the *political* institution of the *Komsomol*, producing an ostensibly monolithic discourse on youth.

The implications of these differences will be discussed at length below, but first the paradigmatic lines of the discussion must be drawn. Although undercurrents of familiar paradigms such as 'youth-as-object-of-social-control' and 'youth-as-passive-consumer' (Hebdige's 'youth-as-trouble'/'youth-as-fun' binary) are evident in the Soviet-Russian youth debate, to simply apply this model from the West would lose the peculiar *overdetermination* of the Soviet debate by the political moment. Different paradigms are required through which to elucidate its development, and the ones which will be employed here are those of 'youth-as-constructors-of-communism' and 'youth-as-victims-of-Western-influence'.[1] These are not discrete paradigms of course, but rather act as part of an indissoluble binary and, despite a shift in emphasis from the first to the second of the two paradigms in the post-war period, elements of both can be traced throughout Soviet history.

It will be argued, however, that the political moment only overdetermines and does not determine wholly the Soviet-Russian debate on youth. Moreover, given the institutional weight behind the dominant paradigms, it is the undercurrents in the debate which are often most illuminating and indicative of emergent directions. The discussion which follows will thus aim to reveal the complexities of the Soviet youth debate by outlining not only how the dominant paradigms have been constructed and institutionalized, but also the roots of alternative or only semi-consistent approaches and their development throughout the Soviet period.

## 'FATHERS AND SONS': YOUTH IN PRE-REVOLUTIONARY RUSSIAN CULTURE

As in the West, Russian youth culture has been viewed as a product of twentieth-century urban life. Studies of pre-revolutionary peasant culture suggest distinct traditions and norms amongst the youth of a village but no distinct way of life. This is partially explained by the fact that the pattern of rural life included only a very short period of youth (two to three years) which made it difficult to establish a distinct culture or way of life.

It would also appear, however, that the practices of Russian peasant youth – especially their control of the process of courtship and marriage – were primarily orientated precisely towards their rapid and successful completion of the move into the adult world. On the one hand, the *khorovod* (round dance)[2] was much more than a group for round-dancing and the evening, festive *posidelki* (working bees or evening gatherings of young people) allowed young people to engage in intimate games and dances which sometimes went beyond the bounds of what adult society felt to be decent (Gromyko 1986: 161; Worobec 1991: 131). Some of their activities, such as the singing of frivolous *chastushki* (spontaneously composed songs of rhyming couplets), were disapproved of by the older generation (Semenova 1990: 27), and thus might be seen as evidence of resistance to adult norms by the youth of the village. Nevertheless, the *khorovod* and its *posidelki* were also crucial institutions of socialization, tying young people firmly into the village and its way of life. The *posidelki* were not only festive occasions but working bees organized by the unmarried girls of the village and involving the performance of essential agricultural tasks (Worobec 1991: 130–1). Even the festive, evening *posidelki* had an important social role: they acted as the first stage in the courting process which led to marriage and signified the attainment of adulthood for both women and men. In this sense the control of the process of courtship and marriage exercised by the youth community did not resist but ensured its incorporation into the dominant culture.

To suggest a completely smooth passage of generations would be to present an idealized vision of social and cultural harmony in pre-revolutionary Russia, however. Amongst the intelligentsia generational continuity had already been seriously disrupted by the rapid social change which had ensued from the emancipation of the serfs (in 1861), and the radical intelligentsia movements of the 1860s and 1870s had torn fathers and sons, as well as mothers and daughters, apart. In the villages, the apparently smooth transition of social power between fathers and sons was predicated on the subordination of women as mothers, wives and daughters. Moreover, the emergence of urban centres offering employment and cultural opportunities encouraged significant migration or semi-migration out of the villages and began to bring serious conflict between generations (Bestuzhev-Lada 1987a).

Nevertheless, it is true to say that on the eve of the revolution capitalism was still weakly developed and peasant youth was largely incorporated into the life-activity of the community from an early age. Young people's leisure time was integrated into the seasonal labour patterns of the rural community and their activities were not peripheral or subcultural but, on the contrary, aided the social and cultural reproduction of the community (Frank 1992: 712). In explaining the lack of youth cultural resistance to the power of the 'fathers' it is also important to note that this culture was one not only of paternal hierarchy and prohibition but also of celebration and festivity; 132 days per year were devoted to celebration in rural Russia (713). These celebrations were times at which established hierarchies were turned around and elemental feeling ran free.

In contrast to this cyclical pattern of social and generational power, the revolutionary paradigm of youth was premised upon the institutionalization of a momentary inversion of hierarchies (the revolution) after which there was to be an unerring continuity of generations in an unswerving march towards progress.

## THE CONTINUITY OF GENERATIONS: FROM REVOLUTIONARIES TO CONSTRUCTORS OF COMMUNISM

> The entire purpose of training, educating and teaching the youth of today should be to imbue them with communist ethics . . . the generation of those who are now fifteen will see a communist society, and will themselves build this society. This generation should know that the entire purpose of their lives is to build a communist society.
>
> (Lenin 1976: 13, 21)

These words, taken from Lenin's speech 'On the tasks of the youth leagues', are generally understood to be the essence of the Soviet approach to youth. They lend themselves to an interpretation of the Soviet period as a gradual incorporation of a vulnerable section of the population into the tasks of the construction of communism, during which rulers have used instruments of control and indoctrination to impose certain patterns of behaviour and attitudes on young people in order to 'strengthen and perpetuate their regime' (Fisher 1959: ix). In contrast the present author aims to explore the youth paradigm of 'constructors-of-communism' in a way that illuminates not only the process of transformation from revolutionary utopianism to pragmatic state-building but also the social and cultural roots of its other key elements. At the heart of the 'constructors-of-communism' paradigm, it will be argued, lies the conjunction of the symbolic importance of youth in the process of state-led modernization with a labourist, progress ideology. At the same time, it is recognized that this paradigm was not monolithic in nature. As Bolshevik ideals interacted with the reality of post-revolutionary Russian society the themes of social control, poverty and juvenile crime also came to shape the post-revolutionary construction of youth in practice, if not theory. Herein lie the roots of the second youth paradigm – 'youth-as-victims-of-Western-influence' – which will be discussed in the second half of this chapter.

### 'The future belongs to youth': Lenin, the revolution and the cultural construction of youth

In existing explorations of the youth question in the revolutionary period, its political determination is understood in a narrow sense. Fisher, for example, interprets early Bolshevik thinking on youth as the elaboration of the necessary means for winning over youth to the revolutionary cause (Fisher 1959: 2). This is understandable since, as in other areas of his work in the pre-revolutionary period, Lenin's chief concern was indeed the explanation of the roots of capitalist exploitation in the Russian context and with mobilizing the population into a revolutionary stance. In relation to his direct concern with young people, it is generally noted that it was upon Lenin's initiative that a resolution was taken at the Second Congress of the Russian Social Democratic Labour Party (RSDLP) (1903) 'On the attitude to studying youth', which aimed to alert the party to the need to recruit youth in order to prevent them from falling prey to 'false friends' (Lenin 1977: 79). Concrete demands for the improvement of the socio-economic position of proletarian youth (which would give them a vested interest in revolution) were incorporated into the First Programme of the party and, as revolutionary agitation grew, efforts to encourage students and young workers into the revolutionary cause were intensified. In a pamphlet published in June 1917 (entitled 'Materials relating to the revision of the party programme'), Lenin called for a number of measures to improve the living standard of students and protect young people at the workplace (Lenin 1977: 55–6). Indeed, the party declared itself to be 'well aware of the immense importance of youth for the working-class movement as a whole' and in the famous resolution of the Sixth Congress of the RSDLP 'On the youth leagues' (August 1917) party organizations were ordered to give their maximum attention to assisting the establishment of socialist organizations of youth (Krivoruchenko 1976: 37–8). The organizational attention paid to youth by the Bolsheviks appeared to pay off in terms of support for the party; during the course of 1917, in both Petrograd and Moscow, Bolshevik youth organizations outmanoeuvred more pluralistic and independent groupings (Baum 1987: 11; Fisher 1959: 5).

The degree to which young workers and students were callously manipulated into the ranks of the Bolsheviks as a kind of revolutionary ballast is questionable, however. Tirado argues that, in practice, the pro-Bolshevik youth movement received little attention from the party either during the months before the October revolution, or immediately after it (Tirado 1988: 178). Avtorkhanov also remarks on the numerous independent organizations of youth which existed well into 1918, all of whom resisted pressure to adopt the term 'communist' in their names (Avtorkhanov 1959: 9). Thus the tension between the role of the youth revolutionary movement as an 'integral part of the larger workers' movement' and its 'expression of autonomist, potentially "syndicalist" forces within the revolutionary process' remained unresolved even after the revolution (Tirado 1988: 203).

This tension finally came to the fore in August 1919 when a joint resolution of the Central Committee of the Russian Communist Party and of the Young Communist League of Russia (RKSM) declared the Central Committee of the RKSM to be immediately subordinate to that of the Russian Communist Party, and the local organizations of the RKSM to be under the control of the local party committees, thereby abolishing the independence for which the First Congress of the RKSM had voted unanimously in August 1918 (Avtorkhanov 1959: 9). This subordination was resisted by a group of leading *Komsomol* members (headed by Dunaevskii, Polifem and Iakovlev) who formed an alternative organization – the 'League of Soviet Working Youth' – in September 1920 (9–10). Dunaevskii and his group were condemned for 'youth syndicalism', however, and removed from their positions within the *Komsomol*.

The accusations of youthful maximalism or youth syndicalism levelled at young revolutionaries might be compared to those of 'bourgeois feminism' raised against leading Bolsheviks who struggled for women's rights. Indeed the whole dual approach to youth displayed by the party – enfranchisement (legal empowerment) plus protectionist labour policy (effective disempowerment) and organizational tutelage – is very similar to that which it applied towards women.[3] This is consistent with Bolshevik analysis of the situation of both women and youth who were seen as constituting particularly disadvantaged sections of the proletariat due to their (natural) physical weakness and their (social) financial and emotional dependence. The psychological peculiarities ascribed to young people by the First Secretary of the Central Committee of the RKSM, Lazar' Shatskin, in his speech at the Third Congress of the RKSM in 1920 is particularly telling:

> [they show] a prevalence of feelings over rationality, [they have] an enthusiasm and a preparedness for self-sacrifice, and a certain frivolousness'
> (cited in Sundiev 1990: 4).

In this way both youth and women were seen as possessing an important revolutionary potential but also needing careful and separate attention either because of their perceived political backwardness (in the case of women) or political naivety (in the case of youth). This materialist approach imbued at the deepest level with essentialist premises lay at the heart of Bolshevik attitudes to women and to youth and was the source of their symbolic importance. In the new order, women's 'backwardness' came to symbolize continuity with the past, connection to the land (and its people), stability and comfort in the brutality of rapid transformation and civil war. The 'naivety' of youth, on the other hand, meant that it became the symbol of the 'bright future' (*svetloe budushchee*), the life-blood of the emergent new society as well as its physical constructor. This material and symbolic connection is evident as early as 1906 when Lenin declared:

> We are the party of the future – and the future belongs to youth. We are the party of innovators, and youth is always more open to innovation. We are the party of selfless struggle with old evil, and youth is always the first to take up the selfless struggle.
> (cited in Strokanov and Zinov'ev 1988).

As is patently obvious, this symbolization of both women and youth is far from unique to Soviet society or to Marxist ideologies. Moreover, it was not new to the period of socialist construction but part of an existing 'modernization consciousness' (Astaf'ev 1989: 5). In the forging of the new, modern society youths were dually important: as the youngest, most educated, and most modern elements of society they were seen as vital to the natural, linear *progression* of society, but as the natural representatives of the youthful and backward society, their precociousness, intuition and even maximalism might allow Russia to evade the mistakes of the older generation of modern societies and leap-frog into a better society. In youth, the irrational, the past, the Russian merged with the rational, the future and the internationalist. In effect youth constituted the body and mind of the new society.

## Creating a new culture: continuity and change

The tension between 'law-governed' behaviour and voluntarism, between orthodox Marxism and Russian revolutionarism, between continuity and rupture came to the fore in the period immediately after the October revolution, when the practical tasks of forging the new society had to be confronted. Even the celebrations of revolutionary victory in October revealed an uneasy mixture of carnival and sobriety neither repeating the carnival atmosphere of the public celebrations of March 1917 (the so-called 'Revolution Days' following the February revolution) nor conforming to Marx's view of revolution as a 'tragedy of the proletariat' (Stites 1989: 97–8). For Lenin celebration had to be purposeful, i.e. harnessed to the building of a new order (ibid.), and, just as he struggled against the anarchists on issues of politics and state, so too he vehemently opposed any form of cultural nihilism and sought not the wholesale destruction of bourgeois culture but to 'build upon' its best traditions.

Exactly which traditions were the best and just how they should be built upon, however, remained a subject of much debate – a debate often referred to as that of Proletarian Culture (*proletkult*). *Proletkult* was founded in 1917 and consisted of an uneasy mixture of elements of pre-war high-culturalism, the vaguely defined revolutionary proletarian culture associated with the Left Bolsheviks and independent worker initiatives (40). As such it was united in its hostility to commercial culture but racked with internal disputes both among its own intellectual leaders and between intellectual and worker activists in the movement (ibid.). As a mass organized movement *proletkult* was at its height during the civil war, when it looked like there might indeed be a short-cut to communism, but by the end of the war its role as the major mover in the founding of a new culture had been taken by the Commissariat for Education, *Narkompros* (Mally 1990: 256). The movement remained active throughout the 1920s, however, and this helped keep alive the issue of proletarian culture, in particular through the well-publicized debate in the early 1920s between Lenin and Bukharin on the possibility of building from scratch a specifically proletarian culture.

Lenin had persistently denied that a purely proletarian culture could be constructed after the old bourgeois culture had been smashed and continued to do so even in the midst of civil war (Lenin 1987: 27). Whilst at this time Lenin was clearly concerned with organizational questions, especially retaining control of *Proletkult* by *Narkompros* (Biggart 1987: 234), nevertheless his clear rejection of any notion that the new society could 'invent its own culture' had two fundamental premises.

The first was related to the materialist concept of culture. For Lenin culture was not only the changing by human beings of nature, but also the changing of those individuals themselves in this process (Oizerman 1983: 76–7). The relation between the two, therefore, was not one of subject–object (a crude materialist and rationalist position) but of subject–subject. This has important implications when extended to the wider understanding of culture in the post-revolutionary society. Culture was envisaged not simply as the product of the interaction between people and nature (the artefacts of everyday life) nor the treasure trove of that which is valued by the society of the day, it was rather the sphere of the living interaction of society and its subjects. With regard to youth, the subject–subject relation meant that youth was not treated as 'raw matter' for social training (*vospitanie*), or as Fisher suggested for 'indoctrination' and cultural 'imposition'. In fact *vospitanie* was envisaged as a two-way process providing a constant dynamic interaction of young people with the social system. Youth was a subject of social activity and this activity reacted back on society as a whole (Ikonnikova 1974: 9–10).

The second premise was rooted in the progress-orientated concept of historical materialism which accorded little weight to the social reproduction of labour, and envisaged a simple process of the transferral of the best traditions (the 'progressive') from the old culture into the way of life of the new society. This is best summed up by Marx and Engels in *The German Ideology*:

> History is nothing but the succession of the separate generations, each of which uses the materials, the capital funds, the productive forces handed down to it by all preceding generations, and thus, on the one hand, continues the traditional activity in completely changed circumstances and, on the other, modifies the old circumstances with a completely changed activity.
>
> (Elster 1986: 182)

From this Soviet culturologists developed three key concepts for understanding post-revolutionary culture: 'continuity' (*preemstvennost'*), 'social inheritance' (*nasledovanie*), and generation (*pokolenie*). 'Continuity' united the past and the future and was thus essential for the transfer of social experience and for social progress (Rozova 1988: 30–1). This process was termed 'social inheritance' (*nasledovanie*) and necessitated the presence of a collective subject–successor in order to ensure the transfer of the achieved level of development of material and spiritual production, forms of communication and cultural values (Ikonnikova 1974: 22–3). This subject was the generation (*pokolenie*). The delineation of generations did not imply the existence of generational conflict, however, since in socialist society, it was argued, both each generation and the totality of generations were characterized by an internal, socio-political and ideological unity. The uniqueness of each generation lay only in its inheritance of a certain level of development and the possession of its own specific historical tasks (ibid.).

The theorization of the role of youth in the formation of post-revolutionary socialist society then, can be summarized by the following principles:

- the individual interacts with nature as a result of which nature is transformed and the individual (*lichnost'*) is formed[4];
- in this way culture – in its material form – is developed;

- history moves in a linear fashion and progress is achieved through the social inheritance of the cultural values of the previous era;
- generations are the vehicle of this social inheritance and socialist society is characterized by a continuity not a conflict of generations.

Bearing this in mind, it is possible to begin to re-read Lenin's statement that 'this generation should know that the entire purpose of their lives is to build a communist society'. At the heart of it lies not the desire 'to control the behaviour of the new generations' as Kassoff suggests (Kassoff 1965), but the dialectical relationship between object of education and subject of historical activity embodied in the principles set out above. What Lenin intended by his words was that there could be no point in didactic approaches; simply teaching young people communism would not make them communists. Nor should young people be used as a cheap labour force to carry through rapid modernization – to build the new society – for this would repeat the mistakes of capitalism. In contrast, it was the *process* of the construction of the new society – the construction of communal property, in a communal way for the common good – that would form the 'new person' in the new society. The construction of communism then was not the first cynical act of a government that would soon turn voluntary labour into forced labour, but the concrete task of a particular generation – the means by which communism became 'accessible to the working masses, as their own business' (Lenin 1987: 36). In this sense Lenin's much cited words really do articulate the essence of the paradigm of 'youth-as-constructors-of-communism'.

### The Komsomol: institutionalizing youth construction

It was the institutionalization of this active learning and teaching process through the *Komsomol* organization that was to lend the 'youth-as-constructors-of-communism' paradigm its political overdetermination. Although no detailed historical account of the formation and development of the *Komsomol* is offered here, its central organizing and articulating role in the post-revolutionary youth paradigm cannot be ignored.

Founded officially in August 1918 as an independent organization of youth whose aims were 'in solidarity' with the Bolsheviks but whose organization was independent, the *Komsomol* was envisaged as an avant-garde of youth, which was itself 'the vanguard of the social revolution' (Tirado 1988: 177). This is not to say that the *Komsomol* is to blame for the ideologization of the youth paradigm or for the manipulation and coercion of the mass of Soviet youth into state construction tasks. The post-revolutionary generation was suddenly faced with the possibility of immediate change and the participation by young people in the construction of a new life was voluntary, desired and spontaneous (Kozlova 1990: 15–16). As the memoirs of *Komsomol* members reveal, young people were not coerced into the revolutionary movement but were eager to become part of the 'struggle for a bright future' driven by their belief 'in the possibility of realizing the people's eternal dream of a free and prosperous life' (Lunev 1959: 24). While this recollection may be somewhat romanticized, it is certainly true that the *Komsomol* offered many young people the possibility of organized social activity, the opportunity to better themselves both through education and employment, and an appealing ideology of social justice.

By the end of the civil war, however, the *Komsomol* had become both the main source of reserves for the party and a powerful institution of the emergent socialist state (Tirado 1988: 205). According to Tirado, the main reason for this was the decision taken by the leaders of the youth movement that in order to achieve their aims they must first of all defend the revolution (175). In practical terms this meant filling the ranks of the Red Army and the new state administration with *Komsomol* members. Virtually all its members in provinces close to the fighting went to the front, while even *Komsomol* committees in provinces at the rear sent as many as 30 per cent of their members into battle (Avtorkhanov 1959: 7–8). But *Komsomol* activists were also rewarded with important administrative and agitational positions and, after the civil war, entrusted with the most important political tasks of the day such as shock construction and collectivization. On the one hand this secured the position of the *Komsomol* in the post-revolutionary order as the right hand of the party – and thus at least gave youth a prominent position – but at the same time it increased its dependence on that organization. *Komsomol* ranks were physically depleted as its members left to defend the revolution and as a result the party had to be relied on to stop its decline by recommending that all young party members also joined the youth organization and by taking responsibility for new recruitment to the *Komsomol* (Tirado 1988: 179). The *de facto* influence of the party on the *Komsomol* became enshrined at the latter's Second Congress when it ratified the earlier Instructions adopted by the party in August 1919, which confirmed the autonomy of the *Komsomol*, but not its independence, and required that all party members under the age of twenty join the youth organization (182).

But the statization of the role of the *Komsomol* must not be seen in isolation or as a particular weakness of the organization's leaders. Although the physical construction of communism was to weave together the people and their new society, there was always the inherent danger of this living link becoming a binding chain. At times even Lenin's vision of the creative interaction of individual and society melted into an instrumentalist exploitation by state of labour in which communism was equated with 'the management of state construction' (Lenin 1987: 36). Just how the *Komsomol* became woven into the starched fabric of the Stalinist state will be dealt with below.

## NEP – A temporary lull in the construction of communism

The period of the New Economic Policy (NEP)[5] marked a temporary downing of tools by the foremost constructors of communism. Disillusionment and relative inactivity of the *Komsomol* during NEP was reflected in a levelling-off of interest in, even an exodus from, the organization. During the civil war membership had rocketed from 22,000 in 1918 to 400,000 in 1920, but by 1922 numbers had fallen to just 247,000. This fall is attributed by Avtorkhanov to disillusionment as a result of the loss of independence of the youth organization and the 'retreat' into NEP (Avtorkhanov 1959: 10).

Certainly there was a fear that the revolutionary vision of young people would turn into mass pessimism – hence the seriousness with which the so-called *Eseninshchina*[6] was treated by leading Bolsheviks such as Bukharin (Karpinsky, Mokeev and Pisigin 1988). The confusing nature of the post-civil-war period is noted in the autobiographical account of Nikolai Bocharov who describes the different reactions among *Komsomol* members to the changes wrought by NEP:

> The oldest *Komsomol* members . . . saw in this a return to the older order. Some of them took to drink. Some of them gave up their work in government establishments and left town . . . I remember how the head of the local district police, an old party member and a hero of the civil war, began to appear in the streets in a state of intoxication . . . I often saw policemen dragging him home half drunk, while he shouted . . . , 'Comrades! Is this what we shed our blood for? For painted tarts? So that the merchants can get rich?' On the other hand there were *Komsomol* members among us who saw in the new policy the triumph of the workers' and peasants' revolution. . . . Delicious things to eat . . . appeared in the town. There was even a movie theatre in which one could be whisked off to the alluring life of the American prairies. For me this was already a sort of conquest of the revolution.
>
> (Bocharov 1959: 47–8)

The lull in the forward movement towards communism also highlighted the emergence of other youth problematics and the activities of the *Komsomol* of the 1920s illustrated how the 'constructors-of-communism'/'victims-of-Western-influence' binary interacted. First, the struggle to build communist morality was accompanied by a struggle against bourgeois *im*morality. At one level this took the form of campaigns against alcoholism and moral decadence as the *Komsomol* sought to reinforce discipline, character and moral excellence (Baum 1987: 16). But more usually utopianism and puritanism were deeply intertwined. For *Komsomol* members in Kharkov in 1922, for example, realizing the principles of communism meant, 'if anyone had two suits or two pairs of shoes, he kept only what was most essential and gave the rest to his comrades' (Lunev 1959: 31). But the issue was not always so clear cut, as was revealed by the story of another early *Komsomol* member who recalled how, as *Komsomol* cell secretary, she bore responsibility for expelling another young woman member from the organization for 'bourgeois decadence' after she had turned up to a meeting in a silk dress from her grandmother's salon. Because the young woman concerned was so upset about the decision, the secretary referred the matter to the First Secretary of the party who decided that the girl should not be expelled because 'there will come a time when we will all wear silk dresses' (Alekseevich 1987).

The issue of dress is more generally indicative of the puritan element of *Komsomol* ethics as well as the confusion of the 'one step backwards' period of NEP. In the face of the new class of NEP-men, *Komsomol* activists adopted a plain and untidy style which acted as a visual reminder of their commitment to social equality (Stites 1989: 132), whilst at the same time envisaging a future in which this 'levelling down' would be replaced by an abundance which would give access to all to that which had earlier been the exclusive culture of the rich and powerful.

A second tendency to emerge in this period was that of the role of the *Komsomol* in preparing young people for class struggle. This took the form of the development of competition in sports and military training. This may be read as a way of channelling growing desires among young people to be active (like their predecessors in the civil war period) in a period of frustrating political stagnation (Baum 1987). It might also be read within the context of a puritanization of morality in general as a growing sublimation of the energies of youth. Aron Zalkind suggested that sexual behaviour should be governed by the securing of the continuity of generations. In his book *The Revolution and Youth* he argued that, 'one's sexual life is for the creation of healthy revolutionary-class descendents, for the correct, militant use of all the energies of the individual, for the organization of one's joys in pursuit of revolutionary aims' (Zalkind 1925: 76). Others reacted less radically to the perceived sexual anarchy which had followed the struggle against bourgeois morality. Bukharin, for example, argued that to talk morals was wrong because this fetishized the issue in a way which was not necessary for the working class and recognized that passions did not need to be sublimated but fostered since they 'united' and 'educated' (Bukharin 1988).

A third marked tendency was towards monopolization and was characterized by a desire on the part of the *Komsomol* leadership to absorb or outlaw all alternative youth organizations. Although in the immediate post-revolutionary period both pre-revolutionary and newly-formed voluntary and independent organizations flourished, by the 1930s the only widespread form of independent social initiative among youth consisted of criminal and courtyard-based (*dvor*) gangs whilst the space for socially-approved initiative of youth had narrowed to the confines of a few official organizations (Sundiev 1989: 58; Semenova 1990). It was not only alternative political associations that lost their right to act, but any organization that threatened the position of the *Komsomol* as the 'only form of mass movement of working youth', which it had declared itself to be at the Fourth All-Russian Congress of the RKSM in September 1920. A case in point is that of VTOPAS (All-Russian Society of Educational-Production Associations of Youth In Pre-Conscription Military Training) founded by Podvoiskii to help group together 'street' teenagers in associations. VTOPAS had expanded to incorporate fifty provincial branches with 100,000 members. However, playing on fears of the revival of petit-bourgeois values especially among youth, the *Komsomol* accused it of youth syndicalism and, with the help of Molotov, it finally managed to ban VTOPAS along with another thirty organizations (Dolgov 1989).

Finally, the *Komsomol* was employed in the construction of communism via the eradication of bourgeois influence from within. This took the form of the mobilization of urban *Komsomol* youth into campaigns for the collectivization of the peasantry. This was a particularly disillusioning experience for many members since they met stiff resistance not only from village heads but from young people themselves. One young activist described his humiliation when, having been invited to a village youth *posidelka* after an agitational meeting, he found himself unconscious at the bottom of a pit when he was not forewarned that the house into which he had been ushered had no floor in the entrance hall. He also described how peasant youth, especially girls, resisted anti-religious propaganda and would sing pointed *chastushki* when *Komsomol* members passed (Bocharov 1959).[7] Such tribulations were trivial, however, in comparison to the resistance met by later *Komsomol* activists who were drafted into the campaign of mass, enforced collectivization and were often beaten up and besieged by angry peasants (Viarich 1959: 67).

By the beginning of the First Five Year Plan, therefore, not only was the *Komsomol* clearly out of touch with the peasant population, but it had become a tool of an increasingly coercive state.

## THE FIRST FIVE YEAR PLAN: THE PHYSICAL CONSTRUCTION OF COMMUNISM

The Union of Communist youth should act as an example in practice for young workers and peasants. . . . How this is handled organizationally, how it should be implemented I cannot say . . .

(Desiaterik 1988)[8]

[the Komsomol is] only the reserve of the party and an instrument in its hands.

(Strokanov and Zinov'ev 1988)

These definitions of the role of the *Komsomol* were articulated just four years apart. The first by Lenin in 1920 clearly assumed the organizational autonomy of the youth organization, whilst the second, given by Stalin in 1924, sees its role as both the training ground for obedient party members and a key organ of the execution of the party's will. Not surprisingly, then, it has become accepted, even ritualized, to depict the period of the First Five Year Plan and the subsequent launch of Stalinist terror through the prism of the gradual whittling away of the autonomy of the *Komsomol*, its take-over by 'big brother' (the party) and its inclusion in the ever-expanding and increasingly monolithic state apparatus.

This was certainly the view expounded in the glasnost press which echoed the Gorbachev government of the time in calling for the 'end to deformations' and the 'return to Leninist principles' as the way out of the malaise and cited Bukharin's criticisms of the bureaucratism of the *Komsomol* leadership of the time (Karpinsky, Mokeev and Pisigin 1988). According to this scenario, Stalin consciously set out to curb the independence of the *Komsomol* and achieved his aim by writing into its programme and statutes that it was a non-party organization, by preventing alternative organizations of youth emerging (such as an organization of peasant youth) and by making *Komsomol* committees directly subordinate to party ones. The implication of this was that the *Komsomol* began to perform an executive rather than a political role; its chief task becoming the participation in the implementation of economic targets set by the party. Moreover, it was argued, the *Komsomol* itself had become an object rather than a subject of the terror. Evidence of this was that 80 per cent of its own central organs were repressed (including former heroes such as the Moscow metro constructor Aleksandr Shashirin) and that individual units of the organization – such as the Voronezh 'Communist Party of Youth' – had worked underground to struggle against the Stalinist terror in the post-war period ('Eshche raz o "dele KPM" ' 1989; Iakovleva 1988; Iakovleva and Muratov 1988). This circumscription of the autonomous space of the *Komsomol* is contrasted to the position under Lenin when youth questions were regularly considered in the highest forums of the party, and the party acted as an ideological and political guide to the *Komsomol* but observed its organizational independence and its right to decide upon its own forms and methods of work (Strokanov and Zinov'ev 1988).

The gradual incorporation of the *Komsomol* by party and state, however, serves only an illustrative not an explanatory function in understanding Soviet youth paradigms which were rooted in a more fundamental reconstruction of the social body in the late 1920s and early 1930s.

Revolution and civil war had seriously disrupted the social fabric of the country. In 1921, the country's population was about thirty million less than would normally have been expected due to the loss of sixteen million people in war, civil war, famine and epidemics as well as a fall in the birth-rate which reflected the poverty and insecurity in which people lived (Lewin 1978: 42). The effects of NEP were also mixed. On the one hand the working class began to grow again, but so too did the ranks of the unemployed, the *otkhodniki*[9] and the criminal subculture (47–8). Post-revolutionary society thus appeared far from the utopian ideal fought and died for, and 1928 was to mark the beginning of a painful process of the purging of the Russian social body accompanied by its massive and rapid reconstruction.

The physical departure of millions of people to the great construction sites of the First Five Year Plan was accompanied by a mass culture which 'fused national accomplishment, social mobility, and personal success' (Stites 1992: 65–6). The images employed in this mass mobilization exercise were ones of military valour, valiant trail-blazing and production heroism. The construction of communism was also laden with images of youth. Young people were portrayed as being *essentially* connected to the values of the time, which were considered to be optimism, love of life, progressiveness and love of work (Astaf'ev 1989: 5). At the Eighth Congress of the *Komsomol*, Stalin formally assigned the *Komsomol* the task of 'socialist construction' and its leader, Chaplin, appealed to the membership to initiate a massive volunteer programme to draw millions of young people into the push for production. Combat jargon filled the youth newspapers of 1928 as activities undertaken by *Komsomol* collectives were labelled in military terms such as 'light cavalry', 'brigades' and 'fronts' (Baum 1987: 24). The NEP lull in *Komsomol* activity came to an end and in 1928 membership jumped to two million (13).

But why was youth so central to the First Five Year Plan campaign? The cynical answer would be that for any state, young people are an important and valuable strategic resource with the help (or exploitation) of whom it becomes possible to conquer new territories and accelerate economic progress with comparatively small outlay on infrastructure. Baum, however, sees a more historically rooted reason. By 1927, she argued, the *Komsomol* was steeped in military discipline, frustrated by its lack of action since the end of the civil war and thus not only prepared, but eager to fulfil Stalin's appeal for 'soldiers' in the drive for rapid modernization (18). Thus, the 'shock brigades' of *Komsomol* workers were a natural extension of the military role the organization had already played in the civil war and which had been kept alive via a network of military-sports clubs established by the *Komsomol* from 1920 and united in 1927 into a single mass society called *Osoaviakhim* (the Society for the Promotion of Defence and of the Aviation and Chemical Industries) (20–2).[10]

While Baum's fundamental point that the *Komsomol*'s participation was eager rather than reluctant is surely correct, nevertheless, the historical preparedness of the *Komsomol* was not the cause of, but only the organizational mechanism through which a mass social and cultural movement was structured. Just like the individual heroes of labour who were celebrated to the point of virtual deification,[11] the participation of the *Komsomol* in the construction of socialist society was, above all, symbolically important; by participating in the shock construction and production movement – and by

1932 over two-thirds of *Komsomol* members were doing so (Kononov 1989: 54) – youth and the communist future became entwined. The dawning of the new society could only be symbolized by the young people who would live to witness it. Moreover the victory of the proletariat could only be secured by its efforts alone and, at the beginning of the First Five Year Plan half the Soviet working class were young people (under 30 years of age) and a quarter were under 22 (Serebriannikov 1967: 24). Finally, the task of the time demanded those qualities which were seen as inherent in youth: self-sacrifice, enthusiasm and maximalism. The speed of construction meant not only extremely hard work but movement to far-flung corners of the Union, undesirable, heavy manual labour and poor living conditions. This kind of sheer self-sacrifice and enthusiasm was an option only for those who had no dependents and who sought new lives for themselves, and was realistically palatable only for those who would live to receive a return on that sacrifice.

Baum argued that it was precisely the enthusiasm which the *Komsomol* could instil which was so valued by Stalin since it constituted a well of energy to be tapped. Indeed the enthusiasm of youth embodied the spirit of the time and was captured in the pictures of enthusiasts which abounded, the March of the Enthusiasts and the naming of avenues and roads after the 'enthusiasts' (Kononov 1989: 53). Their enthusiasm also carried *Komsomol* members in their thousands to the massive construction projects of the time. These included the Stalingrad tractor factory (employing 7,000 *Komsomol* constructors), the Gorkii car factory (8,000), the construction of the Urals–Kuzbass industrial complex (66,000), forest clearing (20,000), the coal mines of the Donbass (36,000) and the Moscow underground (13,000) (Serebriannikov 1967: 49). Indeed almost half (47 per cent) of the workers on the Moscow underground were young people under 23 years of age (Kosarev and Kraval' 1936: 34). The memoirs of *Komsomol* members of the time best capture the mood:

> Remember, only the short-sighted moan. Let your imagination go free, its strength is exceptional. We will teach ourselves a sense of time and a sense of the future!
>
> (from the diary of a *Komsomol* constructor in
> Komsomol'sk-na-Amure on the Far Eastern taiga,[12]
> cited in Serebriannikov 1967: 29)

> I believed that the construction of socialism in our country would radically change the future of the nation, and that by a high degree of mechanization of labour and scientific achievements the doors would be flung open to cultural growth and a life free of care.
>
> (A *Komsomol* organizer describing his experience
> at the Kharkov tractor factory construction site in 1930,
> cited in Lunev 1959: 34)

Since this future was based on a dream of technologism and the mastering of machinery, the *Komsomol* also played an important role in the development of the education of youth. The first task the *Komsomol* took upon itself was that of the liquidation of illiteracy. In 1922 (at its Fifth Congress) the *Komsomol* resolved to form peasant schools and in 1928 it declared war on illiteracy, drunkenness and filth and sent out 100,000 'cultural soldiers' to carry through this task. By the following year there were a quarter of a million in their ranks (Serebriannikov 1967: 114). By 1936, the state could boast that 73 per cent of young workers read the newspapers regularly as did 78 per cent of young collective farm workers, although not as frequently as their urban contemporaries[13] (Kosarev 1936: 64–5). Another symbol of the future was the 'young specialist' and the enthusiasm of the *Komsomol* in conducting crash education programmes meant that by 1933 over 60 per cent of specialists working in industrial enterprises were young people (Kosarev and Kraval' 1936: 178).

These construction campaigns, brigades, marathons and competitions played another important role; they brought a symbolic order to what in reality was the chaos of the First Five Year Plan. The flight from famine, the slaughter of livestock, the mass deportations became encoded as a steady flow of young hands to the edges of the Union where new territories were being forged:

> We are going. We, the generation of the thirties. Before us are construction sites, wars, experiences. We will take it all. Nothing, except our belief in socialism, is forcing us to leave our native regions and we go where our motherland and the revolution calls us. . . . We are going. Long live socialism!
>
> (Inscription against picture of young workers off to a construction site, in Serebriannikov 1967: 23)

This image of the planned and directed location of thousands of voluntary, young workers eager to participate in the construction of the new society thus became superimposed on the reality. In 1931 alone about seven million *otkhodniki* moved around the country. In the cities, the unanticipated influx made poor housing conditions unbearable and as personal relations took the strain there was a growing incidence of neurosis and anomie, culminating in an alarming fall in the birth-rate and leading to the outlawing of abortion in 1936 (Lewin 1978: 54). Far from being the firm bedrock of the future socialist state, then, Russia of the early 1930s is characterized by Lewin as a 'country of vagrants' and a 'quicksand' society (Lewin 1978: 56).

## On the streets of Soviet Russia – the besprizornik

The picture of youth pacing the front line(s) of battle or agitating among their more backward peasant sisters and brothers then is only half the story. Even in the urban areas, alongside the 'trusted reserves of the party' eagerly fulfilling their role in the construction of the new society, there was a very different urban youth culture to be found on the streets of the country's cities. Urban subcultures, even gangs, developed around groups of urban residents working in the same factory, coming from the same rural region or living in the same area of town. Sometimes such gangs would engage in semi-organized brawls with each other (Stites 1992: 11). Courtship also played an important part in youth cultural activity, just as among peasant youth. Urban youth promenaded round the town and gathered in streets, gardens, taverns or dance halls with the purpose of making new acquaintances (ibid.). If it was the hooligan who caused English society to shudder in the early twentieth century, however, Russia's social plague was that of the *besprizorniki* and a brief survey of this social phenomenon serves to illustrate some key undercurrents to the dominant youth paradigm of the post-revolutionary period.

Strictly defined a *besprizornik* is 'one deprived of family or domestic care' (Bosewitz 1988: 1) in other words an 'orphan', 'waif' or 'foundling', and the term was used to describe an acute social problem which afflicted Russian society from well before the revolution until after the Second World War. Even before the beginning of the First World War there were an estimated two million *besprizorniki*, largely due to children being driven out of or running away from home. By 1923, as a result of the catastrophic combination of the ravages of the First World War, the October revolution and ensuing civil war, the Ukrainian and Volga famines of 1920–2 and the growing unemployment of the NEP period, this number had grown to seven million, according to Krupskaia, or nine million, according to Lunacharskii (Bosewitz 1988: 158; Juviler 1985: 276).

The *besprizorniki* were an unprecedented social phenomenon in Europe not only in numerical but also cultural terms. They were similar to other European subcultures in that they were to be found primarily in large urban centres, they tended to gather into hierarchically structured gangs, they were closely linked to the criminal world and they instilled fear in the 'respectable' urban dwellers. Nevertheless, they also revealed some subcultural peculiarities. The most significant of these were the wandering tendencies of the waifs. The *besprizorniki* would travel the length and breadth of the country in search of food and a more clement climate, but the travelling became part of the culture itself. The skills of clinging onto the underside of moving trains, for example, became part of the initiation into the subculture. This permanent movement between large cities persists in some contemporary youth cultural practices such as the taking to the *trassa* (road) by hippies and the *gastroly* (tours) of the *gopniki*.[14] In some respects, then as now, this movement was necessitated by the weather and by the need to find work or better pickings. Nevertheless, as a cultural practice it was also certainly fuelled by a romanticism of travelling, of being 'on the road' and free. In addition, the high level of mobility had two important social consequences: it made the phenomenon seem even greater than it actually was, since it was not localized in slum areas of large cities; and it made the task of those trying to rehabilitate the *besprizorniki* in stable communities even more difficult.

The waifs appear to have had no distinctive subcultural style, but were identifiable rather by the scruffiness of their clothes and their dirtiness, a product of the poverty in which they lived. In the cities the *besprizorniki* would gather in railway tunnels, at stations and in cellars or dens they had constructed. Particularly appealing to them was the *kotel* which was a cauldron used during the day to prepare pitch for road surfacing and thus sought after by *besprizorniki* at night since it provided somewhere warm to sleep. The term subsequently became used to mean a group of *besprizorniki* rather than the place they slept[15] (Bosewitz 1988: 13).

A third peculiarity of the *besprizorniki* concerns the economic motivation of their delinquent behaviour. The most common crime recorded by Juvenile Commissions in 1921 was food theft – of 11,000 children apprehended 7,510 had stolen food and had migrated from the famine region of the Volga. A similar conclusion – that crime was essentially committed out of need – was reached by a larger study of *besprizornik* crime in the Moscow region conducted by Popov in 1926–7 which showed that almost two-thirds of all detected crime was economic (Bosewitz 1988: 31–4). This is consistent with Juviler's conclusion that the phenomenon was primarily fuelled by poverty not criminal romanticism (Juviler 1985). Nevertheless, within an established *besprizornik* group or gang, crime and other delinquent behaviour such as alcohol and drug abuse (the use of cocaine for example was widespread) became systematized and ritualized.

Societal response to the *besprizorniki* reflects to some extent these peculiarities but also illuminates some important cultural specifics of the youth paradigms emerging in post-revolutionary Russia. First, unlike the hooligans of turn of the century England, the *besprizorniki* were seen (at first) not as perpetrators of mindless anti-social behaviour but as victims of an oppressive system (the old capitalist system) who must primarily be helped in material terms. Consequently, by the provisions of the first Code of Family Law to be passed in Russia after the revolution (in 1918), the state assumed responsibility for all children considered to be in need (Stolee 1988: 67). This approach was also evident in the organizations and methods employed to help alleviate the problem. In January 1918 a decree was issued which raised the age of criminal liability from 10 to 17 and stipulated that juvenile offenders should not appear before courts but have their cases heard by special bodies – the Commissions on Juvenile Affairs (*Komones*) – which had representatives from the medical, educational and health professions as well as judicial and social welfare personnel (Juviler 1985: 263). Moreover, as far as practically possible given the poor institutional base for this, children judged to be in need of correction were sent not to prison but to special homes operated by the Commissariat of Social

Welfare (Stolee 1988: 67). The aim was to avoid sending young people to prison where older and more established criminals would socialize them into the criminal underworld, and instead, to provide socially-positive environments for their education and upbringing.

The early 1920s saw a massive increase in the scale of the problem of *besprizornost'*, however, due to the combined effects of the civil war and famine.[16] The desperation of the homeless children rose and they increasingly took to crime. Consequently the government appointed Feliks Dzerzhinskii of the Cheka to organize the Commission for the Improvement of Children's Lives (*Detkomissiia*) in January 1921 and in the following years efforts focused on rounding up the *besprizorniki* and placing them in suitable institutions including special children's homes, colonies, communes and cities which aimed to remove the children from the delinquent environment and reintroduce them to mainstream society (68).

The real change in attitude to the *besprizorniki* came in the mid-1920s as the numbers of homeless children continued to spiral and the state institutions could provide only a fraction of the places needed. The problem was different from that in the first years after the revolution not only quantitatively but also qualitatively: the children now on the streets were no longer the war orphans or victims of the earlier social crises – they were newly homeless. Analysis by the Commissariat of Education suggested that these children: had fled from poverty and suffering at home in search of excitement and employment in the urban areas; were a product of the disintegration of family caused/encouraged by the revolution; were the result of the incorrect upbringing of children and the exploitation of their labour by parents; and could not be sufficiently accommodated in appropriate schools for normal and special-needs children (70). The implications of this analysis were that the children were no longer victims of capitalist exploitation or even of the horrors of civil war, but of poor upbringing in their families. Consequently a new approach was adopted which treated the problem as one not only of *besprizornost'* but also of *beznadzornost'* ('unsupervisedness'). The notion that it was parental inattention which was to blame for the vagrant children not social phenomena or catastrophes had been reinforced by the discovery by the Moscow Juvenile Affairs Committee that 72 per cent of the juveniles brought before it lived with their parents and not on the streets. This led to a situation in which the child who turned to begging or theft to support her/himself became increasingly indistinguishable in the eyes of the state from the child who became a hooligan out of boredom and/or lack of supervised activities (71). Both came to be seen as juvenile delinquents who should be rehabilitated through socially useful work in factories, vocational schools, trade union and agricultural co-ops (for those over the age of 12) and in labour colonies for those under 12, or in need of stricter supervision (ibid.).

On the surface the new approach was successful; the beginning of the

First Five Year Plan in 1928 provided jobs for older children and educational opportunities for younger ones and this, together with the additional effort made by members of the criticized organizations, meant that the numbers of *besprizorniki* were reduced to 'manageable proportions' by 1930 (ibid.). However, in reality the period did not mark the end of the problem but its reconfiguration. In the 1930s a new wave of *besprizorniki* emerged as a result of the policies of collectivization and liquidation of the kulaks (richer peasants) which reached its peak in 1932–4 when there was a major famine in the grain-growing regions (72). But, unlike in the 1920s, these children were not seen as victims, but as parasites avoiding participation in socialist construction. As such the children were quickly picked up and sent to establishments under the control of the OGPU (formerly the Cheka).

In the late 1930s this tendency was intensified with increasing percentages of young people committing crimes being punished as criminals rather than re-educated as victims. In April 1935, the age of criminal responsiblity was reduced from 16 to 12, the *Komones* were disbanded and juveniles in legal difficulties had to appear before regular tribunals. Thus whereas in 1934 less than 17 per cent of those brought to court for juvenile offenses were sentenced to labour colonies, by 1938 the figure had risen to 66 per cent (74). By a decree on the 'Liquidation of children's *besprizornost'* and *beznadzornost''* of May 1935, measures against the problem were strengthened and the local police were given the additional right to fine negligent parents up to 200 roubles (or even remove the children if the negligence continued) if their children were found unsupervised on the streets. Finally, in 1936 the attainment of socialist society was declared by Stalin and the problems of the past – which had no place in such a society – were decreed out of existence. Consequently, the *Detkomissiia* was dismantled on 25 August 1938 with its tasks apparently fulfilled (75).

## YOUTH IN SOCIALIST SOCIETY: VICTIMS OF WESTERN INFLUENCE

The pronouncement of the attainment of socialist society in 1936 marked the dawn of a new cultural era. With regard to the cultural construction of youth it meant that the paradigm of 'youth-as-constructors-of-communism' could no longer coexist with that of youth as victims of the vestiges of the former system (as it had done in the case of the *besprizorniki*). The roots of existing social problems were now traced to deviant elements within the new society, and any deficiencies in social relations were no longer to be attributed to 'vestiges of the past' but each socialist individual was held responsible for her/his own actions. One consequence of this was that increasingly parents were blamed for negligence (*beznadzornost'*) and children who fell foul of the law during their street-life were punished as juvenile delinquents. In the early 1930s, alongside the *besprizorniki*, many other segments of the criminal underworld were also swept off the streets and into jails and camps, giving rise to prison camp culture (*blatnaia kul'tura*) (Stites 1992: 97) whose influence over the youth sphere remains today as strong as ever (see Chapter 4).

The declaration of socialism also had serious implications for the role of the *Komsomol*. Its original task – the protection of young workers and peasants from exploitation – made no (logical) sense in a society already half-way to communism and whose state was an organ of the proletariat. At its 1936 Congress, it became apparent that the new role of the *Komsomol* was to be one of a mass organization whose prime responsibility was to inculcate in youth as a whole the same dedication to the socialist state that its avant-garde already showed (Fisher 1959: 180–210). But as the cult of Stalin grew, individual responsibility turned into collective guilt. In November 1938 all the members of the Secretariat and Bureau of the *Komsomol* Central Committee were arrested as 'enemies of the people'. Those shot included its First Secretary, A. Kosarev, who had conducted the mobilization campaigns to which young people had flocked in order to construct socialism (Avtorkhanov 1959: 15), and who less than a year earlier had been promoted first to the Supreme Soviet of the USSR and then to its Presidium (Fisher 1959: 212). This was not the first purge of leading *Komsomol* members – in the period 1928–30, Shatskin and Chaplin among others had been denounced for Trotskyite leanings (280) – but it was the most far-reaching. This time a similar purge of leading *Komsomol* members was carried out in all republics, regions and districts and ordinary members were left confused and bewildered as the leaders they had admired were denounced as traitors, saboteurs and wreckers (Lunev 1959: 35–6). In addition, those *Komsomol* members who were of dubious social origin and who had joined the league primarily in order to continue their education lived in constant fear of being discovered and denounced (Hryshko 1959: 90–110).

The German invasion in June 1941 turned the main focus of the campaign against the enemies of the motherland to the threat from without rather than within. Once again the *Komsomol* was enlisted in the mobilization campaign and its military role returned to the fore. More than ten million *Komsomol* members fought in the war and more than 3,000 underground *Komsomol* organizations were active in the partisan movement in Nazi-occupied territory (Krivoruchenko 1976: 252). Self-sacrifice returned as a key theme, and images of young heroes prepared to give their own lives in order to defend the nation abounded (Stites 1992: 99).

The immediate post-war period saw the launching of a harsher than ever policy of cultural conformity, led by Zhdanov who called for a fusion of politics and culture, the hegemony of the party over art and of the 'mass interest' over the whims of artists. In particular it was the dangers of 'high culture' and of 'foreign influence' that concerned him and he not only forbade dissent but demanded positive political correctness, ruling anything else to be outright 'ideological diversion' (Stites 1992: 117; Starr 1983: 219). Despite Zhdanov's sudden death in 1948 (attributed to 'cosmopolitan plotting' by a group of Jewish- and American-employed doctors), he had an important impact on Soviet culture, beginning, in the late summer of 1946, a new onslaught on jazz which culminated in the early 1950s in the sacking and arrest of thousands of jazz musicians and the denouncing of jazz as a 'tool of American imperialism' (Ryback 1990: 11).

This hard line from above accompanied a growing interest in Western music and style among members of the cultural intelligentsia and well-positioned urban youth which had become established even before the famous 'cultural thaw' (*ottepel'*) of the Khrushchev leadership. The most obvious sign of this was the emergence of the first recognizable youth cultural group – the *stiliagi*. The *stiliagi* had their own style (*stil'*) which was an interpretation of American rock'n'roll styles and their own jargon. They represented an alternative avant-garde of youth to the *Komsomol* since they constituted the front line of ideological subversion rather than purity. As early as 1949 the satirical journal *Krokodil* was parodying such blind followers of fashion – who knew all the latest Western dances but not the most famous works and figures of their own cultural heritage – comparing them to barren ears of rye which stood out from the mass because they were tall and beautiful but did not contain kernels and thus could not give bread (Beliaev 1983: 170–3).

At the same time the Eleventh Congress of the VLKSM stressed the personal self-sacrifice which youth was prepared to make. The *Komsomol* (now referred to as the 'Leninist-Stalinist *Komsomol*') was awarded the Order of Lenin for its services to the motherland and in its address to 'Comrade Stalin – leader of the peoples, teacher and friend of Soviet youth', the *Komsomol* swore that it would 'dearly love its socialist motherland and hate its enemies without fear of struggle', and that the younger generation would fulfil all the orders of Stalin, the party and the Soviet government ('Vozhdiu narodov, uchiteliu i drugu sovetskoi molodezhi – tovarishchu Stalinu' 1949). Whilst the post-war period for Western youth signalled a new freedom for young people, for Soviet youth it began in an atmosphere of conspiracy, suspicion and subordination to the wishes of the state, and its leader.

## The 1950s: thaw or Cold War?

Although the Khrushchev period is generally considered to be an era of cultural thaw, when the Soviet Union opened up to itself and to the world, it was also a period of intense international mistrust. Despite the death of Stalin in 1953, the equation between anti-Soviet behaviour (manifesting itself in the prioritization of the citizen-consumer over the citizen-worker) and the infiltration of Western trends developed unabated. Soviet youth was no longer seen so much as the victim of *bourgeois* norms which had survived from the past but of contemporary Western, bourgeois influence.[17] Of course this paradigm had roots further back. There had been sporadic attacks on jazz and Western dances as a source of mass corruption as far back as the 1920s and, following Gorkii's equation of jazz with 'homosexuality, drugs and bourgeois eroticism' in 1928, *Komsomol* patrols began an active campaign to rid public dance places of its evil influence (Stites 1992: 49,73). Nevertheless, even in the early 1930s (known as the red jazz age) both European and Soviet jazz bands were widely listened to (Stites 1992: 74; Starr 1983: 107–29). Thus it was only in the 1950s, and specifically around the figure of the *stiliaga* that the 'youth-as-victim-of-Western-influence' became a fully-fledged paradigm through which youth issues were viewed. But why was it that the *stiliagi* became the symbol of the first wave of the contemporary informal movement?

First, the *stiliagi* were a serious challenge to Soviet ideology, not because they were numerous or powerful, but because they were the first manifestation of a new phenomenon for which the country was ideologically unprepared. The *stiliagi* were very much confined to central, large and well-developed urban areas, and in their desire to 'stand out' they marked a new age of urban youth cultural strategies. Their emergence coincided with a renewed surge of urbanization following the end of the war and with the reduction of the working day from eight to six hours for 16–18 year olds in July 1956. The *stiliagi* were quickly followed in the 1960s by the *bitniki* (and their rivals the *shtatniki*) and subsequently the hippies. In the 1970s, rock music became a general youth language and the repeated waves of hippies were joined by heavy metal fans, bikers, punks, and various pop music and movement fans.

Second, despite the limitations of the Khrushchev 'thaw', it did mark a period of opening up which helped foster these strategies in a Westernizing direction. The occasion of the Sixth World Festival of Youth and Students held in Moscow in the summer of 1957, for example, was a major channel of information and access for Soviet young people to the latest music and styles.

Third, the urban sophistication with which the *stiliagi* were associated became part of an invective against elitism and inequality which also characterized the Khrushchev period. In 1957, for example, new rules were introduced for entrance to higher education giving priority to those who had already worked in production for two years. In contrast, the *stiliaga* was portrayed primarily as a privileged student of a higher educational institute who had lost her/his sense of taste and been 'entranced by the vulgar music' (American foxtrots and boogie-woogie) and who, unless stopped, would become 'an over-refined intellectual with petit-bourgeois tastes and propensities' (Ivanov 1954: 11).

Fourth, the macro-political environment of the Cold War made the association of deviant youth styles with Western subversion highly appropriate. Youth came to be seen as a prime target of the Cold War, whose combatants fought not for the territories of Central Europe but for the airwaves which crossed them. The anti-Soviet nature of the music listened to by young people was seen as an integral part of this struggle; one performer popular with the *stiliagi* of the time, for example, was described by a *Komsomol* organizer as 'a White emigre who sold himself to the Hitlerites and performed anti-Soviet songs for them' (ibid.).

A massive campaign was conducted against the *stiliagi*. *Komsomol* brigades were established to conduct an ideological struggle against them, and in the cities of Sverdlovsk and Ul'ianovsk these patrol groups were reported to have cut both the trousers and the hair of local *stiliagi* (Pochivalov 1958). The press was also used to ridicule the young people, equating them with cheap speculators who hung round foreign hotels hassling foreign visitors and who sold the name of the Soviet Union for little more than chewing gum (Kruzhkov 1957; Shatunovsky 1959). The centrality of the interaction with foreigners was twofold: on the one hand the *stiliagi* were accused of sullying the reputation of the Soviet Union in front of foreigners, whilst, on the other, never achieving their aim of appearing like their idols, since foreigners themselves saw them as hopelessly out of date (ibid.). Not surprisingly, a common solution to the problem was to remind young people what it was to be Soviet by sending them 'to the north, to the taiga wilderness, where they will find it easier to learn how to respect human labour' (Shatunovsky 1959).

By far the most famous images of the *stiliagi*, however, were derived from the cartoons featuring them published in the satirical magazine *Krokodil*. Since *Krokodil*'s audience was older, these articles had a less didactic tone than those cited above taken from the youth newspaper *Komsomol'skaia Pravda*. They also tended to be more orientated to the parents of the offenders. Hence one featured a *stiliaga* sitting on a bar stool smoking and sipping a cocktail with the caption 'At 2am, the doorman says: Excuse me, your mother phoned. She's worried about whether you did your homework' ('Concerning the family, the school and children's upbringing' 1954), while another simply shows a youth in *stiliaga* style with a Pobeda car in the background and is entitled 'Daddy's Triumph' (*pobeda* means 'Triumph' and was a Soviet made car popular at the time) (ibid.).

Attempts were also made to restrict the attack on youth culture to rock 'n' roll, by distinguishing between acceptable jazz orchestras (popular among the respectable intelligentsia) and 'the music of lunatics and paralytics' which had originated in 'North American bars and dance halls under the intoxication of liquor and narcotics in a collapsing decaying capitalist world' (Zakharov 1954: 11). The latter, it was claimed, leads to convulsive body movements, 'is alien to us' and 'evokes nothing but disgust' (ibid.). In order to discourage young people from rock 'n' roll, dance schools were to be expanded in order to teach young people ballroom dances and a dance director was to be appointed at every young people's dance who would (with the help of *Komsomol* members) draw up the dance programme (ibid.). Discussions were also held on taste and manners in which young people themselves criticized those among them who kowtowed before 'the American way of life' (Rymashevskaia and Rubetskaia 1959), and programmes were launched 'to raise the cultural level of young people' through the building of clubs, houses of culture, cinemas and libraries ('Young Communist League Cultural Campaign' 1958).

The development of the 'youth-as-victims-of-Western-influence' paradigm did not simply replace that of 'youth-as-constructors-of-communism', but reinforced it since – as one police officer quoted by Stites put it – every ounce of energy used on the dance-floor was energy which could, and should, have been invested in building a hydroelectric power station (Stites 1992: 133). That youth was still required to construct the new society was evident at the Twelfth Congress of the *Komsomol* (March 1954), where it was economic matters – in other words the role of the *Komsomol* in fulfilling party-determined production plans and targets – that governed the content and tone of debate (Fisher 1959: 255). Directly recalling the *Komsomol* mobilizations of the First Five Year Plan, volunteers were now called upon to put their hands to the development of socialist agriculture by participating in the reclamation of the so-called 'Virgin Lands' of the Urals, Kazakhstan and western Siberia. This project was central to Khrushchev's social and economic development plan and its immediate success in bringing bumper harvests from hitherto infertile areas of the country was lauded as a great socialist achievement. The *Komsomol* played no small role in this success, since between 1955 and 1966 it was estimated that 500,000 *Komsomol* youth had responded to the party's call and had volunteered for assignments (*putevki*) to the Virgin Lands. In addition 400,000 *Komsomol* members had responded to the appeal of the party to move to new construction projects and 15,000 were involved in the construction of the Bratsk hydroelectric power station (Pavlov, S. 1959: 26).

Once again, the *Komsomol* was decorated with the Order of Lenin for its role in the latest achievement of socialism (Krivoruchenko 1976: 252; Fisher 1959: 258). In a message from the Central Committee of the CPSU to the All-union Conference of Young Builders in March 1961 acknowledging the role of young people in the construction projects of the current Seven Year Plan, the full rhetoric of the paradigm is displayed; likening the Soviet Union to 'a vast construction site of communism', the message notes that:

> The Leninist *Komsomol* and all the Soviet youth are actively involved in translating the breathtaking plans of capital construction into reality. Young people are a great force in construction. . . . They are upholding and enriching the splendid traditions of the builders of Komsomol'sk-na-Amure, the Dnieper Hydropower Station, the giant steelworks in the Urals and the Kuznetsk Basin

and ends with:

The party is confident that the Leninist *Komsomol*, our splendid youth will give all their strength and energy to the great and lofty cause of building a communist society in our country. Glory to Soviet builders! Long live the heroic Soviet people building communism!

(Krivoruchenko 1976: 116–7)

It was not only in material construction, but in spiritual and cultural construction, that the Khrushchev years were ones of 'a great leap forward'. Ever since the declaration of socialism by Stalin in 1936 it had been important that citizens of the Soviet Union – especially young citizens, since they had known no other society – manifest their dedication to socialism not only physically (through military service and labour) but mentally, by displaying the characteristics of the new socialist man/woman. In 1961, however, when Khrushchev announced that Soviet society had entered the period of 'full-scale communist construction', the ideological soundness of the younger generation took on a new importance. Although the Leninist dialectic which envisaged the new person being forged through her/his active participation in communist construction remained the central principle of youth education, the party now considered it its paramount task to help that process along. This was to be achieved by: educating all working people in a spirit of ideological integrity and devotion to communism and cultivating in them a communist attitude to labour and the social economy; eliminating completely the survivals of bourgeois views and morals; ensuring the all-round, harmonious development of the individual;[18] and creating a truly rich spiritual culture (ibid.). Henceforth it was a matter of national pride and integrity that not only the communist avant-garde (the party and the *Komsomol*) but all those being brought up in socialist society displayed a 'communist consciousness'.

This indicated a significant new direction in concerns about youth and its development – not only was youth to be mobilized, but also controlled. Since the 1949 VLKSM (All-Union *Komsomol*) Congress, there had been increasing emphasis on the preservation of political orthodoxy and ideological purity, the suppression and control of antisocial conduct and the supervision of leisure and recreation. From 1955 this took the more direct form of the *Komsomol*'s role in the suppression of minor infractions, including rowdyism and hooliganism, through its own patrols (Kassoff 1965: 118). The *Komsomol* also tried to control increasing numbers of youth by incorporating them into its own ranks; by 1958 enrolment had soared to 18.5 million and by 1962 to 19.4 million. Thus, Kassoff concludes of the *Komsomol* and Pioneer organizations of the Khrushchev period, that they were 'not organizations of or for youth but the agencies of the Communist Party and Soviet government. They block the open formation of dissident youth groups and therefore back up the system' (171).

The 1950s and 1960s then was a period not of thaw but of an unsettled climate. It was during this period that the first independent youth groupings emerged, such as the communards movement (a legalistic movement which emerged to combat the power of the territorial gangs), the Nature Protection Volunteers (*Druzhiny Okhrany Prirody*), the folk clubs *Klub Samodeiatel'noi Pesni* and *Klub Turisticheskoi Pesni* as well as spin-offs of the *Komsomol* such as the NTTMs and Schools of Young Rationalizers. It was a time of greater intellectual freedom and the emergence of independent literary and arts associations. At the same time, it was a period of renewed commitment to ideological unity and purity. It was under the leadership of Khrushchev that the hounding of the *stiliagi* was encouraged and the *Komsomol* significantly expanded both its membership and its sphere of activity which, henceforth, included the task of controlling young people in their leisure time.

## SOCIOLOGISTS, SURVEYS AND 'DEVELOPED SOCIALISM'

The relaxation in the political climate and the limited opening up to the West during the Khrushchev period had a further important implication for the construction of youth paradigms that was to become highly significant in the years which followed. This was the emergence of a new institutional interest with the revival of sociology as a branch of academic study.[19] The interest of sociologists in the problems of youth was not completely new. In fact, according to Zhitenev, 'the creative co-operation of the *Komsomol* and academics had been established in the first years of socialist construction', and in the mid- to late 1920s, studies of aspects of the lives of working youth, school pupils and *Komsomol* members were conducted (Zhitenev 1978: 13–14). Following the virtual disappearance of sociological work in the Stalinist period, it was not until the early 1960s that sociology departments and research centres emerged in Soviet academic institutions. Their impact on the study of youth was important, since until 1960 sociological work on youth issues had been restricted to the themes of 'communist education', 'moral education', 'education' and 'work' (Boriaz 1973: 41), which were deemed important to Soviet economic and social development by the CPSU. In contrast, the work of the new sociologists – Grushin, Iadov, Zdravomyslov and Shubkin – was focused on the study not of social classes but individuals, especially via public opinion research, and, as sociology became more accepted as a discipline, serious empirical studies including on the sociology of labour, leisure, education, national relations, mass media, propaganda and art were conducted (Shlapentokh 1987: 33–51).

### The role of sociology in the creation of youth paradigms

The importance of sociology for the study of youth was its premise – the heterogeneity of society – which meant that youth was no longer seen

simply as the first in the queue of the masses clamouring to participate in
the construction of communism, but as a distinct socio-demographic group
with its own problems and needs. But did the rise of academic input into
the youth paradigm mean the end of its political overdetermination?

The results of thirty years of the sociology of youth was summed up by
Blinov as leaving 'no doubt that contemporary Soviet youth is characterized by remarkable ideological and moral qualities – fidelity to the ideals of
communism, devotion to the interests of Soviet society and an ever-
increasing social activism' (Blinov 1983: 6). This conclusion reflects the
decline of Soviet sociology through the 1970s and early 1980s which
resulted in the sociology of youth being restricted to three main trends:

- a tendency to concentrate on survey analyses with no clear theoretical
  implications beyond the fulfilment of the *sotsial'nii zakaz*;
- a tendency for those who were interested in theoretical issues to be
  drawn into the (highly critical) study of Western theories of youth;
- and a tendency, sometimes through conviction, sometimes through
  default, to adopt an essentially structural-functionalist interpretation of
  youth, albeit couched in Marxist language.

These characteristics of Soviet sociological work on youth culture will be
explored below.[20]


## The sotsial'nii zakaz

Although by 1970 the most frequently published themes in the study of
youth remained those of work, communist education and education, the
development of the sociological interest had produced some new key
issues. These were the study of life plans, interests and ideals of youth,
leisure, the social activeness of youth, the all-round development of the
individual and the relationship between the collective and individual, and
delinquency and criminality (Vasil'ev, Kulagin and Chuprov 1967: 11;
Boriaz 1973: 41). This period also saw the gradual increase in studies of the
effectiveness of propaganda and the attitude of youth to various channels
of information as well as a growing interest in the peer group and its
influence on teenagers.

The early 1970s, however, witnessed a sea change in Soviet sociology as
liberal academics such as Levada, Iadov, Grushin, Shubkin and Kon were
ousted, and empirical sociology frowned upon for its attention to individuals and individual interests rather than global aggregate concepts such
as class (Shlapentokh 1987: 43–55). The new sociologists who replaced the
'founding fathers' were involved in 'social planning' work, that is the
setting of goals for the social sphere as part of the Five Year Plan. As
intellectual employees of the state, sociologists were expected to fulfil the
so-called *sotsial'nii zakaz* (social order) which was generated by the 'law-
like development' of socialist society. In particular the earlier generation of

sociologists was criticized for its inattention to questions of consciousness such as the problem of the assimilation of communist philosophy by various categories of youth, the influence of the means of mass information on this process, and the study of the moral qualities of the individual and his/her adaptation into work collectives and vocational training colleges (Zhitenev 1978: 15). This criticism reflected a new era embodied in Brezhnev's notion of the 'Soviet way of life' (*Sovetskii obraz zhizni*), in which the superiority of Soviet society was proven via its level of moral rather than economic progress.[21]

In an attempt to rectify the apparent failure, a co-ordination council on the research of problems of communist education of youth was set up in 1976 – under the Central Committee of the *Komsomol* and the Academy of Pedagogical Sciences of the USSR – comprising seventeen sections and bringing together more than 500 leading academics in the country (Zhitenev 1978: 19; Il'inskii 1985: 34). This built upon existing links with the *Komsomol*. In 1965, at the request of the Central Committee of the *Komsomol*, the Presidium of the Academy of Sciences of the USSR had opened four youth laboratories in its existing institutes which fulfilled the orders of the *Komsomol* and, by 1967, sociological institutes, laboratories and groups had emerged under more than fifty city, regional and central committees of the *Komsomol* organizations of the Union Republics and about 850 academics collaborated with the Central Committee of the VLKSM (Vasil'ev, Kulagin and Chuprov 1967: 9). The result was a sudden surge in publications on youth problems; a survey of academic publications revealed that over the period 1953–70, 74 per cent of all books, 80 per cent of all articles and 93 per cent of all conference and seminar materials on youth were published in the three years between 1967–70 (Boriaz 1973: 35).

The 1970s also witnessed a strengthening of the trend for the ideological control of sociological work. In 1982 Blinov noted that the Eighteenth Congress of the *Komsomol* devoted much attention to the questions of the sociological study of young people and that research was being carried out to serve the needs of *Komsomol* organizations at various levels (Blinov 1983: 16). By 1985, there were 10,000 people working on youth problems in four major centres: two academic (the Academy of Pedagogical Sciences of the USSR and the Institute for Sociological Research of the Academy of Sciences of the USSR) and two party (the Academy of Social Sciences under the Central Committee of the CPSU and the Institute of Marxism-Leninism under the Central Committee of the CPSU). In addition there were seventy academic laboratories and groups acting under the Central Committees of Union Republic and regional committees of the *Komsomol* (Il'inskii 1985: 32).

### Critique of bourgeois theories

A second trend in the sociology of youth was theoretical hesitancy. Even the identification of youth as a distinct group continued to cause social scientists both methodological and theoretical problems. Most chose to simply avoid defining their object of study, while those who did tackle the problem focused on the need to define the upper and lower limits of the group being discussed and to differentiate between the physiological and social categories of youth. The distinction is clearly an important one – Kon and Ikonnikova rightly recognized that since the experience of youth (*molodost'*) differed according to circumstance, one could not talk about youth (*molodezh'*) as a whole but only about youth as a part of certain classes and social strata (Ikonnikova and Kon 1970: 10). The issue was not just an academic, but a political one. Consequently, the different experience of youth (*molodost'*) among Soviet youth (*molodezh'*) was largely ignored, while that between Soviet and Western youth was magnified. Hence, it was argued, the category of youth may be a 'specific socio-demographic group with general socio-psychological characteristics and value orientations' but its social content was determined not by its 'youthfulness' but by 'the character of social relations' (14). In other words, class remained the determining factor and youth in socialist society was qualitatively different from youth in capitalist societies; whereas the social antagonisms of Western societies evoked deep psychological dissatisfaction, unemployment-free socialist society opened up wide opportunities for youth (13).

A second implication of the hesitancy in developing a genuinely alternative theoretical perspective on youth was that those interested in theoretical issues often turned to the study of Western literature. The requirement that this literature was assessed negatively, means that in order to ascertain some of the new tendencies in thinking on youth culture, a good deal of ritualized critique must be endured. This sector of the academic field is inhabited not only by sociologists but also culturologists and is centred on the refutation of the 'youth as revolutionary class' theories which are associated with the 'New Left' of the 1960s. Since works on this subject follow an almost set format, the components of the argument can be summarized quite briefly and generally:

- In the 1960s bourgeois ideologists saw youth as a class, often even a revolutionary class, confronting the older generation. This was expressed in the theory of the 'conflict of generations' – which falsely replaced class struggle as the motor of history – and in theories of the 'counter-culture' which saw a section of youth to be adopting a lifestyle which kicked against the norms and values of bourgeois ways of life. These approaches were the product of both a lack of Marxist theoretical analysis as well as a conscious attempt to distract youth from their real revolutionary interests.

- The counter-culture began under the New Left movement but rejected the political orientation of youth protest whilst at the same time assimilating its metaphysical content. Its form of protest was that of the inner revolution (using magic, occultism, yoga and drugs, sensuality, mysticism and sexual revolution). It blamed the scientific-technical revolution for the deficiencies of contemporary civilization, but replaced it with nothing more than an abstract humanism which ignored the real antagonistic contradictions of capitalist society. Since it was directed only at the self-consciousness of the individual and ignored the class struggle, it created only an illusion of a radical break with bourgeois society and reflected a crisis of socialization characteristic of a specific part of Western youth (especially from the middle and upper-middle classes) and which retarded the formation of class consciousness of youth.

- In order to neutralize the political protest of the younger generation in capitalist countries, the term 'youth culture' was coined and promoted. It was premised on a Western bourgeois understanding of culture as consisting of various subsystems (subcultures) based on territorial, professional, religious and national, age and sex factors. This emphasis on the importance of the cultural sphere helped to promote illusions that the class structure of society could be challenged simply by changing manner, style or clothes. Thus the term 'youth culture' was employed in two ways. First it was seen as a unique form of adaptation of youth to the norms, values and way of life of contemporary capitalism and was used in order to encourage consumerist orientations and thus confine youth to the spheres of entertainment, fashion and personal interests and away from politics. Second, and under the growing influence of socialist ideology, it began to be seen as housing oppositional ideas and rebellion against mass culture.

- The early 1980s were characterized by a new conservative tendency among youth in reaction to the radical revolt of counter-cultures of the 1960s. This was seen in the growth of 'yuppies' and neo-Christian movements proposing to resolve the problems of social reality through a moral-religious reconstruction of the human spirit. It was also evident in disco-culture which gave an illusory sense of freedom and choice when in fact the individual character of members of the disco subculture was subjected to a levelling down. The increasing exclusion from the production process due to rising unemployment was in fact leading to a growing sense of superfluity and the turning away of youth from the state, large monopolies, political parties and trade unions and towards alternative, social movements such as ecologists, squatters, antiauthoritarians, and greens. The attractiveness of 'irrationalist' (alternative) movements was also due to the failure of bourgeois rationalism and was particularly attractive to the young middle classes who lived by selling their labour power – predominantly of an intellectual kind – but who, by their position in the process of production, level of income, degree of organization of the division of labour, were close to the working class.

• Contemporary alternative culture shared much in common with the subcultures of the 1960s: both were formed as a result of a crisis in the socialization of youth; supporters of both cultures tried to stand out from the general mass; both promoted the task of 'the liberation from rationality' because reason was the chief obstacle in the path of mystical consciousness. The difference was that the subculture was a product of the relative revitalization of the capitalist economy and the New Left was optimistic about the possibility of social change, whereas the alternative culture was the result of the deepening of its crisis and this deprived the new generation of any optimism about the future that awaited it.

(Davydov 1977; Ikonnikova 1974; Ikonnikova 1976;
Khudaverdian 1977; Khudaverdian 1986; Kurbanova 1985;
Kurbanova 1986)

Although this interaction with Western theoretical work was ostensibly used to criticize capitalist society and its bourgeois theorists, in so doing Soviet sociologists of youth sometimes employed arguments advanced by Western sociologists themselves. In particular the notions of the illusion of protest and the massification of originally rebellious cultural forms built on the Gramscian informed studies of dominant and subordinate cultures described in Chapter 1. To this end the work of Willis, Clarke, Brake and Cohen was cited to suggest that youth culture in Western societies might reflect a form of class consciousness of young people shut out of the truly liberatory sphere of production (Luk'ianova 1986: 115). Moreover, some of those who had begun with a study of Western literature went on to advance interesting interpretations of Soviet youth culture (see Chapter 5).

## Slide into structural functionalism

The adoption of elements of a neo-Marxist critique of subcultures however was not commonplace. On the contrary, the failure to develop a distinctive materialist theory of youth and its culture meant that Soviet sociologists presented an interpretation of youth culture that was closest to the structural-functionalist approach (see Chapter 1). By this is meant that the dominant approach to youth cultural practice was concerned with its role in the socialization of young people, and to this end the success of Soviet society in integrating its younger generation was contrasted to the experience of capitalist societies which were facing critical ruptures.

Nevertheless, socialization was seen to be increasingly problematic, even in socialist society. According to two leading academics this was because:

there was a growing gap between physical and social maturity; the increasing complexity of the social roles of the adult person meant that longer professional and social education was required than previously; socialization was complicated by the increasing autonomy of youth and the growth of influence of various youth groups and organizations at the expense of the family; and the acceleration of social development which had led to an increasing gap between older and younger generations (Ikonnikova and Kon 1970: 3). These were all social phenomena associated with modern industrial societies, and given the relative youthfulness of the Soviet Union as a predominantly urban society, a central part of this debate was occupied by the study of the implications of urbanization for the socialization of young people.

The significance of patterns of rural–urban migration in determining the forms of youth cultural activity adopted by young people was a theme developed by youth cultural theorists in the latter part of perestroika (see Chapter 5). Even before this watershed, however, it was recognized that it took a number of generations to adapt fully to urban life, before which society could expect to confront some dislocations in the socialization process (Grigor'eva 1985: 60). An early study of informal groups of teenagers in an urban environment conducted in 1977, for example, showed that not only had the increase in the gap between physical and social maturity caused new tasks for the organs of socialization, but that there were specific problems related to those teenagers migrating into urban areas from rural districts in order to study. This was due to the new social environment they found characterized by overcrowding, an intensity and anonymity of communication, the territorial division of work and leisure, and the sharp reduction in direct visual control of teenagers' behaviour (Alekseeva 1977: 60). In order to manage this new environment, Alekseeva's study suggested, young people developed 'informal groups' which fulfilled, above all, an elementary need for interpersonal communication. She found that 90 per cent of teenagers (in Moscow) belonged to relatively stable informal groups (*kompaniia*) usually of between four to six people and that the main motivation for participation was a desire for meaningful communication (69). Not surprisingly, the reverse side of this was an expression of negative attitudes towards organized leisure and the fact that the meetings of young people generally took place outside the sphere of social control was a cause for concern for the author. The means advocated to restore such control of youth leisure were through 'the development of "voluntary work" and a restructuring of leisure facilities, especially cafes' (ibid).

Despite the problems associated with urbanization, it continued to be viewed as a precondition for the development of socialism, since the alternative was the 'idiotism of rural life' of which Marx had spoken. For youth, in particular, the urban environment broadened the space and lengthened the time of active self-improvement of the subject since it offered a greater plurality of social activities, forms of communication and sources of information than could the social rhythm of rural life determined as it was by nature (Grigor'eva 1985: 44–5). In seeing a disruption of 'generational rhythms' in modern urban society, in which the father and son had been replaced as the key players by the teacher and pupil, Grigor'eva's approach was close to that of Margaret Mead (35), although she did not go as far as to suggest the roles of teacher and pupil had become inverted (see Chapter 1). In relation to the increasing importance of the peer group at the expense of the family in socializing young people, Grigor'eva cited Eisenstadt and argued that the peer group might have either an integrating function or disintegrating function (83–4), thus also building on notions of the role of circumstance and role model in the development of criminal activity.

Summing up the structural-functionalist variant of Soviet sociology on youth then, the urban environment – the movement away from the confines of 'direct collectivity' and locality in village culture – was considered to be a prerequisite for the emergence of the socialist, all-round developed individual. The city with its concentration of people and cultures broke down old norms and created new and progressive ones and thus produced a new type of *lichnost'* who recognized her/himself as the subject of history and culture (Grigor'eva 1985: 115). The urban environment was the site of the concentration of key social institutions of 'socialist spiritual production' (political and social organizations, theatres and cinemas, museums and clubs, scientific and educational establishments) which became increasingly important as society developed (Levicheva 1988: 23). These institutions of spiritual production were particularly important in the process of the socialization of youth and in the stimulation of further social and economic development. The problem was, therefore, simply one of the stage of development; the fragmentation of contemporary urban culture was a temporary phenomenon which would be overcome with the further development of socialist society (Grigor'eva 1985: 164).

## FROM BREZHNEV TO GORBACHEV: THE WAKING STATE

Under the Brezhnev administration, discussion of the relationship between youth and the state had concentrated on the rights enjoyed by youth under the Soviet constitution (the right to work, education and labour protection) and the 'active' part young people played in politics and government. Youth had the right to unite in organizations according to their interests and needs, and the *Komsomol* was simply the largest of these independent organizations whose work was based on the 'active initiative and independent action of its members' (Reshetov and Skurlatov 1977: 39). If the principle that the *Komsomol* was an independent organization of youth reflecting the needs and interests of young people is accepted, then one could applaud with Reshetov and Skurlatov the fact that:

> *Komsomol* committees are directly involved in solving problems concerning young people. They play a part in the recruitment and dismissal of young people at work, decide on all kinds of transfers for young workers (promotion, demotion, awarding ratings etc.). . . . It also has its representatives in many leading bodies of state institutions and public organizations such as Ministries of Education, Higher Education, Culture, Council of Ministers etc.
>
> (Reshetov and Skurlatov 1977: 41)

If the premise is not accepted then it appears that the *Komsomol* had become an integral part of an intrusive state. Of course the only real way to make an informed decision on this is to evaluate the degree to which the organization played the role of representative of young people or the role of an organ of social control, keeping in check 'youthful maximalism'.

Under the old informal quota system, young people fared well in terms of their representation in parliament. In the elections of 1974, 305 deputies under 30 were elected to the Supreme Soviet – nearly one-third of the number of Supreme Soviet members – and about one-quarter of those elected to regional, city and rural soviets were young people (46). Youth affairs commissions operated in both chambers of the USSR Supreme Soviet, providing the opportunity for the raising of issues specifically related to young people. In addition, the *Komsomol* had the right to initiate draft laws, resolutions and other acts (41). But despite this formally strong representation, the interests of youth appear to have been subordinated to the interests of the state. Attempts to adopt a law on youth had been made in 1966 and 1977, but although their drafts were approved by the chambers of the USSR Supreme Soviet, they never made it to the statute book (Vasil'ev and Zhavoronkov 1988). The role of the *Komsomol* as the executor of party resolutions and as a training ground for party cadres also minimized any independent, interest-representing function it might once have had.

If passivity characterized the Brezhnev era, however, his death in 1982 heralded a period of ideological vigour and more active state intervention. In the youth sphere this was witnessed in a renewed concern with the social control of young people, mentally through improved ideological training and physically, through the greater regulation of their leisure time and activity. It was the party, naturally, which concerned itself with the ideological purification of young people, making a broad attack on 'ideological slackness' among youth and its organization, the *Komsomol*, at the CPSU Central Committee Plenum in June 1984.

In particular, the ideological offensive was to be fought on the music front and in July 1984, the Ministry of Culture issued a directive entitled 'On the organization of the activities of vocal instrumental ensembles and improving the ideological-artistic level of their repertoires' in response to the party's criticisms. The thrust of this directive was to gain greater control over what young people listened to. This was done first by tightening laws against the underground recording and distribution of unofficial music and the issuing of unofficial blacklists of songs and bands which were not to be played at discos. *Komsomol* detachments were even charged with conducting raids against those trading in Western records and tapes (Pavlov, A. 1984). Second, Soviet rock groups were to be better screened though the establishment of a commission to review professional groups (leading to between one-third and one-half of rock groups being disbanded), and an order was issued demanding that 80 per cent of the material performed at concerts be written by members of the Union of Composers (Ryback 1990: 220–1). The concern was that subversive texts were being let in through the back door by allowing rock music to flourish and young people were berated for allowing themselves to fall under the 'narcotic of mass culture'. Those newspapers who pandered to such tastes by giving extensive coverage of Western rock music and using English slang terms – such as *Moskovskii Komsomolets* as well as numerous provincial papers – were also criticized for their lax approach (Kuniaev 1984; Geiko 1984).

This campaign was clearly infused with the 'victims-of-Western-influence' paradigm; in the final analysis the distortions in young people's tastes were portrayed as a product of the fact that the standards of bourgeois mass culture (consisting of unchecked violence and shameless eroticism) had penetrated the Soviet Union through music and other media forms (Nozhin 1984). But this paradigm consisted not only of the argument that the ideological staunchness of Soviet youth was being whittled away by its exposure to the false lure of mass culture, but that Western intelligence services were conducting an active campaign to win it over. One article compared the current era to that of the Second World War when the US secret service used American popular music hits and Broadway shows of the 1930s and 1940s to demoralize Germany's population, instil in the enemy's mind the basic postulates of the American way of life and thus lessen its will to resist. This war effort, the author claimed, had now been switched to the Soviet Union and NATO's Council on Youth Affairs had declared its goal to be 'to captivate the young people of the USSR with the ideals of the West' through propagandizing an aggressively independent way of life through rock culture that they saw as characteristic of the young (Filinov 1984). Thus rock music and the youth culture surrounding it came to be seen as outright 'psychological warfare' aimed at shaking young people's confidence in communism. According to one academic, the campaign conducted against the Soviet Union was engaged in by 'thousands of specialists', co-ordinated personally by the leaders of the imperialist powers and used 'everything from the most advanced technical means to rumours and jokes'. Above all, however, it employed radio broadcasts.

Voice of America, it was argued, had 'two clearly delineated tasks: to extol the American way of life, on the one hand, and to slander the Soviet Union in every conceivable way, on the other'. These efforts were focused on young people because their 'heightened susceptibility, emotionality and forthrightness were sometimes combined with psychological instability, negativism and the confusion of ideals with illusions' (Nozhin 1984: 3).

Since the campaign was an ideological one, it was to be resisted on an ideological level. The first priority was to improve political education and so better prepare young people to resist the onslaught. In this task the help of academics was mobilized and a number of surveys were carried out in order to test the 'level of understanding of the class approach' among young people. This was done by calculating how many young people scored correct answers when their responses were tested on questions of economic, socio-political and ideological events and the conclusion was that a minority of 'asocial' youth strove to receive information from foreign sources and actively sought out contacts and dubious acquaintances. This, it was suggested, could be counteracted through a campaign to 'raise the class approach in the communist eduction of youth in the current stage of development' (Blinov 1985). Since bourgeois ideology could only be fought with socialist ideology, a second measure was to raise the production of Soviet fashionable youth clothes (Logachev 1984), which would have their own logos and slogans with revolutionary and patriotic themes, pictures of scenic places and the heraldic crests of ancient cities, local nature scenes, sports and various professional occupations to counteract the fashion for banal, Western-style ones (Romaniuk 1984).

A third, although far from new, concern was that of the social control of youth. Taking up the party's call, the Presidium of the USSR Supreme Soviet passed its own resolution 'On the soviets' tasks stemming from the CPSU Central Committee's resolution "On further improving ideological and political-upbringing work" ' and youth affairs committees considered reports on the progress made by regional councils. The conclusion of one such meeting (considering the situation in Odessa, Murmansk and Riga) was that the leisure time of a large part of older teenagers (especially technical college students and those already working) was poorly organized. This meant that young people were being left to their own devices and thus fell under the influence of undesirable members of society, spending their time in small groups in which drinking, gambling and hooliganism often flourished. The committee's recommendations were: the setting up of a special institution to train personnel for upbringing work with young people at the neighbourhood level; the drawing up of rules of behaviour for teenagers in public places which would help state agencies and public organizations maintain law and order; and to open up existing leisure facilities – for example in schools – for wider use (Mogliat and Khlystun 1984).

The essence of the approach by the legislators was to exercise greater control of youth through: the professionalization of youth work; greater legislative control of behaviour; and the expansion of the network of controlled spaces available for youth leisure. This approach reflected a growing concern with the influence of 'the street' on young people, where it was estimated teenagers spent two-thirds of their time (Belaia 1987). Academic research had suggested that the contemporary planning of new city housing developments (*mikroraiony*) was partially to blame; the absence of a central closed-off space (the courtyard or *dvor*) which might act as a focus for youth meant that teenagers were being pushed onto the street (Grigor'eva 1985: 90). The restructuring of urban space in the 1970s and 1980s emphasized individual comfort and privacy and thus favoured individual flats over communal ones (*kommunalki*) and quiet streets and avenues over the traditional courtyard formation. The loss of the four walls of the courtyard signified the physical loss of the old forms of rural interaction and social control and – since youth was unprepared for the individual responsibility this necessitated – it led to an increase in juvenile delinquency (Bogatyreva 1990: 53).

As was noted above, however, it was not only the geographical space of the street that was considered to be leading young people into delinquency, but the people who controlled it. According to the Deputy Head of the Juvenile Department of the USSR Ministry of Internal Affairs' Chief Administration for Criminal Investigation, the problem was twofold. First the street was the collecting ground for people with criminal records and, second, the street was controlled by 'group mentality' which often led 'normal' youngsters to act uncharacteristically (Balkarei and Zhavoronkov 1984). One of the chief problems in rectifying the situation appears to have been the lack of clarity regarding which of the many organizations responsible for young people was to blame: schools, the housing management offices or the *Komsomol* detachments (which were reported to have almost two million young communists engaged in controlling the street). But even if all were active, there was the problem of the effectiveness of that activity. The practice of setting up 'red corners' by housing management office educational organizers was particularly notorious for its formalism, often involving little more entertainment than lectures on the evils of drink (ibid.). Moreover, these organizations continued to focus their efforts on club work despite the fact that research into youth leisure preferences had shown that clubs and 'circles' held little attraction for contemporary youth.

Direct control of the streets was also attempted. In 1984 the Leningrad City Council adopted a number of additional rules designed to control the behaviour of children and teenagers in public places. These established that: those under 16 were not allowed on the streets unaccompanied after 9 p.m. (during school holidays after 10 p.m.);[22] the managements of trade and public-catering enterprises were liable for ensuring that no one under 16 was in a restaurant or bar where alcohol was on sale, or after 9 p.m.; and parents were responsible for their children being found on the street at an unauthorized hour or visiting places forbidden to them – and as such were liable for any fine imposed. Parents were also liable for the payment of compensation for material damage caused by their children through vandalism (Mikhailov, M. 1984).

The liability of parents for their children's behaviour was a natural progression of the emphasis on the micro-social environment as the site of social distortions which had begun in the 1930s, but which had been strengthened in the 1970s as the retreat into the family gathered pace. The claim that it was parents who had the greatest influence on children's behaviour (Il'inskii 1985: 35), meant that the superior nature of socialist society as a whole could continue to be proclaimed whilst individual *parents* were punished for their failure to bring up their children as good socialist citizens. Some deviance theorists did continue to argue that all 'deviations from the norms of the socialist way of life' must be attributed to 'vestiges of the past' rather than current social conditions since they were committed by individuals not social groups (Plaksii 1985: 17–22). Others, however, saw two sets of factors as essential in analysing juvenile delinquency: the macro-environment, i.e. the forces and relations of production in society, needs, interests, political and other social relations, legal norms and moral principles; and the micro-environment such as school, place of work, the family, daily-life and intra-personal factors (Batku 1984: 32–3). Nevertheless it was the inadequacies within the micro-social environment that were judged to be the major cause of juvenile delinquency whilst the existence of anti-social behaviour *per se* in socialist society was explained by imperfections in the system in the current 'lower phase' of communism and the 'concrete-historical conditions' in which the development of the new society was taking place (referring, one presumes, to the negative influence stemming from capitalist culture) (26).

On the eve of perestroika, then, interest in the culture or way of life of youth reflected concern about the continuity of generations within socialist society. This continuity depended upon the successful 'socialization' of young people into society which consisted of the formation of the individual as a *lichnost'* and the overcoming of the marginality of the biological and social position of youth (Grigor'eva 1985: 19). The culture of youth was central here because cultural norms both channelled individual actions in accordance with the main goals of society and guaranteed the possibility of individual expression (Volkov 1989: 18). In this sense 'cultural norms' were seen as a simple extension of 'social norms', which were the mechanism of the transfer of social aims, goals and desires into the action of individual agents. They were the concrete forms of social behaviour which realized the principles of the society (e.g. socialist morality, humanism, collectivism and internationalism). Thus whilst traditions and rituals transmitted social experience from generation to generation, social, and cultural, norms brought this experience from society to the individual. Where a non-correspondence between norms accepted in society and the real behaviour of people was experienced, 'social control' and its sanctions were applied (11–32).

## CONCLUSION

This chapter has attempted to outline the paradigms that have housed the youth debate in post-revolutionary Russian society and not the real social experience of young people over seventy years of Soviet history. This corresponds to the aims of Chapter 1 although, since the social experience of young people in Russia will be less familiar to the reader than that of youth in Western societies, where possible the gaps between the representation of youth and their actual experience have been flagged. The paradigms of 'youth-as-constructors-of-communism' and 'youth-as-victims-of-Western-influence' are somewhat crude – as paradigms they must necessarily be so – but they provide a useful framework for tracing the changing discourse on Soviet youth.

In the Soviet tradition, youth was attributed specific psychological traits which set it apart from the adult population, but the primacy of class analysis meant that young people appeared as a demographic stratum of separate classes (both within Soviet and between Soviet and Western, capitalist societies). As such, the possibility of a distinct 'youth culture' was rejected since in a non-antagonistic society the 'socialist way of life' was common to all. More important than the class (or rather non-class) position of youth, however, has been the role youth was seen to play in the historical process. The 'continuity of generations' in a non-antagonistic society replaced the struggle between classes as the motor of history. This meant that the drive for ideological 'purity' amongst youth was greater than amongst the adult population, since dissidence could be either tolerated or physically alienated, whereas a generation gap would wreck the very means of the development of socialist into communist society; it would disrupt the laws of history themselves. The emphasis on the non-conflictual nature of socialist society together with the rejection by Soviet sociologists of Western neo-Marxist (and thus revisionist) theories of youth and youth culture meant that the undercurrents within the academic debate leant heavily towards structural-functionalist interpretations of youth culture, which, ironically, were criticized at the time in the West for being premised on the stability and natural reproduction of capitalist society.

The 'constructors-of-communism' paradigm was not simply an ideological justification for the economic exploitation of youth labour in the fields of the Virgin Lands and along the railway tracks of the Far East, however. It was rather the physical embodiment of the construction of the new society and of the continuity of generations. As the advent of communism retreated into the increasingly distant future and the money for key projects such as the Baikal–Amur railway dried up, however, young people found themselves stranded in half-built cities permanently lodged in their temporary self-sacrifice. Not only were they on the 'road to nowhere' but they had built that road with their own hands.

Alongside their incorporation into the tasks of the day, however, youth also developed its own ways of life which expressed themselves both as generational identities *vis-à-vis* the adult population and more localized (regional and class) identities *vis-à-vis* other youth cultures. The former's manifestation in a post-war interest in the West, especially America, evoked a strong reaction from above and led to the evolution of the paradigm of 'youth-as-victims-of-bourgeois-influence' into that of the 'victims-of-Western-influence'. Youth cultures as the manifestation of differing youth identities, however, remained articulated only in relation to localized problems of delinquency and hooliganism to be tackled by calls for greater social control of youth whose marginalization was a product of rapid urbanization. Thus, by 1985, although the 'youth question' was not considered 'solved' altogether, the picture of Soviet youth elaborated was one of a mass of youth successfully socialized into society, and eagerly taking up the baton of the construction of communism, alongside a small minority of 'problem teenagers' who had been failed by their micro-environment. Society, then was ill-prepared indeed for the advent of glasnost and the non-homogeneity of the youth sphere which it revealed.

# Part II

# Reconstructing Soviet youth 1985–91

# Introduction

In April 1985 a major attack was launched on 'old ways of thinking' in the Soviet Union. The rallying call for the 'acceleration' of socio-economic progress was accompanied by a new attitude to the individual; socialism was to be constructed not at the cost of the people but for the people. This new 'socialism with a human face' involved a redefinition of relations between state and individual. Institutions of the state, and their representatives, were to become genuinely accountable to the people whilst individual citizens were asked to recognize their obligation to the state. Consequently, over the six years that can now be characterized as those of perestroika, the institutions which had framed the debate on youth and its culture – the party, the *Komsomol*, parliamentary and government committees, academia and the various organs of social control – changed significantly, both internally and in their relative centrality to the youth debate. The aim of this second part of the book is to explore these changes in order to assess: to what degree the youth paradigms were reconstructed or restructured in the period 1985–91; what the key moments in this restructuring were; and whether it is now possible to talk of a post-perestroika youth paradigm in Russia.

Chapter 3 will consider the early perestroika period and trace the impact of glasnost and party self-criticism on the youth debate. It will be argued that the core binary outlined in Chapter 2 was not fundamentally changed in the 1985–6 period. The key themes of youth as constructors of communism and youth as prone to diversion by Western consumerism were played out through a limited exposé of the 'real conditions' of Soviet society, without challenging the belief that these could be put in order through an improvement in the ideological work of the *Komsomol* and the encouragement of youth into more active forms of leisure pursuits.

Chapter 4 will trace the politicization of the youth debate in the period 1987–9 and the *neformaly* theme that dominated this process. This period is characterized by the recognition of alternative cultural formations in Soviet society and attempts by state institutions to gain contact with them and to guide them. This was evident in the elaboration of a 'differentiated approach' to the *neformaly* which was used by the *Komsomol* and other formal institutions in order to classify the multifarious informal groups as 'positive', 'neutral' or 'negative'. Towards the end of this period, concern over the 'cancerous' spread of negative (politically antagonistic or delinquent) groups was replacing fascination with the neutral (spectacular subcultural) groups as the chief focus of the perestroika youth debate. Chapter 4 also analyses the extent to which one can talk of a 'moral panic' over the phenomenon of teenage gangs in Russia during this period.

Chapter 5 considers the collapse of the VLKSM and, with it, the old paradigms of the youth debate. In this period, alongside the sociological and criminological inputs to the debate, there emerged a school of socio-psychological study of the *neformaly*, and the new directions this brought are analysed. The debate is followed through to the beginning of 1992 by which time new institutional and ideological frameworks to house the discussion of youth appeared to be emerging. Youth cultural groups began to be interpreted as evidence of youth's peripheral social position, and youth as a whole was seen not as the vanguard of the construction of communism but as a social metaphor for a collapsing society and the object of a paternal social policy. Youth entered the post-perestroika era, it will be argued, not as the constructors of the 'bright future' but as a 'lost generation' which had neither present nor future.

**A note on sources and methodology**

The conclusions drawn in Part II of the book are based on the study of the treatment of youth issues in the press, film and other popular art forms, in academic literature (from the disciplines of sociology, social psychology, criminology and pedagogy), and in CPSU and *Komsomol* resolutions and reports. The survey of material covers the period 1 January 1985 to 31 December 1991, for which period all issues of three newspapers were read: *Komsomol'skaia Pravda*, an all-Union newspaper under the Central Committee of the *Komsomol*; *Moskovskii Komsomolets*, the Moscow paper under the Moscow city and regional *Komsomol* committees; and *Sobesednik*, the weekly, illustrated colour supplement of *Komsomol'skaia Pravda*. These are by no means representative papers but were chosen with reference to their peculiarities.

*Komsomol'skaia Pravda* was interesting because of its extreme popularity and wide circulation which, at around twenty million earned it an entry in the *Guinness Book of Records*. A study of the youth press conducted in 1987 revealed that 77 per cent of young people in Ukraine were regular readers of the paper, whilst only one in ten were regular readers of its republican-level equivalent, *Komsomol'skoe Znamia* (Kostenko 1990: 82). Since its founding in May 1925, *Komsomol'skaia Pravda* has also been the definitive source of VLKSM Central Committee views. In contrast, its weekly supplement *Sobesednik* was founded only in February 1984 and was one of a new generation of publications being printed in colour and focusing on feature journalism of an adventurous kind. Its small circulation (1,300,000) and availability only on open sale (rather than through subscription) meant that it had a substantially smaller and narrower readership than its big brother daily. The readership is well educated; the single largest category has been that of the technical intelligentsia aged between 26 and 40, and 50 per cent of all readers have higher education ('I eto vse o nas' 1990).[1] It also has a predominantly Russian, urban readership: 70 per cent of readers live in the RSFSR, 63 per cent live in large cities and only 9 per cent in rural areas (ibid.). The narrowness of the readership, however, did serve to maintain the youth profile of the magazine; the *Sobesednik* editorial board, which commissioned the above survey, was itself surprised to find that 57 per cent of its readers were under 30 (24 per cent under 20), since they feared that the paper was being read mainly by pensioners who tended to be the first to get to the kiosks where it was on sale (ibid.).

*Moskovskii Komsomolets* provides a more popular interpretation of events, being significantly more light-weight than the two other papers. Indeed it prided itself on its reputation for scandal-seeking, especially when it was directed against those whom the paper felt were retarding the process of perestroika (Dmukhovskii 1989). As a local newspaper it has been relatively free from central control yet, as an organ of the Moscow *Komsomol* committee, more vulnerable to shifts in the balance of power at city level. According to the paper's chief editor, the appointment of Boris Yeltsin as First Secretary of the Moscow Party Committee, for example, allowed the paper to enter a period of 'the quest for closed themes', whilst his replacement by Lev Zaikov at the end of 1987 rapidly closed this space again (Gusev 1991).

Despite their different profiles, the three papers shared two things in common. First, they were all 'youth papers' (*molodezhnaia pechat'*).[2] This was important not only because greater attention was paid to youth issues, but because the role of the institution of the youth press itself was likely to be central to any new youth paradigm formed. Second, all three papers were considered to be of a 'progressive' tendency. In particular *Komsomol'skaia Pravda* was soon being heralded as the flag-ship of the more ambitious reformists, especially from 1990 onwards when Gorbachev's own position became less than clear. Whilst this is hardly representative, it was important for the purposes of this particular study to follow the debate in those papers which were actively taking up the challenge of glasnost, not those which were more or less actively resisting it. Nevertheless, articles on youth and youth culture were also followed in less radical papers such as *Pravda*, *Izvestiia*, *Literaturnaia Gazeta*, *Sovetskaia Rossiia*, *Moskovskaia Pravda*, and in weeklies and journals such as *Novoe Vremia*, *Iunost'*, *Molodoi Kommunist* and *Nedelia*.

During neither periods of field work was regular access to a television possible and, for this reason, the study is confined to the press, although where the findings of other studies based on alternative media forms either confirm or refute those from the press, they are cited. Reference is also made to film, theatre and other popular art forms where appropriate.

The academic literature analysed focuses on youth culture but situates its discussion in the wider debates on the *neformaly*, the restructuring of the *Komsomol* and the socio-economic position of youth. Indeed, the different ways in which the debate has been framed are a central part of the analysis. Institutional and political affiliations of the authors of academic studies are also explored, especially where changes in this area affect the nature of the debate. The journals used include *Sotsiologicheskie Issledovaniia, Voprosy Filosofii, Obshchestvennie Nauki* and *Dekorativnoe Isskustvo* as well as numerous academic brochures and books. Official policy and how it is formed is followed through documents relating to plenums, congresses and resolutions issued by party and *Komsomol* organizations and parliamentary and government youth committees. The results of policy-making and to some extent the conflicts in the process of its formulation have also been reflected in the youth press, which has been institutionally controlled by the *Komsomol*.

In the analysis that follows, therefore, the relative autonomy of media, academia and state institutions is explored but so too are the areas of overlap and influence which have helped shape the changing youth paradigm of the perestroika years. Texts produced by these institutions are read paying particular attention not to any coded messages they might contain, but to their production and consumption; it is through this social contextualization that the shaping of a new youth paradigm is traced.

# 3 Youth under the spotlight of glasnost 1985–6

The policy of glasnost ('openness' or 'voicing') metamorphosed the style and content of media reporting on Soviet society both within and beyond the USSR. Glasnost cannot, however, be simply equated with the liberal notion of the 'freedom of the press' but must be seen in its social and cultural context.

'Glasnost' was not a new concept for the Soviet press,[3] and its earlier usage had included both a positive openness about the progress of the construction of the new society, in order to provide a model for emulation, and a critical appraisal of negative phenomena (McNair 1991: 29).[4] The re-emergence of glasnost in the perestroika period, therefore, must be seen in the context of this wider application to public administration and political activities. It was certainly a much more meaningful concept than the *ottepel'* (thaw) of the Khrushchev era, for it entailed not just the toleration of the right of the intelligentsia to freedom of expression, but was an integral component of a much broader social, economic and cultural programme of change. At the heart of this lay the realization that – as the government had been warned more than a decade earlier (Sakharov 1974) – the 'relations of production' were slipping behind the 'forces of production' and halting the latter's development. In effect the failure of the Soviet Union to move into an intensive rather than extensive form of production – a switch closely linked to the introduction and expansion of information technology – was preventing the continued growth of the Soviet economy and the qualitative improvement of life for Soviet citizens.

While glasnost was much deeper than the notion of cultural thaw, however, it was also much more instrumental. Its aim was not only to allow a greater freedom of the press and speech but to expose the 'real' state of affairs and, still more importantly, to create a climate in which solutions to the problems uncovered might be more readily found. The start of the glasnost campaign was thus characterized by attention to the publication in the newspapers of the critical opinions of workers. These themselves became an important aspect of the party-led labour discipline and anti-alcohol campaigns and calls for the moral strengthening of the family unit. The essence of this gamut of campaigns was not only to revive Leninist traditions against the distortions of Brezhnev and Stalin before him, but to return responsibility to the individual (to 'activate the human factor' in the language of Gorbachev) and create an environment in which initiative was seen to be rewarded rather than punished.

That the party retained its ability to control both the depth and breadth of glasnost was evidenced in not only the partial nature of glasnost, but also the unchanged institutional position of the media. The abolition of preliminary censorship by *Glavlit* (the official censorship body) from 1 August 1990 (Wedgwood Benn 1992: 178) may have removed all ostensible censorship but, as journalists admitted, the internal censor continued to operate. Moreover, as elsewhere, censorship in the Soviet Union was only an extreme measure, and the party controlled the media much more effectively through: its control of access to media facilities; its control of the paper supply and printing facilities; its subsidy of the prices for newspapers; its control of media policy-making; its power over appointments to senior media positions; and its direction and supervision of journalistic training (McNair 1991: 49). Thus, although the implementation of glasnost did have a tangible impact upon the media (especially in its eradication of many of the 'blank spots' of Soviet history, the 'de-shelving' of previously banned works of film, art and literature and the removal of the old guard in the key artists' unions), nevertheless the continuity in the institutional position of the media ensured that glasnost remained a reform weapon rather than an end in itself. It was not until June 1990, when the long-awaited law on the press was finally passed, that party control of the media was brought to an end. Rather like the long-overdue emancipation of the serfs in the previous century, however, the freedom gained was very partial; for many papers the new law just added financial crisis to ideological tutelage.

The ideological, and later institutional, changes associated with glasnost in the mid-1980s, therefore, did not sweep away the old media system built on the principles of propagandizing, mobilizing, partiality, objectivity, accessibility and openness and replace it with the principle of exposing the truth. Rather the emphasis was switched away from propagandizing, partiality and objectivity and towards openness and accessibility whilst retaining a strong mobilizational intent (and effect). The result was not an anarchic polyphony but a widening of the spectrum of voices being heard as well as the emergence of a peculiar glasnost voice or agenda. It is the nature of that agenda in relation to one specific issue – youth and its culture – which will be explored in this chapter. The question to be addressed is to what extent the advent of glasnost disrupted or continued the paradigms of the youth debate outlined in Chapter 2.

## YOUTH AS RECONSTRUCTORS OF COMMUNISM

The politically overdetermined base binary of 'constructors-of-communism' and 'victims-of-Western-influence' remained intact throughout 1985 and 1986. The 'constructors-of-communism' paradigm was most overtly continued through the reporting of grand projects and campaigns designed to speed the construction of 'developed socialist society' in which the activities of student-youth brigades, socialist youth labour competitions and shock youth or *Komsomol* brigades featured prominently. It was equally evident, however, in the formation of economic and social policies that continued to approach young people not as individuals with distinct needs, but as a generation whose duty it was to make a specific contribution to society at the current stage of its development.

### Advances in the construction of communism

Student brigades were ritually thanked for their participation in bringing in the harvest, which remained a symbol of the coming together of urban and rural areas – of peasant and worker – as well as being essential if a large part of the harvest was not to rot in the fields. The work of student-youth brigades on All-Union projects such as the Baikal–Amur railway line (BAM) was acknowledged (Gorin 1985), as were more local efforts such as the development of the village economy (Liuboshchits 1986). Socialist competition was portrayed as being alive and well; in 1985 *Moskovskii Komsomolets* ran a series of reports on the 'Stakhanovites of the eighties' and featured the first regional competition of metal-workers (Nikolaev 1986). A shock *Komsomol* brigade of the Moscow City *Komsomol* organization – rather unimaginatively called 'Stakhanovite' – was also reported to have been dispatched to the Tiumen' region to help build the new town Munavlenkovsk.[5]

Another important aspect of socialist competition was its role in aiding the selection of candidates to participate in youth housing projects (*Molodezhnie Zhilie Kompleksy* or MZhK).[6] But there were also a number of important social spin-offs. During the competition for admission to the Stupino MZhK, for example, productivity was raised (after a year candidates for the MZhK project were producing 140 per cent of their previous output), there was increased social activity (candidates on average had two permanent social/public commitments), and there was a marked improvement in labour discipline (Alpatov 1986). MZhKs were also reported to have a positive effect on the family. At the Sverdlovsk MZhK, the number of divorces was six times lower than the average (Petrov 1986). Karelova also notes the positive counterweight of the MZhK in the social chain of housing shortage–divorce–reduction in birth rate. The social responsibility that constructing and living in an MZhK induced, she reported, had led to an increase in the number of children per family from 1.3 to 1.6, while almost half the families in the MZhK had two or more children (Karelova 1987: 15). Finally, the MZhK was seen to have a correcting role in the battle against the slippage of gender roles within the family. The MZhK, it was argued, could help restore male authority – seen to have declined due to the alienation of men from familial functions together with the increased public role of women – in so far as men usually participated in building the MZhK and thus increased their contribution to the organization of family life. Moreover, the participation of male residents in the children's clubs of the MZhK should help compensate for the absence of male influence (in one-parent families), and eliminate the consequences of 'feminized' child-raising in such families (Gurko, Matsovskii and Solodnikov 1987: 23). These reports indicate that the importance of the MZhK was not only material but also educative: the process of the construction of the MZhK taught people the principles of communist morality while the community which develops acted as an example of the virtues of the socialist way of life for the rest of society.[7]

At the same time, the MZhK was an important ongoing construction project of developed socialism. In 1985 the USSR Council of Ministers adopted a resolution requiring that USSR ministries and departments and Union-republic Councils of Ministers make provision in their draft plans for the construction of MZhKs and young people's housing construction co-operatives, and authorizing enterprises, institutions and organizations to use their assets to lend financial help to employees who were members, or potential members, of the young people's housing-construction co-operatives ('On the construction of housing for young people' 1985). The desire to improve the housing situation of young people – especially young families often forced to live much of their early married life with their in-laws – was given special emphasis at the Twenty-seventh Congress of the CPSU in February 1986. Immediately after the Congress, the Central Committee of the CPSU adopted a resolution 'On basic guidelines for accelerating the solution of the housing problem in the country', which included the recommendation to expand the MZhK project as part of a series of measures designed to provide all families with separate flats by the year 2000 ('In the CPSU CC' 1986).[8]

The ideological and material thus remained entwined in the 'constructors-of-communism' paradigm which still shaped the youth debate. Articles in the press continued to cite young people's work on 'the grand construction sites of Siberia, the Far East and the North of the country' as evidence of their ideological firmness and support for the Soviet government (Khaitina 1986), and to encourage other young people to take up the baton for the next lap of the ongoing race towards the communist future (Sokolov 1986).

Nowhere was the symbolic and material construction by youth of the future society more clearly stated, however, than in the new CPSU pro-gramme and statutes published after the Twenty-seventh Party Congress in

1986. The role of the *Komsomol* was essentially unchanged: it 'helps the party to instil a spirit of communism in young people, to enlist them in the practical construction of a new society and in the administration of state and public affairs, and to mould a generation of comprehensively developed people prepared for labour and the defence of the Soviet homeland.' ('Communist Party Programme and Party Statutes' 1986). Gorbachev, as leader of the party, was no dissenter from this position. Replying to a question as to whether it was true that Soviet youth was uninterested in politics and socially inactive, he declared that, 'Young people go willingly and enthusiastically to those parts of the country where it is necessary to work (the North, Siberia, the Far East). There are currently half a million young people working on these sites.' (Gorbachev 1986: 13). There were some new emphases however. The stage of socio-economic development reached by 1985 – embodied in the policy of 'acceleration' (*uskorenie*) – meant that it was less the physical power to construct that was needed from youth than its dedication to the acceleration of scientific-technical progress (Solomkin 1986). Since youth constituted the most educated portion of the population, and some tasks – such as computerization – could be solved by youth alone, it was youth's ability to develop and introduce new technology to industry which was portrayed as the appropriate 'heroism of our time' (Il'inskii 1987a: 4–5).

If young people were to be able to fulfil the economic 'task' assigned to them, however, the education system had to prepare them for it. Given the nature of the task, this entailed not only improving educational standards in general, but tying the individual young person's rights and choices to the social good. In fact, the 1984 education reforms had done much of Gorbachev's work for him. These reforms were concerned with the choice of educational path made by young people at the age of 15. The problem was that annually about 60 per cent of pupils chose to remain at general secondary school, which was the most academic option and the usual route into higher education (Muckle 1988: 21), and this was considered to have helped fuel the overproduction of specialists in the economy. The 1984 reforms thus aimed to upgrade the prestige of the vocational-technical college or PTU (generally considered to be the dumping ground of the Soviet education system) by allowing students to graduate with a certificate of secondary education and thus the right to apply for higher education. The idea was that the secondary vocational-technical college or *SPTU* would come to replace the general secondary school as the standard choice for 15 year olds, thereby boosting the numbers of skilled workers so urgently required in the economy (Dunstan 1985: 164).

Glasnost did little to challenge these reforms, despite their unpopularity among both parents and pupils. The rubrics in which issues specific to young people were discussed in the youth press mirrored their position in the education system, denying the possibility of any common youth interests and encouraging young people to think of themselves in terms of their

social position and role.[9] The real issues of concern such as the dissatisfaction of young people with time spent on military training, compulsory
vocational training, dictatorial classroom methods and even corruption
among teachers were not voiced.[10] As a result of the 1984 education
reforms young people were also worried about the increasing difficulty
of gaining acceptance at an institute of higher education – not only because of the encouragement of vocational education but also the reassertion of 'social criteria' in the competition for higher education places. It
was stated by the Minister of Higher Education, Iagodin, for example,
that in considering applications particular attention would be paid not to
ability but to 'achievements in improving production, efficiency and
inventing, victories in competitions in maths, physics etc., employment
and military service records' and, above all, *Komsomol* reports (Korsakova 1986).

The 'activation of the human factor', with its emphasis on individual
responsibility and ability, thus still envisaged that the individual's activity
should be directed to the predetermined social good, which, of course,
might be in conflict with the individual's perceived interests. The early
glasnost period saw the voicing of little challenge to key social institutions,
which remained dedicated to producing the kind of workers and citizens
needed by society in transition.

### Setbacks in the construction of communism

The glasnost agenda nevertheless meant that whilst quantitatively stories
of production and labour may still have dominated the press, qualitatively
they had changed. In line with the advocacy of criticism and self-criticism
(especially of formalistic or bureaucratic management), the press began to
highlight not only the successes of the labour feats of young people, but
also the difficulties faced. In 1984 the construction of the giant tractor
factory in the city of Elabuga was declared to be an All-Union shock
*Komsomol* construction project (*udarnaia komsomol'skaia stroika*) since
two-thirds of the 5,000 workers there were youth and *Komsomol* members.
But not even such a prestigious construction project could escape the
blockages of the Soviet planning system; it became caught up in disputes
between the two responsible ministries resulting in serious supply shortages and work being conducted without a clear plan target (Kozin 1987b).
The MZhK projects often ran out of steam because of problems with
funding (the work was essentially voluntary) and, consequently, the motivation of participants suffered. Alternatively, participants dropped out due
to pressure at work; many rose quickly up their professional ladder and
soon had too much responsibility to be able to devote time to work at the
complex (Vlasov 1984). The Kaliningrad MZhK was found to have been
badly planned – containing too many one-room apartments which soon
became too small for growing families – while the Sverdlovsk complex

was criticized for its underrepresentation of members of the social class of workers (Kravchenko 1985).

As the symbol of the continuity of generations, the Baikal–Amur railway project (BAM) came in for particular attack (Sungorkin 1988; Nikolaev 1987).[11] It was claimed that workers sent to the region found there was no real provision for them. The cities which housed the construction brigades had been built on the assumption that the population would be a temporary one of single men, and consequently there had been no provision for family accommodation. Poor housing conditions, low levels of recreational facilities and high overstaffing levels (17 per cent) led to low morale, massive personnel turnover and poor economic results (Druzenko and Ezhelev 1984; Ordzhonikidze 1985). The cost of rectifying the planning mistakes already made was estimated at 866.9 million roubles (Koveshnikov and Cherniak 1988), and the catastrophic situation was once again blamed on poor co-ordination between central and regional planning. Although formally the local soviets were responsible for the social welfare of the residents of BAM towns, in practice BAM was built by USSR ministries and departments who funded only production units, not sociocultural infrastructure and who were not subordinated to the local organs of power (ibid.). This situation led sociologist Mikhail Topalov to question the necessity for such 'heroism' by contemporary constructors of communism. Surely, he argued,

> under socialism the person is not for the sake of the state, but the state is for the sake of the person, not the person for BAM but BAM for the person, not the person for victory but heroism in the name of humanity.
> (Topalov cited in Koveshnikov and Cherniak 1988)

Despite the new critical approach to the BAM construction project, however, throughout 1987, the press continued to follow in great detail such events as the election of a new leader of a *Komsomol* office to oversee youth participation in the BAM project (Vishnevskii and Utekhin 1987c; Medvedev 1987; Utekhin 1987b; Utekhin 1987c; Vishnevskii and Utekhin 1987a; Vishnevskii and Utekhin 1987b), and the economic development of the BAM region was declared to be 'one of the most important tasks for *Komsomol* members' and 'a glorious *Komsomol* construction' (Utekhin 1987a).

A theme little touched upon in the early glasnost press, but undoubtedly reflecting a very real problem, was that of the resentment of incoming 'shock brigades' by the local population. This was revealed in a report published from the plenum of the Khabarovsk regional committee of the *Komsomol* on the subject of a reprimand issued to the First Secretary of the regional committee (*kraikom*) following an incident in the city of Komsomol'sk-na-Amure in which a group of local teenagers fought with a 'Constructors of the *Komsomol*' youth brigade which had arrived from Kazakhstan. The police had been forced to issue 'warning shots' in order to disperse an angry crowd which gathered. In a separate, but not unconnected incident, a virtual riot ensued when the police arrested two youths for disturbing public order – a group of young people headed towards the police station overturning cars and throwing stones through windows (Mironova 1987).

A third concern to be voiced concerned the poor management of student work brigades. Bad management meant that before their arrival detachments had no idea of the volume or nature of the forthcoming work and so could not rationally distribute their manpower, thus the first days were wasted in redeployment (Pristupko and Elkind 1985). Moreover, students were both discriminated against and exploited in the labour market. The reluctance to hire students on the part of enterprise directors meant that in the Moscow area in 1985, 30,000 students were looking for work but only 8,000 managed to find it, despite the fact that economists calculated that the city had a net labour shortage ('Between lectures' 1985). Those that did find work with student brigades generally earned only 200–300 roubles for their two months' work (if they were employed in construction at their own institutes, as was often the case, they were paid even less) and many collectives devoted part or all of their earnings to social funds such as children's homes or the peace movement (Pristupko and Elkind 1985).

The problems faced by student brigades sent to collective farms to help with harvests were the most notorious. Despite the supposedly voluntary nature of this work, students had little choice but to participate and their resentment was only heightened by the bad management which made their efforts seem worthless.

### Glasnost as 'voicing', but whose voice?

What is most noticeable from the youth debate in this early period is the continuity of themes such as production and labour from the pre-glasnost days and the virtual absence of the opinion of youth itself. This is confirmed by content-analysis studies of the youth press. The Ukrainian study of the All-Union paper *Komsomol'skaia Pravda* and the republican paper *Komsomol'skoe Znamia* cited above analysed 540 'problem situations' which were discussed in the papers in the period 1986–7, and found a striking similarity in the themes that appeared. In both papers most space was given to issues of production, *Komsomol* work and the moral education of youth – themes fully consistent with the press of the pre-perestroika era (Kostenko 1990: 83). New themes such as that of the informal youth associations in the leisure sphere came around half-way down the list of theme-categories, while those associated with the democratization of the public consciousness – such as the electoral system, the broadening of rights and freedoms of the individual and the improvement of the legislature – remained peripheral (84). While the two papers analysed were fairly consistent between themselves in the prioritization of particular themes, when these themes were compared with data taken from public opinion surveys of youth, there was a significant discrepancy. Precisely those issues which were peripheral in the press were seen as the most important in the public opinion survey, while issues such as 'irresponsibility at work', 'school reform' and 'the creative initiative of youth at work' (all in the top five priorities in the press, clearly reflecting the 'activation of the human factor' programme) did not feature at all in public opinion (85). This led the authors of the article to conclude that the current organization of the youth press continued to encourage the defence and popularization of the positions of the papers' owners (various levels of *Komsomol* committees) and thus left intact the propagandistic model of the press (87).

At the same time, the authors detected the adoption by editors of a list of priorities formed on the basis of what editors often referred to as the '*sotsial'nii zakaz*' (see Chapter 2). The *sotsial'nii zakaz* in this case was a kind of ideal model of democratization and was determined, not from below but from above, through reference to party documents of recent years. This *sotsial'nii zakaz* of specific themes and issues to be dealt with was then filtered through the other pressures on the editors (the traditions of the paper, the norms of behaviour and models of journalism and the information needs and interests of the readers) (83). The result, in the authors' opinion, was an unhappy state of affairs whereby the same newspapers were being asked to simultaneously fulfil the demands of three separate subjects of communication: the ideological institutions forming the *sotsial'nii zakaz*; the publishers; and the broad spectrum of the youth audience (88).

The continuity with pre-glasnost practices was not only one of content, but also of tone, however. Another survey based on a content-analysis of two local youth papers, Moscow's *Moskovskii Komsomolets* and the Krasnodar paper *Komsomolets Kubani*, concluded that the media was failing to fully bring to light the problems of youth. The lack of independence of the press from the *Komsomol* determined its outlook. The content-analysis revealed that 44 per cent of the material was considered in its ideological-moral aspect, 19 per cent was from a socio-political viewpoint and 50 per cent considered issues at the level of individual enterprises and organizations. The failure to adequately reflect social reality, the author claimed, was responsible for a decrease in the trust of information in the papers – only 49 per cent of readers said that they trusted the information provided by the media (Loshkarev 1989: 55).

The 'voicing' taking place during the early period of perestroika then was not the result of an opening up of the media to allow young people to air their views on their own situation, since the institutional organization of the youth press could not allow for this. It was rather a publicizing of the ways in which youth could participate in the new stage of socio-economic development and thus the texts which emerged were as much, or more, part of a discourse on labour discipline and individual responsibility as on youth issues. It appears, however, that in the non-written forms of the media, the stranglehold was looser. One notable example is the youth television programme 'Twelfth Floor' which began broadcasting in January 1986. The programme not only discussed topical themes but openly encouraged young people to express their viewpoints, and not from the controlled environment of a television studio but from the streets and courtyards of the country's cities. The discussions that ensued were often highly critical of the *Komsomol* and other official organizations supposedly dealing with youth issues (Mickiewicz 1988: 172–8).

One of the reasons this programme, as well as 'View' (*Vzgliad*), which began broadcasting in 1987, was so successful was that it managed to get immediate feedback from young people. The only real access to youth opinion which the press had was through letters sent to the editors. Although these came in floods – in 1987 *Komsomol'skaia Pravda* received over six million letters, of which 2,447 were published (Kozyrev 1987) – they were generally of little use in indicating youth opinion since, editors admitted, they were mostly written by pensioners, party members or *Komsomol* activists (Mickiewicz 1981: 121). Those that were written by young people were predominantly about their personal situations, about loneliness and lovelessness. This may help explain to some extent the shock caused by Juris Podnieks's film released in 1986 *Is It Easy To Be Young?*. Although, in retrospect, it remained rather controlled and didactic, the film was astonishing in both the issues it dealt with (hooliganism, rock fanaticism, the death of young people through wrong treatment in hospital, juvenile crime, subcultures such as the punks) but more importantly in the scope given to young people to talk about themselves. In so doing they revealed their real concerns about school, work, the army and finding partners, rather than the worldly concerns of internationalism and socialism. These fleeting insights revealed the cracks in the old youth paradigms; flouting any ideological commitment to the construction of communism, for example, one young man explained his plans to go to Siberia to build roads before going on to study as being motivated by the desire to enter higher education 'financially secure'.

## CONSUMED BY CONSUMPTION? THE DEBATE ON YOUTH LEISURE

What has been argued above is that, despite the note of self-criticism which the early glasnost period brought to the youth debate, the paradigm of 'constructors-of-communism' essentially remained intact. The next question which must be posed is, how well did the 'victims-of-Western-influence' paradigm withstand increased openness and the 'activation of the human factor'?

Of course, as was suggested in Chapter 2, the attribution of problems in the youth sphere to ideological diversion instigated by the West did not prevent the assertion of the responsibility of micro-level social institutions (the family, school, work collective and youth organization) for failures in the upbringing of children. In the same way, the 'activation of the human factor' – an ideological slogan used extensively at the Twenty-seventh Congress of the CPSU and afterwards – was able to coexist happily with a youth paradigm of the 'victims-of-Western-influence'. Indeed the two reinforced each other as was made clear by Kravchenko:

> the improvement of the socialist way of life is inseparably connected to the increase in effectiveness of work, with the development of socialist culture, with the increase in socio-political activity of workers and with the fight against petty-bourgeois psychology.
>
> (Kravchenko 1988: 97)

The understanding of culture had not changed, it remained a strategically important sphere which allowed the smooth historical progression of socialist construction. The duality of cultures – socialist versus bourgeois – was reasserted, indeed the importance of the cultural sphere as the *site* of that struggle was heightened since culture acted as the means of socialization of youth (Askin 1988: 6). In this section, therefore, an attempt is made to show how the campaign for the 'activation of the human factor' worked *within* the 'youth-as-victims-of-Western-influence' paradigm to shape the distinctive formulation of the youth question in the early perestroika period as one of inadequate leisure provision.

Concern about the provision of organized leisure for young people had been voiced well before perestroika (see Chapter 2) but in the early glasnost period it became the central theme of the youth debate. A reading of the press debate in conjunction with the policy priorities being outlined by the party and *Komsomol*, however, suggests that this concern was born not of a response to voiced criticisms or demands from young people themselves, but was a product of the restructured *sotsial'nii zakaz*. Indeed, the debate on youth leisure provision exemplifies the continuity of the 'victims-of-Western-influence' paradigm of youth in a perestroika coating. Its elements followed a standard 'activation of the human factor' format recognizable in campaigns such as that for labour discipline and against alcoholism, unearned income and the double burden of women. This consisted of: an identified social malaise (in the case of youth, the growth of consumerism); a subject of this malaise (the mass of Soviet youth symbolized by the *dvor* group); and a combat task (to turn youth as passive consumers into active constructors again).

This format marked a deviation from the traditional mobilization campaigns in the level of self-criticism voiced by those defining the debate, but there was also much continuity. The 'problem' – the growth of consumerism – was discussed less in terms of the objective social conditions which might influence change in leisure behaviour than in its ideological aspect (the influence of the West) and implications (the diversion of the mass of Soviet youth from socialist construction). The 'combat task' also remained defined and led from above; the limits of and absences in the debate reveal how the spotlight of glasnost was manoeuvred as considered necessary for the illumination of specific issues rather than used to expose the whole of society to the light of a new era.

### The 'teenage consumer'

That a society known to have a constant shortage of consumer goods should suffer from the teenage-consumer syndrome might seem strange at first. In fact, however, post-war industrial societies both East and West had much in common. In 1960 the seven-hour working day was introduced in the Soviet Union and in 1967 the five-day week (for 16–18 year olds this happened even earlier, see Chapter 2). Since then there had been a steady rise in the free time enjoyed by young workers; between 1975 and 1985 the amount of leisure time available to young workers increased by six to eight hours per week (Pishchulin 1985). This, combined with the rapid development of a host of forms of accessible mass information, led to concerns on both sides of the Iron Curtain about the growth of a passive, consumerist attitude to leisure (see Chapters 1 and 2). Whereas in Britain the fear of the growth of passive cultural consumption was associated in popular consciousness with an Americanization of culture, in the Soviet Union it was a more general 'Westernization' or 'bourgeoisification' that was feared, since this threatened to undermine the notion of the superiority of the 'Soviet way of life'. This was, of course, linked to the popularity of Western radio channels, primarily the BBC and Voice of America, which broadcast into the Soviet Union and were seen as the transporters of alien styles and youth cultures to Soviet youth whose political naivety led it to 'imitate' them. Thus there were two aspects of the Soviet teenage consumer which caused concern: first a tendency amongst young people to consume rather than create their own entertainment; but second, the content of that which they were passively consuming was fundamentally opposed to and subversive of the socialist personality (*lichnost'*).

The first was a problem because it disrupted the dialectic of the construction of communism and broke the link between active physical involvement and active ideological engagement. On a theoretical level these issues were dealt with by the concepts of 'free time' and 'rational needs'. These concepts started from a class approach to free time which saw it as consisting not only of freedom but also of 'responsibility', with its content being determined by the system of social relations. Thus, in socialist society, free time consisted of the activities which assisted the all-round development of the individual (*lichnost'*) (Tishchenko 1989: 20–3). There could, however, be distortions in socialist society. In particular, the rapid rise in the material well-being of young people, as well as their level of education and culture, was seen to have increased their demand for the consumption of spiritual artefacts (cinema, concerts, theatre and fashion) (Plaksii 1983: 35). The failure to meet these heightened demands hindered the rational use of free time and thus the development of the individual (Tishchenko 1989: 31). In particular the migration of young people from rural areas to towns and cities was attributed to the very poor recreational and leisure provision in the countryside. Consumption of leisure artefacts therefore was considered a normal part of activity, and was sharply contrasted to 'consumerism' which represented the disharmony of material and spiritual demands, of personal labour contribution and spiritual needs and which turned people into the slaves of things. The development of rational needs was the way in which consumption in socialist society was differentiated from the 'consumerist psychology' alien to socialism. Rational needs were those which: ensured the conditions for life activity of the individual; which facilitated the all-round and harmonious development of the individual; and which did not contradict the demands of society but facilitated its progress (Kozlov and Lisovskii 1986: 92–107).

On a practical level youth leisure became another combat task defined by the party. On 12 June 1985, the Central Committee of the CPSU adopted a resolution which set out the urgent task of 'the improvement of forms and methods of the work of cultural establishments in the organization of the leisure of the population, the raising of the role of trade unions and *Komsomol* committees in the improvement of their activity, and their more active participation in the creation of various amateur (*liubitel'skie*) associations, circles and interest clubs for youth and constant control of their activity' ('O problemakh, zadachakh i perspektivakh molodezhnogo dosuga' 1985). The task of securing this improvement was assigned to the existing cultural organizers, the *Komsomol* and the trade unions, and they wasted no time in adopting the required rhetoric. At the plenum of the Moscow City Committee of the *Komsomol* which took place later the same month, the First Secretary, Smirnov, highlighted three priorities of the *Komsomol*: socialist competition and the activation of the human factor; improved ideological work by local committees; and the need to ensure that how young people spent their leisure time coincided with the growth of spiritual culture (Smirnov, S. 1985).

The youth press also had a role to play here and new rubrics soon appeared to perform it. Throughout 1985, 1986 and 1987 *Moskovskii Komsomolets* ran a front-page rubric entitled 'Youth leisure – experiences, problems, tasks and prospects' which was devoted to exploring the problems and successes of leisure organization in different districts of Moscow as well as further afield. This was matched in *Sobesednik* by a section entitled 'You and your leisure'.

These rubrics provided the perfect opportunity for the local and national *Komsomol* committees to propagandize their programmes designed to tackle the identified problems. The Moscow City *Komsomol* Committee, for example, published its programme on 'The work and leisure of young people' in advance of its discussion at its forthcoming plenum. The programme aimed to create much wider leisure opportunities in the local area for Moscow youth by: transforming empty first-floor and basement rooms for youth leisure purposes; building simple sports facilities in every district; making wider use of existing school and college sports halls; organizing and improving existing circles, clubs, etc.; developing defence-sports camps and car, motorbike, shooting and parachuting types of sport; creating additional amateur associations and clubs according to interests; opening (the much delayed) Palace of Youth; holding regular festivals of literature, music and art; developing a chain of district youth centres, clubs, cafes, and theatres; and creating a self-financing voluntary organization 'Youth Initiative' which could invest in slot machines, table games, discos and video clubs ('Nashi plany i nadezhdy' 1986).

The particular forms of youth leisure encouraged for development were not new. Sports clubs, especially defence sports, had been promoted as early as the 1920s, while interest clubs and circles also had a long history. Greatest emphasis though was laid on the provision of youth cafes and clubs. Although the level of provision was undoubtedly appallingly low – in 1986 there were just six cafes which were open on a daily basis in the whole of Moscow – the concern was indicative of the more general desire to create controllable spaces in which young people could gather, for fear of what they would get up to if left to the influence of the street (see Chapter 2). This was also reflected in the attention paid not only to the forms of leisure to be developed, but to the process of their development. The guiding principle of the Moscow programme was that youth should actively participate in this process itself; following the Leninist dialectic described in the previous chapter, youth of the 1980s would become active partakers of leisure not passive consumers only in the process of actively making their own leisure (ibid.). The Novosibirsk city *Komsomol* Committee even set up a 'Fund of Youth Initiative' in order to help realize the ideas of young people themselves on improving leisure facilities.

The second problem – of *what* not *how* youth consumed – was even more directly linked to the 'victims-of-Western-influence' debate and envisaged young people as ideologically ill-prepared to resist the onslaught of diversive bourgeois culture. In the early part of perestroika, this problem focused on the discussion of rock music.

Glasnost did not revoice the invective against rock music of the immediately preceding period, in which it was declared that Soviet young people must be trained in 'ideological immunity' in order to withstand the psychological warfare being conducted by the West (Nozhin 1984: 1). On the principle that 'forbidden fruit is always sweeter', arguments working on the purely ideological level were replaced with an acceptance of the popularity of rock music, alongside attempts to control its worst excesses. The prime task was thus to 'educate' young people in what was and what was not worth listening to and what the 'subliminal messages' of Western rock might be.

In this cause, use was made of the puritanical American backlash to rock and of academic research. One author, for example, quoted American sociological research to prove that the latest pop stars (those cited were Phil Collins, Madonna and Michael Jackson) had no special talent and were popular only because of their 'image' and 'packaging'. She went on to argue that this music was threatening to produce a whole generation brought up on sadism, violence, sexual perversion and drug abuse as was indicated by current crime figures in the USA. Hence, she concluded, 'music has become the field not of the critic but of the psychiatrist as these perversions have become an epidemic penetrating the heart of the American character' (Gapochka 1986).

As elsewhere in the world, most criticism was levelled at heavy metal music which, at best, was described as 'senseless guitar noise' (Iudanov 1987) and had become popular in the West because of the decline in interest in 'boring disco' (Platonov 1987: 30). Sarkitov (writing in the journal of the Institute of Sociological Research) cited Adorno to support his claim that the most popular forms of music encouraged social passivity through a process of gradual 'stupefication' (*effekt oglupleniia*) (Sarkitov 1987: 94). In particular, however, he condemned heavy metal, arguing that groups such as Kiss, Iron Maiden, ACDC and Van Halen 'are the true "heroes" of the destruction of culture, the only aim of which is commercial success with the mass, undemanding consumer' (ibid.). The same conclusion was reached by representatives of the medical sciences. A physiologist (and academician) supported Sarkitov's stupefication theory, arguing that 'sharp strong movements and loud music ultimately dampen all emotions . . . One must understand clearly that rock, hard rock, ruins the brain. If you look closely at rockers' faces you will see that they are dispirited' (Bekhtereva 1988). Whilst rock was essentially stupefying, however, Soviet young people were warned to be aware of its subliminal messages. One author claimed heavy metal music was specifically exported by an American company wishing to exploit its texts which incited anti-Sovietism and fascism (Naloev 1986).

The combat task with regard to rock music had two goals: to control the use of rock; and to encourage a more ideologically acceptable rock. The first of these aims, it was hoped, could be achieved by the re-siting of the consumption of rock in controllable spaces. Initiatives for drawing young people back into organized clubs (which were two-thirds empty) by turning them into self-managing associations where existing networks of friends who liked listening to and swopping records could meet, were praised. Such clubs, it was claimed, would prevent vulgarity and tastelessness in the practice of music listening (Filinov 1986). Most typical of this approach, however, was the case of a group of *Komsomol* activists at the Zhdanov district *Komsomol* in Moscow, the leader of which, Vadim Avilov, was a self-confessed 'reformed hippy'. The aims of the group were: to study the negative interests of teenagers in Western symbols and fashion; to destroy young people's false heroes through helping people see what was genuinely good and what was just commercial, rubbish or provocation; and to reveal the perniciousness of the propaganda of the way of life behind the curtain (Vasilov, Kupriianov and Cherniak 1986; Avilov 1987).

The second approach to rock in this period – the encouragement, or at least tolerance, of a more ideologically-acceptable rock – could be seen in the everyday reporting of the Soviet rock scene such as in the '*Zvukovaia Dorozhka*' (Sound Track) rubric in *Moskovskii Komsomolets*. The opening of the Moscow Rock Laboratory – a joint-initiative of the Moscow City *Komsomol* Committee and the department of culture of the Moscow City Council designed to keep tabs on the numerous unregistered rock groups which were appearing – was spoken of approvingly by the First Secretary of the Moscow *Komsomol* committee (Smirnov, S. 1986). *Sobesednik* also responded to complaints they had received from readers about the small number of records for youth released by the state recording company *Melodiia*, noting that it was the Ministry not *Melodiia* which set figures for release (Komarov 1986).

As perestroika developed, the youth press increasingly discussed the latest developments in Soviet rock as well as carrying stories on Western rock stars in a similar way to Western youth magazines. At the academic level, attempts to classify young people's musical preferences continued and the results even used to challenge traditional classifications of music (Kataev 1986; Meinert 1987). Attempts were also made to theorize the importance of rock music, especially in its relation to subcultural and countercultural ways of life. Foreshadowing the major debate of 1987 and 1988, a round-table discussion chaired by the editor of the sociological journal *Sotsiologicheskie Issledovaniia* argued over whether rock music was a weapon of inter-generational conflict (the fathers and sons syndrome of the late twentieth century) or intra-generational conflict, i.e. the kind of rock music listened to reflected a whole way of life, based on social position and opportunities as well as individual preferences (Batygin 1987).

Although by the late 1980s rock had ceased to be a major ideological battlefront, the attack on rock was taken up by the emergent Russian nationalist, high-culture lobby. The most succinct expression of this came in a letter to *Pravda* by three Russian writers in which they labelled rock music 'the propaganda of anti-culture' which was causing untold 'psychological and moral damage' by 'alienating young people from true culture [and] turning them towards spiritual primitiveness' (Bondarev, Belov and Rasputin 1988: 6). Also in 1988, the highly conservative journal *Nash Sovremennik* published three biting attacks on rock music and youth culture. Claiming that form and content could not be separated, the authors argued that rock music was not simply a modern form of music to be considered alongside classical music but that it was inherently bourgeois (Gun'ko 1988: 122). Rock, it was claimed: had the same effect on the brain as cocaine; was primarily designed 'to help destroy rationality'; was 'used by Western special agents to propagandize psychological war against the USSR and Soviet youth'; and destroyed people's ability to appreciate the most important cultural values through inculcating blind consumerism (Chistiakov and Sanachev 1988). Finally, and inevitably, the task of saving children from the terror of rock music was laid at the door of women whose 'well-known conservatism' and 'natural calling' made them particularly suited to saving people from the 'threatening evils of our time' (Chirkin 1988: 146–7). This formulation of the problem is indicative of the gendered nature of the debate on youth as consumer in which the 'numbing' effect of rock music was seen to endanger male rationality whilst young women's consumption not of music but of the 'high life' in general was perceived as evidence of their moral laxity.[12]

### The subject of 'the problem': the dvor group

The desire to create spaces in which young people could spend their leisure time in an organized way was not only fuelled by a need to project the socialist way of life as superior, but by the fear of what would happen to that youth if their leisure time was left uncontrolled.

This concern was most directly associated with the ongoing deviancy debate and the fear of the slide of youth into drugs, alcohol and crime. Numerous articles in the 1984–6 period registered concern about: drinking by schoolchildren at discos (Iliin 1984); the effects of alcohol on the unborn child (Balaian 1984); the medical consequences of juvenile alcoholism and drug addiction (Gindikin 1985); the links between alcohol and juvenile crime (Volkova 1985); and the psychological causes and consequences of drug addiction ('Ia ne broshu tebia v bede' 1986; I.S. 1986; Svetlova 1986). This reflected the priorities of the contemporary anti-alcohol campaign, but at the same time, the fact that incidence of delinquent behaviour continued to be attributed primarily to distortions in the micro-social environment (see Chapter 2). In particular, crime was associated with drink and 'problem families'. According to the criminologist Karpets, for example, almost three-quarters of all those who broke the law were people who started drinking between the ages of 14 and 17, and 75 per cent of all juvenile offenders and 90 per cent of the teenagers who committed violent crimes came from 'troubled families' (Smirnov, V. 1985).

But the concern was not only for those young people with serious addiction problems – it was a general concern about the influence of the street, which could best be fought by the greater effort of *Komsomol* organizers in encouraging young people into organized forms of leisure (Bortsov 1985). In calling for tighter control by the *Komsomol*, and other appropriate cultural agencies, of the repertoires of vocal and instrumental groups and the standard of dancing in discotheques, a *Komsomol* Central Committee secretary noted:

> the more effectively ideological upbringing work and young people's leisure-time activities are organized, the more productive the struggle against law-breaking, drunkenness and other antisocial manifestations among young people will be.
>
> (Fedosov 1985: 8–9)

In the meantime, the problems were to be tackled by the employment of so-called detachments of volunteers (working in conjunction with the police and *Komsomol*) and conducting 'raids' on known hang-outs of teenagers or leading general round-ups of any young people appearing to be drunk.[13] It is worth noting that the main criticism levelled at Ziukin and other *Komsomol* officials in the article on the riot in Komsomol'sk-na-Amure referred to above was that, despite the city having one of the largest *Komsomol* organizations, at the time when the fight broke out in the park, there was not one *Komsomol* mobile detachment (*operativnii komsomol'skii otriad*) present nor one *Komsomol* worker or activist amongst the crowd of youth (Mironova 1987).

The concern with the street and with creating a positive leisure environment for young people also revealed a tacit acceptance that 'deviant' behaviour was not just the result of individual 'distortions' but formed part of a whole way of life. Karpets noted that more than half the crimes committed by teenagers were committed in socially heterogeneous groups of youngsters with their own leaders (Smirnov, V. 1985). Another author brought to life the statistics by recounting details of a trial of two teenagers who drank and then tried to steal a car. What emerged from the case was that the issue at stake was more than that of what drinking might lead to (or as the trial judge put, another 'teenagers-wine-crime story'). The young people concerned had attempted the theft because they needed to pay back a debt which one of them had incurred when he had borrowed money to buy a cassette of his favourite hard rock band (Volkova 1985). This gives some insight into the role of debt in Russian youth culture, especially in the provincial interior cities of Russia which was later seen to be central to youth cultural forms of the gang type (see Chapter 4).

The subject of this unspoken youth culture was the *dvor* (courtyard) group. The planning model of Soviet towns and cities whereby blocks of flats were built around a central piece of communal land, or *dvor*, meant that there was a natural meeting ground for young people. When weather permitted they often gathered outside and, when not, in the entrance ways to individual blocks of flats, or in the basement flats which were generally left empty and unused. *Dvor* groups were not spectacular subcultures, but the most unspectacular phenomenon of all: groups of bored teenagers (Belaia 1987). But it was this apparent boredom which was threatening to the adult world, because it made young people open to suggestion and, most importantly, influence. The concern over the influence of the group and the street on teenagers was explored in *Komsomol'skaia Pravda* in a special rubric devoted to this theme (*Ulitsa, kompaniia, podrostok*) as well as in a series of special assignment articles. These articles revealed two central (and not unconnected) themes common to the discussion of these unspectacular *dvor* groups: the decline of morality and the abuse of girls.

One article from the *Komsomol'skaia Pravda* rubric related the story of a group in the city of Voroshilovgrad who gathered in an empty flat. The group (led by three lads) drank, stole and abused a number of girls (beating and raping them). The girls were viewed less as victims, however, than as conspirators of this moral perversion. It was a girl who was labelled the 'proprietress' of the flat where the group met and was condemned not only for her part in the proceedings, but for having drawn her sister into the group. Moreover, it was the girls who were seen to have committed the most treacherous breach of morality; in the fantasy that was played out, the girls were called 'instigators' and bore the names of three of the Soviet Union's most famous and beloved war heroines who had taken part in the underground *Komsomol* organization 'Young Guard' (see Chapter 2). Thus, in commenting upon the trial of the young men involved, the journalist felt compelled to note:

> Let us recall that both morality and the law forbid the coercion of girls, regardless of whether their behaviour is good, dubious or the sort that leaves no room for doubt. In this instance, we are dealing with the third type.
>
> (Lesoto 1985: 13–14)

But extreme tales of grotesquely deviant acts undertaken by the groups' members were generally avoided in favour of the publication of letters or stories from young people who had mended their ways. These stories were clearly designed to act as inspiration for anyone in the same situation, suggesting that a way out of this vulgar environment could be found simply through an individual's strength of character. In March 1986, Lavrova reported stories of how young people who were dissatisfied with street life and falling into crime, with the support of their loved ones, were trying to, or had managed to escape their situation (Lavrova 1986). The issue was essentially one of moral conviction and strength and young people in similar situations, it was hoped, would be encouraged by stories such as one entitled 'You are needed, you can do it', which evoked the desolation of the superfluous teenager and pointed to a way forward ('Ty nuzhen, ty mozhesh'' 1986). The moral conviction needed to 'do the right thing' was also the essence of a remarkably frank article by Lavrova on *dvor* based gangs in Kharkov. In this article the journalist attacked what she called the superficial morality of the adolescent group, which divided the youth world according to apartment buildings, schools and streets and which labelled those from other territories as 'strangers' to be beaten up on sight. Equally false was the prestige granted to those who drank, got into trouble with the police and humiliated others since real moral strength was shown by those who broke out of such an environment and established their own identity (Lavrova 1985b). This was not to say that group activity *per se* was negative; another group she reported on had been set up originally to defend its members from bullying at school but later developed into a force for positive change when it took up the task of struggling against the bureaucracy and personal selfishness (Lavrova 1985c).

In a rare exploration of the *dvor* theme in its social context, one article told of a group of lads who appeared to be model students (*otlichniki*) at school – even being active in the *Komsomol* – but outside this formal environment drank, smoked, idolized rock idols and were generally cynical and morally corrupt (Kupriianov 1985). This 'dual morality' resulting from the atmosphere of lies and hypocrisy of the Brezhnev period was later to become a common theme of the academic literature of the perestroika period. The moral degradation of the groups however was generally indicated not by their own behaviour but by their attitudes to 'the weaker sex'. Occasionally a strong (almost Madonna-like) girl in the group was seen to act as the central pillar and source of moral strength for the group (Lavrova 1985a). But this was clearly the exception which proved the rule: the girl concerned in the above article also talked about another, more typical group which she had visited once where the group drank, idolized the group 'KISS' and the girls smoked. Of course, the boys also smoked but this was irrelevant since: it was the girls' behaviour – as guardians of morality – which determined the moral tone of the group; and because the girls' smoking was a signifier of moral laxity and, as such, suggested the beginning of the descent into moral degradation.

That girls' downfall began with their entrance into *dvor* groups was suggested by many articles. Typically, the process began with the girls learning to smoke and drink and ended with them becoming little more than unpaid prostitutes within the group. One article recounted the story of a girl who extracted herself from such a group after visiting a pioneer camp where she realized her true vocation was to work with children. After her return she found the strength to break with the group, give up drinking, start work as a teacher and feel herself to be a fulfilled person (Lavrova 1987). Another article, based on a letter received by the newspaper *SPID Inform*, described how a 17 year old girl who learnt to smoke and drink in a group was raped by four lads from the group after they had got her so drunk that she fell unconscious. They subsequently blackmailed her with photographs which they had taken of her (with a penis in her mouth) and forced her to do exactly what they wanted her to. When she became pregnant they found themselves a younger (14 year old) girl and left her in peace (Kirillovy 1990). The moral of the tale, though, was the admission by the girl that when, after two months she had no money left, she 'went to the station and picked up clients', and finally, the chain of moral corruption is complete.

The early discussion of youth culture articulated through the concern over *dvor* groups thus remained firmly within the leisure problematic. The groups, it was posited, were a sign of kids 'having nothing to do' and this aimless passing of time in the group often led them down the slippery slope to delinquent behaviour. For girls the slope began with smoking and ended with common prostitution. The conclusion was simple: it was morally healthier for young people to be occupied in organized leisure spaces.

## THE STRUGGLE TO RECAPTURE YOUTH: THE ORIGINS OF THE NEFORMALY DEBATE

In the course of 1986 the struggle by the *Komsomol* to reorientate the leisure of youth began to be articulated via a debate over the competition between 'formal' and 'informal' (i.e. state and non-state) organizations for control over youth. In fact, this debate had been prefigured by a similar discussion of 'informal groups' at the end of the 1960s, which showed an awareness of the low popularity of officially organized clubs and the need to 'recreate the psychology of informal groups' within official groups (Detraz 1992: 176). The failure to put these words into practice, however, meant – according to one *Komsomol* official – that 'a large sphere of youth leisure has been shaped in isolation from the *Komsomol*' (Smirnov, S. 1986).[14] At first, the issue was treated within the 'victims-of-Western-influence' paradigm which expressed itself most clearly in the *nash/ne nash* ('one of us/one of them') debate, that is whether these groups were simply imitating Western subcultural groups, or whether they had social origins in contemporary Soviet society.

The first serious attempt to deal with the problem of the *neformaly* by the youth paper *Moskovskii Komsomolets* had no difficulty taking a stance on this question. The article reported a round-table discussion, including on its panel a number of journalists, current affairs commentators, specialists on juvenile crime and an organizer of a breakdance group. The contributions included frequent reference to the negative phenomena (drug abuse, crime, sexual licentiousness) prevalent among these informal groups. After watching the performance of a breakdance group invited to the round-table, one of the commentators called it 'just the rehashing and depressing repetition of Western forms . . . our so-called "informal" youth associations are only a mindless imitation of something Western . . . it's about time we remembered the dignity of our nation and state'.[15]

Moreover, although 'mindless', these groups were not benign; according to one of the *Moskovskii Komsomolets* journalists on the panel, the way heavy metal fans dressed, for example, indicated membership of a clan and must therefore be seen as 'aggressive' and designed to issue a 'challenge' to the rest of society. Not satisfied with the comments of the panel, the editors of the paper added their own postscript which warned the *Komsomol* that although all *neformaly* were essentially imitations of groups existing in capitalist societies, and would therefore eventually disappear, this did not solve the problem of the *neformaly* (ibid.).

In the second half of 1986, however, there emerged the first signs of what was to become known as the 'differentiated approach' to the *neformaly* (see Chapter 4). This involved an assessment of the relative levels of social danger or social good individual groups of *neformaly* presented and facilitated the discussion of groups individually and some preliminary judgements of them. The clearest evaluation was that given of fascist groupings. Having published a letter reportedly sent by a group of young people from Novokuznetsk who claimed solidarity with 'such youth tendencies abroad as the hippies, punks, skinheads and bikers' and thus with 'fascism' (Misiuchenko 1986), *Sobesednik* received a large response from readers who called such people 'traitors to the motherland', suggested that they be sent to Afghanistan to learn from the good example of Soviet youth and that the *Komsomol* 'take action' against such people who were 'not fit to live alongside us'. Other groups, however, were portrayed as relatively benign: roller-disco, aerobics, skateboarding and breakdancing which appeared to have no obvious ideological motivation, were accepted as 'harmless fashions' (Lugovaia 1986). Some groups – such as the initiative groups which formed in order to preserve historic monuments (such as Shcherbakov's house in Moscow which was due to be pulled down to make way for a third ring road) – were even applauded (Kukeva and Mikhailov 1986; Mikhailov, K. 1986). This was also true of the initiative groups of *Afgantsy* (returnees from Afghanistan) who were seen as having a special sense of justice and communist morals that must be channelled in the right direction (Snegirev 1986).

Other manifestations of informal groups caused more uncertainty in evaluation. This was certainly true of the Bulgakov fans who gathered at no. 10 Bol'shaia Sadovaia (flat number 50 was where the plot of *The Master and Margarita* had taken place and thus was supposedly inhabited by an evil spirit). One journalist reported that the Bulgakov fans were evidence of a new type of 'desire for independence' on the part of young men and women which reflected self-assertion rather than passive consumption of leisure (Kulikov 1986a). On the other hand, others saw the Bulgakov fans as nothing more than 'hooligans who graffiti and break things' and, it was noted, that a club set up of 'Bulgakov lovers' had soon collapsed. Thus, the author concluded, there was a real or potential anti-social tendency among informal groups which it was the task of the *Komsomol* to prevent flourishing (ibid.).

The *nash/ne nash* debate was essentially aimed at the exclusion of those groups found to be ideologically unacceptable. On the positive side, though, it at least demanded that each group be looked at in isolation and judged on its merits. This, in turn meant the appearance of articles in which young people from individual groups were allowed the opportunity of explaining why they were members, even if the journalist still had control over how their words were interpreted and used. Perhaps the most active journalist in allowing young people to speak for themselves was Iurii Shchekochikhin whose contributions to the paper *Literaturnaia Gazeta* struck a memorably different tone than most others. His concern with youth issues led him to set up a telephone line for young people who phoned him to talk about their subcultural groups and many of the conversations were reported in his book aptly entitled *Hello, we can hear you* (Shchekochikhin 1987a).

This new kind of article not only quoted members of the groups but described some of their way of life. Thus the heavy metal fans described in one article were said to meet in 'bunkers', give each other nicknames and get 'high' (*baldet'*) on heavy metal music (Kulikov 1986b). Moreover, these articles actually inspired young people to reply – a week later *Komsomol'skaia Pravda* published a selection of readers' letters confirming that such *metallisty* and their bunkers were commonplace ('S "metal-lom" v golose' 1986). The other group to receive attention was the *rokery* or bikers who hung out, at that time, at the Luzhniki (adjacent to the Lenin sports stadium). In an uncharacteristically objective article the positions of both the traffic police and the *rokery* were put forward as the issue of night-riding was discussed. Moreover, space was given to one biker to explain why they refused to join the organized motorcycle clubs (the creation of which was one of the aims of the leisure policy of the *Komsomol*). This, he said, was because they would not be able to ride together since you could only register for a club in the district where you were officially resident, and because they did not allow racing, which was a key part of their enjoyment. Thus, turning their criticism on the official institutions, the journalists noted that despite the existence of the *rokery* for eight years, neither the *Komsomol* nor DOSAAF had understood how to work with them and that in their desire to chase and catch the *rokery*, the police had forgotten their social and educational function. The consequence of this 'undeclared war' with the night riders was that the informal association was being turned into a negative phenomenon (Kupriianov and Iakovlev 1986).

An earlier article by Kupriianov had gone still further in rooting youth cultural activity as a 'home affair' and in criticizing the *Komsomol* for its heavy-handed approach. The article discussed an armed fight involving about 100 teenagers which took place in a provincial mining town in which two young people were injured. What was shocking was not that this had happened, but that it was a regular event after clubs or discos came to an end and was, he said, part of the tradition in the town of celebrating the achievement of mining records with vodka sessions along the principle of 'work hard, play hard' (*udarno porabotal – udarno otdokhni*) (Kupriianov 1986). Evidence from Vorkuta also suggested that 'battles' on dance floors between groups of teenagers were commonplace at the end of the 1970s and the beginning of the 1980s. Special, and illegal, dens for body-building – as well as drinking and speculating – were set up in order to train (Rogozhuk 1987: 26).

This linking of youth behaviour to a wider, and well-established, masculinist, proletarian way of life was supported by Kozlov and Lisovskii in their brief discussion of a similar phenomenon in the city of Kazan'. They argued that the deviant nature of street groups often developed out of a desire not to look weak or 'girlish' and a belief that the most important thing was to be the strongest and that this had become institutionalized in strict behaviourial norms and sanctions. To illustrate their point they drew on the earlier Kazan' phenomenon of groups of *telogreechniki* (*telogreika* is a padded jacket) who insulted, beat up and humiliated others who came from different areas of the city (Kozlov and Lisovskii 1986: 123).

The symbolic use of the *telogreika* was also central to the clashes described by Kupriianov between the so-called '*fufaechniki*' and '*ital'iantsy*'. The former were groups of teenagers who turned the *telogreika* (also known as the *fufaika*) into their symbol, decorating it with lightning. The latter were the trendy youth who listened and danced to Italian pop music which often dominated the discos and their scorn of the former often incited the fights. Rather than berating the *Komsomol* for not having had more brigades patrolling though, the journalist noted that its lack of contact with young people (except for disciplinary reasons or to collect membership dues) often meant that the organization had little idea of the real issues and how they might be tackled. The city committee of the *Komsomol* had initiated a campaign called 'basement' (*podval*), for example, which aimed to bring young people into clubs and circles, but this failed to take into account the socio-cultural reality (*sotskultbyt*) of the town where there was a high rate of alcohol abuse and domestic violence. As a result of the distance between them, *Komsomol* activists did not know how to talk to the *neformaly*, while the latter's suspicion meant they refused to give their names and did not turn up for arranged meetings. Even when young people were successfully brought out of their dens and into properly equipped sports centres, they invariably soon returned to their own basements (Kupriianov 1986).

## CONCLUSION

By 1986 the unnameable had been named. Two terms began to appear in press articles to refer to the whole range of youth groupings which had been a part of Soviet life for a number of years but which had been absences in the discussion of youth issues: 'informal associations of youth' (*neformal'nie ob"edineniia molodezhi*); and 'independent associations of youth' (*samodeiatel'nie ob"edineniia molodezhi*). In true glasnost style, once the problem had been named, forces were mobilized to rectify the situation. The head of the research centre of the Higher *Komsomol*

School, for example, set out in the pages of the CPSU theoretical journal *Kommunist* his suggestions on what needed to be done so that the creative forces of youth would once again be realized 'in the interests of the building of a new society'. His programme had six points: a state programme to combat problems faced by youth; the creation of a fund which would finance this programme; the co-ordination of legislation on youth in a single law; the encouragement of responsibility and independence among young people; the improvement of sociological work on youth, which was poorly developed because it was not a prestigious area of research; and the activation of *Komsomol* (Il'inskii 1987b). That, at this stage, this need not have threatened the old youth paradigms of 'constructors-of-communism' and 'victims-of-Western-influence' is revealed clearly in the words of the Central Committee of the *Komsomol*:

> The *Komsomol* organizations must direct the work of the independent associations of youth towards forming among young men and women a high political and moral culture, a demand for scientific-technical creativity and physical and spiritual improvement. They should be used as an effective form of struggle against the penetration of bourgeois ideology, consumerist psychology, religious prejudices and anti-social manifestations and to propagandize a sober way of life . . . *Komsomol* workers should participate in the work of the groups themselves and make sure that they do not allow apoliticalness, immorality and blind imitation of the Western way of life to creep in amongst youth.
>
> (Buro TsK VLKSM 1986: 1)

The new climate of coexistence prevented any move towards the prohibition of independent groups, which, it was accepted, would only push them underground and possibly make them more rather than less attractive. The prime cause of the emergence of the groups was still considered to be the inadequate provision for already existing leisure demands, and, it was posited, the formation of 'formal' (i.e. publicly organized) leisure groups would lure the waiverers into their camp. Consequently, what appears as almost a plan target for the creation of such leisure associations was suggested: in order to fulfil the demand, the number of associations in the fields of music, artistic and technical creation, cinematography and photography and history would have to be increased by two and a half to three times and in sport the number would have to be doubled (Levanov 1987a: 89). On the other hand, coexistence did not rule out ideological struggle and the *Komsomol* was instructed by the party to give the informal groups 'more ideological-political and ideological-moral direction' (87). It was not expected that these kinds of spontaneous groups could ever be made completely redundant, but it was up to the *Komsomol* to ensure the balance of power remained in its favour. By the beginning of 1987, then, the ground had been prepared for the political battle to follow.

# 4 The politicization of the youth debate, 1987–9
## The neformaly

Towards the beginning of 1986 the first signs of a new youth agenda had appeared. Between 1987 and 1989, however, not only did there emerge a specific perestroika debate on youth, but that debate itself became a central perestroika theme. As part of this process, the issue of the social and cultural activity of youth became politicized (as opposed to ideologized) in a way that had not been the case since the mid-1920s. The vehicle for this politicization was the polemic surrounding the so-called *neformaly*;[1] the discussion of the 'positive' and 'negative' aspects of the emergence of informal and independent organizations. This chapter analyses how the theme of the *neformaly* was constructed in academic, political and media discourses, what this tells us about changing approaches to youth and youth culture, and how this is related to economic, political and social changes taking place during the three key years of perestroika, 1987–9.

The analysis is presented in three parts. In their first manifestation, the *neformaly* appeared as the living embodiment of the process of democratization; they occupied the space opening up between state and individual. As such, they presented a challenge to the existing state and social organizations which, in accordance with the principles of 'socialist pluralism', were asked simultaneously to encourage such manifestations of pluralism but also to keep them within the bounds of that which was acceptable to the 'socialist way of life'. The first part of the analysis below considers the importance of the discussion of socio-political informal groups in the light of the unfolding official discourse of 'democratization' while the second part addresses the impact of the emergence of the *neformaly* on the *Komsomol* and other official organizations responsible for young people. Another important element of the state and individual debate was that of individual responsibility towards the state (civic responsibility) and the problems of both its under-development and over-development. This issue was central to the discussion of the warring youth factions of *neformaly*, i.e. the 'Westernizers' (punks, hippies, etc.) who wanted the freedoms but not the responsibilities of citizenship, and the over-enthusiastic defenders of the socialist way of life (the *liubery* and others). In the third section of this chapter, therefore, the politicization of this aspect of the youth debate is taken up through a study of the moral panic about the *liubery* and provincial street gangs, revealing, as it does, some important undercurrents of the debate on youth. It should also be noted that in this period, new academic studies of youth culture suggest a growing interest on the part of psychologists and culturologists in the *neformaly* and a new attempt to understand them, not as the politically conscious reserves of perestroika but as 'distinct ways of life'. Since this tendency became fully developed later, it will be discussed in Chapter 5.

## THE NEFORMALY: CAUSE OR EFFECT OF DEMOCRATIZATION?

The beginning of the democratization stage of perestroika is generally attributed to the 1987 January Plenum of the Central Committee of the CPSU when Gorbachev suggested the need to discuss the questions of internal party democracy and the balance of institutions in the national political sphere. It was at the Nineteenth Party Conference in June 1988, however, that serious reforms in this area were proposed. The promotion of a pluralism of opinions encouraged the 'mushrooming' of informal groups (*neformal'nie ob"edineniia*) of people who wished to state their own views, standpoints and candidate preferences in the public sphere. The social significance of these *neformaly* was that they epitomized the Gorbachev dilemma. On the one hand they took up the call for individual responsibility and civic initiative but, on the other, they soon began to challenge the one-party system. In this sense the issue of the *neformaly* was *the* political issue of the 1987–9 period and the initial reporting on the informal groups clearly reflected all the ambiguities of the wider democratization discourse. As tangible evidence of 'social activation' and 'civic initiative' informal groups were praised, but only in so far as the social forces activated were perceived to be 'socially desirable'.

The press reported the contribution of the *neformaly* to perestroika in raising issues of local and national heritage and civic pride. The Club for Social Initiatives (CSI), for example, was given positive coverage as an umbrella or co-ordinating organization designed to encourage independent civic initiative, co-operation and civic mutual support. It also channelled the energies of young people away from conflict (fights between heavy metal fans, bikers and *liubery*) into positive action in *subbotniki* and other joint actions (Pel'man 1987). Indeed the CSI consciously fostered its role as a social mobilizer for reform by declaring its aim to be the formation of a social base for perestroika. It was the CSI which was the initiative behind one of the major events of 1987: the first All-Union meeting of informal groups which took place in Moscow in August. Although the meeting was not uniformly applauded, the leading glasnost papers gave it both extensive coverage and a basically positive evaluation. In line with Gorbachev's concept of democratization at that time, *Ogonek* declared the meeting to be the beginning of the learning curve of democracy: talking and listening in order to come to the truth (Iakovlev 1987b). Although the goal itself was not up for discussion, nevertheless, the very existence of the meeting illustrated that the party was willing to enter into dialogue before it decided on the way forward.

A key problem of this period in relations between the new informal groups and the existing authorities was that of defining what constituted permissible and desirable activity. A common criticism levelled at the groups was their concern with scheming and faction-forming and their preference for talk rather than action (Iakovlev 1987b; Plaksii 1988b: 18). From more critical quarters this led to accusations of power and publicity-hunger among leaders of informal groups at the cost of little positive input to perestroika (Gubenko and Piskarev 1988). On the other hand, where direct action was taken, the response was also mixed. A number of campaigns initiated by local informal groups aimed at preserving historical monuments aroused both support and criticism.

One such action was the attempt to save the Angleterre Hotel in Leningrad organized by a group called 'Salvation' (*Spasenie*). The campaign attracted many young people to the site of the building (where the poet Esenin had committed suicide), but despite their efforts the building was bulldozed. The issue of the fight for the preservation of the Angleterre revealed the growing divisions amongst the once monolithic press of the Soviet Union. Central, perestroika-orientated papers heartily supported the informals (see, for example, Academician Likhachev's defence of the Salvation group in *Literaturnaia Gazeta*, Likhachev, 1987). In particular, the central newspaper *Izvestiia* took up the group's cause criticizing other organs of the media for directing unjustified insults at the young people (Ezhelev 1987a), and taking the city council to task for bureaucratic intransigence and failing to take into account public opinion in planning decisions (Ezhelev 1987b). The local papers, on the other hand, remained strictly the organs of the party. The Leningrad city council used the local paper *Leningrad Evening News* (*Vechernii Leningrad*) to accuse the 'Salvation' group of refusing to co-operate with any public organizations, of challenging the city council's right to manage the city and of being anti-Soviet and even fascist (Ezhelev 1987c).

This last accusation shows how the arguments over the Angleterre action had a wider political resonance than might first have appeared. The reason for this was that during 1987 it became evident that the social activity of the *neformaly* was not confined to progressive, civic actions but had also taken the form of extreme right-wing, 'national-patriotic' movements. In particular the organization 'Memory' (*Pamiat'*) received considerable media coverage and its leaders even managed to gain an audience with Moscow city party and council leaders Yeltsin and Saikin. However, Yeltsin's successor as head of Moscow city party committee, Lev Zaikov, was not as tolerant of the new informal groups and warned the city *Komsomol* committee, on the occasion of the opening of the long-awaited Palace of Youth at the end of January 1988, to be 'on its guard' against anti-social elements in them who were trying to use glasnost and democratization in pursuit of their own, anti-perestroika, goals (TASS 1988).

## Socialist pluralism: defining the boundaries

The continued growth and diversification of the informal groups meant that the CPSU came under pressure to adopt a clearer position in relation to them. In mid-1987, the party theoretical journal noted that the number of informal groups in Leningrad had grown to around 2,000, uniting more than 100,000 people, mainly youth. Moreover, it claimed the party had taken steps to enter into dialogue with them and was well aware of the less attractive side to some of them (Kadulin and Kolesnikov 1987: 48). In particular, the national patriotic groups discussed above and the 'Democracy and Humanism Seminar' (later to become the 'Democratic Union') were singled out for criticism, being considered beyond the bounds of socialist pluralism (Ponomarev 1987). Meanwhile, Gorbachev himself applauded the activities of the young restorers, seeing in their activity a clear example of efforts to preserve the link between generations and thus the fabric of society. In a direct reference to the Angleterre incident, he called upon young people to continue their work – even if it meant moving the bulldozers out of the way (Gorbachev 1988).

In extreme cases (groups which were openly anti-semitic or rejected the October revolution *per se*) the party had little problem in exercising their powers of definition as to what was and what was not acceptable to the socialist way of life. In other cases, however, where political aspirations were not part of the overt identity of the informal group, they needed to recruit expert help. Soviet social scientists thus found themselves with a new *sotsial'nii zakaz*; the definition of which of the *neformaly* were 'socially positive' – and thus within the bounds of socialist pluralism – and which were 'socially negative' and therefore beyond these limits. The early media discussion of the *neformaly* then was politicized in the sense that it often focused on groups with political goals which, it was suggested, were a direct product of the activation of political initiative under perestroika. At a deeper level, however, the issue of which groups were supported and which denounced, was also a matter of some political significance.

In order to aid the CPSU and the *Komsomol* in determining their position towards individual groups, social scientists were encouraged to engage in classificatory studies of the new informal groups. Such studies emphasized less the causal role and more the fostering role of perestroika in the emergence of the groups, rooting their origins more socially and historically. The factors cited included general socio-cultural or socio-psychological ones such as:

- urbanization, the growing importance of peer-group relations and weakening influence of traditional institutions and ideology on the norms of young people's behaviour;
- scientific-technical progress, which had led to an increase in the role of mass communications, leisure time and the length of compulsory education;
- the increasingly complex social structure;
- the natural desire for self-realization among youth;
- objective global problems including the nuclear threat and the ecological crisis.

More specific political factors were also cited, including:

- alienation of youth from politics during the period of 'stagnation' due to the poor representation of youth in leading managerial positions, a state social policy which disadvantaged youth, the overqualification of young people, poor housing and dependency on parents;
- the failure to satisfy demand among youth for leisure facilities;
- the formalized and bureaucratic nature of youth organizations (including the *Komsomol*, DOSAAF and VOOPIK);
- the growing contradiction between production and consumption in the early 1980s.

Despite this emphasis on long-term social change, however, the importance of perestroika in providing greater opportunity for civic initiative and independent action, and thus encouraging the proliferation of informal groups, remained central to the analyses. Indeed, even these sociological studies remained highly politicized, for two reasons. First, since democratization was so associated with the emergence of these groups, they, in turn, came to be seen as an indicator of the level of democratization of society (Nevar 1989: 14). Seen in historical perspective, the existence of informal, independent youth associations, in the post-revolutionary and Khrushchev periods, was said to have reflected the democratic health of society (Kononov 1989). In the current period this youth initiative took the forms of new co-operatives, self-financing organizations and social and political initiative and was seen as central to the future of perestroika (69). The second political significance, therefore, was that informal youth organizations were not only a sign of a democratic society, but the means of bringing it about. Since informal groups fostered horizontal rather than vertical social links, they created the kind of social relations which constituted the preconditions for democratizing the political structure (Topalov 1988: 132).

For some sociologists this meant that the groups were an end in themselves; the social activity of youth was better realized in the informal groups than in formalized structures where that activity had determined forms (ibid.). In the majority of academic works written in this period, however, the pluralism of informal groups was seen to be meaningless without its socialist orientation. Perhaps the starkest formulation of this position is by Komarova who argued that:

> the evaluation of any association should be . . . according to the criterion of whether or not it acts for perestroika and how it does this, i.e. how far its activity corresponds to the ideology of renewal.

> (Komarova 1989: 100)

This led her to draw up a typology of *neformaly* consisting of three 'directions': positive (socio-political groups, production groups and sports groups); neutral (punks, metallists, pop groups, Krishna groups); and negative ('alternative' and anti-social groups such as pro-capitalist political groups, nationalist and fascist groups) (111). This typology agreed in all but terminology with that of Lisovskii, who called the directions 'pro-social', 'asocial' and 'anti-social'. The implications of these typologies were that informal groups had one of two opposing functions in society: they could propagandize socio-political values, replace outdated conservative relations and stimulate the activity of youth; or they could spread anti-socialist propaganda and extremist views. Consequently the *neformaly* debate was also a politicized debate in so far as the groups became defined in relation to their perceived political stance and evaluated according to how far this was deemed compatible with the party-led programme of perestroika.

This approach was most pronounced amongst those social scientists employed in CPSU or *Komsomol* institutions. The research centre of the Higher *Komsomol* School (NITs VKSh) was one of the first organizations to carry out extensive surveying of informal groups and it was their findings, from research done in 1985 and repeated in 1987, which were most frequently cited in more popular articles in the press. Their adoption of survey as opposed to ethnographic methods showed a clear orientation towards establishing how widespread informal groups were as well as their 'typical' characteristics. Although individual sociologists interpreted the results of the surveys differently, the questionnaires employed show that their chief considerations were: the number of informal groups; the motivations of young people in joining informal groups; the relations of informal groups with the *Komsomol*; the goals and activities of groups; the structure of groups including the role of leaders and their relations with other groups; the personal attitudes of young people participating in informal groups to perestroika and their general political orientation; and the extent of deviant activity among informal groups.[2] The results of the Higher *Komsomol* School surveys, as presented in the press, academic journals and papers can be summarized as follows.

Around 60 per cent of youth (aged 17–30) considered themselves to be members of informal groups (Plaksii 1988a: 84; Plaksii 1988b: 7; Rubanova

1988). The reasons cited for joining groups were predominantly those of leisure; 47 per cent of those surveyed in 1987 said they joined informal groups in order to satisfy their leisure interests (Plaksii 1988b: 12). Moreover, this was directly linked to dissatisfaction with formal social institutions, especially with the *Komsomol*; only 15 per cent said they were satisfied with the leisure provided by Houses of Culture, clubs, etc. (Rubanova 1988). Even less, 7 per cent, said they were 'satisfied' with the *Komsomol*'s work in the sphere of leisure, and only 6 per cent felt their opinion could influence the work of the *Komsomol* (Plaksii 1988a: 84; Plaksii 1988b: 11). Hence, the activities of the *neformaly* were seen as being a product of dissatisfaction with existing institutions and were essentially goal-orientated in their desire to rectify the situation. Additional evidence was the finding that only 2 per cent of those surveyed said they joined the *neformaly* for pleasure reasons alone (*pobaldet'*).

The majority of groups were found to be small, of between ten and twenty people meeting in flats or basements, and lasted on average two to three years (Rubanova 1988). Only one-third of groups had rules of membership and the same proportion had a recognized leader – almost always male (ibid.). Groups were prepared to interact with other organizations in order to realize their aims: 56 per cent had links with other informal organizations, 23 per cent had gone to the *Komsomol* for help and 13 per cent had received that help (ibid.). Moreover, the tendency was towards formalization via the formation of co-ordination centres, organizational committees and the definition of general social problems which needed to be solved (Levanov, Levicheva and Rubanova 1989: 53). The number of groups not against legalization rose between 1985 and 1987 from 38 per cent to 50 per cent, while 40 per cent of *neformaly* said they were prepared to work with the state establishments and one-third wanted the association to be recognized officially (Levanov 1987b; Il'inskii 1987a: 6).

For these reasons, it was suggested, the groups should not be seen as a wholly negative phenomenon since many contained social potential and only about 7 per cent of groups could be considered anti-social. Figures were somewhat varied on this issue, however. According to Rubanova (who included hippies, punks, Nazis, *liubery* and 'high-lifers' in her classification of anti-social groups) this figure was up by 1 per cent on 1985 (Rubanova 1988), but Levanov suggested the figure had risen from 6 per cent to 12 per cent (Il'inskii 1987a: 6), whilst Plaksii simply cited the proportion to be 'less than 10 per cent' (Plaksii 1988a: 88). Amongst these groups there was a higher level of organization – 73 per cent had links with other groups, 40 per cent had rules of membership and one-third had leaders (Rubanova 1988). The single greatest factor differentiating them from the positive and neutral groups, however, was that more than double the number than in other groups listened regularly to radio programmes of capitalist countries which, it was suggested, was evident in the significantly lower level of ideological and political knowledge among anti-social groups (ibid.).

Rubanova predicted that over the next five to ten years there would be an increase in the number of *neformaly* and a broadening of the spectrum of direction of their activity and interests. At the same time the number of socially beneficial groups would increase whereas the number of anti-social groups would decrease (ibid.; Levanov, Levicheva and Rubanova 1989: 53). Levanov agreed that the press was highlighting interest in groups such as the punks and Nazis whose lack of ideology or organizational unity in fact meant that their base of growth had already been exhausted (Levanov and Levicheva 1988: 22). Thus it was groups that had a socio-political orientation, or could motivate people around a more spiritual ideology such as the religious and mystical groups which would increase (Levicheva 1988; Grishina 1988).

For *Komsomol* workers on the ground, this academic work was translated into what was known as 'a differentiated approach' to the *neformaly*. This meant that informal groups were not seen to be inherently opposed to the *Komsomol* or other social organizations, but simply outside officially existing social institutions (Plaksii 1988a: 89). Consequently, many co-operated with the *Komsomol* and where this was the case the official youth organization was encouraged to make use of the fact that half the members of informal groups remained *Komsomol* members in order to establish for itself a co-ordinating role. Moreover, informal group leaders who were dedicated to perestroika might even be attracted into full-time *Komsomol*, trade union or council work where they could exercise their authority in the interests of the social good. Where groups were of an anti-social nature, *Komsomol* workers were instructed to struggle against their leaders (88–9).

Whilst the *Komsomol* articulated its approach to groups in terms of political principles, to some informal group members the *Komsomol*'s division between social and anti-social groups appeared as one between 'submissive' and 'non-submissive' ones. Socially acceptable groups were those which agreed to recognize the leadership of the *Komsomol* whilst those which did not were subject to attempts to subordinate them by the *Komsomol*, regardless of their social character (Beliaeva 1988: 14). The question of the 'differentiated approach' to the informal groups, therefore, was a political issue in one further way; it was closely bound up with attempts by the *Komsomol* to confront the dilemma of its own political position.

## RESTRUCTURING THE KOMSOMOL

> sometimes it seems that young people are walking down one side of the
> street and *Komsomol* activists down the other, and in the opposite
> direction.
>
> (Gorbachev 1987a: 24)

As the 'reserve and trusted aid' of the party, the *Komsomol* was responsible for executing the party campaign for democratization. In order to do
this, however, the youth organization had to subject itself to a painful
process of self-criticism and a campaign of 'going to the people' which
aimed at one and the same time to renew the *Komsomol* through greater
input from below, yet also to maintain its monopoly position as the only
mass, organized youth movement. This had been necessitated by the
transformation of the *Komsomol* from a political avant-garde of under
500,000 (2 per cent of the eligible population) in 1920 to nearly 41 million
(or 65 per cent) in 1987 (Riordan 1989: 22), with a concomitant consolidation of an *apparat* of privileged *Komsomol* workers who used the
organization as a rung on the political career ladder and were removed
from the everyday interests and needs of young people. The *Komsomol*
thus had to relearn the language of youth in order to cross to its side of the
street and establish some kind of *modus vivendi* between formal and
informal youth organizations.

### Criticism and self-criticism: the Twentieth Congress

In theory the *Komsomol* had always been open to outside scrutiny; by 1987
almost 1,000 dissertations had been written on the history of the organization. In practice, however, the vast majority of these had been devoted to
the theme of the 'party guidance of the *Komsomol*' and contained little
objective critique (Galgan 1987), whilst the real issues in the lives of young
people had been kept 'out of bounds' (Il'inskii 1988a: 9). This did little for
the image of the organization; a public opinion survey conducted on the
eve of the Congress revealed that 79 per cent of young people saw the
*Komsomol* as a formalistic and paper-shuffling organization, 65 per cent
thought it to lack initiative in presenting and deciding complex questions
and 65 per cent thought it showed a lack of knowledge of the interests and
needs of youth (10). The run up to the Twentieth Congress of the VLKSM
in April 1987 therefore, witnessed the first open discussion of youth affairs
and the *Komsomol*.

In an atmosphere of anticipation of fundamental change, the youth
press published harsh criticism of the privileges enjoyed by *Komsomol*
leaders, their hypocrisy and phrase-mongering and their kowtowing to
party directives (Riordan 1989: 29). In an attempt to overcome the embedded lethargy, the *Komsomol* paid attention to the question of cadres. In

July 1986 a new, and, at 33, young First Secretary was appointed – Viktor Mironenko – to replace the incumbent Viktor Mishin. Two years later he was to report that more than 3,000 full-time *Komsomol* workers had been dismissed over the previous five years due to abuse of position (Mironenko 1988a: 36). The report and election campaign in Moscow in 1987 resulted in 128 *Komsomol* committees receiving unsatisfactory evaluations of their work and at the Twenty-seventh Conference of the city *Komsomol* organization, the importance of bringing in new and talented blood and strengthening the organization at the bottom was emphasized ('Otchetnii doklad' 1987). The debate over new and old methods in the *Komsomol* was vividly illustrated by an article published in 1987 carrying interviews with 'two very different *Komsomol* leaders' (both working in the same district). The first demanded strictness and discipline and emphasized attention to *Komsomol* finances, socialist competitions and political education, while the other saw talking to young people on the street as the organization's priority and wanted to help build a club for the local lads (*patsany*) (Cherniak 1987).

The official agenda of the Twentieth Congress was to revitalize the organization both internally and externally; it was to confirm the support and help of the VLKSM in the implementation of perestroika in the country at large whilst recognising that the youth organization had not escaped the deformations of the Brezhnev period and thus that it also must implement an internal restructuring.[3] Despite the reform rhetoric, however, the promise of more fundamental change, which had been on the unofficial agenda in the run up to the Congress, did not materialize.

In particular there had been much speculation about the possible transformation of the *Komsomol* from a political organization enmeshed in the structure of the Soviet state into an umbrella organization of interest-based clubs (Kushnerev 1987). The informal group *Obshchina*[4] even proposed an alternative draft of the VLKSM statutes which, had it been accepted, would have abolished the territorial-production basis of primary cells and replaced it with an interest-based organization (Bychkova 1989a). Not only would this have set a dangerous precedent for the CPSU – since there were already calls for it to cease activity at the work place – but it would also have entailed the right to free exit from the *Komsomol* which its *apparat*, fearing a mass loss of membership, rejected out of hand ('Vopros, kotorogo byt' ne dolzhno' 1987). Mironenko, therefore, acknowledged the need to encourage new political clubs and amateur associations but declared that the *Komsomol* remained 'an inseparable link of the political system of Soviet society'. Moreover, he saw no change in the relationship between the CPSU and its youth organization; the strength of the *Komsomol*, he said, lay in 'party guidance' (*rukovodstvo*) and the whole purpose of its activity lay in the implementation of the programme of the CPSU. The single veiled criticism of the party was in the call for party committees to 'trust *Komsomol* committees more in the resolution of youth problems' – something already promised by Gorbachev on frequent occasions.

Whilst the party remained beyond criticism, however, state organizations did not enjoy the same privilege. Mironenko claimed that the
opportunities for participation of youth in the management of state and
public affairs were not being fully utilized and called for more effective
forms of joint work between the *Komsomol* and the Committees of Youth
Affairs attached to parliamentary bodies. Particularly worrying, he said,
were signs of the fusion of the *Komsomol* bureaucracy and the bureaucracy
of the ministries and departments (there were commissions of youth
attached to twenty-nine ministries and departments) to the detriment of
the interests of young people. The *Komsomol*'s role was limited by the fact
that it did not control state funds and finances but had to ask enterprises
and trade union committees to support youth initiative, and their decisions
were often taken not on the basis of social need but as a result of the
personal disposition of individual leaders. This, together with the failure to
implement many of the disparate laws on youth, meant that the *Komsomol*
was in a weak position to defend the rights of young people.

The outcome of the Twentieth Congress, therefore, was that of the two
options open to the VLKSM – to remain a mass organization but take on a
consciously non-political, leisure-based profile, or to return to the Leninist
norms of a small political avant-garde – the latter was ostensibly chosen.
This was reflected in an amendment to the party statutes, which redefined
the *Komsomol*'s position; it was no longer 'a social organization embracing
the wide mass of progressive youth' but 'a socio-political organization
embracing the advanced section of youth' (Riordan 1989: 36). This was in
tune with the key theme of democratization at the time, which, as
Gorbachev spelled out in his own speech at the Congress, was that 'more
democracy' meant 'more socialism' and that democracy was 'inseparable
from honesty, orderliness, responsibility and strict observance of laws and
norms of socialist living' (Gorbachev 1987b).

The practical results of the Congress were modest: a programme of
perestroika in the *Komsomol* was created, the socio-political role of the
*Komsomol* was strengthened and concern with the real problems of youth
was expressed. But calls for the *Komsomol* to stay out of economic matters
such as MZhKs and construction brigades and to concentrate on charity,
ecological and cultural-historical issues in order to regain authority among
young people went unheeded. Thus the Twentieth Congress, according to
one Moscow *Komsomol* secretary, had indicated only what the *Komsomol*
should not be like, not what it should be like (Apresian, Gusev and
Bazhenov 1988).

### Defining the role of the Komsomol: economic or political power?

Although the Komsomol had chosen to emphasize a return to its original
political role, it had studiously avoided weakening its economic position.
In March 1988, the Politburo accepted proposals put forward by the

Central Committee of the *Komsomol* to facilitate and strengthen the organization's role in the economic sphere. The new rights gained were: to conclude economic contracts with managements for the manufacture of products (especially youth goods) during after-work hours; to set up a central office for organizing voluntary youth labour and to finance youth co-operatives; to establish enterprises to render services to, and manufacture goods for, children and young people; and to engage in foreign trade. All these activities were to bring considerable new resources to the VLKSM and by the end of 1989 its fixed assets were estimated at 615 million roubles. These assets included 600 enterprises; three publishing houses, 248 local newspapers, twenty-nine national magazines, two national newspapers, thirty-six museums, seven campaign trains, two campaign vessels, seventeen youth centres and seventeen leisure-time facilities; forty-four republic, zonal and regional *Komsomol* schools, five training and methodological centres, and the Higher *Komsomol* School of the VLKSM Central Committee; thirty-eight tourist centres, five vacation homes, two national and three republican Young Pioneer camps, nine hotels, and the *Sputnik* youth travel office ('On extending the rights and possibilities of the Komsomol in tackling socio-economic tasks' 1990).

Far from curtailing economic activity, the *Komsomol* hoped to encourage such initiative through measures of 'self-financing'. This meant that primary *Komsomol* organizations would have full control over the money they earned and an experiment to this end had been established in fifty-six large primary organizations (Mironenko 1988a: 124). The most significant change wrought by this was that income from membership subscriptions was no longer used to maintain the *apparats* of city, republic or All-Union committees nor to support large-scale events. Previously, of the sixteen million roubles earned from membership subscriptions in Moscow, seven million remained in the city and nine million went into the budget of the Central Committee. From 1988, it was decided that only 5 per cent of the combined income of the city *Komsomol* should be paid to the Central Committee.

The budgets of *Komsomol* committees were also to come under greater scrutiny. The draft budget of the VLKSM for 1989 – showing a 10 per cent reduction in spending on the maintenance of the Central Committee – for example, was discussed at length in *Komsomol'skaia Pravda* ('Kuda idut nashi den'gi' 1989). The Moscow city *Komsomol* committee also published a detailed breakdown of its intended budget for 1989 which showed that 65 per cent of membership subscriptions would remain in the district and primary organizations (Blinkov 1989).

The programme for the development of commercial ventures (production units, voluntary labour organizations and youth leisure facilities) did not undermine the ideological goals of the *Komsomol*, but combined them with its economic interests. As the First Secretary of the Moscow *Komsomol* Committee argued, 'we will not achieve the goal of ideological-educational work if we do not possess the sphere of young people's free time . . .' (Chepurin 1987), and so at the forefront of this programme was the creation of self-financing cafes and youth centres that would simultaneously secure the position of the *Komsomol* and bring young people into a controlled leisure environment.

In Moscow, these two aims were embodied in two programmes of the city *Komsomol* committee: its resolution of August 1986 'On the broadening of the network of youth cafes and the improvement of their work'; and the two-year, city-level programme called 'Teenager' (*Podrostok*) introduced in spring 1987 and aimed at attracting as many teenagers as possible to clubs, sections and other amateur organizations in order to lower the juvenile crime rate. In order to make these 'self-financing youth associations' more attractive for teenagers, they were to be made more modern and be given more financial independence.[5] The 'Metelitsa', 'Prospekt', 'U Fontana' and other cafes were opened in Moscow providing premises for live bands to play as well as disco nights for fans of heavy metal, pop and rock'n'roll music. Initiatives by young people themselves – such as that of student groups in setting up youth cafes – were also welcomed and the importance of the *khozraschet* (self-financing) basis of the cafes in ensuring their success was stressed.[6]

On 12 July and 8 August 1988 the 'Draft Statute of the Youth Centre' and the 'Standard Statute for the Headquarters of Voluntary Youth Work Associations' were adopted by the VLKSM Central Committee Secretariat and these resolutions paved the way for the rapid development of youth centres at town and district level. According to a Central Committee secretary of the Belorussian *Komsomol*, this was linked to the new approach adopted towards the *neformaly* which saw leisure developing on the basis of self-financing youth cultural centres which built on the positive potential of informal youth associations; the youth centre attached to its Central Committee was just one of sixteen such formations in the republic (Samofalov 1988). Youth centres also often developed out of what were known as 'funds of youth initiatives' which had developed to support 'worthy' youth initiatives as part of the differentiated approach to informal groups described above. The first such fund had been set up in Novosibirsk, but since then they had spread to a number of other cities where they helped organize and materially support amateur associations and clubs involved in the organization of leisure, self-financing centres of scientific-technological creation of youth and youth co-operatives (Churbanov and Neliubin 1988). In Novosibirsk, the fund was directed, organized and controlled by the city *Komsomol* committee although the relationship between the two was far from unproblematic. The difference between the funds and the *Komsomol* was that the funds were not socio-political organizations and did not have the right to initiate legislation or participate in the administration of state and government. Nevertheless, there were fears that the funds might set themselves up as an alternative to the

*Komsomol* and this prompted Mironenko to directly state that the two were not in competition at the Twentieth Congress of the VLKSM.

The formation of youth centres and other *khozraschet* units was actively promoted and in 1989 the Central Committee boasted that 'virtually every one of the 4,130 regional and city *Komsomol* committees had youth, revenue-and-cost accounting units,' and in the Moscow, Leningrad and Tomsk regions alone there were 383 youth centres, eleven headquarters of voluntary youth work associations and thirty-three joint ventures ('On extending the rights and possibilities of the Komsomol in tackling socio-economic tasks' 1990: 130). The most developed area of the youth centres' activities were repair and construction jobs and cultural recreation services, while *Komsomol*-owned enterprises had much wider involvements including the production of clothes, haberdashery, wooden souvenirs, computers, medical instruments, farm machinery and materials and other industrial equipment (ibid.). In the Babushkinskii district of Moscow the youth centre had three main briefs: to promote leisure, via its youth cafe, dance hall and studio (which had run discos in the 'Metelitsa' cafe); to engage in production, through an association of young artists, a boutique making youth clothes, a recording studio and a youth repair and construction section; and the development of amateur associations, including the support of unofficial military-patriotic clubs, setting up facilities for bikers and the establishment of a centre for work with juvenile delinquents (Dudukina 1988).

Despite this, the units were not bringing the economic rewards expected. In 1989, youth centres, and other enterprises of the *Komsomol* were budgeted to raise fifty-five million roubles (already considerably less than their potential) but the budget showed a deficit of 108 million roubles. The reason for this was said to be the thwarting of their potential by departmental interests represented in state normative documents and financial instructions which curtailed their freedom ('Kuda idut nashi den'gi' 1989). The *Komsomol* also identified problems in the implementation of tax relief for social initiatives and charity work and threats to the tax privileges enjoyed by *Komsomol* enterprises ('On extending the rights and possibilities of the Komsomol in tackling socio-economic tasks' 1990).

Consequently, the Central Committee of the VLKSM began a campaign to protect its favourable tax status and this was to become an important issue at its Twenty-first Congress in 1990.

## GOING TO THE PEOPLE: IMPLEMENTING THE 'DIFFERENTIATED APPROACH' TO THE NEFORMALY

No amount of self-criticism on the part of the *Komsomol* could re-establish authority for it; it also had to directly approach young people and win them back to the fold. This it attempted to do by applying its 'differentiated approach' to independent, or informal groups of young people which consisted of: the support of groups considered to be ideologically compatible with the *Komsomol*; attempts to make contact with socially 'neutral' or 'passive' groups; and an ideological struggle against anti-social or negative groups.

### Informal groups accepted by the Komsomol

A number of informal groups lent themselves to direct support from the *Komsomol* and such groups received not only ideological backing but material help. In 1988, the Central Committee of the VLKSM directly helped the internationalist movement (*interdvizhenie*), military-patriotic clubs, centres and funds of youth initiative, clubs of nature conservation volunteers, the 'Charity' movement and the movement of young military reservists (Filatov 1988a). Many of those singled out for support were groups which had a history in the pre-perestroika period, such as the movement of the ecology of culture (founded in 1971) and nature conservation volunteers (founded in 1960). Others were supported because they were seen as ideologically compatible with the *Komsomol*. This is especially true of the internationalist 'interbrigades' defined as 'a movement of solidarity with those fighting for the freedom and independence of the peoples of Africa, Asia and Latin America'. The Central Committee of the VLKSM helped organize an All-Union meeting of such clubs in Moscow in October 1987 attended by representatives of seventy-seven clubs of internationalist friendship, interbrigades and clubs of political song from forty-two cities of the country (Plaksii 1988a: 85; Utrenkov 1987). Following the meeting the Central Committee resolved that VLKSM committees should not only render the youth internationalist movement help but learn from its twenty-year experience of organizing support campaigns and protests, and a year later the second All-Union meeting of such clubs was held (Filatov 1988b).

A second kind of group to receive significant support from the *Komsomol* was the clubs of 'military reservists' whose initiators and activists were predominantly returnees from the war in Afghanistan. An All-Union gathering of young military reservists supported by the Central Committee of the *Komsomol* was held in November 1987 ('My ne proshchaemsia rebiata' 1987; Korsakova *et al.* 1987). Such clubs were centred on the use of sport and defence skills in preparing young people for service in the armed forces and thus had a direct socializing role for the state. Individual clubs, such as the club 'Duty', based in the Perovo district of Moscow, even co-operated closely with social control organs in the prevention of juvenile crime and the organization of leisure (Plaksii 1988b: 19–20).

Often these groups sprang up in areas where there was a high degree of social tension in the youth sphere. The group 'Kaskad' (named after a military operation in Afghanistan) in the city of Kazan', for example, was established on the initiative of a *Komsomol* district secretary who invited a returnee from Afghanistan to set up a group where he trained young men in self-defence and talked to them about his military experience. The group quickly grew to about 100 people and came to be respected as the defender of the victims of the 'kings' of the street (Kozin 1987a).

Whether run by Afghanistan veterans or not, military-sports clubs were seen as a positive means of preparing young men for military service and channelling their energies away from the street (Voronkov 1987). Such clubs often trained young men in self-defence sports (*sambo*) which, unlike the highly popular but officially disapproved Eastern, combat sports such as karate, were seen to be essentially non-aggressive and thus ideologically acceptable.

A third type of informal activity to be considered socially positive was that of political clubs where young people could ask questions and discuss issues of the day. The aim of such clubs was to raise the theoretical level of discursive culture and to increase the active co-operation of young people in perestroika. One such club, called 'perestroika', established by a group of young academics developed into an impressive think-tank on contemporary political theory and practice (Komissarenko 1988). In an attempt to bring the 'formals' and 'informals' together the Central Committee of the VLKSM hosted an 'All-Union Meeting of Political Clubs' in October 1988 in a symbolic re-enactment of the First Congress of the RKSM on its seventieth anniversary ('Kak zakaliaetsia mysl'' 1988; Tepliuk and Chudakov 1988). This was a particularly symbolic act since it referred back to the time when the *Komsomol* had been a genuinely independent umbrella organization (see Chapter 2).

The success of the meeting was primarily in the genuine nature of the discussion which avoided the kind of self-congratulatory celebration associated with the bureaucratized *Komsomol* organization. Some genuinely interesting initiatives also arose out of the meeting, however. The first was a 'bank of ideas' which had been established during the course of the meeting and which the Central Committee of the VLKSM gave an undertaking to consider (Tepliuk and Chudakov 1988). Arguably the most important result of the meeting, however, was the emergence of the first faction within the *Komsomol* since such signs of disunity had been prohibited following the Tenth Congress of the Communist Party in March 1921. This grouping – calling itself the 'Democratic Faction of the VLKSM' and led by Andrei Isaev – had its roots in the Federation of Socialist Clubs (FSOK) which had formed in August 1988. The 'Democratic Faction' aimed to act as an internal oppositional force designed to criticize and improve *Komsomol* policy – its members remained active in their own local *Komsomol* organizations but simultaneously participated in the informal organization. In particular, the faction campaigned for the abandonment of the territorial-production principle of organization of the *Komsomol* in favour of collective membership based on independent youth organizations with their own structures and programmes. They also favoured the tackling of youth issues via the parliamentary system rather than the party system, and wanted to mark this by transferring the leadership of the VLKSM from its First Secretary to the leader of the parliamentary group of *Komsomol* deputies (Sibirev 1988).

All these groups, alongside the economic groups such as the NTTMs, MZhKs and youth co-operatives, were thus seen as not only harmless but as positively, socially useful. At the Second Plenum of the Central Committee of the VLKSM in 1987, Mironenko had declared the right of *Komsomol* members to satisfy their personal interests and leanings in any association or social grouping outside the organization as long as its activities did not contradict the constitution of the VLKSM (Plaksii 1988a: 89). Indeed such groups showed dynamism and initiative and the *Komsomol* was keen to be associated with them and emphasize the overlap between formal and informal organizations. A clear example of this was evident in an interview with Mironenko following the All-Union political clubs meeting during which he declared his attitude towards the 'Democratic Faction' to be positive since it united people in the *Komsomol* who wanted to push forward democratization. Moreover, he claimed, he supported 60–70 per cent of the faction's ideas and acknowledged that it had been more consistent in conducting its policy than many *Komsomol* workers (Mironenko 1988c).

**Making contact with socially 'neutral' or 'passive' groups**

In contrast, the socially neutral or socially passive groups had to be worked on as well as with.

The policy developed by the *Komsomol* and other responsible organs towards such groups as the punks, heavy metal fans, breakdancers, hippies and bikers during the 1987–9 period was based on an understanding of informal youth groups as a part of the socialization process in society (see Chapter 2). To this end it was emphasized that informal youth groups had always existed (even in the 1930s there were fans and *dvor* groups), but that both social and political changes had increased their importance today. The former consisted of the increase in free time due to the success of the scientific-technological revolution and the lengthening of the period of compulsory education, while the latter consisted of the over-formalization of the *Komsomol* and other official organizations. Subcultural activity, according to this interpretation, should not be seen solely as being imitative of Western groups but as a product of the cultural-historical process of societies which had rapidly developed material wealth but had not yet developed the corresponding mechanisms of social homeostasis (Andreeva, Golubkova and Novikova 1989).

According to this analysis, until the end of the 1950s, society had been united through the imperative of need, youth had been incorporated into working life early and there was no problem of continuity (ibid.). The problem, it was suggested, was that the first subcultural groups began to appear before the old prohibition model of socialization had been replaced by more 'normal mechanisms of socialization'. Consequently, youth had been pushed out of more significant spheres of life and into the sphere of leisure where informal groups began to develop as deviant counter-cultures (ibid.; Bestuzhev-Lada 1987b: 29).

This process was sometimes referred to as one of the marginalization or alienation of youth as a result of stagnation and frustrated expectations among youth. These frustrations were borne of the overproduction of graduates who were subsequently forced to take manual jobs, the formalism of social organizations, and of distortions of social justice, which bred a kind of infantilism among young people (Sundiev 1987; Nastichenko 1988; Grishin 1989). The solution, it was suggested, would be the transformation of all but the anti-social *neformaly* into formal (although not formalistic) associations. Such interest-based clubs and associations, it was thought, would help incorporate youth subcultures more organically into the dominant culture of society.

The role of the restructured formal organizations then should be to help these informal groups out of the 'underground' and direct their activity in a socially progressive way. Groups such as the bikers and heavy metal fans were seen as having gone underground as a sign of protest at adults' failure to understand their interests, and the task of party and *Komsomol* was posited as lending them 'an appropriate ideological direction' ('Utverzhdat' novie podkhody v rabote s molodezh'iu' 1988). Examples of their success in this aim were cited at length. The creation of rock laboratories and clubs (in Moscow, Leningrad and Sverdlovsk) to support some of the more acceptable home-grown rock bands, for example, was viewed as a means of counterposing an alternative Soviet rock tradition to that of the West and thus of encouraging heavy metal fans and others to listen to '*our music*' (Filatov 1988a). Co-ordinating organizations of voluntary associations were also set up by the *Komsomol* in Khabarovsk and Sverdlovsk where informal umbrella organizations had not been so quickly generated as they had been in Moscow and Leningrad (ibid.).

As had been recommended by the *Komsomol* sociologists, youth workers paid particular attention to establishing authority among informal groups, either by winning over existing leaders and using their authority to channel the group's direction or by putting their own leaders in place. In Novosibirsk, a former worker of the regional committee of the VLKSM became president of the rock club and proved that good *Komsomol* workers could win the trust of both formals and informals, while the Second Secretary of a district committee in the city managed to develop contacts with the heavy metal fans of his district and eventually become their leader (Nazarov 1988). In particular, the 'taming' of the bikers (*rokery*) was seen as a victory for ingenuous and courageous *Komsomol* workers. The success of various city committees, including Sevastopol' and Riga, in establishing courses and clubs for bikers was emphasized although a more mixed experience was reported from Astrakhan. There the First Secretary of the city *Komsomol* committee, having decided to make an informal contact with the local *rokery*, went to meet them in his official Volga and, not surprisingly, his suggestion that they meet with *Komsomol* leaders was rebutted. A local journalist, however, took up the challenge, donned biker gear and joined them on a bike. After a while he became accepted (especially after he was stopped along with them by the traffic police). He soon learned that any self-respecting biker should have a girl behind him on his bike and one night he turned up with a female passenger, much to the approval of the bikers who now saw him as a real *roker*. The young woman was in fact the head of the propaganda department of Astrakhan regional *Komsomol* committee. This truly informal first interaction, however, meant that the bikers felt they could talk to her and the first steps were taken towards setting up a club for them and establishing co-operation with the traffic police and the DOSAAF organization (Strynin 1987).

But those with initiative on the ground were often frustrated by middle-level authorities. In Kirovograd a young woman took the call of the *Komsomol* to mobilize *neformaly* into socially useful activities quite literally – she began inviting heavy metal fans, skateboarders, bikers and the like off the street to help set up a theatre and discotheque. But her action met resistance from the local *Komsomol* organization and the cultural administration evicted the theatre from the building in which it was housed. A journalist from *Komsomol'skaia Pravda* travelled to the city to try to intervene on the activist's behalf, but the *Komsomol* postponed the arranged meeting (Virabov 1987). This experience was in marked contrast to that of the director of the *Komsomol* theatre-studio 'Na Krasnoi Presne' in Moscow. The theatre had made contact with informal associations including bikers, breakdance and heavy metal fans who both took part in the shows and helped out in their production. As a result, a special decision by the executive committee of the Moscow city council led to the injection of money into the theatre.[7]

The theme of resistance to perestroika-orientated reform then was very much associated with the provinces and was also depicted in Iurii Shchekochikhin's film *Shchenok* (Puppy) of 1989, whose hero was a young progressively minded teenager who attempted to fight passivity and corruption in the Voronezh region. Another example from the press concerned a *Komsomol* secretary from Belgorod region who narrowly escaped being dismissed from his post following the introduction of radical changes in the style of his work. He had begun by going out onto the streets and meeting the *rokery*, eventually succeeding in organizing a motorcycle race dedicated to the memory of victims of the Second World War and establishing a fully legal and official youth club for them known as '*rokmoto-banda*'. The same secretary also persuaded a group of delinquent teenagers to set up a sports club, used the district committee music equipment to create a dance floor in the square next to the *Komsomol* building and organized a shock labour brigade which took young people out to collective farms at the weekends to work. His success, it was reported, was that he offered bored local youth something to get involved in, but his methods did not meet the approval of all and he was asked to resign. His obsession with leisure, it was claimed, had led him to neglect his administrative duties such as the writing of reports and the collection of subscriptions. However, after a large number of young people threatened to resign from the *Komsomol* if he was forced out of his job, he was allowed to stay and remained an example of a 'new type of *Komsomol* leader' (Morozov, I. 1987).

In fact, neither the problems nor their proposed solutions were new. In 1966 in the city of Pavlodar a young man was released from a juvenile colony where he had been serving a sentence for armed robbery in order to set up a club for young people which would take them off the streets and prevent them being drawn into the criminal world. The club (with 150–200 members) was a self-administering organization in which the structure, administration and rights of members were decided by the young people themselves. It was sited in an empty basement belonging to a tractor factory which the members had found and renovated themselves. The club ('Grinabel') achieved its aim: within months the area had been made safe from street groups (since their members had all joined 'Grinabel') and disputes began to be settled through discussion rather than physical violence. Nevertheless, the club leader's efforts were eventually thwarted by the *Komsomol* when all funding was withdrawn from the project after he was accused of making a cult of his own personality and was criticized for the fact that the club did not include enough *Komsomol* activists. After eight years, the city *Komsomol* committee decided to replace him with a new leader and when the club's members refused to accept the person appointed, its building was repossessed and the club collapsed (Eremin 1987a; Eremin 1987b).

The concern of the *Komsomol* with 'going to the people' was not only fuelled by a desire to prove itself to be at the forefront of perestroika, however, but also the result of the fear that, if it failed to find a common language with young people, it would lose control of them. On Moscow's Arbat – where youth of different groups gathered regularly – for example, in just eight months 3,000 people (80 per cent of them under 30 years old) had been detained for offenses related to street disturbances (usually unauthorized gatherings) (Avdeev *et al.* 1987).[8] In the city of Cherepovets a youth crowd expecting a disco became uncontrollable when it turned out that the event was a *Komsomol*-organized contribution to the Festival of Soviet Youth. Although the situation was eventually calmed and damage was minimal, the embarrassment caused to the *Komsomol* (whose leaders were forced to abandon their speeches) led to a thorough investigation of the causes. Although they had expected to find a handful of *neformaly* behind the incident, it was proved that those who had taken part were in fact the 'normal youth' of the city. For local leaders the incident revealed how out of touch with youth issues they had become and, subsequently, a centre to study teenage problems was set up and *Komsomol* actions which would be of practical help to youth were planned (Pankratov 1987).

But could the *Komsomol* ever hope to recapture the street from the informal groups? As one article pointed out, for every 'difficult teenager' on the street there were, on average, already fifteen 'educators' supposedly working on her/him, including those attached to schools, colleges, places of work and young people's hostels, instructors from voluntary associations, full-time *Komsomol* workers, juvenile workers, educational workers, and members of councils of assistance to the family and school attached to enterprises and trade union clubs (Ladatko 1990).

But the issue was not only that the *Komsomol* was unlikely to succeed where all these others had failed, but a question of whether one could channel youth into the 'right' path at all (Poliakov 1987). As Paul Willis argued of informal groups amongst British youth (see Chapter 1), the 'informal group' (whether or not it adopted a shocking or spectacular style) was the material base or infrastructure of the informal sphere into which young people retreated in order to evade the rules, hierarchies and physical structures of the formal world (Willis 1977: 23). What Willis had to say about school and counter-school culture might equally apply to the *Komsomol* and informal group activity. The two were not mutually exclusive – in his study 'the lads' still went to school, just as the *neformaly* often remained members of the *Komsomol* – but it would be naive to expect that they could be simply won round and their activity channelled into socially-useful activity, since they felt that their interests were not served by the formal structure and thus *chose* [my emphasis] to withdraw into the informal sphere (22–3).

**Anti-social or negative groups**

Despite the 'differentiated approach' of the *Komsomol* to the *neformaly*, there remained some confusion over which groups should be fought and which worked on. Rubanova, for example, included hippies, punks and high-lifers in her estimation of the number of anti-social groups while Komarova saw them as neutral (see above).

In media reporting, it was the *rokery* or bikers which received the most consistent treatment as a problem of social control. This was clearly the product of repeated, direct clashes between the *rokery* and the agencies of social control – specifically the traffic police (*GAI*). In 1987, in the popular paper *Arguments and Facts*, the head of the road patrol service of the

Moscow police blamed the *rokery* for causing 327 accidents in the first six months of the year, in which twenty-four people had died and 317 had been injured. Moreover, he claimed, twenty of their core were convicted criminals (having served time for crimes including group rape) and had a bad influence on others (Butakhin 1987). The solution he posed was a typical one; the creation of isolated and controlled spaces for the bikers by building a motordrome outside Moscow, allowing them to use a pitch of the Lenin sports stadium and encouraging DOSAAF to find the money to build a motorcyclists' club.

The same themes reappeared in an article in the local Moscow youth newspaper *Moskovskii Komsomolets*: the *rokery* clashed with the police and with taxi drivers; they had links with the criminal world (since the bikes they rode were too expensive for them to have bought legally, they must have obtained either the money or the bikes by illegal means); and, although the *rokery* denied having leaders, the role of key members, such as the Zakharenkov brothers, was clear (Lapin 1987). Criminologist Revin confirmed the importance of leaders in lending groups an anti-social atmosphere. According to him over 50 per cent of leaders of anti-social groups such as the *rokery* had criminal records and almost a third had been convicted on more than one occasion (Revin 1991: 299).

Despite the resolution of the Moscow city council in February 1987 on 'The prohibition of group motorcycling', the traffic police had been helpless in stopping them since no detailed instructions or extra powers had been given and the *rokery* simply refused to stop when flagged down. Efforts to provide the bikers with a place to train and a cafe at the Luzhniki had come to nothing partly because the traffic police had insisted that they also agree to join a registered club and end their night-riding. Finally, Lapin also claimed that the *rokery* were getting the better of the police. They did not only refuse to obey orders, he claimed, but demonstrated their refusal to subordinate themselves and turned clashes to their own advantage – if one hit his head on the police windscreen, he was seen as a victim of police brutality, for example. At the same time, the bikers teased the police; one female biker was quoted as saying, 'we try to get his stick, or stop and then pull off just as he comes up to us. It's fun . . .' (Lapin 1987).

Another story linked the *rokery* to gang fighting when it described how a group of about seventy bikers, armed with metal bars, stones and sticks, had marched on a local youth disco and ended up in a brawl with the police when the latter intervened to stop fighting within the gang. Two police cars were smashed and eighteen people were detained for investigation. At about 1 a.m. 100–150 motorcyclists met again armed with sticks and metal bars but this time the group was dispersed peacefully.[9]

The *rokery* then were seen alongside teenage gangs as a problem of social control; in a criminological study of informal groups published in 1991, the bikers were one of two groups of *neformaly* singled out for discussion in a section entitled 'One step away from breaking the law, and that step has been taken' (Igoshev and Min'kovskii 1991). The growth of inter-gang fighting was a particular concern of the time and included fights between youth of different districts and streets at discos and between locals and groups coming to Moscow from outside the city. This raised the profile of criminologists in the study of youth culture, not least since areas of professional responsibility – between the juvenile sections of the police and the *Komsomol* - needed to be determined.

Opinions among criminologists themselves varied considerably, however. Some saw law-breaking (of a petty nature) as being inherent in the activity of informal groups. Solntsev (head of the juvenile department of Moscow city Administration of Criminal Investigation), for example, saw informal groups as uniting around a lack of desire to work or obey norms of behaviour. The crimes committed by such groups (hippies, bikers, football fans) varied according to the individual group and, he argued, the press gave too much attention to such groups, blaming everyone and anyone for their actions except the young law-breakers themselves who, after all, were no different from any other young hooligans (Solntsev 1988).

Others, however, considered informal groups to be united not by a common 'deviant' behaviour pattern but by their display of initiative or independence (*samodeiatel'nost'*). Sundiev, for example, criticized approaches premised on the belief that informal groups were imitations of Western subcultures or that they were formed from 'the dregs' of Soviet society and had been allowed to develop because of the inadequate work of the *Komsomol*. His typology of groups included: political initiative groups (pro-perestroika groups, political clubs, funds of social initiative); social initiative groups such as ecological and charity organizations; economic initiative, especially co-operatives; associations of cultural initiative which both created culture themselves and which serviced others; spectacular (*epatazhnie*) subcultural groups which challenged social norms through their clothes and hairstyles and whose purpose was self-assertion (punks, heavy metal fans, etc.); and finally groups of 'aggressive initiative' which had primitive hierarchies (*dvor* gangs, the Kazan' formations and groups participating in aggressive sports) (Sundiev 1989). Sundiev posited no direct relation between informal groups and criminality – criminal behaviour could exist in any or all of the groups he classified.

According to Vladimir Ovchinskii, however, Sundiev's views were unrepresentative of the academic collective of the Ministry of Internal Affairs (MVD) who, on the whole used the term 'non-traditional groups of teenagers' and 'youth of an anti-social direction' rather than 'informal groups' to describe these young people (Il'inskii 1987a: 17). In his view such non-traditional groups of youth were inherently orientated towards Western mass culture which was a breeding ground for deviant behaviour (speculation, drugs and alcohol use and abuse) (Ovchinskii 1988: 114). Such activity also led them into connections with the criminal world by whom they were greatly influenced (115). Thus although their style was not deviant in itself, it was important to provide controlled places for their activity and to 'neutralize' their leaders and reorientate groups to socially-useful activity (120). But the *Komsomol* approach, he argued, based as it was on the question: 'What percentage of *neformaly* are law-breakers?', was the wrong one. The figure – of 6 per cent – that they arrived at was meaningless, since they grouped together as *neformaly* the whole spectrum of informal groups – from hooligans at football matches to girls in sewing and knitting circles (Ovchinskii 1989: 63). Instead, he proposed, research should be focused on the opposite question, that is: 'What percentage of law-breakers are *neformaly*?'. Only having answered this question, could one progress to the second one of establishing whether or not the law-breaking activity was actually associated with membership of that informal group.

The conclusions he drew on these issues, based on research conducted by MVD academic institutions, were that, in general, the *neformaly* came into conflict with the *local authorities* (especially concerning the right to meet and demonstrate) rather than the *police*. Of young people registered with juvenile departments for offences in the Moscow region (outside the city) on average 10–15 per cent could be called *neformaly* (mainly heavy metal fans, breakdancers, bikers and members of territorial groups) although this fell to the odd individual in some areas whilst in others, such as the Moscow suburb of Liubertsy, it rose well above the average (65). In the city of Kazan', in contrast, 30 per cent of juvenile offenders were members of an informal group with an anti-social direction. Moreover, the crimes which they had committed were directly related to membership of these groups, whereas in the Moscow region the two were unconnected, with the possible exception of Liubertsy (ibid.).

Ovchinskii fundamentally disagreed with the *Komsomol* sociologists on one other issue: that of future trends. Whereas the research centre of the Higher *Komsomol* School had suggested that anti-social groups would decline, Ovchinskii predicted a decline in groups such as the hippies, punks and heavy metal fans but a rise in the hierarchically organized, oppressive and criminally influenced groups of the type prevailing in Kazan' and Liubertsy. This prognosis was based on a much wider study of juvenile delinquency which was felt to be sweeping the country, and it is this phenomenon which is analysed below.

## THE LIUBERY AND OTHERS: PERESTROIKA'S MORAL PANIC?

In 1972 Stanley Cohen's seminal study of British society's reaction to the 'mods' and 'rockers' – or more specifically their reported gang fighting and hooliganism at the country's southern coastal resorts – suggested two important principles about modern society's treatment of juvenile delin-

quency. First, in order to understand such phenomena not only the delinquent activity itself but societal reaction to it must be studied. This includes
the role of the media in exaggerating, distorting and creating symbolic
representations of the perpetrators (the creation of 'folk devils') and the
control culture which grinds into action as the public and social agencies
are sensitized to such activities (beginning to see evidence of it in unrelated
incidents) and exploit them for commercial or ideological purposes.
Second, his work suggested that themes associated with youth – in this case
affluence and youth – can come to sum up the social changes of a particular
period in time (Cohen, S. 1987: 191). Both of these mechanisms lead to the
original 'deviance' becoming amplified, and the control culture – originally
invoked to deal with the 'problem' – comes, in fact, to encourage it.

The analysis undertaken here of youth gang fighting as reported in the
glasnost press will broadly adopt Cohen's deviancy amplification model,
although paying particular attention to the socio-cultural factors which
make specific elements of the model inapplicable in the context of Soviet
reality. The phenomena under study are the so-called *liubery* from the
Liubertsy suburb of Moscow and the inter-gang fighting in a number of
provincial cities of Russia.

### Initial problem and solution

The first two stages of the deviancy amplification model concern the nature
of the phenomenon itself. Early journalistic reports concerning the *liubery*
suggested the following elements to their behaviour:

* they came from the town of Liubertsy, about 20 kilometres south-east of
  Moscow;
* Liubertsy had a culture of physical strength and this encouraged lads to
  practice boxing, karate and body-building in unofficial establishments
  (usually in empty basements and known as *kachalki*);
* such practices began anywhere between eight and fifteen years ago;
* they travelled to Moscow (and other nearby towns) in order to beat up
  those of their contemporaries who did not meet their approval;
* those they did not like were generally *neformaly* such as heavy metal
  fans, football fans, punks and hippies;
* although they themselves used stimulants and hormonal drugs to
  enhance their strength, they were strongly opposed to the use of drugs
  and alcohol and their actions against the *neformaly* were motivated by a
  desire to help administrative organs do their job (Ovchinskii 1991).

Police reports confirmed cases of group hooliganism in Moscow committed
by groups of teenagers chanting 'Liu-ber-tsy' and beating up local teenagers. Furthermore, statistics suggested that residents of Liubertsy committed over a third more crimes in Moscow in 1985–6 than residents of
other areas on the outskirts of the capital. This tendency was not only

confirmed but more pronounced for juvenile crime. Figures on juvenile crime for 1987–8 showed that residents of Liubertsy committed 2.5–3 times as many crimes as the residents of other similar areas (Ovchinskii 1991: 263–5).

But the case of the *liubery* was only a very visible example of a much wider phenomenon which also first began to receive attention in the press in the mid-1980s and which was widely known as the 'Kazan' phenomenon'. In fact it was not confined to Kazan' but was part of a general problem of street gangs (*ulichnie gruppirovki*) which had become a serious social concern in a number of cities, especially Dzerzhinsk, Ioshkar-Ola, Kazan', Ul'ianovsk, Petrozavodsk, Cheboksary and Cheliabinsk (Baal' 1991: 283). The chief characteristics of such street gangs were:

- gang fights;
- more recently (and in order to counteract police efforts to end group fights) the formation of small, more mobile groups carrying out attacks on individuals. In the first half of 1989 there were more than sixty such attacks in Kazan' and 'tours' to other cities were conducted;
- territorial allegiance – gangs were based on the *mikroraiony*, quarter, street, courtyard or house. In Kazan' by mid-1989 there were sixty-three gangs (of 10–100 members) known to the police, incorporating about 1,700 core, active members but involving about 6,000–8,000 people in total. In Dzerzhinsk in 1989 there were thirty gangs involving 900 people, in Ioshkar-Ola eleven groups incorporating 600 and in Naberezhnie Chelny, fourteen groups with a total membership of 540 people;
- members of the gangs (whom in general could be called *gopniki*) pressurized those not wanting to join (*chushpany*) by threats and violence;
- once a member, it was possible to extract oneself only by paying large sums of money;
- gangs had an internal hierarchy based on age and (criminal) experience. In Kazan' about 60 per cent of members were under 18 (mainly 16–17 year olds), 6 per cent of whom had criminal records. The remaining 40 per cent were mainly 18–25 years old, of whom 28 per cent had criminal records;
- each gang had its leaders which consisted of the *avtory* (a shortened word derived from 'authorities' consisting of between one and three people) and their closest 'reserve' (ten to twenty-five people). The *avtory* were generally 18–25 years old;
- the majority of members of gangs practised some kind of strength sports often in unsanctioned *kachalki*;
- the gangs almost always had some system of collecting money for the material support of gang members serving sentences in corrective institutions or for the funerals of those who had died in fights. In fact,

though, the money often went straight into the pockets of the leaders. Money was also gained through theft, robbery and muggings;
- groups were increasingly taking up arms;
- there were strong links between leaders of groups and the professional-criminal world. This was especially true of Kazan' although much less true of Ioshkar-Ola where fights were less planned or organized;
- the prohibition of the use of alcohol to younger members (although this depended on overall importance of leaders in the gang structure) and a system for punishing those who broke gang traditions;
- a growing tendency for girls to participate (Baal' 1991; Kashelkin and Ovchinskii 1991).

The chief difference between the *liubery* and the Kazan' gangs (apart from the scale of the phenomenon) appears to be the targets, or victims of the aggression. In the case of the former, the targets were Westernizing youth groups, whereas in the latter the gangs fought between themselves. The above 'facts' are clearly not objective nor outside the debate under analysis, but they should at least provide the reader with an outline of the social phenomenon under discussion and are drawn from academic writings of the period after the 'moral panic' had already subsided.

In fact, of course, in the first stage of Cohen's model, it is precisely the role of the media in laying out 'the facts of the matter' which is scrutinized. He suggests that in reporting the events the media show three tendencies: exaggeration and distortion; prediction of future such events (which become self-fulfilling prophesies); and symbolization, by which certain objects (of hair and clothing) become symbolic of those who wear them and their 'delinquent' behaviour. The application of this stage of the model (which Cohen refers to as the 'Inventory') is perhaps the most unsatisfactory in the Soviet context. Although aspects of all three elements can be traced, the very different heritage of the role of the press in the Soviet Union makes it unlikely that the model could be strictly applied. In particular, the educative rather than interest role of the newspapers tended towards a more serious and analytic approach than the sensationalist reporting which lies at the heart of the 'exaggeration and distortion' elements of Cohen's inventory stage. The agitation and mobilization role which the press continued to play even in the glasnost period, also meant it unlikely that the 'prediction' element of Cohen's model would be confirmed; the essence of glasnost was the identification of problems for the facilitation of the location of solutions. Moreover, the legacy of the persistently 'bright future' remained strong and whilst the recognition of existing social problems was accepted and even encouraged, the prediction of the spread or growth of negative phenomena remained taboo. The analysis of the 'inventory' phase developed below, then, will deviate significantly from Cohen's model in order to express the Soviet context, although this model will be drawn upon where it can aid analysis.

Central to the glasnost agenda was the restoration of the press to a role of giving people the truth (*pravda*) rather than the distortion (*krivda*) to which they had been subjected for so long.[10] This meant that the dominant theme of the inventory stage of the *liubery* phenomenon was the establishment of whether or not the *liubery* constituted a phenomenon at all.

Those who argued that they were an important part of contemporary Soviet reality were most inclined to exaggeration, distortion and symbolization in the elaboration of these 'folk devils'.

One of the key articles in the creation of the moral panic about the *liubery* was that by Vladimir Iakovlev published in *Ogonek* in January 1987. This article performed much of the symbolization function spoken of by Cohen. It associated the *liubery* with a 'uniform' of white shirts, narrow black ties and wide, checked trousers. Together with their gait (hands firmly behind their backs) and their muscles 'bulging through their shirt sleeves', this uniform symbolized something rather clownish and provincial, but nevertheless serious. Key to this is the association of the orderliness in dress with a particular ideology and organizational strength. Iakovlev argued that the *liubery* were not isolated groups of young thugs, but 'an office' (*kontora*) with leaders and a plan for 'cleansing Moscow' of undesirables, for which purpose they travelled to Moscow and 'scattered throughout the centre of the city in small groups'. The leaders ('kings') of the *liubery* were not the chief ideologues of this plan, but cynical manipulators of young people. They had criminal pasts and could rally over 200 lads to do their bidding within a couple of hours. They did not adopt the uniform and did not lower themselves to taking things from hippies and punks but focused their own criminal acts on more lucrative targets, primarily speculators (Iakovlev 1987a).

Although in contrast to the distortion and exaggeration of the Western press, Iakovlev's article appears mild, it was a sensation in the Soviet press of the time, not least because of the unorthodox journalistic techniques used in order to create the required effect. The article began with an account of how the journalist himself had been set upon by a group of *liubery* after being approached because he was wearing a rock-festival badge. In addition, the article was accompanied by a photograph of two extremely muscular young men, one of whom appeared to clench his fist in a symbol of open and outward aggression. (In fact, the fist was probably clenched in order to enhance the display of muscle.)

This 'sensationalist' approach to the discussion of the *liubery* was criticized by Aleksandr Kupriianov, writing in *Sobesednik* shortly afterwards, who, although also asserting that the *liubery* were a real phenomenon, approached the issue from a very different angle. However, whilst openly rejecting the organized violence element of Iakovlev's interpretation, in fact Kupriianov simply diversified the symbolization. In his analysis, the proletarian checked trousers symbolized the 'revenge of the provinces' for the years of privilege the capital had enjoyed. Hence the *liubery* were referred to in the subtitle of the article as 'the capital's stepchildren' and were portrayed as gathering into groups to overcome their inferiority complex *vis-à-vis* the capital and defining themselves as *liubery* only when they were directly oppressed by those who saw themselves as superior (Kupriianov 1987).

Kupriianov himself was criticized for failing to differentiate between different kinds of youth in Liubertsy and thus treating as one the *liubery*, body-builders (*kachki*) and groups of lads who simply went to Moscow in the evenings in search of entertainment. Moreover his photos were declared to be unrepresentative of Liubertsy youth, since they showed 'half-developed alcoholics' and thus reinforced stereotypes of provincial poverty and cultural backwardness (Epifanov 1988).

Where Kupriianov played up the provincial motif in his discussion of the *liubery*, Osin focused on the ideological theme. Linking the *liubery* to a general growth in nationalistic and fascistic views, he argued that the tacit support of the police for the activities of the *liubery* was exploited by the latter who began to beat up other young people at will knowing they would not be punished. This, he argued, was the main reason why the groups grew so rapidly. Moreover, the organs of social control not only turned a blind eye to the activities of the *liubery*, but sometimes also lent material support by issuing them passes as voluntary police (*druzhinniki*). The ideology of the *liubery*, therefore, was not only anti-*neformaly* but also directed against non-Russians and linked to the 'Memory' (*Pamyat'*) organization (Osin 1989). Following a similar line of analysis, Kaplinskii likened the uniform of the *liubery* to that of Mussolini's blackshirts and rooted their emergence in the Stalinist period which had created the preconditions for neo-fascist movements (Kaplinskii 1988: 76). Hence, journalists who argued that the *liubery* phenomenon was a real problem with roots in contemporary socio-political reality also indirectly accused those who claimed they were a media myth of effectively supporting and even encouraging the exploits of the *liubery* for political reasons.

Indeed, the myth of the *liubery* argument was primarily put forward by various organs of social control. The reaction of the *Komsomol*, for example, was the calling of a joint leisure evening between youth of the Volgograd district of Moscow and of Liubertsy designed to show what good neighbours the two sets of youths were. In an article on the meeting published in *Moskovskii Komsomolets*, the First Secretary of the Liubertsy city *Komsomol* committee complained about the 'distorted portrayal of problems connected with youth in Liubertsy given by recent press articles' and the journalist covering the meeting summed up its conclusions thus: 'in search of sensation, from partial facts, journalists extracted a phenomenon which was never inherent in the youth of the Moscow suburb' (Beslov 1987). As Ovchinskii noted, this conclusion was ironic since only a few days earlier the same newspaper had published a report of the Moscow

City *Komsomol* Committee which had referred to the problem of the *liubery*.

The police also denied that the city was really under threat from the *liubery*. In a famous interview published in the conservative newspaper *Sovetskaia Rossiia*, a spokesman for the Moscow police, Goncharov, denied reports of clashes with the *liubery* in the city centre and argued that Liubertsy had one of the lowest rates of juvenile crime in the Moscow region. He played down the phenomenon of secret *kachalki*, claiming that there were only fifty-six in the city involving, at most, 500 youths. He attacked the *Ogonek* publication and claimed that the two supposed *liubery* photographed were in fact completely respectable students who had been asked to pose, and were told that the article would be one in defence of Liubertsy sports groups. Thus, he claimed, the ideological motivation of the *liubery* had been created by journalists and these kinds of articles had actually caused any problems which might now exist, since they resulted in notices being sent by *neformaly* to schools and districts calling for joint efforts to beat up the *liubery*. He also denied that the police tacitly supported the *liubery*, saying that they had contacted informal groups and assured them of the support of the police if they were attacked (Gutiontov 1987).

What is astonishing about the case of the *liubery* then is that the moral panic emerged with very limited press coverage using, comparatively, few mechanisms of exaggeration, distortion and prediction. This probably reflects the fact that the period of glasnost itself helped realize the unifying potential of media culture; the new excitement about the press and its role in bringing the truth meant that people read and discussed the same papers and articles. The discussion of these articles is particularly important since the oral transfer of information remains stronger in Russian culture than elsewhere in Western Europe due to the combined effect of relatively recent urbanization and, until the advent of glasnost, the scarcity of news and information.

By the beginning of March 1987, then, the liberal press was warning that ill-considered articles had inflamed a moral panic about the *liubery* which might be manipulated by the opponents of perestroika to close down the new freedoms won. Iurii Shchekochikhin's 'hot-line' on youth issues, for example, revealed that at one school parents had been ordered not to let their children out on the streets at the weekend for fear of attack. Meanwhile a resident of Liubertsy complained that at his school, attendance at the school disco on Saturday had been made compulsory. Neither of these cases were unique. Moreover, district *Komsomol* committees were preparing their voluntary police detachments (*druzhinniki*) for the expected onslaught. In one district of Moscow, it was reported, the civil defence system had been put on alert (Shchekochikhin 1987b). In this case the prediction did not manifest itself as a self-prophesying one – there were no reported incidents of violence that weekend. Undoubtedly, though, the fact that a virtual curfew for teenagers was imposed in areas adjacent to Moscow, whereby 14–17 year olds found on the streets after 10 p.m. were dispersed, increased tension (Epifanov 1988).

In the case of the *liubery*, both the sensationalist reporting of the press as well as the tacit support of the organs of social control encouraged a moral panic about attacks by the *liubery* and thus aggressive responsive action by those groups who felt victimized. The creation of the 'folk devil' always remained partial, however. It was never certain whether or not they actually existed, and, if they did, whether they were really devils or in fact heroes in devils' clothing. This ambiguity resulted from the ideological colouring to the discussion. First, the symbolization of the *liubery* was not wholly negative since it conformed to an image of the provincial working class which had constructed the Soviet Union. Second, it had to be read against the already existing 'folk devils' of the Westernizing *neformaly*.

One of the results of the activation of the societal control culture in reaction to the moral panic about the *liubery* was the spread of discussion from the local level (Moscow) to the national arena. The first manifestation of this was the growing concern with 'bored teenagers'. Teenagers left to their own devices, it was feared, would inevitably turn their frustration into violence. In this discussion the old term from earlier deviancy work of 'difficult teenagers' (*trudnie podrostki*) resurfaced but without its qualifying adjective. Thus the use of the word teenager (*podrostok*) as opposed to youth (*molodezh'*) located the discussion clearly in a discourse of social control. This was evident in an article in *Komsomol'skaia Pravda* in 1989 on the creation of a 'Moscow Union of Teenagers' to tackle the issues that adults had left unsolved. Although the article was essentially enthusiastic about this initiative, it was published with three photographs of teenage lads smashing up furniture and boxes in a courtyard and sitting around what appeared to be their own basement; the impression created was that they had recently been released from a remand home (Orlov 1989).

The major manifestation of this concern, however, was the emergence of a wide debate on the gang fighting in the city of Kazan' and other central Russian cities. Here all three elements of the inventory part of Cohen's model are much more apparent than in the discussion of the *liubery*.

The debate over the Kazan'-type gangs was characterized by a much greater sense of 'loss of control'. This emanated from the emphasis of the seriousness, the scale and the all-encompassing nature of the phenomenon. Seriousness was indicated by frequent reference to the use of weapons (especially metal and spiked objects) and to the number of people killed and injured in the fighting. A common opening to such articles would be a description of the funeral of one of the victims of the gang fighting (Morozov, N. 1988) or a recent murder case. This could even lead to metaphors of civil war in which the lads were seen returning from battle to have their wounds dressed by their women (Likhanov 1988), while civilians dared not go out onto the street without bullet-proof vests (Orlov 1990).

The implication of the war metaphor was that the moral codes of 'normal life' had been suspended. Shchekochikhin, for example, described two incidents where moral guardians had been attacked; the first was a case of a young man who had been killed when he was set upon whilst walking his girlfriend home, the second that of a policeman who had been murdered by a group of teenagers (Shchekochikhin 1988a). Other articles taking up the war motif noted the effective curfew after 9p.m. in many districts of Kazan' (Likhanov 1988: 22), the fact that in Dzerzhinsk 'even adults are afraid to go out at night', and that virtually all discos and clubs had been closed because of the fights (Dolgodvorov 1988). But it was also a war without measure and without end. The former was expressed by a journalist who noted that the spread of violence to include the mass violation of girls had been shocking even to citizens of Kazan', while the latter is best articulated by the words of one of the members of the gangs: 'the fights will never end. That's how it's always been and will be!' (Shchekochikhin 1988a).

The scale of the phenomenon was suggested by references to the numbers involved and the fact that the influence of the gangs had spread from the street to inside the schools. In Kazan' in 1986–7 there were 181 group disturbances of the peace including fifty-one group fights in which six teenagers died, seventy-three were hospitalized with serious injuries and 193 received less serious injuries (Shchekochikhin 1988a). In particular, the rate of growth of gangs and criminal incidents was stressed; the number in Kazan' was said to have doubled between 1987 and 1988 (Kozin 1988). Towards the end of 1987, knives, metal balls, knuckledusters, sharpened steel instruments and home-made explosives began to be used and consequently, in the first four months of 1988, six people died in fights (Shchekochikhin 1988a).

The strongest theme in the discussion of the Kazan' groups, however, was the power of the groups which, it was suggested, had allowed them to become a world unto themselves beyond the control of official institutions. They constituted, according to one author 'a state within a state' (Likhanov 1988: 21). This image was portrayed, first through an emphasis on the high degree of organization of the gangs. Gangs were organized territorially – at the lowest level two to four neighbouring houses formed a *korobka*, several *korobki* formed a *kust* and several *kusty* formed a *kontora* or *gruppirovka* with a defined territory and name. The internal organization of each gang was hierarchical according to age: *shelukha*, *skorlupa*, *gorokh* (10–13 years old); *supera* (14–16 years old); *molodie* (17–18 years old); and *starshie* or *stariki* (above 18 years old) (Shchekochikhin 1988a; Podol'skii and Zhukov 1989; Mialo 1988b: 41). Commitment to the group was expected to be for life and anyone attempting to leave was treated harshly.

Second, the gangs were difficult to control because they had leaders who had strong links with the professional criminal world. It was they who organized the collection of money ostensibly used to help victims of fights and to give to the mothers of those killed. Most fights in Kazan' were premeditated and gangs had their own armouries (Shchekochikhin 1988a). This integration into the criminal subculture made the groups very difficult to control. Threatening them with prosecution had little effect since many lads preferred to go to prison rather than serve in the army, and two-thirds of those who were not in prison when their call-up papers arrived could not serve anyway because injuries already received made them unfit for conscription (Tsukerman 1990: 30). Thus they learnt the ways of criminal life in prison and returned as leaders to inculcate what they had learnt amongst the younger members.

The sense of loss of control is most potently elucidated by Vitalii Marsov, however, who estimated the existence of 150 groups in Kazan' (two and a half times more than all other estimates). Moreover, he said, where they used to fight with fists, they now fought with metal weapons; where participation in gangs used to be voluntary, members were now recruited by violent means and, as a result, 'a significant proportion' of teenagers in Kazan' were forced, whether they wanted to or not, to subject themselves to the laws dictated by active participants in gang fights. This meant two things: first the problem had spread from the deviant or potentially deviant minority to the majority of honest, respectable youth; and second that the gangs had 'brought the law protection agencies in Kazan' to surrender'. This was important in itself because it revealed another aspect to the exaggeration and distortion element of the setting out of the facts. Marsov saw the very fact of the phenomenon being away from Moscow as contributing to its 'out-of-control' nature. He accused the Kazan' police of covering up the real rise in crime figures in order to suggest that they had the situation under control, when in fact the number of groups had been underestimated by two times and the number of participants by between four and five times. It wasn't until five teenagers were killed in a short period of time, he argued, that the local police asked Moscow for help and a special brigade of the All-Union Ministry of Internal Affairs could be brought in to restore control (Marsov 1988).

The framing of the issue as being a problem of the provinces is most clearly seen in the process of symbolization. One article described how a group (*motalka*) descended on Moscow from the provinces: 'the lads look like something from a Mosfilm movie on *besprizorniki*. You can tell *motalki* above all by their trousers – they are made of a dark woollen material in a particular fashion – resembling wide [Turkic] trousers (*sharovary*)' (Podol'skii and Zhukov 1989). The other most commonly mentioned artefact was their wide flat caps which symbolized simultaneously their provincial, working-class and Eastern origin.

The main concern of the Moscow law enforcement agencies appeared to be to return them from whence they came; the lads were rarely charged with crimes, only with the violation of administrative rules for visiting the capital (Podol'skii and Zhukov 1989). Thus, it does not need wild claims – for instance that the CIA was behind the gangs as it aimed to control and buy off the youth of the city (cited by Likhanov 1988) – to suggest mechanisms at work in the presentation of the issue of the Kazan'-type gangs which encouraged a sense of the loss of control in the provinces, whereby territory was divided up between warring gangs and normal life was disrupted, if not destroyed.

## Opinions and attitudes

In the second stage of his model Cohen analyses the opinion and attitude themes which run through the reporting on the mods and rockers. These themes are expressed in general orientations towards the identified 'problem' and are reinforced by key images of the participants as well as explanations of the reasons for the emergence of the phenomenon. This part of the model was extremely useful in analysing the Soviet debate on the *liubery* and Kazan'-type groups, especially since Soviet press reports tend toward opinion more than news reporting anyway. In the analysis below, the orientations adopted and the images through which these were expressed are described before a discussion of the causal explanations offered is attempted.

### Political struggle

One orientation has been to view the *liubery* and other groups as 'fighters for socialist morality'. Thus in his speech at the Twentieth Congress of the *Komsomol*, Victor Mironenko noted that he applauded the 'noble impulse' of groups which had taken it upon themselves to fight against people in society who flouted the norms of socialist life, but not the means employed by them (Mironenko 1988a: 83). In this interpretation they are often associated with the so-called vigilante groups, and even the *Afgantsy*. Among the more extreme examples of this kind of activity reported in the press was that of the group of teenagers arrested at the market in the city of Barnaul for pouring sulphuric acid over speculators, explaining their actions as a fight against the shadow economy (Kuz'min 1990). Equally disturbing was a report from the town of Volzhskii on groups of so-called *striguny* (hair-cutters) who cut off the hair of girls known to be going out with foreign workers at the nearby Italian car factory. Calling themselves 'fighters for morality', the lads claimed that their action protected the city from AIDS (Ratvanin 1987). The fact that the principles if not the methods of such groups were approved of by the formal social control institutions is evident in this case: the *Komsomol* tried to form the group into a brigade to fight prostitution in the city.

By far the most common acts, however, were ones aimed at curbing the influence of *neformaly*, especially those involved in speculation and drugs (Radov 1986). When groups that learnt Eastern martial arts and unarmed combat in order to 'give a sound thrashing' to a group of dope smokers in their block of flats, are evaluated as having 'noble intentions' and 'clean hands' (ibid.), it is not hard to see why the *liubery* might expect the same kind of approval for their attempts to deal similarly with *neformaly* such as the punks, hippies and heavy metal fans.

However, there were two main differences between these groups (which were generally given a positive, though conditional reception) and those like the *liubery* and the Kazan' groups on tour to other cities. The first is that the *liubery* and their like not only attacked their ideological opponents, but confiscated their attributes such as badges, jewellery and leather jackets which could be sold on the black market. Their own motivations were therefore subject to some doubt. Second, they were outsiders. Thus, whereas the former were portrayed as noble, even if misguided warriors, the latter were seen as provincial thugs whose trips to Moscow were motivated by the desire to steal clothes, personal stereos and other fashionable items which they then justified by the empty claims to be concerned about social injustice.

## Centre versus provinces

The second orientation was to see these claims of rectifying social injustice to be of significance and thus to interpret the phenomenon as an issue of an aggressive provincial culture which was antagonistic towards the centre. This was particularly prevalent in discussion of the 'tours' of provincial gangs to the capital. Ovchinskii, for example, explained the recent surge in street robberies in Moscow as being due to the fact that members of youth gangs from other cities – not only Kazan' but also cities like Voronezh – travelled to places where living standards were higher and justified their crimes with reference to the violation of social justice. For Ovchinskii, however, the teenagers were not fighters for socialist morality but victims of older gang leaders who organized their 'guest performances', tried to cultivate criminal communities of youngsters and deliberately exploited the lower prison sentences for juveniles by using 16 year olds to tackle the most dangerous jobs. Young people were lured into the net by the promise of financial wealth if they succeeded, and, if they did not, only a short prison term, the help and protection of the gang and financial reward after release. In Dzerzhinsk, for example, it was claimed, 70 per cent of crime was committed by first-time offenders, mainly juveniles (Dolgodvorov 1988).

The tight structure of the gangs meant that as soon as a teenager entered the group he became a debtor (*dolzhnik*) (Kozin 1988), and although some groups allowed members to buy their way out (often itself leading to crime), others permitted them to leave only 'feet first' (Tsukerman 1990: 30). The oppressiveness of the territorial gang structure was described by a young person from L'vov (in Ukraine) who had struggled to extricate himself from the gang structure.[11] The teenager, he wrote, 'has no choice', if he does not enter the group, his life will be made hell, but once he has entered it is considered the most terrible treachery to leave (Zakharov 1987). The gang bosses also used young people to protect themselves. They orchestrated large-scale fights between teenage gangs in their home town in order to distract the police whenever they were coming close to uncovering some major case of corruption, drug trafficking or speculation.

Despite Ovchinskii's concern with the organized nature of the crime committed, one of the factors he saw as pre-determining the growth of juvenile delinquency was the underdevelopment of the social sphere, the sharp contrasts between the capital and the provinces, between downtown areas and the suburbs (the habitat of most youth gangs), and between the various social strata (Radyshevsky 1989). Mialo also argued that not enough attention had been paid to the impact of so-called 'closed' cities whose residents had had a privileged status and who treated those who lived on the periphery of the cities with the same instinctive hatred as skinheads addressed to Turks in Germany (Mialo 1988b). The reaction, according to one author, was that young people sometimes came with the intention of bringing Moscow to its knees, as became clear when a co-ordinated police operation between Moscow, Kazan' and Naberezhnie Chelny resulted in the arrest of 417 teenagers armed with guns and other offensive weapons (Podol'skii and Zhukov 1989).

Adopting this orientation, then, groups are seen as a phenomenon specific to the development of social relations in and between centre and periphery. This includes some sympathy with claims of social injustice although also tends towards seeing the provinces as a wild and uncontrollable hinterland where local 'bosses' control and exploit the younger generation, thereby also ensuring the reproduction of the criminal underworld.

*Alienation*

The third and most frequent orientation towards the Kazan' groups has been to see them as a general symbol of the times, as an expression of 'the collective aggressiveness of young people in the face of social problems' (Shchekochikhin 1988a). This orientation shows many of the features located by Cohen in his analysis of reaction to the mods and rockers. In particular the gang fighting is seen to be indicative of a general social and moral decline. According to Mialo, the groups are evidence that, in the face of the disintegration of society, there has been a reversion to the social structure of the middle ages, in other words, a return to the 'pack' and 'gang' social formation. This disintegration is the result of a growing tendency towards marginalization in the last two decades as cities have grown without a properly developed socio-cultural sphere. The consequence has been the formation of groups organized around a leader and a tendency towards criminality. In other words, the formation of ghettoes as youth groups grew alongside the creation of new districts in the 1970s

(Mialo 1991: 193; Kruglov 1988). Young people were easy to lure into the mafia-controlled gangs because they had lost their place in society, had become marginalized and alienated.

What the *kontora* gave teenagers was what society had denied them: financial independence, collectivism, an opportunity to improve physical fitness in underground training gyms, and to make a career by rising from the bottom to the top through taking risks and gaining experience (Pankratov 1990). The young people involved tended to come from poor families and had watched their parents slave on the factory floor all their adult lives with little in return. The *kontora* on the other hand offered a chance to get on in life, to get a car, earn a decent wage, and not live in fear of going out at night (Tsukerman 1990: 32; Orlov 1990).

The implications of this are twofold. First, the gang structure was not only forced on young people but was attractive because it provided material security. The economic function of the *motalki*, claimed one author, was what differentiated them from previous forms of *dvor* gangs (Gatov 1988). Second, the socialization which the state should provide was actually found in the *kontora* which guided the teenager's entrance into adult life (Pankratov 1990). This is confirmed by Eremin, who saw it as one positive side of the gang structure (Eremin 1988). For young people in the cities affected, however, it was a socialization process which left them no choice; for many there was only one path – into a colony for juvenile offenders (Dolgodvorov 1988).

The second familiar element of this attitude theme was its portrayal of the problem as a disease which had not been confined and was now spreading. According to Shchekochikhin, Kazan' was just an extreme example of a phenomenon taking hold of the entire country (Shchekochikhin 1988a). Pankratov also noted that the upsurge in youth crime had moved on to take Cheboksary, Ioshkar-Ola, Izhevsk, Dzerzhinsk and Gorkii and that the residents of these cities lived in daily fear of 'disaster' (Pankratov 1990). For him the disaster was most likely to take the form of the use of the groups to play out inter-ethnic tensions (ibid.). Youth crime, moreover, was just one manifestation of a disease gripping the whole social body (Podol'skii and Zhukov 1989).

The alienation approach suggested that the Kazan' phenomenon was just the beginning of a new and much more widespread youth plague, which unless stopped, would take the whole country. Kazan' was thus indicative, on the one hand, of the same thing beginning to emerge elsewhere and, on the other, of different but related social diseases. This theme is clearly close to the 'state of things' approach which Cohen found to be prominent in his analysis of the mods and rockers.

## Causation

Opinions about the causes of the gang phenomenon have two main themes: they are young people's reaction to the general social malaise; and they reflect the reaction of criminal subcultures to the changing social environment. Many interpretations include both themes, but lay greater weight on one or the other.

Few observers doubted that the gangs, including the *liubery*, had connections with the professional criminal world, but some saw the role of the criminal subculture as being a causal one. In the case of the Kazan' groups, the emergence of the problem was generally related to the appearance of an armed gang (*banda*) known as the 'Tiap-Liap' in the Teplokontrol' district of Kazan' in 1978 (Kozin 1988; Likhanov 1988: 21). This gang acted as a prototype for later groups and they and their activities became mythologized and romanticized by younger lads who turned them into Robin Hood figures. The gang's activities came to an end after an incident in which one passerby was killed and several others injured and which led to the leader of the gang, Zavdat Khantimorov, being executed and other members of the gang being imprisoned. A second factor used to explain the re-emergence of the Kazan' gangs, therefore, was that following the release of many criminals from this era as the result of a general amnesty, many had returned to the area and begun working as leaders of new groups or at least as their consultants (Kozin 1988; Likhanov 1988: 21). A third factor is noted by Eremin; the policy of sending juvenile criminals to colonies effectively trained them in the criminal subculture and, when they returned, they imposed this knowledge and experience on society at large (Eremin 1991b).

The links of the *liubery* with organized crime became evident at the trial in February 1991 referred to as the 'Liubertsy case' which focused attention on the activities of criminal groups from Liubertsy operating in Moscow (A.F. 1991). Some commentators suggested not only links between the criminal world and the *liubery*, however, but that the whole *liubery* phenomenon was the outward manifestation of the reaction of the criminal world to the emergence in society of new sources of income. According to this interpretation the hippies and heavy metal fans were no more than 'easy targets' in a struggle for spheres of influence between the old Brezhnevite mafia and a new, younger generation of the criminal subculture (Koshelkin 1991).

The second explanation for the rise of Kazan'-type gangs is closely related to the 'alienation orientation' (described above) in that it emphasizes the socio-cultural roots of the phenomenon. Such explanations generally include some or all of the following factors:

- the poor material provision of provincial cities which mean that residents have to stand in long queues even for the most basic goods;

- the extremely poor ecological situation in the cities;
- the pressures on mothers, especially single mothers, which did not allow enough time to bring up their children properly;
- the weak influence of the family in comparison to the peer group;
- the failure of teachers to take time to understand the environment in which their students live outside school;
- the extremely limited opportunities for young people to find work;
- the almost non-existent leisure provision for young people.

The most thorough socio-cultural explanation is offered by Mialo who, above all, points to the marginalization of young people as massive migration into cities was allowed to take place without adequate planning, leaving new urban dwellers to cope as best they could in their new ecological and socio-cultural environments. At the same time, the country was experiencing a general crisis in social values and ideals due to the fact that the growth of consumerist orientations in the 1970s and 1980s had been accompanied by rising social inequality. The gang phenomenon had emerged primarily in provincial and peripheral areas, therefore, because this was where the inequality was felt most acutely, breeding a thirst for social revenge among those from the least well-off families (Mialo 1988b: 41). A more journalistic variant of this approach was evident in an article concerning the activities of female gangs in Cheboksary. One group of girls, who were standing trial accused of attacking other girls and stealing their clothes, were motivated, according to the journalist, by the fact that 'They feel insulted by life: there is nothing interesting to do for young people nor nice clothes – yet surely they want so much to dress smartly, nicely and their parents of course are unable to clothe them' (Ivanova 1990).

### Rescue and remedy

The final level of Cohen's model directly concerns societal reaction. It includes opinions about how to rescue the country from its social crisis as well as measures taken to this end. The first aspect of this process is referred to by Cohen as 'sensitization'. This refers to a heightened sensitivity to anything which appears to be similar to the moral panic under question and it leads to events previously unremarked coming to be considered as examples of the phenomenon under discussion.

There is some evidence of this process taking place in former Soviet society, as indeed there was a more general sensitization to crime and social tension as perestroika progressed. In particular, those incidents of fighting at discos which had earlier been seen as an extension of the 'work hard, play hard' provincial culture (see Chapter 3) began to be interpreted as manifestations of a heightened social tension. New rubrics devoted to crime stories highlighted the exploits of teenage groups threatening public order. One such story from Moscow talked of a group of 250–300 teenagers gathering at a metro station, drunk, with the intention of planning a fight with another group from a suburban state farm.

But even non-aggressive gatherings of young people at metro stations, where they met, chatted, smoked and, sometimes, drank were seen as a growing problem. The same article noted that in 1988 alone there were 2,860 arrests of juveniles for administrative offences.[12] One investigation of the circumstances of 15,000 cases of juvenile offences established that more than a third of the offenders had been unlawfully arrested and taken into custody, often on patently absurd charges, such as 'being idle' or 'drawing on the road' or 'rummaging in dustbins for sweet wrappers' or were simply detained for 'identification purposes'. It was even suggested that quotas were set in some places for the arrest of juveniles and the police station's effectiveness was judged by the achievement of these targets ('Minor abuse' 1990).

By far the most relevant of Cohen's categories to the Soviet situation, however, concerns the activation of the societal control culture, involving diffusion, escalation and innovation of social control activities.

At the first level, the effectiveness of police control was criticized, in particular in the Tatar Autonomous Republic (now Tatarstan) for not bringing the situation in Kazan' under control (Likhanov 1988: 22; Morozov, N. 1988). This led to some policing innovations such as the introduction of a special unit created in Moscow to fight 'out-of-town' juvenile crime. The only one of its kind in the country, it was reported by the end of 1989 (around six months after its creation) to have made 2,000 arrests (Podol'skii and Zhukov 1989). A special subdivision for fighting organized crime was also formed in Kazan', and brigades of volunteers were used to patrol residential areas in the evenings (Morozov, N. 1988), although, it was also claimed these were useless since they consisted of elderly people who would not have stood a chance against the teenage gangs.

The *Komsomol* was also heavily criticized for its inertia and it responded by promoting the formation of defensive youth groups to struggle against the gangs and encouraging those concerned with law and order – especially the *Afgantsy* – into work with local teenage gangs (Antonova 1990: 81). The most famous of these were the 'Kaskad' group and the 'Dzerzhinskii Brigade' in Kazan'. The former consisted of sixth-formers of a school, the latter was attached to one of the city's vocational technical schools (SPTUs) (Gatov 1988: 7). The problem with these alternative gangs was that they had no official powers, were often met with a lack of understanding by teachers, police and cultural workers and had no content of their own beyond opposing existing groups (Kozin 1988). Despite the *Komsomol*'s hope that they would be seen as more authentic, they never had any real authority and, by July 1988, it was reported that they had collapsed (Likhanov 1988: 22). The experience of self-defence brigades in

L'vov suggested that, since essentially they opposed force with force, in the end there was little difference between them and the gangs they started out to fight. Moreover, they could never attract enough people to effectively fight the gangs since, 'not everyone wants to sacrifice their own entertainment to fight negative phenomena' (Zakharov 1987).

The second area to which the *Komsomol* channelled its efforts was directing the energies of young people to more positive ends. Two problems were identified here: the need to end the deficit of youth cafes, sports halls and other leisure facilities; and to convince young people already involved in gangs to leave them. Morozov, for example, noted that fifty teenage clubs in Kazan' had transferred to the youth initiative centre in the belief that well-organized leisure could attract teenagers off the street. The problem, as he saw it, was the lack of sufficient leisure opportunities and inadequate quantity and quality of equipment – one motorcycle club, for example, had one bike for every six members (Morozov, N. 1988). The problem of resources was also mentioned in reference to work in Cheboksary. Here limited success had been achieved by attempts to localize teenagers and confine them to their own district. Nevertheless, the idea of opening a 'military-tourist camp' for 16–17 year olds in the Chuvash republic remained a 'dream' of local juvenile crime workers (Kruglov 1988). Another article, however, claimed that although a local youth centre (previously a military-patriotic association) in Naberezhnie Chelny had been given almost 500,000 roubles to build a sports complex, the lads who were members of the *kontora* said that, no matter how wonderful a sports complex was built, they would never join (Orlov 1990).

A third remedy was the articulation of more integrated social policy programmes. Often called simply 'Teenager', these were introduced in a number of cities including Moscow, Cheboksary and Dzerzhinsk and included leisure programmes, help-lines and tele-bridges, work-placement schemes for the summer holidays, educational offices at large enterprises, parental patrols, weekly meetings of co-ordinating committees on youth work in city party committees, and the propaganda of information on teenagers and the law (Kruglov 1988; Dolgodvorov 1988).

Many, however, felt that the situation had gone far beyond building clubs, playgrounds and sports centres. A striking feature of the rescue and remedy debate was the appeal to the more general level; above all what was needed, it was claimed, was the restoration of moral order (Pankratov 1990; Gatov 1988). This argument was indicative of a much wider moral panic; panic in the face of the imminent collapse of a whole social order which threatened not only to cause economic dislocation and political upheaval, but to hurtle society back into the past, a past which was not only pre-modern but also 'pre-moral'.

**The liubery and others: glasnost or moral panic?**

But to what extent did societal reaction to the teenage gangs actually constitute the phenomenon itself? It is certainly true to say that specific approaches fostered the groups rather than discouraged them. The reporting of the *liubery* as being ideologically motivated, for example, helped create the distinct *liuber* identity. As one former member of the *liubery* explained, it was only after these articles that the notion of an ideological mission against the *neformaly* was articulated:

> That was all nonsense. Maybe, later, after the newspaper articles, some began to think of themselves as fighters for an idea. But really, they just huddled together for courage. They beat up everyone, without distinction – heavy metal fans, punks and hippies. They were asserting themselves.
>
> (Koroleva 1991: 2)

*Komsomol* efforts to re-channel energies also backfired. The campaign in Kazan' to open school gyms in order to allow sports clubs to gather in the evenings, for example, led to the formation of pseudo-sports associations led by people who had neither sports nor pedagogical education and whose motives were dubious (Tsukerman 1990: 30). In effect, the *Komsomol* was aiding rather than controlling the gangs by providing them with premises and the opportunity to practice defence sports. The same could be said of the encouragement of defensive gangs (see above), while the labelling of gang members could also lead to discrimination and expulsion from school which increased young people's sense of alienation and reduced their interaction with positive, socializing institutions (Likhanov 1988). Further evidence suggesting the construction of the 'Kazan' phenomenon' appeared in an article in the newspaper *Izvestiia* early in 1993 in which the author declared that many of the gangs had collapsed and that the 'Kazan' phenomenon' itself no longer existed (Bronshtein 1993).

However, whilst displaying many of the thematics described by Cohen, the glasnost press never reached the heights (or depths) of the role played by the British press in amplifying the moral panic of the mods and rockers. In way of a conclusion to this section of the chapter, some tentative reasons why this might be so are suggested. These reasons fall into two categories: the different role of the media in former Soviet society; and the different nature of the general 'social crisis' which the moral panic about youth was symbolizing.

Despite the metamorphosis of the media following the introduction of the policy of glasnost in 1985, they retained very different priorities and emphases to those associated with the popular or tabloid press in the West. These included a leaning towards opinion and analysis rather than 'facts', which greatly reduced the sensationalist event-orientated reporting factor so important to Cohen's analysis. Indeed, many of the newspapers carrying teenage gang stories were weeklies or were published three times a week and thus adopted a more in-depth analysis approach than would a daily. The pressure for 'new news' was absent in any real sense since it was not until the end of 1991 that the media came under any real financial pressure to win readers. The glasnost agenda also significantly shaped the reporting of stories. Whilst investigative reporting meant exposing the 'truth' and uncovering the hidden social problems of Soviet society, it also meant encouraging their solution. This led to a greater tendency to employ expert opinion in writing articles and to propose constructive measures to ease problems rather than focus solely on how bad they were. Finally, the role of the newspapers in reflecting the opinions of 'the people' also led to a more sympathetic approach to the problems faced by young people; one local Cheboksary newspaper even published the letters of young people who talked about how gang fighting affected their everyday lives.

This sympathetic approach is indicative also of the different nature of the wider social crisis felt to be gripping society. As is clear from the explanations offered of the causes of the teenage gang phenomenon, the adult population did not feel so much affronted by youth, but to blame for the problems they faced. In particular, while the distortions of social justice and the collapse of morality during the Brezhnev period might be blamed abstractly on 'a corrupt ideology', at an individual level, every parent faced the question of: 'What did you do about it?'. Unlike post-war Britain, therefore, the general social crisis was not one of the advent of new values and behaviour based on a general rise in affluence. In the Soviet Union, the crisis of youth symbolized the end of the bright future, it presaged the much grander civil war which so many expected to engulf the whole country and the return to a pre-modern and pre-moral society under the rule of local warlords.

## CONCLUSION

During the period 1987–9, the theme of the *neformaly* dominated the discussion of youth and its culture. The term itself had an important political resonance. Although generally translated as 'informal groups' in fact the groups were not necessarily *in*formal in their organization or activity (by the end of this period some had grown to become national movements) but *non*-formal. What the *neformaly* signified was the existence of a sphere of activity which was outside the realm of the private but was also consciously not incorporated into the state or formal sector. Since this 'initiative from below' was a central part of the discourse of democratization, the fate of the *neformaly* was viewed as an indicator of the success of perestroika. At the same time, the term itself was a legacy of the past, when 'beyond the state' also meant 'beyond the law'. Moreover, the failure to legally guarantee the civic rights of the *neformaly* meant that the groups remained at the mercy of the political wind of the day. Nevertheless, the desire of the state to harness the forces for initiative led key social institutions, such as the *Komsomol*, to seek to determine those elements which were 'politically progressive' and to incorporate these into their own structures. In this way the issue of the *neformaly*, although helping to de-ideologize the youth debate, did not disrupt its political overdetermination. The 'differentiated approach' adopted in relation to the *neformaly* in fact revealed that only a minority (around 10 per cent) of informal groups were socially or politically orientated and, worse still, that around 6 per cent were directly anti-social or criminal. This meant that the vast majority of young people participating in non-formal activity were not engaging in the struggle for socialist pluralism but simply living a socio-cultural pluralism.

Since at this stage of perestroika pluralism remained a means to an end and not an end in itself, the apparent disengagement of youth from the current tasks of restructuring led to growing fears among politicians about the social marginalization of young people which would only add to the growing social disunity. This led to the rise of a discourse on youth that had always been present, but never dominant: the discourse of social control which stressed the marginal position of youth in contemporary society and the weak authority of all the key socializing institutions. As the social crisis deepened in the years to come, it was this discourse which became definitive.

# 5 Youth as object of social policy, 1990–1

The rise of the social control discourse was associated not, as might be expected, with the strengthening but with the weakening of the state. The centrifugal forces pulling the Soviet Union apart, together with deepening economic and social crisis increased the state's concern with securing its national future. This meant it paid additional attention to the material position of young people as well as solving those 'youth problems' (drug addiction, alcoholism, juvenile crime) which threatened the health and strength of the future nation. Such a dramatic change could not be contained within the old paradigms of the youth debate and the first part of this chapter will chart the collapse of the *Komsomol* and with it the paradigm of youth as the vanguard of the construction of communism. The second part will go on to detail the elaboration of a new but equally paternalistic approach to youth, which saw it first and foremost as an object of social policy. By the end of 1991, it will be argued, youth had become not the symbol of the bright future in a new society but 'the lost generation' and as such a social metaphor for a collapsing society.

## IN SEARCH OF A FUTURE: THE DEMISE OF THE VLKSM

The campaign of 'going to the people' embarked upon by the *Komsomol* failed to revive the moribund organization. From the beginning of perestroika to the end of 1989, ten million members left (Sibirev 1989b). Table 5.1 shows the extent of the decline in membership since the Brezhnev era.

Table 5.1 shows that the annual intake of new membership in 1989 was less than 40 per cent of that in 1982. In practical terms this meant that 58,000 organizations, including more than 1,000 school organizations, had not admitted a single person that year (Mironenko 1989b), and that 40,000 primary organizations had ceased functioning altogether (Sotnikov 1990). But the net loss of members was not the only problem facing the *Komsomol*. A more detailed breakdown of new membership shows that it was also losing the wrong kind of members. Amongst those in full-time education, new membership in 1989 was 46 per cent of its 1982 level while

*Table 5.1 Komsomol* membership 1982–90

| Year | Membership (millions) | % of CPSU members | % of women | New members (millions) |
|------|------------|------------|------------|-----------|
| 1982 | 41.36 | 3.6 | 52.5 | 4.37 |
| 1983 | 41.80 | 3.6 | 52.3 | 4.12 |
| 1984 | 42.01 | 3.6 | 52.4 | 3.69 |
| 1985 | 41.94 | 3.6 | 52.7 | 3.78 |
| 1986 | 41.94 | 3.6 | 52.8 | 3.25 |
| 1987 | 40.85 | 3.4 | 53.3 | 2.28 |
| 1988 | 38.31 | 3.1 | 54.0 | 2.42 |
| 1989 | 35.62 | 2.7 | 54.6 | 1.74 |
| 1990 | 31.20 | 2.1 | — | — |

*Source: Molodezh' SSSR – Statisticheskii Sbornik* 1990: 151–4

among industrial workers it was just 7 per cent. In other words, where the principle of mass membership still applied – in schools where whole classes joined *en masse* and amongst students who were not sure whether they still needed a *Komsomol* recommendation to gain entrance to higher education – membership held up best. However, at the workplace, where the *Komsomol* would have to be strong if it was to realize its stated desire of becoming a smaller, but committed political avant-garde, membership had been decimated. The exit from the *Komsomol* therefore did not signify a shedding of the 'ballast' in the move towards a more streamlined and politically committed organization, but a critical loss of authority especially in those areas where the *Komsomol* sought it most.

The exit from *Komsomol* organizations in the non-Russian republics was even more dramatic. Between 1988 and 1990, membership of the Latvian LKSM fell by almost 100,000, leaving only one-third of its original members. Meanwhile, new membership in 1989 stood at only one-fifth of the level of the year before (Markarian 1990). In Lithuania, recruitment in 1988 was only one-third of that in 1986, and a poll taken in 1989 revealed that only 11 per cent of young people (mainly the ethnic Russians in the republic) thought that the Lithuanian *Komsomol* should continue as a member of the VLKSM (Girnius 1989: 21).

The second major problem for the VLKSM, therefore, was that the growing mood of independence among the republics had punctured the unity of the organization. The first indication of this came from Estonia when an emergency plenum on the future of the republic's *Komsomol* failed to bridge the split which had emerged over its attitude towards the degree of independence desirable for Estonia (Teterin 1988). By the time of the Eleventh Congress in November 1989, members of the Estonian *Komsomol* had decided to go it alone, withdrawing their membership from the VLKSM (Sibirev 1989c) and resolving that after a transition period of three months, the Estonian Young Communist League would be dissolved and then re-formed on the basis of new statutes and programme. The refounded organization had a membership of just 30,000 (compared to 165,000 in 1987) and existed alongside an Association of Youth of Estonia and the Fund of the Youth of Estonia (Mironenko 1990a; Solnick 1990: 10).

The Lithuanian organization in contrast simply split; at an extraordinary congress held in June 1989, it transformed itself into an independent organization – the Communist Union of Lithuanian Youth – and, subsequently, those who wished to remain part of the VLKSM formed a separate organization which remained within it (Mironenko 1990a). The formation of the new organization was intended to mark a return to the independent *Komsomol* that had existed in Lithuania between 1919 and 1940 and which, the First Secretary Alfonsas Macaitis declared, had been illegally incorporated into the VLKSM (Girnius 1989). The statutes of the new independent Communist Union of Lithuanian Youth (*Kommunisticheskii Soiuz Molodezhi Litvy*) replaced traditional goals such as 'the further progress towards communism' with the 'defence of the sovereignty of the Lithuanian SSR . . .' and 'democratic centralism' with the principles of collegiality, personal responsibility, free exit and the right to participate in other groups (Bychkova 1989b; Sibirev 1989a; Pal'tsev 1989; Girnius 1989: 22).[1] The new Communist Union of Lithuanian Youth lasted just fifteen months, however; in October 1990 it changed its name again, this time to the 'Youth Forum of Lithuania' and resolved that the property and duties of the former *Komsomol* of the republic would be transferred to the youth forum (Informatsionnoe Soobshchenie 1990).

By the time the Latvian *Komsomol* came to discuss its future, then, it had two possible models to choose from. In the event it chose neither of them, or rather a mixture of both of them. Making a mockery of the principles of democratic centralism, the Latvian *Komsomol* declared it would have its own rules and statutes, but did not withdraw from the VLKSM (Arifdzhanov 1990; Markarian 1990).

The former Baltic republics were not alone in their desire for greater independence, however. In October 1990, having already changed its name to the Union of Armenian Youth, the former Armenian *Komsomol* dissolved itself. The Georgian *Komsomol* preferred a slow death; its Thirty-fourth Congress decided to allow a period of three months of 'self-determination' during which time free exit from the *Komsomol* would be permitted and new youth organizations created (Mikeladze and Mursaliev 1990; Tskhvaradze 1990). In Ukraine too, the *Komsomol* had already come under direct attack when groups such as the Union of Independent Ukrainian Youth (SNUM) had tried to burn *Komsomol* membership cards in L'vov (on 14 October) and in Kiev (22 October) (Matvienko 1989).

The rush for independence begun by other republics, and the growing sense of the implosion of the VLKSM, left *Komsomol* supporters within Russia – the only republic within the Soviet Union never to have had its own republic-level *Komsomol* organization – fearful of their position, and calls for the creation of a Russian *Komsomol* were soon heard. Following a congress of *Komsomol* organizations of the RSFSR in February 1990, a voluntary association on the territory of the RSFSR was agreed and the election of organs and adoption of programmes and statute documents was set for June of that year (Mironenko 1990a). The inaugural First Secretary of the Russian *Komsomol* (RSFSR LKSM) was Vladimir Elgin, the former First Secretary of Orenburg (Tsotsuev 1990). But not even the newly formed Russian *Komsomol* could escape the trend towards factioning and its split was concurrent with its formation. At the 1990 Congress not one but two new organizations were formed: the LKSM RSFSR; and the Russian Democratic Socialist Association (*Rossiiskaia Demokraticheskaia Sotsialisticheskaia Assotsiatsiia*, or RDSA) (Khaitina 1990d). The founders of the latter grouping argued that since no rule of the subordination of the minority to the majority (democratic centralism) had been agreed by the congress, the two organizations must be considered equal and the RDSA intended to set up primary cells and branch headquarters in a number of Russian cities (Bek, Graivoronskii and Romanov, 1990).

This split must be seen against the background of events in the CPSU where, by January 1990, 'Democratic' and 'Marxist' Platforms had emerged in the run up to the February Plenum of 1990 and the formal discussion of the future of Article Six which had hitherto guaranteed the monopoly status of the CPSU as a political party. The 'Democratic Platform of the CPSU' (the first organized faction of the CPSU since the 1920s) was supported by those favouring a multi-party system (e.g. Iakovlev and Yeltsin), while the alternative 'Marxist Platform' called for a return to 'classical, critical Marxism' rather than social democratic revisionism. One congress delegate declared that the RDSA felt itself to be broadly aligned with the Democratic Platform of the CPSU and claimed its only point of difference with the LKSM RSFSR was its rejection of the principle of democratic centralism (Ul'ianov 1990). Others, however, had a more radical stance and did not hide their support for the pro-democracy umbrella organization Democratic Russia. They argued that the RDSA advocated: the abolition of a rigid *Komsomol* apparatus and the introduction of full independence for primary organizations; the delegation of election by secret ballot of all co-ordinating organs; the end of democratic centralism; and the ownership of all resources by primary organizations (Khaitina 1990b). As political opinion polarized in the country as a whole – with Gorbachev swinging from left to right and back again between the autumn of 1990 and the spring of 1991 – the RDSA also began to radicalize and its aim shifted towards the foundation of an alternative non-communist youth organization along the lines of an association of 'Democratic Youth of Russia' (Khaitina 1990f).

By the time the Twenty-first Congress of the VLKSM met in April 1990, therefore, it did so in a radically different political environment from that of just three years before, when it had held its previous congress. In order simply to live to see a Twenty-second Congress the VLKSM would have to succeed in suppressing internal divisions along both political (radical/ conservative) and national lines. Only with this unity could it set about the task of devising a strategy to head off attacks on its privileges (its virtual monopoly of the youth sphere both politically and economically) and to secure its place in the future political structure, whatever that might be.

### The Twenty-first Congress: to be or not to be?

In the opening words of his speech to the Twenty-first Congress of the VLKSM, its First Secretary, Viktor Mironenko, referred to the congress not only as an 'extraordinary congress' (since it had been brought forward) but also an 'emergency congress'. Given that at the time he was speaking, there was not one youth organization left in Eastern Europe still under the name of communist union of youth, he had good reason to be worried.[2] Consequently, debates in the run up to the Twenty-first Congress of the VLKSM had not been concerned so much with reform as with a much deeper existential question: 'To be or not to be?'

At the Eighth Plenum of the Central Committee of the VLKSM (in the summer of 1989), there was already talk of crisis and it was decided that the next congress of the VLKSM should be brought forward to spring 1990 and that a 'programme' should be established ('Diagnoz postavlen. Trebuetsia lechenie' 1989; Sibirev 1989b). The importance of the decision to draw up a programme was twofold. First, its content became the focus of struggle for different factions within the *Komsomol*. Second, it indicated that as far as the Central Committee was concerned, the decision about what shape the organization should take had already been made; the drawing up of a programme indicated that the VLKSM was to remain a single, united body with greater political independence, including the right to defend its own particular platform. The significance of the latter will be discussed in greater detail below, after the struggle over the programme has been considered.

The return to business as usual after the Twentieth Congress did not please the more radical reformers within the *Komsomol* and in the autumn of 1988, a second faction formed around leading reformist members. Since its founding meeting was to be held in the Siberian city of Surgut, it became known as the 'Surgut group'. The group used the decision of the Fourth Plenum to strengthen the rights of 'temporary *Komsomol* organizations' (Kirin 1988), in order to establish itself legally within the *Komsomol*. The group consisted of 'authentic *Komsomol* leaders' and their meetings aimed to raise for discussion key questions not resolved by the Twentieth Congress (Baikov *et al.* 1988). Its attempt to foster a populist and authentic image was evident in the slogans used at its first meeting which included anti-*apparat* sentiments such as 'Not a penny of our subs to the *Komsomol* bureaucrats' (*Komsomolskim biurokratam – ni kopeiki vznosov!*) and 'We want change' (*My khotim peremen!*), the latter borrowing the title of a popular song by the Leningrad rock group 'Kino' (Kozheurov *et al.* 1989). Although the vast majority of young people undoubtedly would have preferred to listen to Viktor Tsoi's version of change than the *Komsomol* radicals', nevertheless, the Surgut group effectively kept debate alive in the organization between congresses and helped provide a focus for opposition to the limited reforms proposed by the Central Committee. By August 1989 it declared itself to have outgrown its temporary *Komsomol* organization status and gravitated to calling itself the 'Surgut alternative' or 'Surgut movement'. By this time it already had its second generation of leaders – Maksim Sotnikov, Aleksandr Bek, Aleksandr Fomin, Nikolai Brusnikin and Pavel Romanov amongst them – whose ambitions had grown to include the possibility of progressing from a *Komsomol* faction to an alternative youth movement (Khaitina 1990a). It was these people who were to feature in the struggle over the new statutes and new programme of the VLKSM.

Whilst seemingly an open debate – discussion of four draft versions had already begun at the Eighth Plenum and had been published in the press after the plenum ('Programma VLKSM: Vozmozhny varianty' 1989) – in fact, the Central Committee of the VLKSM remained firmly in control. At the Ninth Plenum (held at the end of October 1989) Mironenko simply declared that none of the variants were adequate for adoption as the *Komsomol* programme and the Central Committee had instead decided to issue a Programmatic Statement (Mironenko 1989b). Nevertheless, the discussion of the programmes had revealed the fundamental issues of struggle in the *Komsomol* which re-emerged at the Twenty-first Congress the following spring.

First, there was the issue of the structure of the *Komsomol*. The actions of individual republican *Komsomol* organizations meant that by the time the Twenty-first Congress met, the VLKSM was already redundant; the least the congress could do was to reflect the existing state of affairs. This is what it did, adopting a federal structure which made the *Komsomol* organizations of the union republics independent socio-political organizations whose participation in the VLKSM was to be voluntary and on a basis of equality. Effectively, however, just as at the Twentieth Congress, the VLKSM had rejected the idea of transforming itself into a federative organization of political and interest-based organizations in favour of retaining a smaller, but better, politically motivated organization with significantly more independence from the CPSU.[3]

The second major issue to surface was that of *Komsomol* funding and finances. The greater financial independence of the primary organization had been a major theme of the previous congress, and, at the Fourth Plenum after that congress, the Central Committee declared that it would prune the top layers of the *apparat* by 30 per cent before 1st April 1989

('Postanovlenie IV Plenuma TsK VLKSM "O dal'neishei demokratizatsii zhizni Komsomola" ' 1988). Nevertheless, more radical members remained deeply unhappy about the continued top-heavy nature of the VLKSM which drained the organization's resources (Sotnikov 1990). At the Twenty-first Congress Maxim Sotnikov criticized the proposed new statutes (drawn up by Ziukin) for stopping short of the point where the position of the Central Committee might be threatened. His alternative statutes proposed to make the highest body of the organization its congress, not the Central Committee ('Vasha pozitsiia?' 1989).

The extent to which the Sotnikov group saw the issue of organization as being an anti-*apparat* one can be seen in the bitter tirade launched against the Central Committee by one of its members, Viktor Graivoronskii, shortly after the congress had ended. His first accusation was that despite the declining membership of the *Komsomol*, the Central Committee *apparat* continued to grow – by 300 people in the previous year alone. Second, he claimed, the Central Committee *apparat* was using the creation of self-financing centres and associations to employ the former VLKSM nomenklatura. Third, he suggested, *Komsomol* money was being used to finance the Central Committee's lifestyle rather than worthy causes and that investment had not been made in the infrastructure of the country but in institutions for the reproduction of the Central Committee *apparat* (Graivoronskii 1990).

The outcome of the Twenty-first Congress was essentially as unsatisfactory as that of the Twentieth. In the run up to the congress two ways forward had been suggested: turning the organization into an elite group of young communists only concerned with political matters (à la Ziukin); or forming a broad youth movement on the basis of the existing *Komsomol* (à la Sotnikov) (Potekhin 1990). Neither one nor the other was adopted and the new statutes emerged as an unsatisfactory hybrid. The ideological position of the post-congress *Komsomol*, for example, was highly confused: it was referred to as 'communist', 'socialist' and 'for democratic socialism'. The relationship with the CPSU also remained unclear. Although, as Ziukin put it, 'The kind of *Komsomol* whose relationship with the Communist Party was defined by the length of the leash and the strength of the collar that one apparatus placed on another no longer exists' (Ziukin cited by Solnick 1990: 12), nevertheless, there was still talk of 'solidarity with the CPSU' and 'active participation in the elaboration and realization of the policies of the CPSU and of other socio-political and state institutions addressing the problems of youth' (Solnick 1990: 12). Despite the clear desire for independence among most of the republics, the *Komsomol* remained essentially a unitary organization. Mironenko's belief that 'a strong centre consists of strong organizations in the provinces' (Mironenko 1989a) followed Gorbachev's vision for the Soviet Union of a strong centre plus strong republics and, as it turned out, both were doomed to failure. Finally, the issue of whether the organization was primarily an elite political organization or a mass one remained unresolved. Despite Mironenko's citation of sociological research which suggested that the *Komsomol* could only rely on the support of 10 per cent of young people and that only 53–5 per cent of young people supported even a broadly socialist perspective (Mironenko 1990b), he continued to equate the interests of *Komsomol* members with those of youth in general.

## YOUTH, THE KOMSOMOL AND THE STATE: DEFINING A NEW RELATIONSHIP

The real significance of the adoption of a *Komsomol* programme at the Twenty-first congress was that it reflected a manifest desire by the *Komsomol* to establish a new political role for itself, without relinquishing any of its existing political or economic power. This was to be achieved by a redefinition of its role; it was to become 'the defender of youth interests', the representative of youth in parliamentary and state organizations and the organizer, co-ordinator, and future owner, of youth leisure and labour facilities. This was not a sudden change of strategy but the culmination of a long process of the reorientation of *Komsomol* activity necessitated by the fundamental changes in the balance of political power taking place in Soviet society under perestroika.

Central to Gorbachev's democratization programme had been the clearer delimitation of the role of the CPSU to be achieved through the prevention of its interference in the everyday running of the country by increasing the self-financing and self-administration of enterprises and councils and by upgrading the role of the parliamentary bodies. These reforms were embodied in a new electoral law and a number of amendments to the constitution which were published in October 1988 and approved in December of the same year. Recognizing that it was to be the bodies of parliament and government rather than those of the party which were to assume the central role in Soviet politics, the *Komsomol* had begun to manoeuvre itself into a new position as early as the Twentieth Congress in 1987, when it passed a resolution declaring the need for 'close cooperation between *Komsomol* committees and committees of people's deputies' (Kalinin 1987).

Included in the constitutional changes elaborated in 1988 was the creation of a new highest organ of power in the country – the Congress of People's Deputies – whose major responsibility was to elect from amongst its number 542 members of the Supreme Soviet. The latter body was to become a proper working parliament as opposed to the rubber-stamping body for politburo decisions which it had been earlier. Of the Congress's 2,250 deputies, for the first time, 750 were to be elected not by popular vote but from All-Union public organizations including seventy-five from the VLKSM. Radical reformers were highly critical of this amendment since it effectively reserved seats for conservative organizations such as the

CPSU, the *Komsomol* and the trade unions. The Lithuanian *Komsomol* refused to nominate deputies in this way for its own republican Supreme Soviet at its congress in June 1989. The VLKSM, however, welcomed the new system, arguing that the additions to the constitution provided the *Komsomol* with new opportunities to conduct youth policy and defend the interests of youth in the highest organ of state power ('Postanovlenie IV Plenuma TsK VLKSM "O dal'neishei demokratizatsiia zhizni Komsomola" ' 1988). In March 1989 the deputies who were to represent the *Komsomol* were duly elected, fifty-seven of them simultaneously being members of the party.

Despite the seeming advantage won for young people, it is doubtful whether they gained significantly in representation from the reforms. In the last pre-perestroika election, 15 per cent of USSR Supreme Soviet deputies had been *Komsomol* members (Zhuganov 1988: 26), while in 1989 the number of deputies elected to the Congress of People's Deputies under 30 years of age was 187, or 12 per cent.

By the time the Twenty-first Congress of the VLKSM gathered in April 1990, the urgency of the task of re-establishing the *Komsomol* at the centre of a very different emergent political system was clear. Article Six of the constitution had already been abolished and the sacrosanct position of the party (and thus also the *Komsomol*) was no more. The way forward for the *Komsomol* was outlined by Mironenko in his speech to the Twenty-first Congress; the new organization was to be 'non-dogmatic' and to attach great importance to defending the interests of youth (Mironenko 1990c).

To mark the break with the past and the beginning of a new era, Mironenko decided to withdraw his candidacy for re-election as First Secretary of the VLKSM. Nevertheless, of the three front-runners for the post, it was the one most closely tied to the interests of the Central Committee, Vladimir Ziukin, who won, whilst Andrei Sharonov (a people's deputy from the *Komsomol* and at 26, ten years younger than Ziukin) and Maksim Sotnikov (a leading member of the Surgut alternative) came second and third respectively (Arifdzhanov, Bykov and Dmukhovskii 1990). Ziukin's three years in the Central Committee had been preceded by the post of First Secretary in the Khabarovsk region, where, as reported in Chapter 3, he had been reprimanded for 'the low level of moral education of youth' following two incidents of street disturbances by youth in the city of Komsomol'sk-na-Amure in which one youth had died. As regards his potential as a radical, *Sobesednik* reported that he had been nominated by its readers to attend the Surgut alternative meeting but had been 'prevented from doing so by illness' (ibid.).

Ziukin's vision of the future role of the *Komsomol* was well known. Criticizing the Sotnikov model of a loose structure of interest-based organizations, in an article published in February 1990, he posited the priorities of the *Komsomol* as:

- political struggle for state power in order to realize the goals of the organization, to create and implement a state youth policy, and to defend the rights and interests of youth;
- participation in the activity of soviets at all levels, including participation in legislative and socio-economic planning activity, and in executive organs of state power and in self-management of enterprises;
- the implementation of a social programme based on the *Komsomol*'s own organizational and material resources including the development of MZhKs, NTTMs, youth tourism and youth centres (Ziukin 1990a; Ziukin 1990b).

The future of the *Komsomol* envisaged by Ziukin then was as an organization *for* and not *of* youth. It was an organization which 'should care about the young person, guarantee his interests, and be a political instrument for solving the social problems of youth'. This would be achieved by establishing a system of social protection for youth which would grow into a social-state one including a chain of information centres, social, legal, psychological services and clubs where young people could obtain information and qualified help on work, study and recreation (Bychkova 1990b).

The ambitions of the *Komsomol* were not unfounded since its former position as *the* recognized representative of youth meant that it had the right to initiate legislation and conduct state policy. Moreover, its newly elected deputies were in a strong position to maximize the use of this privilege. The Central Committee proposed the creation of a more effective Committee on Youth Affairs of the USSR Supreme Soviet and strongly supported the need for a USSR law on youth ('Postanovlenie IV Plenuma TsK VLKSM "O dal'neishei demokratizatsiia zhizni Komsomola" ' 1988). The proposal suggested that deputies from both houses of the Supreme Soviet should participate, but that the prime participants should be deputies elected from the VLKSM. This would provide a secure base of representation of youth and its inclusion in the discussion of any state plans for social and economic development of the country and state budget where the interests of youth were concerned, and of draft laws and other legislative acts related to it (Mironenko 1988b). Such a committee – possibly including representatives not only of the *Komsomol* but of other youth organizations registered with the local administration – it was argued, could become a much more effective way of conducting youth policy (Lukov 1988).

However, although a new Chair of the Supreme Soviet Committee on Youth Affairs – Valerii Tsybukh, the 38 year old First Secretary of the Ukrainian *Komsomol* – was elected in June 1989, the passage of the Law on Youth proved more difficult than anticipated. Attempts to adopt such a law had already failed in 1966 and 1977 (see Chapter 2), but the issue had been taken up again in 1985 and a draft version of the law had been due for publication by the end of 1988. This draft was worked on by a special Supreme Soviet commission, a *Komsomol* commission under the chairmanship of Viktor Mironenko and a group of specialists on youth problems at the Research Centre of the Higher *Komsomol* School (Vasil'ev and Zhavoronkov 1988). Nevertheless, the preparation of the law met serious problems.

The first problem was that the law became a focus for the struggle over the monopolistic position of the *Komsomol*. Many feared the law privileged the organization as the single representative of young people and thus made their rights effective only through it (Il'inskii 1988b), while others attempted to use the discussion to raise again the question of abolishing the territorial-production principle of *Komsomol* organization (Vasil'ev and Zhavoronkov 1988). Second, the law was seen to privilege young people by establishing their legal right to state support and thus to encourage dependency on the state (Tsybukh 1990). The experience of other socialist countries who had passed such laws (Hungary 1971, GDR 1974, Poland 1986), it was argued, had been negative and, in the current climate, such a law would appear to be allowing youth to live on the back of society whilst solving none of its problems (Os'kin 1990).

The third, and probably most widespread, objection to the law was that it was simply pointless and a deflection of concern away from the real issue of the need for a radical change in the role of the *Komsomol* (Osin 1991). By the time the 'Law on the Fundamental Principles of State Youth Policy in the USSR' was finally passed on 16 April 1991, indeed, it probably was. This was because in order to secure its passage, the section concerning socio-economic guarantees for youth which had been included in the first drafts had to be removed because (according to Mironenko) this would have required resources which the state had not got (Zaripov 1990). But without these guarantees, the law contained little more than abstract principles, and certainly did not live up to Tsybukh's vision of 'levelling the playing field' for young people (Tsybukh 1990).

Beyond the rhetoric, the law contained two concrete commitments. First, it stated that tax and credit concessions for registered youth organizations, to encourage youth initiative and entrepreneurship, would be continued. Second, it envisaged the creation of a state youth service at All-Union, republican and local levels in order to implement state youth policy and the defence of youth. This service would include bodies coordinating youth policy as well as a number of social services providing information about young people's rights, psychological and pedagogical services, legal and drugs advice, help for disadvantaged children, programmes of social work for young offenders and rehabilitation programmes for young people ('Ob obshchikh nachalakh gosudarstvennoi molodezhnoi politiki v SSSR' 1991).

The failure to establish any real mechanism by which to resolve the problems facing young people did nothing to allay the fears of those sceptical about the new position of the *Komsomol*. Critics saw the new line of the *Komsomol* as simply a means for the *Komsomol* nomenklatura 'to retain power and to preserve its position' (Bek 1990). Indeed, the *Komsomol* had done little in the past to enable its own deputies elected in 1989 to work effectively through parliament; from an *apparat* of 100,000, the *Komsomol* had allocated only four positions to help the *Komsomol* deputies in parliament (Graivoronskii 1990). One of these deputies made clear the feeling of abandonment at the Twenty-first Congress of the *Komsomol*; thirteen months after their election, he claimed, the *Komsomol* Central Committee had met with them only once (Solnick 1990: 12). This deputy was Andrei Sharonov, whose failure to be elected as new First Secretary of the *Komsomol* also cast serious doubt on the VLKSM's real commitment to shifting the prime orientation of the *Komsomol* to its parliamentary role.

The period after the Twenty-first Congress was one of struggle for both economic and political control of youth policy. In economic terms, the *Komsomol* was concerned to protect the favourable tax status given to its enterprises; a statement had been sent from the Twenty-first Congress to the Supreme Soviet protesting the latter's proposal to increase the tax rate on *Komsomol* enterprises from 35 per cent to 55 per cent (Bychkova 1990a). The *Komsomol* was also concerned that any precedent of state appropriation of its resources set in the republics might snowball and Mironenko had argued at the Twenty-first Congress that the organization's resources should not be divided but concentrated on implementing large, All-Union programmes (Mironenko 1990b). Moreover, whilst accepting that the *apparat* must be cut and *Komsomol* workers must increasingly be employed in direct work with youth (in youth centres and complexes), it was argued by those at the top of the *apparat* that the jobs of *Komsomol* workers must be protected, in order that new workers felt they had a secure future (Khaitina and Bychkova 1990).

But it was not only the state which was threatening the economic empire of the *Komsomol*; the directors of youth centres and other enterprises originally set up by the *Komsomol* were also beginning to have a vision of the future without 'big brother'. When they had started up, links between the *Komsomol* and the youth centres had been mutually beneficial since the former had benefited from the progressive image of the centres, while the latter needed the *Komsomol* to defend their interests especially in the negotiation of favourable tax status. Although most youth centres had originally been set up by the *Komsomol* and around two-thirds of their directors were its former employees, they expanded and diversified quickly; one survey conducted in 1990 showed that 86 per cent of youth centres had a production base and more than a third had rented factories or parts of factories (Sidorov and Krasner 1990). As the centres developed, they outgrew the *Komsomol* and many directors began to seek the kind of guarantees and regulations which applied to other kinds of small enterprises (ibid.). Threatened by this stance, in August 1989, the *Komsomol* issued a resolution which strengthened its own influence over the centres, and the directors responded by forming their own association which aimed to define the legal and financial position of the centres more clearly (Kuznetsov, Nikiforov and Krasner 1990). The issue at stake was the control of both property and production bases which the *Komsomol* still considered to be its own.

Third, and most importantly, a struggle began for the control of the new state youth service and existing property which had always been under the control of the *Komsomol*, but which had mainly been financed by the state (including houses and palaces of youth and many *Sputnik* facilities). Even before the passing of the law on youth policy, city and regional councils had begun establishing their own commissions on youth affairs with corresponding departments or committees in the executive structure (Anokhin 1991). In Moscow the youth department had thirty-five full-time staff and was involved in elaborating the city's youth policy.

A series of articles in the local youth paper *Moskovskii Komsomolets* revealed the bitterness of the struggle over control of the new service. Outlining the future of the *Komsomol* as an organization defending youth against the state, Aleksandr Artem'ev (chair of the Presidium of the Moscow City Conference of the VLKSM) argued that in the meantime, it was focusing on 'joint programmes', such as giving the state organizations some of the shares in *Sputnik*, MZhK projects and developing an information network and service to help young people find work. Aleksandr Abramov (First Secretary of the Moscow Region *Komsomol* Committee), however, was less compromising. He argued that the *Komsomol* should not suffer financially by any decision on the part of its enterprises such as youth centres and NTTMs to become independent. Criticizing the decision by the co-ordinating council of the NTTMs to transfer its centres to collective property, he maintained that the *Komsomol* should be able to recover the original capital investment it made in the enterprises through receiving a percentage of their profits (Khaitina 1991).

The key point here was the status of *Komsomol* property. Radical *Komsomol* leaders such as Aleksandr Bek argued that the organization's money was essentially state money and that the new state service should be set up on the economic base of the *Komsomol*, entailing the transfer of a large part of current VLKSM property to local councils (Khaitina 1990c). Indeed the *Komsomol* had offered this, the catch was that they wanted the state youth service to be what they called a 'public-state youth service'. The difference was that in the former there would be a strict division of powers: a commission on youth affairs, made up solely of elected deputies, would decide on the nature of youth policy whilst a state youth service (through a department of the executive committee of the council) would implement it. The latter, promoted by the Moscow City *Komsomol* Committee and a group of deputies from the Moscow Council Commission on Youth

Affairs, involved the participation of social organizations in the formulation of youth policy. In addition, there would be a youth fund directed by the council, involving various youth social organizations and funded by profit from enterprises, which would retain their economic privileges and tax concessions (Khaitina 1990e; Bek 1990). The advantage of this proposal was that it envisaged the formation of a public-state youth service without subsidies from the state budget, but financed wholly by social organizations and contributions from youth enterprises to the service (Kolkov 1990).

Criticisms of the public-state conception of the new youth service were twofold. First, the structure envisaged would continue the practice of the fusion of legislative and executive functions. Critics argued that social organizations should be allowed to influence policy only via elections and that there should be a strict division between the body entrusted to devise youth policy and that which executed it. Second, the public-state service meant that the *Komsomol* would retain control over part of the state structure in a way which did not reflect its real rating among youth. The fund would be directed by a council made up of representatives of various youth social organizations in which the VLKSM would have a deciding influence because representation would be organized not on the basis of 'one organization – one vote' but would also reflect the financial contribution made to the fund. The proposed state-public system, Bek argued, was essentially what the country had had for the last seventy years (Bek 1990; 'Nuzhna li molodezhi naiania?' 1990).

## Putting the youth policy into practice

While the Central Committee of the *Komsomol* continued to struggle for political and economic influence at the national level, however, the effective devolution of power which had taken place following local elections in 1990 meant that the struggle had to take place at both national and regional levels. In Leningrad and Moscow there were moves towards the abandonment of the VLKSM structure and the creation of federative organizations of independent groups. In August 1990, a youth parliament of Leningrad was created and a Council of Youth Organizations formed including the *Komsomol* and nine other organizations (Potekhina 1990). By October of 1990 the Moscow City *Komsomol* organization was advocating the development of the organization into a federation of youth organizations – as, indeed, had already happened in some of the constituent districts of the city – which would allow the participation of new kinds of formations (corporative, functional and entrepreneurial) as well as traditional territorial and production organizations and even non-*Komsomol* organizations (Samoilova 1990; Shabanov 1991).

At the same time, however, the *Komsomol* continued to develop its social service role, establishing in many cities, committees and centres of social help for youth as well as information consultation services, child help-lines and a student welfare service (Teletaip TsK VLKSM 1991a; Teletaip TsK VLKSM 1991b). One article, whose aim appeared to be to explain to *Komsomol* workers what the new social service actually was, described the lynchpin of the new service as the district or city-level Centre for Social Help for Youth which would be a kind of 'social polyclinic' for young people – thus underlining the VLKSM's new approach to youth as the sickly child in need of its protection (Aleinikov and Chepurin 1991: 23). The positive experience of a number of cities was cited including Nizhnii Novgorod and Yaroslavl where the VLKSM had become joint founders of centres advising on employment, young people's rights, business opportunities, help for disabled people and psychological counselling and rehabilitation services (24). In Moscow, at least, the ultimate aim of the *Komsomol* policy – to position itself at the centre of the new state youth service – was not realized, however. The Moscow city council rejected the *Komsomol*'s proposal for the formation of a public-state youth organization and opted instead for the creation of a youth service based on the experience of other countries. The draft for this new youth policy was drawn up by the youth sector of the Moscow council executive committee. Youth policy was to be organized through: a permanent Commission on Youth Affairs of the Moscow council (whose role was essentially legislative); a Committee on Youth Affairs attached to the executive committee of the Moscow council (whose role was informational, co-ordinating, organizational and controlling); a Youth Fund (which was to fund projects not included in the budget, and to oversee academic input and training in the formation of youth policy); and co-operative, private and social organizations offering specific youth services. The basic concern of the new policy was to provide young people *on an individual basis* with the basic standards of education, professional training and welfare in order to allow their personal development. This meant a reorientation of social policy away from collectivist principles which, it was argued, had discriminated against young people.

Of course, there could not be an overnight break with the past; many of those central to the formulation of the new youth policy at both national and regional level had come from a background in the VLKSM. Andrei Sharonov, for example, who was to become Chair of the Committee on Youth Affairs of the Russian Federation, had himself stood against Ziukin in the *Komsomol* leadership elections in 1990. Sharonov's defeat, however, in fact relieved him from the task of overseeing the death throes of the VLKSM. By 1991, a street interview conducted by *Moskovskii Komsomolets* among young people in Moscow revealed that the *Komsomol* was already history for young people, some of whom had only a dim recollection of what the organization was ('Ei, Komsomol, ty eshche zhiv?' 1991). Even its First Secretary appeared doubtful about its future. In an article entitled 'There are no careers in the *Komsomol* now',

Ziukin was reported as saying that he anticipated being head of the VLKSM for no more than eighteen months (Ragozin 1990).

In fact he did not even survive that long; at the end of September 1991, the VLKSM held its Twenty-second Congress at which it was declared that 'the political role of the All-Union Leninist Communist Union of Youth as a federation of young communist leagues has been exhausted' (Lebedev 1991). The decision clearly came in the wake of the failed attempted coup in August 1991 which, although not supported by the VLKSM Central Committee, proved to be the final blow to the credibility of the party and its youth league. More than anything the failed coup proved that power and authority no longer resided at the centre, in All-Union organizations. The VLKSM as such was thus dissolved, although a co-ordinating council was set up to regulate relations between republic communist youth leagues and a commission established to divide up Central Committee property.

One faction of the VLKSM – the Communist Initiative – continued to campaign for its restoration, however, and by January 1992, the Moscow *Komsomol* organization had been revived and a new First Secretary – Igor' Maliarov – elected ('Meeting seeks revival of Moscow *Komsomol* organization' 1992). Three months later, on 23 April 1992, a so-called Twenty-third (restoration) Congress of the VLKSM was held in Moscow and attended by more than 100 delegates from various regions of Russia, Ukraine, Belarus, the Baltics, the Transcaucasus and the Dnestr region. The aims of the revived *Komsomol* were stated to be the defence of interests of working people and student youth, its education on the basis of Marxism–Leninism and the cultivation of political activity amongst young people. The main political aim was the restoration of an integral multi-ethnic state of the USSR as a voluntary union of peoples, and the struggle to eliminate all forms of exploitation (Vinitskaia 1992). At the republican level the *Komsomol* continues to exist in the Russian Federation as the 'Russian Union of Youth' with branches at regional and district levels. At this level, the funds and publishing empire inherited from the *Komsomol* allow it to play a 'resource and co-ordinating' function in local politics, acting as an umbrella organization for social initiative groups and lobbying local authorities on youth issues (Leitch 1993: 48).

Despite the stated aims of the VLKSM to become a smaller but politically stronger organization, this path of development was always a much more likely outcome of the ideological impasse. The resources and organizational power of the *Komsomol* are now used by 'expert staff' in order to 'represent' youth interests while the lack of impulse for organized political activity among young people is explained by their past enforced mobilization into state-defined economic and political tasks. In dissolution, then, the VLKSM has reached its logical conclusion; it has become a head without a body.

## YOUTH ON THE MARGINS

The policy-makers were not alone in seeing youth as shut out of mainstream society, the academic world was also moving in this direction. Young people, it was argued, had become second-class citizens or even socially marginalized and as such needed special attention in order to reintegrate them into society. Broadly speaking academic work on youth culture published in the post-1989 period adopted one of two approaches: the moral decay amongst youth indicated the collapse of society at its weakest link and prefigured a general social catastrophe; or the peripheral nature of youth culture signified the possibility of cultural renewal and change. Both approaches were premised on a rethinking of the concept of subculture which had taken place in the 1988–9 period, and the input from psychologists and culturologists at the expense of sociologists in the debate on youth informal groups was notable. Below the history of this process of rethinking is charted before the new approaches which emerged are discussed.

### Informal groups as distinct ways of life: rethinking the concept of subculture

In the pre-1990 period, at the highest level of theoretical abstraction the commitment to the class character of culture – which envisaged Soviet or socialist culture engaged in an ideological struggle against bourgeois culture – remained intact (Kartavaia 1988: 58). Meanwhile, empirical sociological research often remained concerned with indicating the degree to which youth conformed to the socialist way of life (Zborovskii 1989: 101). Nevertheless, even those commentators who devotedly painted the picture of the ideologically correct way of life adopted by Soviet youth began to take seriously the importance of the social environment – not just social institutions – in shaping its cultural practice. According to Blinov, this environment could be divided into micro-environments (the *dvor*, entrance way (*pod"ezd*) and the informal group) and the macro-environment or broader social climate ('Ideino-politicheskoe stanovlenie molodezhi: opyt i problemy' 1987: 26–7). This opened the way to the possibility of seeing Soviet society as having both a set of general cultural characteristics (congruent with socialist society) but retaining a cultural pluralism expressed in national cultures, professional associations, demographic and interest groups. Effectively this meant that subcultures – previously seen as a phenomenon exclusive to Western societies – were evident in socialist society as well, the difference being that whereas in bourgeois society subcultures were born of rebellion against the 'fathers', in socialist society they indicated the uniting of young people for the solution of creative tasks (Kuchmaeva 1987: 5–7).

Kuchmaeva's book was the first to attempt a comparison between Soviet and Western subcultural associations and, although the term 'cultural community' (*kul'turnaia obshchnost'*) rather than subculture was employed in relation to Soviet society, it was nevertheless suggested that the two terms were identical 'in their real content'. This required a re-appropriation of the term subculture which was achieved by distinguishing 'counter-culture' from 'subculture'. The former was applied exclusively to those cultural formations in the West in the 1960s which constituted a 'conscious opposition to norms and ways of the dominant culture', whilst the latter was used more widely to define cultural communities which existed and functioned within culture as a *normal* part of it (Matveeva 1987: 16). The term subculture then was found to be useful since it permitted the classification of different groups in society according to their ways or styles of life, with the proviso that socially-threatening subcultures such as fascist movements, terroristic groups and subcultures of declassed elements of society (criminals, idlers and 'psychedelic subcultures') were declared to be unacceptable to society (Orlova 1987: 8).

Since these ways of life were seen to be born of common interests rather than class position, the acknowledgement of the existence of subcultures did not challenge the accepted version of the fundamental social structure of Soviet society. In fact it was fully consistent with the emphasis during perestroika on the need to identify and harness different professional interests for the general improvement of the economy. Potentially more difficult was the reconciliation of the acceptance of subcultures with the understanding of social and cultural change.

Hitherto, change in socialist society had been seen to be the product of the smooth transition of generations while any notion of change led by a non-class group (such as that put forward by Karl Mannheim) had been heavily criticized (see Chapter 2). This problem was solved by applying the familiar differentiation between classes and 'non-antagonistic' classes to the concept of subculture. Hence, Matveeva argued, in every society there was a core culture consisting of subcultures which together were most characteristic of the given culture and which expressed the general world-outlook, system of values, way and style of life of the majority of the bearers of that culture. In class societies the core culture was relatively unstable and might be opposed by peripheral subcultures which, in times of crisis, might penetrate the core culture and change its nature. In socialist society, however, where there were no antagonistic classes, the core culture was made up of 'organically connected' subcultures expressed in the 'Soviet people' (*sovetskii narod*) and although subcultures could still arise – based on socio-professional groups or along ethnic traditions – their study only illuminated the processes of cultural differentiation and inte-gration (Matveeva 1987).

In relation to youth subculture, this approach was seen to avoid the danger of overestimating the ability of subcultures to challenge or trans-form the dominant culture of which 'bourgeois theorists' were guilty

(Ryleva 1987: 39). At the same time, it recognized the centrality of youth to subcultural activity due to its predilection towards communication in small groups and its tendency to test the strength and boundaries of socio-cultural norms and values in the process of self-determination and identity formation (Shibaeva 1987: 60; Kuchmaeva 1987: 93–8).

This new approach to youth subculture opened the way for the flourishing in the post-1989 period of a notion of youth subculture which suggested that its peripheral nature endowed it with a strong potential for cultural innovation in a positive direction.

## Youth culture and multiple possible futures

The fragmentation and dispersal of political power in the 1990–1 period could not but have a significant impact on the perception of culture and change. The first principle of the former approach to subculture – the uniformity and stability of the dominant culture in socialist society – was symbolized by the unity of the Soviet people and this unity had proven to be both shallow and repressive of natural cultural development. The threat posed to the dominant culture was evident from its own aggressively defensive posturing, examples of which were the *liubery* and the attempted coup of August 1991. The failure of the latter revealed the loss of hegemony of the old guard (who could not even command the full support of the armed forces) but also the failure of Gorbachev to successfully reshape the cultural sphere. The coup underlined above all that the old culture no longer reigned, that the market culture had powerful, but few, supporters, while the majority of the Russian people remained concerned with their own cultural worlds and felt largely removed from attempts to reforge a national culture.

Given the atmosphere of fragmentation and fluidity, it is not surprising that culturologists were beginning to reject the reduction of youth culture to the issue of leisure or to its purely outer manifestation – its jargon, mannerisms and fashion. The cultural sphere, it was argued, had been falsely restricted to a role of leisure or amusement and had been used primarily as a means of social regulation and artificial conservation of the existing state of society, and thus its creative role had been suppressed (Kondakov 1989: 77). The notion of youth culture as a single, socially homogeneous, sexless and nationless phenomenon, which, in the Soviet Union represented a social deviation emerging under the influence of the West, was rejected in favour of seeing in youth subcultures all the contradictions of contemporary social development (Kukhtevich and Dobrynin 1990). In this interpretation, informal groups and youth subcultures were peripheral in the sense that they emerged at the edges or boundaries of formal institutions and of social relations which had failed them. The implication was that since youth cultural groups consisted of those most flexible and receptive to new social technologies, they might give an impulse to society for accelerated social development and facilitate the resurrection of civil society and thus a general reconciliation ('Molodezh' v sovremennom mire' 1990: 25–6; Levicheva 1991: 45).

The groups Levicheva was referring to, of course, were the formerly proclaimed positive or pro-social groups of politically (correctly) orientated *neformaly* and, although more pluralistic in its nature this was essentially a continuation of the old *Komsomol*-promoted line of thought. A similar approach was taken by Sundiev whose exposition of the history of 'informality' (*neformalitet*) in Soviet society clearly rooted him on the '*nash*' ('ours') side of the *nash/ne nash* debate, and whose impressive typology of different forms of informal activity marked him out as one of the Soviet Union's real experts in this area. His evaluation, however, remained firmly locked in the politicized debate of the democratization period of perestroika which meant that above all it was the socio-political contribution of informal groups to the development of society's restructuring which was to be measured and valued (Sundiev 1990).

Potentially more radical were interpretations that focused not on the groups of informals as active political participants, but the cultural moment or activity itself. In rejecting what he, aptly, referred to as the 'Trojan horse' approach of the *Komsomol* to informal groups, Shein argued that the sociological approach to *neformaly* as groups of people was limited and should be replaced with an approach which allowed different informal movements to be viewed as different possible cultural futures (Shein 1990: 11). Asmolov meanwhile blamed the over-politicization of the *neformaly* debate for labelling youth's rebellious behaviour as a kind of counter-culture or culture of protest and thus scapegoating youth in a time of crisis. In fact, he argued, the interest in youth culture had emerged precisely because youth had the potential to lead society's culture in a new direction since rebellious behaviour – be it of vagrants and fools in the middle ages or of dissidents in the second half of the twentieth century – represented not counterculture or even anti-culture but 'variant paths of development' ('Molodezh' v sovremennom mire' 1990: 23–4).

Indeed, even the principle of creating a non-dissenting mass of youth to conduct the smooth changeover of generations began to be challenged. Summarizing the conclusions of a study in Belarus on the effectiveness of the Soviet media in socializing young people into the desired political beings, Manaev criticized the very premise of such studies, i.e. that a dissenting audience was politically negative. The survey showed that 71 per cent of young people usually or sometimes did not agree with the opinions of the media and that there was a significant correlation between those who dissented from, and mistrusted, the media and psychological and moral readiness for perestroika (Manaev 1991).[4]

Thus the division between *nash* and *ne nash* ('one of us/one of them') had to be abandoned in determining cultural policy for, according to Kondakov, such a division was itself culturally disruptive (Kondakov 1989:

82). Instead, the fate of perestroika was seen to depend upon balancing the two fundamental notions of historical progress at work in Soviet society since the mid-1950s: the need for the development of social-practical skills and technocratic knowledge; and the need to develop the creative imagination as the principal stimulus and catalyst of socio-cultural progress (83). The struggle between capitalist and socialist cultures was to be replaced by that between science and nature, rationality and spirituality, continuity and change.

### Subcultures and their members: enter the psychologists

The new possibilities for understanding informal groups provided by the acceptance of the existence of subcultures as distinct ways of life which found expression in a style of appearance and behaviour were exploited above all by social-psychologists, who, hitherto, had played a relatively minor role in the debate on youth culture. The intervention of the psychologists led to two new directions of study which focused, first, on individual and social motivation for joining subcultural groups and, second, on the symbolic systems of particular groups.

The study of motivation paid attention to the psychological make-up of members of groups and suggested that the precise group joined was arbitrary since the group did not express a particular political or philosophical outlook, so much as act as a mechanism or outlet for certain kinds of emotional expression. Bratus, for example, argued that it was not the nature of the activity of the informal group which was important but the need for a group *per se*. In other words, it did not matter whether the members got high on drink, drugs or breakdancing; it was the 'group high' which was important (Bratus 1987). In stark contrast to the political or ideological readings of informal group activity, such interpretations were premised on the notion that different *neformaly* were more like each other than they were like 'normal youth' (Fel'dshtein 1987: 44; Fel'dshtein 1988: 10). Indeed, as one psychologist argued, the *neformaly* were not protesting about anything, least of all the effectiveness of *Komsomol* work (Radzikhovskii 1988b: 17).

Common to the interpretations of psychologists was the claim that many members of informal groups were psychologically abnormal; the fact that members of informal groups were not adopting 'normal' means of making the transition to adult life was, at the very least, evidence that they were experiencing this transition more painfully than average teenagers (Radzikhovskii 1988b: 13). The most frequent suggestion was that they tended towards neuroticism, although some commentators went as far as to suggest that many were simply 'psychologically ill' (Radzikhovskii 1988a: 78). For them, the group was a safe place where they were shielded from normal society. Any beneficial effect of the group, however, was counteracted by the fact that the sense of community created in the group was achieved through opposing the group to the rest of society and this had a negative effect leading to infantilism and aggressiveness (ibid.) Moreover, members of informal groups were more likely to be involved in anti-social acts than non-members and were characterized by asociableness, hedonism and parasitism (Fel'dshtein 1988: 16).

Although for psychologists some forms of subcultural participation might have a social or political significance, therefore, motivation was to be found on the individual rather than the social level. The chief motivations for subcultural activity were suggested to be:

- the adolescent's desire to establish her/his role and meaning in society;
- the transfer of the meaning of life from the unsatisfying spheres of study and socially useful work to informal groups which brought an element of danger, adventure and difficulty;
- conflicts with parents and teachers which occurred during adolescence and which led to psychological tension, worry and neuroticism.

The latter was the subject of a more detailed study by Anna Mazurova and Mark Rozin in which they employed an analysis of stories told by young people in subcultural groups to develop an understanding of parent–adolescent conflicts which might aid psycho-therapeutic practice (Mazurova and Rozin 1991). In such readings of subcultural activity, the theatrical and carnivalesque forms of behaviour in youth groups and its symbolic aggressiveness were seen as providing the opportunity to lessen psychological tension caused by adolescent conflicts (Fel'dshtein 1989). Rather than seeing informal groups as a protest against stagnation, then, their activity, it was argued, was better read as 'symbolic aggression' which signified a protest not about anything in particular but against everything and anything (Rozin 1988: 32).

The most detailed discussion of motivation in relation to youth cultural activity was undertaken by Borisov whose approach posited informal youth groups as mechanisms of dealing with psychological crises (or 'critical situations') in the lives of adolescents. The empirical example given was that of the 'critical situation' characterized by a sense of 'I can but I don't want to', in which the absence of a need leads to the lack of a mechanism for directing goal-oriented, rational activity. The subjects of the study were punks who, it was argued, used the mechanism of 'hedonistic risk' to become 'involved' in life-situations. Hedonistic risk referred especially to the actualization of the needs for self-esteem and security through the creation of a threat to their satisfaction. In the punk subculture hedonistic risk was manifest in the use of objects as weapons, involving oneself in duels or pseudo threats, spitting or verbal/physical attacks on one another or in 'games' especially of chance where the winner had the right to humiliate or abuse the loser (Borisov 1991: 48). Hedonistic risk was particularly spectacularly employed among the biker subculture in the practice of racing (*gonki*), in which death or the possibility of death played a major role (Borisov 1988: 71–2).

Psychologists studying youth cultural activity, thus paid significant attention to the symbolic systems adopted by young people whilst at the same time seeking an explanatory mechanism in individual needs. Rozin, for example, argued that at the root of subcultural activity was the desire for visibility (*zrimost'*), and the informal groups played out their own theatre on the streets of large cities, with passers-by as their audience (Rozin 1988). A key element of this carnival was the magical power of 'conjuring', of 'making things happen', of 'eventfulness', which gave back the possibility of control to young people in a social world in which they were helpless (ibid.). Within informal groups various means were used to conjure up the miracle needed to realize their wishes. In punk and heavy metal groups these included: 'symbolic aggression'; fear, shock and horror; repulsion; the pretence that the world did not exist; and ridicule of the adult world (Rozin 1988: 29). Participation in the hippy movement, Rozin argued, also functioned as a chain of events breaking up the humdrum existence of everyday life, since the internal symbolic order of the hippies functioned to 'make things happen' and bring forward the meaning of life from the distant future (education, career planning, marriage and parenthood) to the present (Rozin 1990: 71).

The complex symbolic order of the hippy culture (non-intervention in life processes, travel romanticism, disrespect for social norms, self-sacrifice and universal love) was thus interpreted as a form of self-presentation. The professed withdrawal from life, passivity and naturalness masked the fact that hippy culture was a symbolic escape which gave meaning to life; it was a playful protest by means of which adolescents acted out their conflictual relations with the adult world as well as being a means of meeting and being with other people and forming friendships (ibid.). Heavy metallists and punks were portrayed as even more directly the product of the working through of compensatory mechanisms. For metallists, it was suggested, the power implied by metal studs and other attributes covered a deep inferiority complex, while punks adorned the mohican as if it were a crown or knight's helmet (Rozin 1988: 29).

Finally, in their symbolic orders, informal groups employed mechanisms of 'victimization' in order to gain sympathy without effort. Punks, for example, played on their hospitalization as psychiatrically ill, while others played on images of the 'misunderstood genius' or the 'gullible emancipator' in order to establish themselves as heroes without having to earn that honour by hard work (Rozin 1988: 30–1).

Zaianaia, on the other hand, interpreted punk cultural activity as a mixture of an unconscious compensatory function (reducing the discomfort the individual feels in society), a more conscious therapeutic function (in which the informal group was used as a means of overcoming discomfort), and an almost wholly unconscious creative self-realization function. For her, punk culture was aesthetically and philosophically rich although largely unrecognized as such, by either the world at large or the punks themselves (Meier *et al.* 1990: 27).

The psychologists' approach to informal groups thus highlighted the functional role of subcultural activity in providing a mechanism for dealing with life tensions at a particularly difficult stage in psychological development. At the same time, however, they warned of the dangers of long-term subcultural participation. Those *neformaly* who had spent a considerable time in the subculture, according to Rozin, experienced significant problems in returning to mainstream society. Many suffered severe depression, alcoholism or drug addiction and ended their lives in suicide. Thus, he concluded:

> whereas a short stay in the counterculture milieu led to psychological effects that were more positive than negative, any deep immersion in this world resulted in grave consequences, so that a person is no longer able to become part of normal social life.
>
> (Rozin 1991: 69)

Ethnographers, on the other hand (who were removed from the social rehabilitation role of the sociologists and psychologists) were able to study the symbolic systems of youth cultural groups as objects in themselves. These systems were interpreted as playing a central role in the functioning of cultural groups and, as the most long-standing and symbolically rich of the Soviet youth cultures, it was the hippie culture or *sistema* (see Chapter 7) which drew most attention from those approaching subcultural practice from an ethnographic standpoint. Shchepanskaia, for example, studied the highly symbolic role within the *sistema* of *fen'ki*. *Fen'ki* were valueless (in a material sense) items – traditionally bracelets made of beads or woven but in practice any small gifts of a symbolic nature – which were given as presents on acquaintance or as a sign of friendship. The symbolic importance of the bestowing of *fen'ki* was twofold. First, it carried some symbolic message itself (in the form of one of the symbols of peace, love, or harmony important to hippie culture) and thus served to transmit those cultural values and norms. Moreover, since *fen'ki* were only bestowed downwards – from the leader to subordinate members of the group – they served to establish channels of control. Second, the wearing of these symbols allowed the recognition of other members of the *sistema* and thus prompted interaction whilst warding off unwanted social interaction with those outside the *sistema* who were repulsed by the outward appearance of the hippies (Shchepanskaia 1991a: 6–9). In other words intra-group symbols performed an important regulating role among groups of people whose marginality meant that conventional norms and mechanisms of control were ineffective (15).[5]

## The 'lost generation': youth as symbol of social disintegration

While the marginality of the subcultural elite might at least be potentially creative and progressive for culture, the marginality of the 'masses' of youth became a metaphor for social disintegration. The kinds of subcultural formations envisaged by culturologists to be potentially progressive were those which acted on the fringes of intellectual circles of the major cities and whose activity was deemed to have some, even if unrecognized, aesthetic value. Such subcultures were born of social plenty rather than social need and in culturally pluralistic society could exist in a non-antagonistic relationship to the dominant culture. The kind of provincial and gang-based subcultural activity discussed in the previous chapter however continued to be seen as an issue of juvenile delinquency which suggested not heightened cultural potential but the collapse of society into pre-cultural formations. Attacking what he saw as 'cultural radicalism' of a Maoist kind, which equated any practice of youth with the new and thus the progressive, Iurii Davydov argued that young people involved in Kazan' type groups had in fact regressed to the 'pack' mentality of animals and needed plain, old-fashioned *vospitanie* (moral training) to draw them back into mainstream society ('Molodezh' v sovremennom mire' 1990: 27–30).

In general, however, sociologists and culturologists were concerned to identify just where the 'old-fashioned *vospitanie*' had gone wrong. Although the appeal to the degeneration of culture due to the authoritarian political system resulting in the 'double-think' of the Brezhnev period still played a significant role in explaining the poverty of moral education (Kondakov 1989: 80), increasingly it was the *social* legacy of the command-administrative system which was considered. Under the old paradigms of 'youth-as-constructors-of-communism' and 'youth-as-victims-of-Western-influence' the social problems of youth had been blamed on weak ideological training or the effect of Western propaganda (see Chapters 2 and 3), but from 1990, Mironenko began to link directly the rise in antisocial behaviour with the socio-economic problems they faced (Mironenko 1990a).

As was argued above, this must be read in the context of the redefinition of the role of the *Komsomol*. The youth organization had a vested interest in fostering the notion of youth as marginalized and in need of a strong and powerful organization to defend its interests which had been neglected, as a 'consumerist attitude' had been adopted *by the state* towards it. The emergent new paradigm of 'youth-as-objects-of-social-policy' was strengthened, however, by the fact that those who sought an alternative to the *Komsomol* as the core of a new youth policy also emphasized the position of youth as 'victims' of the state. The difference was that the latter implicated the *Komsomol* in responsibility for this exploitation as a previously integral part of the Soviet state.

The articulation of this paradigm-switch is considered below through a study of the portrayal of the social problems faced by youth in the late-perestroika period.

## Education and employment

> Youth cannot do the most important thing – it cannot earn itself an interesting life. This is because in order to live an interesting life material foundations are necessary – a good flat, the opportunity to travel, access to information which provides you with new thoughts. We have given them nothing . . .
>
> (Fedorov cited in Mironenko 1990b: 1)

In their working lives, young people were seen to be discriminated against. First of all, they earned only around half of the average adult wage while the level of material provision of the majority of students was significantly lower than the living wage (Mironenko 1990a; Tsybukh 1990; Khaitina and Bychkova 1990). Their labour was exploited in agricultural work for which they received a pittance (Khaitina and Bychkova 1990). Their promotion prospects were not commensurate with their education and skills; the proportion of youth among directors of enterprises, institutions and organizations, for example, fell from 15 per cent in 1980 to 13 per cent in 1985 while over this period the number of young people with higher education had risen by 1.2 per cent. Moreover, the cutbacks in the administrative apparatus meant that a further fall in the proportion of youth among specialists and administrators could be predicted for at least the next ten to fifteen years (Plaksii 1989: 125). This meant that about 60 per cent of young specialists were unable to work in the area for which they had trained and that their standard of living was falling. In 1988 the average wage for young workers rose by 1.5–2 per cent while inflation rose by 3–4 per cent and this encouraged a flow of youth from the state to the co-operative sector of the economy in the hope of better earnings (127–8).

In many respects, then, youth formed part of the secondary labour market to which women also belonged. Like women, youth tended to follow not vertical but horizontal mobility patterns; by the time they were 20, half the young people employed had changed their profession at least once – not because they sought professional self-realization but because they hoped to find a job through which they had a better opportunity of obtaining a flat and of solving their social problems.[6] Youth constituted 65 per cent of the massive turnover of the labour force and often migrated to larger, and more prestigious cities, taking on the kind of work the local population spurned (Sheregi 1989: 130).

A third major problem faced by youth was unemployment. At this time unemployment could be defined in a number of different ways and was extremely difficult to calculate since no figures were comprehensively collected. Thus Tsybukh talked of at least 1.5 million unemployed young people while Mironenko suggested that there were six million young people in Central Asia who neither worked nor studied because there were no opportunities to do so (Tsybukh 1990; Mironenko 1989a; Mironenko 1990a). With regard to youth, it is perhaps easiest to use data on the number of young people having left school who had neither found employment nor entered further education. By 1989 this number had risen from just over 1 per cent of the total number of school leavers to 4 per cent (Krillov 1990). More than one-third of these people were occupied in personal, subsidiary farming, especially in Uzbekistan, Tadzhikistan, Russia and Kirgizia – revealing the regional nature of the problem of unemployment (*nezaniatnost'*). A particular cause for concern was the rise in the number of young people not studying beyond the age of 15 (class 8) since this seriously inhibited their chances of finding work. The number of such people had risen almost four times between 1985 and 1989, but in certain regions by considerably more (in Moldavia by almost twenty times, in Turkmenistan by nine times and in Azerbaidzhan by eight times) (ibid.).

There were also a number of worrying features of the new economic environment for youth. Self-financing meant that directors of enterprises and organizations preferred to take on qualified workers from other enterprises rather than train new workers themselves. Thus, whereas in 1985, 6.9 million workers were trained (including 2.7 million being trained for the first time), in 1988 the corresponding figures were 6.2 million and about 2 million (ibid.). Sociological research showed that enterprises which had switched to self-financing had reduced their spending on improving working conditions by 30 per cent and on training and retraining workers by 20 per cent (Tsybukh 1990). For young people this meant being forced to take jobs left vacant in production where conditions were difficult, wages were low, and there was little hope of gaining a good specialism.

The situation was not wholly negative, however, and the progress that had been made was reported. With regard to the problems of young people at schools and in higher education, for example, the Central Committee of the *Komsomol* eventually supported the activity of student groups in campaigning for a radical change in the teaching of social science, a perestroika in the activity of military training departments and against the use of young people's labour in seasonal agricultural work. Revisions were made which allowed students to defer their call-up to the army until after their period of study had ended and military training in higher education establishments and participation in agricultural work was made voluntary. Student collectives were also given the right to elect their own representatives to academic councils and together with the Ministry of Education and the Central Council of the Trade Unions, the *Komsomol* participated in the founding of an All-Union Student Forum which was to act as an important body for raising the problems of students and pupils (Mironenko 1990a).

The *Komsomol* emphasized its own role in encouraging the establishment of more than 17,000 youth, student and pupil co-operative businesses employing about one million young men and women, and in restricting the recruitment of youth to shock construction projects to a strictly voluntary nature (Mironenko 1990a). The new task of the day was the turning of youth not into good socialist citizens but into a new middle class which would ensure the stability of the country as it had done in the rest of Europe (Rakovskaia 1992: 9). Those still fulfilling the *sotsial'nii zakaz* (such as the Institute of Youth, formerly the Higher *Komsomol* School) suggested that young people were indeed ready to take up the baton of capitalism, being concerned with being allowed to raise their own standard of living through their own efforts. Such a conclusion however clearly flew in the face of the widespread reaction against existing inequality which had been seen to motivate those such as the Kazan' groups (see Chapter 4). Whilst the market might offer real opportunities for a minority of youth well-placed in the old system, others argued that market ideology among youth in fact meant only that teenagers would do anything to escape poverty. At best they might sell newspapers and wash cars, at worst steal – even murder – for money, jeans or trainers (Mochalina 1992).

## Housing

The problem of housing for young people had been on the official political agenda since the early part of perestroika (see Chapter 3), but two new issues emerged in the 1990–1 period.

The first was the hopelessness of the situation. Despite the fact that 35,000 young families had been accommodated in MZhKs (of which there were now 700), about 2.5 million young families were said to be waiting for state housing, with no expectation of receiving it in the near future (Mironenko 1990a). This meant that only one-tenth of young families in the country had their own place to live while two-thirds of young workers lived in hostels, or rented whatever accommodation they could find (Tsybukh 1990).

The second issue was the extremely poor, even inhuman, conditions of many of the hostels in which young people lived. These conditions – including the eviction of young women residents' husbands from the hostel in the middle of the night – led to a spontaneous protest by young workers of the Ufa aeroengine plant (Katoza and Skvortsov 1987). According to Abramov, 70 per cent of young people who changed their jobs or professions did so because of housing problems (Khaitina and Bychkova 1990).

The acuteness of the housing problem had been exacerbated by the failure to solve educational and employment problems. According to Kokliagina, the high levels of poor urban housing for young people had been caused by the introduction of compulsory secondary education without the necessary infrastructural provision. This meant that two-thirds of young people were forced to leave the parental home at the age of 15 in order to continue their education since the necessary institutions were all sited in large towns and cities (Kokliagina 1992: 127). Up to 40 per cent of the total number of pupils moved into hostel accommodation at the age of 15–16 in order to train for their chosen profession. Such young people, Kokliagina argued, remained 'marginals' since they lived 'temporary' lives in temporary accommodation (hostels) cut off from their traditional environment (130).

## Army

By the beginning of the 1990s, the image of the armed forces as a repressive institution which was more likely to turn one into a social or physical cripple than a 'real man' had led to evasion of conscription of a very serious level. Consequently, the state was forced to take seriously the manifold problems young people confronted in the army. The first problem was the period of service which, until recent reforms, was very long; two years for the army and three for the navy. Moreover, young people had no control over where they were posted and might, at the age of 17, be sent thousands of miles to areas either climatically harsh or culturally incomprehensible. Second, the conditions of service were bad; many conscripts were used in construction brigades to perform those labour tasks to which civilians could not be recruited and subjected to extremely poor housing and living conditions.

Third, there was the infamous problem of bullying (*dedovshchina*). In its crudest form this was the subjugation of conscripts in their first six months by those in the fourth and last stage of service. Its most common manifestations were the forcing of young soldiers to do the domestic chores of the older ones, the uneven distribution of food rations and the deprivation of young conscripts of their personal possessions (Deriugin 1990: 112). The origins of the phenomenon were rooted in social changes at the end of the 1950s and beginning of the 1960s – including the amnesty of prisoners following Stalin's death, the youngest of whom were then called up to serve in the army. The practice of shunting responsibility for cases of bullying down the chain of command, the weakening of the authority of the sergeant staff and the rising physical and intellectual maturity of conscripts and thus their growing frustration with the lack of opportunities for self-fulfilment in the army were also cited (109–11).

Nevertheless, the phenomenon of bullying, it was recognized, had been intensified due to ethnic factors. These included the rise in the proportion of conscripts from Central Asian and Transcaucasian regions of the

country from 28 per cent in 1980 to 37 per cent in 1988 and the reinforce-
ment of collectives of mixed nationality. This had led to the increased
emergence of micro-groups formed on the basis of nationality which
initiated bullying practices (114). By the end of the 1980s this ethnically-
based bullying may have superseded that based on length of service to the
extent that first-year non-Slavic soldiers from dominant ethnic groups
might exercise control over older soldiers from a rival ethnic minority
(Gross 1990: 482).

These factors, taken together with the tradition of draft evasion and
desertion established during the war in Afghanistan, meant that by the
early 1990s conscription rates were disastrously low; by the spring conscription of 1992 it was expected that of every 100 young men of conscription
age only twenty-eight would be successfully called up ('Spring conscription
threatened by lack of recruits' 1992).

## Juvenile crime

The most direct link between marginal status and antisocial behaviour was
made in the discussion of the rising juvenile crime rate. Although all
absolute figures for crime were rising in the perestroika period, juvenile
crime was one of the areas where the crime rate was also increasing;
between 1983 and 1989 there was a rise in number of crimes per 1,000
population by 73 per cent (Galinskii 1991: 271). The number of registered
crimes committed by juveniles or with their complicity in 1989 was thus
almost a quarter of a million (223,940) (Karpets 1990).

The primary reason cited for this was the growth in social inequality,
which heightened the contradiction between needs and unequal (legal)
opportunities to satisfy those needs. Growing wage differentials were likely
to negatively affect young people who were a marginal economic group to
begin with and this, it was argued, would be likely to increase the juvenile
crime rate in the future (Arshavskii and Vilks 1990: 59). Attempts to curb
migration into cities also lowered the social status of incomers and encouraged antisocial acts (ibid.).

More specifically, however, the likelihood of young people ending up in
criminal activities was seen by sociologists and criminologists to be
influenced by: family; work position; influence of criminal subculture; and
use of drugs or alcohol. An expert survey of criminologists and those
working with juvenile criminals showed the most often cited factor fostering juvenile crime was belonging to a 'disadvantaged family' (61).
According to Trubin, 40 per cent of teenagers found guilty of crimes came
from incomplete families and many families concerned themselves only
with material care of their children and passed on responsibility for the
behaviour of children to educational and law-keeping institutions. In the
last three years 40,000 parents had been deprived of their parental rights,
many because of chronic alcoholism or drug addiction (Trubin 1990: 2).

Young people who were neither working nor studying were also seen to be at high risk; whilst constituting only 1 per cent of 14–17 year olds, they committed 5–6 per cent of juvenile crime (Arshavskii and Vilks 1990). This was particularly worrying given economic trends which disadvantaged young people in the labour market – the proportion of juvenile offenders not employed in study and work doubled between 1989 and 1990 and without adequate retraining and social protection for unemployed youth this situation could only deteriorate ('O zaniatosti molodezhi, okonchiv-shei sredniuiu shkolu' 1990; Arshavskii and Vilks 1990: 64).

Third, the link between alcohol use and crime was well established in Soviet thinking and, although it was predicted that there would be some reduction in drink-related crime, this was expected to be more than offset by the rise in the level of use of drugs and toxic substances by teenagers (Arshavskii and Vilks 1990: 62). According to Mironenko, 80,000 of a total of 130,000 known drug addicts were young people (Mironenko 1989a).

Finally, there was seen to be a strong influence of antisocial elements and organized criminal groups on juveniles, including informal groups of an antisocial nature, especially territorial groups often originally estab-lished to defend themselves against already-existing gangs (ibid.). Such territorially-based groups were, it was argued, simply a specifically teenage variant of a general social trend which had taken place over the last two decades; the process of the sacrificing of the social interest to the corpora-tive interest in search of self-preservation. The inability to find self-expression at school or in the family meant that young people were attracted to informal groups, despite the fact that even there individual development was limited since the group joined was generally decided by the group, on the basis of territory, rather than by the individual teenager, on the basis of common interests ('Molodezh' v sovremennom mire' 1990: 31–3).

In contrast to the subcultural elites of the major cities, then, provincial youth cultural practices were considered to be not a chosen cultural stance which was evidence of cultural pluralism and movement but a low moral state enforced by cultural marginality. The 'critical moral state' of youth signified, according to Iurii Davydov, 'the first step towards a national disaster and tragedy' (27). This tragedy was the complete collapse of the old social order with no new vision to replace it and thus signifying not a temporary halt on the road to the bright future but a historical regression.

## CONCLUSION

Throughout perestroika, youth had been a prime object of political strug-gle, for, as Fadeev put it:

Like any political project, perestroika is seeking a space for itself in the future, and the future, according to the iron logic of the change of generations, belongs to the young.

(Fadeev 1990: 64)

At the Twenty-first Congress of the VLKSM in April 1990, however, Mironenko declared that it was no longer good enough to say that 'the future belongs to youth', youth needed a present as well (Mironenko 1990b). The abolition of the monopolistic political role of the CPSU earlier that year had already signalled the advent of the post-perestroika era and Mironenko's statement effectively marked the end of the 'constructors-of-communism' paradigm which had for so long shaped the course of the youth debate in the Soviet Union. It did so because it reversed the roles of youth and the state. Youth could no longer be relied on to sacrifice its own present for the future of the state, it was rather the state which was obliged to ensure at least the basic living standards for its young people. In this new order of things it was envisaged that the *Komsomol* should act as a pressure on the state to ensure the fulfilment of these obligations.

Like the CPSU, however, the *Komsomol* had waited too long. By the time of the Twenty-first Congress, it was already simply reacting to events, justifying loss of membership and authority by empty commitments to de-monopolization and voluntary membership (Bunakov 1990). Moreover, while youth might indeed need a present as well as a future, the state was in no position to offer it one. In much of the academic work published in the post-perestroika period, youth became viewed as a 'lost generation' whose social experience had left it marginalized and abandoned on the periphery of society. It was seen as unsocialized into society and unsocializable. In a particularly revealing statement of the collapse of the old paradigm, Meshcherkin and Meshcherkina declared that:

In our restructuring society it is inconceivably difficult to ensure youth a painless 'inclusion' (*vpisyvanie*) into the system (which system?) and the inculcation and transmission of values (which values?) from generation to generation, which is what socialization actually means.

(Meshcherkin and Meshcherkina 1992: 131)

That upon which the 'constructors-of-communism' paradigm depended, therefore, had gone; not communism, nor even construction, but the *continuity* of generations. The result was a vision of youth with neither future nor present.

# Part III

# Deconstructing the constructed: a case study of Moscow youth culture

# Introduction

The deconstruction of the glasnost media undertaken in Part II facilitated the location of the discourses, and their institutional bases, which structured the youth culture debate in Russia during the perestroika years. This says much about the ways in which youth cultural activity is perceived by the adult world, but little about the youth cultural world itself. In the last part of this book, attention must be turned to the 'ways of life' of those young people who appear in the pages of the glasnost press and the restructured academic texts. However, just as glasnost could not confront the lies of the past through 'revealing' Soviet society in its true colours, but only create a new agenda of its own, neither can any claims be made here to present the real story. The ways of life described are not discrete cultural phenomena awaiting their discovery by the intrepid sociologist delving beneath the respectable face of society. They are cultural formations which are created by young people and which act to make sense of the meanings encountered in their daily lives (of school, work, home) and to generate new meanings which sometimes resist, sometimes confirm and sometimes simply sideline these.

The fact that there is no reality with which to counter the constructed fictions of the media, however, does not mean that the researcher must be content with revealing the structures of the text. As was suggested in Chapter 1, the challenges presented by both gender/race-aware critiques of existing theorizations of youth culture and materialist interventions in the post-modernist debate now suggest a need to return to the field. Given the poverty of ethnographic studies of youth culture in the former Soviet Union, it is even more essential to look again at what young people are doing. Indeed, the experience of Russian youth may further illuminate some of the areas which remain underexplored in the Anglo-American tradition of youth cultural studies. In particular, resistance theories of youth culture might be informed by the experience of a non-capitalist society in which the different scope and aims of state institutions highlight the importance of the grey areas between conformity and resistance. The argument developed in this part of the book offers a very different reading from those of other Western analyses of Soviet youth culture which have suggested that the Soviet context has lent non-formal groupings a heightened political meaning, i.e. has made them more clearly resistant than contemporary Western youth cultural groups. On the contrary, it is suggested here, the Russian experience reveals the slippages between *sub*cultural and mainstream cultural activity, and it is precisely because of this that the non-authentic terminology of 'formal' and 'non-formal' activity remains useful. These categories posit a horizontal and interlocking relationship between cultural worlds which may be more analytically productive than more familiar Western ones which suggest a vertical (subcultural) or horizontal, but parallel (counter-cultural) relationship.

In the following chapters the field-work project undertaken in Moscow is set out, with all its acknowledged limitations. Chapter 6 explains the theoretical and methodological framework within which the study was conducted, the problems encountered and the extent to which they were or were not overcome. In Chapter 7 a descriptive representation of the cultural world of the young people who participated in the research is presented. The contours of this world are drawn from the interviews and observations carried out during the field work and the chapter's aim is to introduce the reader to the main players in this world. In Chapter 8, a tentative attempt to understand their world is made. This means that whereas Chapter 7 more or less directly reflects the youth cultural world as it was told to the author, Chapter 8 subjects this construction to a *reading* process aimed at exploring the codes which structure it. This final part of the book therefore makes no claims to paint the 'real' picture of youth cultural activity obscured by the media debates of the perestroika years discussed in Part II. It offers simply an alternative starting point for further study by attempting to understand contemporary Moscow youth culture using urban ethnographic methods and contemporary socio-cultural theories.

# 6 Studying Russia:

## From masochism to methodology

Writing an ethnography is not simply the transformation of field notes into publishable text; it is the process of turning a dialogue between researcher and researched into a narrative. In order for the finished narrative to be understood, the process of its construction must be explored and the terms on which the dialogue took place exposed. It is such an exploration and exposition which this chapter attempts and, since the need for them is rooted in the recognition of the importance of bringing the subject into the ethnographic process, it is a chapter which must be written in the first person.

It did not require an armoury of post-structuralist-influenced ethnographic method to challenge my role as participant observer; this was done by the 'objects' of the observation themselves. Reversing the roles of interviewer and interviewed (and thereby the subject and object of the research), young people participating in the work often demanded that I declare my intention, most frequently by asking what had made me decide to study the Soviet Union. The question was an important one since it revealed a key definer of the context of the research dialogue, i.e. the inferiority complex *vis à vis* the West, which is virtually a reflex reaction amongst young Russians. This is more than a product of consumer envy fuelled by the opening up of communication channels to the West and the consequent exposure to Western lifestyles. That there is a one-directional exchange between Russia and the West is historically and culturally rooted. It is embodied in ideas of Russia as the dark (feudal/autocratic) past of Europe or, still worse, of its potentially darker, *Soviet*, Orwellian future. It is transmitted via images of Russians looking to and learning from the West: Peter the Great tours the shipyards of Europe; Catherine introduces the French language as the acceptable face of Russian culture; Lenin defies the scientific 'laws of history' in order to make Russia jump an historical epoch; Stalin declares war on his own people in order to 'catch up with the West'. Given this context, my desire to *learn* from my interaction with those taking part in the field work appeared either incomprehensible or suspicious. This was articulated by some of the research participants via a normalization or generalization of their activities in defensive statements about themselves such as: 'we are just like young people anywhere'; 'you can find people like us in any European city'.

But Russia is not only the most Eastern edge of the West, but also the most Western edge of the East, and Russians do not only bow to the material success of the West, but celebrate their own spirituality which has not, yet, been devoured by the economic gods. Thus my, at first sight, irrational act of purposeful self-subjection to Soviet reality was also explained by those involved in the project by reference not to my rational or intellectual interest but to an emotional level of involvement. A common second question I was asked, therefore, was whether or not I had Russian blood in my family, since this would give me an organic connection to the country and thus a remnant of that spirituality which could conquer my Western rationality. Those who were deeply involved in the project, however, and who came to know me better, tended to view my desire to study Russia as a kind of rational, compensatory response to an irrational desire. I was seen as responding to a perceived missing element in my own society; periodic immersion in Russian culture was seen as my 'spiritual fix'.

## THE POLITICS OF METHOD

Whatever the source of my madness, it had to have a method – and the question of method was not only a practical but a theoretical and ethical problem whose resolution would crucially determine the conclusions drawn from the research. The problem I faced was twofold: a poverty of methodology in the field of Soviet Studies; and the apparent remoteness of ethnographic methodologies from Soviet social reality.

The first of these problems has been determined to some extent by the nature of the society under study. If the intellectual process thrives on the open exchange of views based on assimilated knowledge, then it is not hard to understand why Soviet Studies has been a difficult area to work in. Access to information, like many things in Soviet society, is not gained without a struggle, and the ideological coating covering much of the work done by Soviet academics has often obscured its value and inhibited debate of the real issues. In addition, the resistance to any research which might reveal that Soviet society was deviating from the path the 'laws of history' had laid down for it, made it very difficult to conduct meaningful research in the Soviet Union itself.

In other respects, however, Sovietologists have isolated themselves from mainstream social science debates over concepts and methods by declaring the experience of Soviet society unique and outside the realm of comparative social science (Fleron and Hoffmann 1991). The result of this has been that Western studies of Soviet society have depended largely upon studies of state-generated statistics, readings of the press and formal interviews with well-known cultural figures and academics. This has rendered social and cultural understanding heavily dependent upon the researcher's ability to 'correctly' read the subtext (*podtekst*) of these texts, which fits uneasily with the 'depthlessness' and plural reading positions of current textual analysis.

The newly exposed polyphony of Soviet politics and society has demanded new approaches and new goals from those wishing to understand them. It can no longer suffice to determine the official line, based on a complex interpretation of what is said and what is meant, facilitated by a detailed knowledge of the balance of power behind the walls of the Kremlin and its regional fiefdoms. But the problem of adapting to the new social reality has been compounded by the lack of a distinct set of tools with which to understand Soviet society. This, I think, is the result of the fact that the interdisciplinary nature of the Soviet Studies project remained at a surface level. There is, of course, evidence of the crossing of disciplinary boundaries. The fusion of polity and economy in the command-administrative system, for example, has demanded a political approach to looking at the Soviet economy and the absence of data on Soviet society has often led researchers to look for social 'types' and social problems in literature and film – necessitating a cultural sociology. Nevertheless, it seems to me that such approaches were felt to be necessitated by 'the system' being studied and were often considered to constitute an unfortunate, inhibiting factor to the exercising of one's 'real' discipline. Hence, the obstacles academics had to negotiate as a result of Soviet reality were overcome via deviations and compromises facilitated by a *multi*disciplinary approach and academic credibility remained rooted in core disciplines.

If Soviet studies offered no off-the-peg methodologies, then this was equally true of other academic fields to which I turned. I had termed my trip to Moscow 'field work' but the methodologies from social anthropology and geography associated with this implied a process of discovering new territories and describing them to an audience remote from the researcher's experience. These methodologies may have satisfied my need for retaining cultural integrity but they could not be adopted wholesale. Although Muscovites are fond of referring to their city as nothing more than a large village, social anthropological methods – designed to capture the way of life and meaning systems of non-urban societies – were simply inappropriate. Rather than attempting to translate a whole meaning-system or culture to an outside audience, my aim was to understand a small part of a society which – thanks to glasnost – people on the outside knew increasingly more about. Furthermore, although accepting that I would always remain a cultural outsider, I was aware that there was a significant amount of shared cultural knowledge between myself and the young people with whom I was intending to work, and I was keen to build on this rather than romanticize the impenetrability of 'Russianness'.

The process of choosing methods to adopt in my research was not simply a pragmatic one – of deciding which tools were best suited to the job – but an issue closely bound up with my research aims. I was not concerned, as many of the quantitative, *Komsomol*-funded surveys had been, with predicting the level of growth of various subcultural groups or of quantifying criminal behaviour or drug and alcohol use/abuse among them. I was also less concerned with making claims about the whole of Soviet, Russian or even Moscow youth than with explaining what young people were doing and how the different elements of what they did fitted into a whole which was meaningful to them. This could clearly only be achieved for a small group and any similar exercise would be highly unlikely to come to the same conclusions. This meant rejecting quantitative research methods and abandoning any claims to the representativeness of the subjects of my research and the generalisability of their behaviour.

There were advantages of adopting a qualitative research methodology, however. I would not be restricted by any original hypothesis which had been generated by a reading process very distant from the social reality of the world I wanted to understand. Qualitative methods would also allow me to adapt the research project as I learned more about the culture, and thus maximize comprehension and explanation. This flexibility was important, since although I had generated some hypotheses about the group on the basis of my interaction with them in the 1988–9 period in Moscow, by my return visit in 1991 the composition of the group and the youth cultural sphere in which they were moving had changed significantly. I needed to be prepared to abandon any of the hypotheses which were no longer relevant and this would have been impossible if they had already been incorporated into printed questionnaires designed to test them out.

The second advantage was the possibility of cross-checking the information being given by informants and interviewees by observing their interactions with other people both inside and outside the group. The greater opportunity to verify data seemed a significant improvement on survey methods – which are forced to take agents' self-descriptions at a given moment in time as truth – since during the course of the research there were significant changes in attitude and behaviour among those with whom I was working. The third advantage of this kind of research was that it made the researcher visible in the research process. This is often a factor used to criticize participant observation since, it is argued, the researcher's presence will affect the interaction within the group and reflect the researcher's greater natural empathy towards some members of the research situation than others. Survey work, however, does not eliminate distortion but simply conceals the strong role of the researcher who has pre-defined not only *who* speaks (the sample), but also *about what* (the questions asked), in what *context* (the formal interview) and *how* (giving pre-defined choices or fitting answers to open-ended questions into a classificatory system). In contrast the presence of the researcher in the research context allows the subject greater freedom to define what is meaningful to the research since it permits the interesting issues raised in conversation to be pursued and irrelevant questions to be dropped. In addition, since the researcher is known to the interviewees, her/his presence is likely to be less inhibitive than an unknown researcher and she/he will be more able to control for this (through feedback), as well as for the influence of different contexts on the behaviour of those interviewed.

My prime concern in adopting the most appropriate research methods for my study, however, was that the people who participated in it were not turned into objects of an abstracted research design whose opinion, behaviour or attitudes were reduced to those of a generalized individual no longer resembling any of the subjects actually participating in the research. Retaining the historical and cultural context of the research subjects and thus allowing them their own subjectivity has an obvious ethical value, but it also has a methodological one. Giving the subjects of research an active role in the research process allows them to take the initiative and guide the researcher around their lives. Especially in the first stages of research this non-interventionist position is important; it allows the building of trust (you are not just another adult defining what is and is not important), and it allows the natural emergence of themes for further exploration. Taking up such a learning position did not mean that, as a Western academic, I did not have certain aims and behavioural patterns that I was forcing upon my subjects (such as insisting on fairly precise times for meetings, orientating my days around work not pleasure, and refusing experience-enhancing substances which others were taking), but it did mean that conversations and interviews were based on what the people to whom I was talking indicated was meaningful, rather than the answers to questions I posed about issues that I felt were important and indicative.

The price that had to be paid for this approach – the loss of all claims to generalization and thus prediction – did not worry me unduly, since my prime objective was explanation rather than prediction. By this I mean that I was not concerned with establishing correlative causal relations but with making maximum use of the explanatory power of qualitative social science by exploring the concepts people have of their action and learning the linguistic and conceptual rules of their cultural context.

## The problem of language and meaning

Language and meaning become central to the research process as soon as one accepts that actions cannot be understood independently of their context, indeed that this context is constitutive of their meanings. A child spitting at another in a school playground, for example, may be rightly interpreted as a sign of contempt, but punks 'gobbing' onto the stage at a gig must be read as ultimate appreciation. Words as well as actions have social contexts and their meaning is dependent on the circumstances surrounding them. This does not necessitate the acceptance of a crude Saussurean view of language as an arbitrary bundle of signifiers and signifieds. On the contrary, the recognition that 'the utterance is a social phenomenon' (Voloshinov 1973: 82) heightens the importance of exploring language and meaning as an area of creative activity. Since the meaning of a phrase is characterized by the use made of it (Wittgenstein 1969: 65), understanding becomes the knowledge of how an expression is used, and how to apply it. The importance of this in my research was that it opened up possibilities for viewing similar artefacts as signifying differently in their own social context rather than representing a surface imitation of Western subcultural styles.

The danger of taking this position too far, however, is that meaningful action becomes identified with rule-governed behaviour and one is led to the same conclusion as Winch, that to understand what someone is doing is to grasp the rule or convention which is being followed (Thompson, J. 1981: 121–3). This would severely constrain the scope of cross-cultural research since it reduces the role of researchers to the determination of the concepts and rules used by actors and leads us down the path to relativism. In fact, of course, it is possible that social relations other than those acknowledged and articulated by the actors exist and explain those actions, often acting as structural constraints on actors. Such institutions and relations include relations of domination and subordination, exploitation, ideology and legitimation, production and distribution. External critique remains a vital tool in allowing researchers to identify such relations and the constraints they place on actors.

How do we retain the importance of language and the concepts used by actors and yet not deny the role of structural aspects of societies in explaining and understanding human action? What is required is an under-standing not only of the utterance as a social phenomenon but also of semiotic exchange as a site of struggle. As we saw in Chapter 1, this has been a key source of debate in contemporary studies of popular culture in general, and in youth cultural studies in particular. In order, therefore, to return to the field at a point beyond seeing Russian youth as just a dry sponge ready to soak up the pulp culture of capitalism (Tempest 1984), or as the new subcultural 'resisters' (Riordan 1988), we must recognize and develop the problematic divide between 'representational and lived social texts' (Roman and Christian-Smith 1988: 8). In other words, we must recognize the interplay between representational texts (see Part II of this book) and lived relations (see Part III) as not just a 'grey area' but as a site of struggle.

This has crucial methodological implications, since it implies that we cannot rely on discourse analysis alone, which, although capable of teasing out relations of power within text, is less able to do so in lived social relations. But nor can we adopt a largely descriptive approach through prioritizing uncommented upon excerpts from interviews. Whereas the former sets us out on the 'road to nowhere', the latter constitutes little more than a 'spurious authenticity' in which the social (and power) relations involved in the creation of the text are ignored (McRobbie 1991: 69). The way out of this methodological impasse is via the recognition of the researcher's role of representing, and of the power involved in this. The researcher becomes narrator of a new text – relating what is voiced to her/him by her/his subjects – but also the interpreter of that text, making visible 'a whole ensemble of meanings and signifying practices that have their own structural and linguistic logic' (Roman 1988: 151), and thus retaining the explanatory power of the research process. The most fundamental implication of such a method is that the positioning of the researcher/narrator within the text under construction is a matter of great importance. It is my own positioning in the research project which I will address in the rest of this chapter.

## RESEARCHING THE RESEARCHER

The history of subcultural studies leads a reading audience to expect from the methods section a long description of the researcher's problems of acceptance by the group. One of the most difficult aspects in relating the experience of my work in Moscow to a Western audience, in contrast, has proved to be explaining not the difficulties of working in the field, but the relative ease with which the relationships developed. This was directly related to a conscious mutual choosing of researcher and subject. From early in the 1988–9 period I was aware that I was learning much more from being with one particular group than from any of the others I had spent time with. In the period out of the field until returning in 1991, I attributed this to my positioning as a female researcher. To put it crudely, I assumed that the large number of girls[1] in the group had facilitated my access and made my presence more natural.

After my second field-work period, however, the gendered nature of the research situation seemed to me to have been a very important, but nonetheless, only one factor defining my relationship with the group. Because being a woman had been a problem for me in past situations with groups, I attributed my sense of well-being with this group to the sense of security I felt among its members. The fact that gender position was the dominant relation structuring our interaction for me, however, clearly does not mean that it was for those I was interacting with. Subsequently, I rethought many of my original assumptions about the power dimensions of the research process and came to see a number of factors as determining the peculiar relationship which developed.

The first is related to the circumstances of our first meeting. While studying in Moscow in 1988–9 I had met a group of young people who called themselves '*stiliagi*' (see Chapter 7 for an outline of the group's style and activities). Since the capacity in which I met them was that of an interpreter for a Western television company, the group saw me as its mouthpiece. Rather than having to fight the image of an intruding

Westerner, I was immediately inserted into the traditional Soviet binary of 'one of us/one of them' ('*nash/ne nash*') on *their* side. This position was further enhanced by the knowledge that, once the bright lights and cameras had gone, I, like they, would remain in Moscow. The readiness to accept my presence was also, to some extent, rooted in curiosity. Whereas it was clear what both the Soviet and the Western media wanted from them, it was not immediately apparent what my interest in them was. As the research developed, members of the group became genuinely intrigued by this new form of representation which was less spectacular than the journalistic forms to which they were accustomed but also less momentary and less beyond their control.

The second, and main, reason for the minimization of problems of acceptance, however, lies in the support and help of specific members of the group at different stages of the research project. In 1989 this was a young woman who had been involved in the group since 1987 and with whom I could go along to group events and simply sit, watch and chat. Such occasions often brought very different insights to the more carefully structured interviews. The importance of being accepted at this level should not be underestimated. Where this had been absent (in groups where my main interlocutor had been male in a male-defined environment), my presence had inhibited normal conversation and my unresolved status in the group remained a cause of unease.

By the time I returned to Moscow in 1991, most of the people I had met in 1989 had left the group. Nevertheless, my contacts with the next generation (who in 1989 had been relatively new members) allowed me to be accepted as somebody with a serious commitment to the group. In fact, since I could remember incidents and figures in the group's history which many of the younger members I was interviewing had only heard second-hand, I was afforded some status within the group by the younger members. This helped limit the intrusive nature of my presence.

**Redefining the research project**

The youth cultural scene in Moscow in spring 1991 was very different from that in 1988–9. The gathering pace of political and economic crisis had sidelined such things as youth culture, which looked increasingly like an outdated leftover from the heady days of the glasnost era. The music scene was in crisis – caught between living off the heroism of its past in the 'underground' and learning to compete with the realities of commercial success. The vibrancy of the early scene had been turned into a nostalgia for the good old days when the *neformaly* were shouted at in the streets, or beaten up after concerts – at least they knew what they stood for then! By spring 1991, the *stiliagi* – who at their peak in the mid-1980s had numbered 200–300 – had been reduced to scattered groups of younger members and a wide network of ex-*stiliagi*.

The possibilities of conducting participant observation in the purist sense, were thus curtailed. On the other hand, the opportunity to follow through the perestroika cycle from beginning to end via the life cycle of one group had presented itself; I now had contact with three generations of *stiliagi* who were willing to talk about their experiences. The fact that most had now moved on to other groups and other lives also allowed me to gain an insight into a much broader youth cultural sphere than I had originally anticipated, and created the opportunity to form an impression both of how the group worked at a particular point in time and how it had changed over time.

The second redefinition of my research emerged in discussion with the three *stiliagi* girls with whom I began my work in spring 1991. Having at first accepted my definition of the project – a cultural history of the *stiliagi* – they soon began to suggest that it might also be interesting for me to meet some of their current group of friends, many of whom had never been *stiliagi*. My initial reluctance to take up their idea emanated from a concern that by diversifying my research I would compromise my prioritization of validity over reliability. I feared that a broader approach might lead to a temptation to generalize and make claims to representativeness, or at least for my work to be read in this way. As the work with the *stiliagi* progressed, however, I found that although I was gaining a clearer idea about what they were, this made little sense without a better picture about what they *were not*. This led me to take up the girls' offers of introducing me to non-*stiliagi* who were part of their current group of friends and allowed me to develop a much clearer idea of how their strategy and style fitted into the wider Moscow subcultural scene (see Chapters 7 and 8).

**Recording the research**

Acceptance by, and mutual trust within, the group was the key to gathering the material which would allow me to gain an understanding of its cultural activity. As a researcher, though, I had an equal commitment to translating that understanding into something meaningful to those outside. This necessitated a carefully thought-out strategy for recording and analysing what I had learned in the field. For the reasons outlined above, I wanted to do this in a way which: allowed maximum control over the research process by its subjects; applied a relational rather than a referential theory of meaning; and displayed a high degree of validity rather than reliability. These criteria drew me towards ethnographic interviewing backed up by non-textual field-work methods.

In all thirty-six young people participated in the research. Twenty-four of them took part in more or less formally structured interviews (nine gave multiple interviews). The other twelve talked to me at length about their lives and activities, although the conversations were not recorded. In addition to these active participants I was able to observe and listen to numerous other young people whom I have not included in my list of 'informants' since they were not consciously approached to participate in the research and thus were denied the possibility of consenting or declining. No attempt was made to sample those who took part for the reasons set out above. Nevertheless, some questions about age, occupation, education, place of residence were built into the interview process (see Appendix).

In the initial stages, interviews were largely unstructured. Informants were asked broad descriptive questions aimed at eliciting: how they viewed their own life-history; how they had become involved in the group; and how they spent their time. Where interviewees clearly found these questions too abstract, a narrower focus would be suggested such as: 'What did you do yesterday?', or 'When did you first come across the *stiliagi*/punks . . . ?'. This narrower focus also had the advantage of ensuring that interviewees used their own categories to describe their activity, since a more abstracted level of description tended to induce less authentic or cliched categorizations of experience. Where these continued to be used, more pointed questioning was employed to elicit authentic categories such as: 'Is that what you normally call . . . ?' or 'How would you refer to . . . ?' (Spradley 1979: 89). On the basis of these interviews, more structured questions were built into the next series of interviews. These more structured interviews aimed at verifying the information from the previous interviews and exploring and establishing boundaries of categories emerging from previous interviews.

Alongside the interviewing process, field notes were kept on all meetings with informants whether or not interviews had been conducted. Such meetings included, trips to concerts, meetings at one of the group's home, walks around the city and visits to cafes. It was often during these chats that some of the important contradictions and ambiguities of the group's activity emerged. For example, virtually all the members of the *stiliagi* interviewed noted that the *stiliagi* was a 'friendly' (*druzhnaia*) group and that members were 'brothers and sisters'. Bumping into an old member, not seen for a long while, at a concert, however, might spark off a conversation about what they really thought of her/him, or some, previously unrecounted and less savoury incident from the group's history. The notes from these meetings, which included not only reports of conversations, but observations of group interaction, attitudes to outsiders, style and behaviour, were written up immediately and accorded equal weight to the more structured texts which emerged from the transcripts of tapes.

Since the group had a highly informal structure, the kind of indirect observations often important to participant observation work (such as rule-books, records of meetings, diaries) were not readily available. One of the members of the group did have a diary containing the names (usually nicknames) and phone numbers of the group's members at its height, and this was a useful aid in sparking crucial insights from memory. I was also allowed access to a large number of letters from male members of the group which had been written during military service. These proved an invaluable source for tapping the feelings of a number of the group with whom I would otherwise have had no contact.

## TEXTUAL ANALYSIS: THE POWER OF INTERPRETATION

It was in the analysis of the texts produced from interviews that the question of the power of the researcher re-emerged. The first question raised was one of method, and the first decision made was that the tape recordings of interviews should be transcribed in full before analysis. This was done despite Hollway's warning that an obsession with transcribing interviews word for word can lead to a form of content analysis which is essentially based on a quantitative rather than qualitative analysis of what people say (Hollway 1989: 20). Whilst accepting her general point, in this instance it was important to have full transcripts in the original Russian in order that analysis could be conducted in the categories employed by the subjects themselves rather than in my own categories derived from Western sociological literature.

The primary method of analysis adopted was Spradley's 'taxonomic analysis' (Spradley 1979). This involved the use of interview texts to define key folk-terms (or 'cover-terms') in the cultural world of the informant. Such cover-terms are the first structural element of a category of cultural knowledge (or 'domain') and, once identified, can be analysed further via the exploration of semantic relationships within the domain (100). The internal structure of the domains are determined via a 'taxonomic analysis' which reveal the meaning of symbols by showing their relationships to other symbols in a domain (155). These relations can be tested by asking inclusion and exclusion questions in order to verify what lies inside and outside a specific domain (157). In order to gain an idea of how these domains fit together, 'cultural themes' are defined. These themes may be more or less explicit and may have to be inferred by the researcher. They can be detected by exploring data not included in the taxonomic analyses, by examining common themes across domains and by using outside knowledge to look for universal cultural themes (186).

The results of this type of analysis will be dealt with in Chapter 8, where I refer to it as a 'synchronic analysis'. Spradley's methods, however, could not satisfy two other needs that were identified in the process of the dissection and reconstruction of the interview transcripts. The first of these was the need for a sense of how the boundaries of established cultural domains differed over time and, very importantly, how the narrative of the group changed in its retelling by different generations of members. The loss of historical context is a drawback of any form of structural analysis and this compelled me to include a second level of analysis, which I will refer to as a 'diachronic analysis'. A third aspect of group life which had emerged from the early interviews, and which had subsequently been incorporated into more structured questioning, concerned the different versions of the *stiliagi* narrative by male and female members and the role the group had played for them respectively. This gendered perspective was very important to the research project as a whole since it not only acknowledged the presence and experience of women in youth culture but also provided a clear example of how both representations and lived cultural practices need to be subjected to serious analysis in order to tease out the structural relations which underlie both.

I had declared my explicit interest in the first two perspectives (structural and historical) to the interviewees at an early stage of the research. Fearing resistance to any overt line of questioning on gender differences, however, I did not reveal my interest in the final aspect until near the end of our work together. I now regret this, since the broaching of the subject with three of the *stiliagi* girls met with an eager response to confirm – as well as qualify – its importance as a component of their activity and practice. Although, at the time, I interpreted my reluctance to declare a gendered perspective as a cultural compromise, recognizing that the backlash to feminism is even stronger in contemporary Russia than it is in the West; in fact, I now concede that it was probably more to do with an internalized guilt that doing feminist research is, on the one hand, a political rather than an academic exercise and, on the other, that it is somehow 'an easy option'. Angela McRobbie sums up the difficult questions here very succinctly: it is important to fight off the feeling that gendered research is a bias that must be eradicated but, at the same time, feminist researchers must acknowledge their own motives and power. Since women are generally, co-operative, good at talking and willing to give up their time for you, McRobbie argues, women researchers may well be in danger of becoming parasites of women's powerlessness (McRobbie 1991: 70). These are important, perhaps the most important questions for a feminist researcher and should have been built into both my research project and process at a much earlier stage.

But is the relationship between researcher and subjects inherently an exploitative one? This brings us back to the issue of the positioning of the researcher, her/his power and how she/he can control its abuse. Although all interviewees were informed of my purpose in interviewing them, I retained the power to deduce meanings from their words which they would neither infer themselves nor necessarily wish to be broadcast to a wider audience. All I could do was employ the mechanisms I was aware of to minimize this abuse of power. To this end, contact with new members and ex-members of the groups was arranged via members of the group already involved in the project in order that those approached felt no pressure to participate. Before, and after, the interview I explained what my interest was and what the material would be used for. The second means of preventing a sidelining of the issues of power in the research process, is to confront the issue throughout that process by employing an active feedback mechanism. By this I mean encouraging the participants to discuss: how it feels to talk about their own lives; their concerns over how I would use the material collected; what they thought I was interested in and how valid this interest was; and what, if anything, they felt they were gaining from being involved in the research.

The part of the research I felt to be potentially most exploitative concerned visual representations of the groups – i.e. taking photographs of them. This was because of the explicit level of objectification involved and the danger of reducing their activity to their style. In fact, however, the groups particularly welcomed photographs being taken of them. They had been highly critical of journalists in the past who had taken photographs and then not fulfilled their promises to send them the results. In the research project, where they had more control, the photographs came to represent something tangible that they could retain from the experience of being involved in the research and something that they valued. I always waited for an invitation to take photographs and so the contexts and the poses struck were very much the constructions of the people involved.

The second area of potential exploitation was my power to interpret the actions of members of the groups in a way which they themselves would not find acceptable. I had been prepared – despite the dangers of too much conscious reflection feeding back into the research process – to discuss with them how I was interpreting their activities. Not surprisingly, there was relatively little interest in this, except for occasional questions about my opinion on the way Soviet journalists had written about the *neformaly*. Despite the numerous criticisms of Soviet journalists they themselves voiced in such discussions, there seemed to be an inherent belief that I was 'different'. Since I had been directly exposed to their versions of what they do, they appeared certain that it would be their voices and not mine which emerged from my research.

One area of concern for the *stiliagi* was that my interest in them did not seem to be rooted in a love of rock 'n' roll music and style – since this was how they defined themselves. After the initial surprise, however, it was simply accepted that I had different musical tastes and there were even suggestions that this apparent lack of concern on my part with the music they listened to and the way they dressed, meant that I was taking them more seriously as individuals – what they thought and did, where they worked and what they were like.

The feedback I gained on what participation in the research meant to them showed quite a marked gender difference (the reasons for this will be explored in Chapter 8). The girls generally welcomed the opportunity to reminisce about what they considered to have been the best times of their life and they repeatedly confirmed their desire to participate, which, they insisted, was rooted in their own interest in the project rather than as a favour to me. This acknowledgement of a self-growth coming from the research process helped me reconcile myself with McRobbie's warning. The interest in them individually, and in the *stiliagi* as a whole, armed the girls with a means of promoting the group (and thus their past) in a positive light to their new friends who were often scornful of it (see Chapter 8). Since the girls' trust and interest in the project enabled me to tackle the more difficult interviews and situations, and encouraged me to continue at points when the task of understanding seemed a hopeless one, the relationship (*to me*) felt less like an exploitation of power than of mutual empowerment. In contrast the lads tended to be less convinced of the value of the research. They were much more likely to suggest that I did not really understand the scene, that I was taking far too seriously what were essentially childish games and that I was not interviewing 'properly' because I was listening to stories rather than asking specific questions. The problem of intimidating one's research subjects was not realized to the extent anticipated. The average age of those participating was 19–20 and they tended to see me as their contemporary, and never more than a couple of years their senior. Nevertheless, my position remained full of ambiguities and my definition of it as 'mutual empowerment' is both a very partial, and a highly optimistic one.

The main locus of ambiguity was my status as a foreigner. On the positive side, being a foreigner overrode all other immediate identity indicators and spared me the resistance on class, race or regional bases that I would have encountered had I been researching in a British cultural context. The fact that I was a foreigner also meant that I was not directly associated with any authority system they might be intimidated by or be resisting.[2]

The other chief advantage of being a foreigner was that my understanding of their culture was always seen in a positive way. Since I was a foreigner, my ability to understand and use their language and concepts constituted a positive understanding (to use their terms '*ia v"ekhala*'). In contrast the understanding that was demanded from any representative of the older generation in the Soviet Union was of a qualitatively different nature, and premised on their *inability* to understand *fully*. Hence it was a negative understanding – in the mode of 'my parents don't *really* understand'. What was demanded from me was essentially verbal (or at most cultural) and not emotional understanding. Having said this, I also think that my closeness to them in age created a certain volume of cross-cultural knowledge to which native Russian speakers of an older generation would not have had access and prevented me from forming questions associated with a parental approach – especially: 'Why do you . . . ?' and 'What's the point of . . . ?' – which naturally generated a highly defensive reaction.

A further advantage of being a foreigner was the possibility of reciprocation. In particular any information I could offer on youth cultures in the West was relished – even in 1991 there were virtually no rock or youth magazines of the kind Western youth is used to. Occasionally I became important in a much more material way – such as the occasion when we were stopped by ticket collectors on a trolleybus on the way to a concert in Gorky Park. The ease with which we evaded the compulsory fine was unanimously put down to the fact that 'these kind of people [the ticket inspectors] do not want to give a bad impression in front of foreigners'. To me, getting away without paying appeared to have been much less to do with my presence, than with the fact that the group had no respect for the authority of the ticket collector and had simply walked away. (Perhaps this might be seen as a concrete example of 'mutual empowerment'.) I was also asked to decipher the texts of songs in English and/or translate them into Russian, although I suspect that this quite often turned out to be a disservice, since once the words were understood the text often seemed less meaningful than it had done before.

Undoubtedly, however, my status as a foreigner was the greatest source of unequal power in the relationship. The inferiority complex *vis à vis* the West evoked a desire to shock among some of the people I worked with. This was certainly true of the punks, who displayed a desire to show that Soviet punks were as 'bad' as Western ones and articulated a concern that they had not been shocking enough – even suggesting that they should invent some tales of their lives so that I would have more to write about. In other cases, the reaction was a need to emphasize that despite their 'unfortunate' position (being Soviet), they knew more, played better and were more authentic than the punks, rockers, or bikers in the West. In any case, this reveals once again that the power I retained to represent them was real and important.

The aspect of my identity which was not concealed behind my Westernness was clearly the fact that I was a young woman. As I have already indicated, my awareness of these issues from an early stage of the research meant that the project had been steered to minimize such problems. The principle of always being introduced to new participants via one of the girls was crucial to my ability to avoid situations in which either I, or those helping my research, felt uncomfortable. It was only when my concern for maximizing information was allowed to override my research principles that I encountered problems. One example was when, after repeated, failed attempts to gain contact with a new group, I decided to go ahead with an arranged meeting even though I knew the girl who had originally set it up could no longer come. The result was that I succeeded only in causing the informant such embarrassment in front of his older, and very scornful mates, that he put off the interview to a later date, and I never saw him again. I then felt bound to abandon further attempts to make contact with this group.

**Unresolved problems**

The aim of my research had been to generate knowledge about a cultural world which was not based on the supposedly productive divisions of hypothesis, data collection and analysis (theory and method) and of researcher (objective position) and respondents (subjective position). The methods that were employed were premised on: the learning not the authoritative position of the researcher; the intertwined and simultaneous processes of data collection and analysis; and a relational theory of meaning allowing the retention of the cultural concepts used by those participating in the research.

Some aspects of the research process, however, remained problematic. The main problem was the contradictory desire to retain the autonomy of the subjects – by not imposing my own interpretations on their actions – whilst at the same time rendering their cultural world meaningful to those outside it. The contradictory pulls between 'allowing text to speak for itself' and dealing with the gaps in shared meaning between readers and producers of the text by intervening with my own interpretations plagued me throughout the research process. On the one hand the problem was an ethical rather than methodological or epistemological one. I was keenly aware that the people who had talked to me expected to see their words reappear in a fairly reflective way – this was evident in their warnings that I ought not to believe everything I was told. Moreover, the people who talked to me, and the texts that were generated by those conversations, were constructed by the context of their creation in which we were all a part. That context is now gone – we have all moved on – but only I retain control of the text produced, and only I have a vested interest in its wider distribution.

On the other hand, the problems which remained unresolved were evidence of the continued vitality of the structuralism/culturalism debate. Despite the acknowledged importance of post-structuralist thinking (see Chapter 1), the ethnographic method employed in the field work and the contextualization and analysis attempted in Chapter 8 reveal a pretension to more than relating just another constructed narrative. Whilst accepting that the peculiar nature of the interaction between myself and those young people participating in the research did indeed result in an unrepeatable text which in absolute terms has no greater worth than any other textual version, the method of my work was guided by two extra-methodological desires. First, to employ the research opportunity in a way which would focus attention on the *activity* of young people, on their capacity for creation and symbolic work. Second, to locate this activity within its social context, in a way which might render it more comprehensible to an outside audience.

The problems, therefore, were not resolved, only dealt with. At the ethical level, all I can do is claim sole liability for the way in which this text finally appears, removing the responsibility for this from any of those who participated in the project. In terms of method, the account which follows claims neither truth nor relativity, and offers no resolution of the structure–action binary; it is quite simply a self-conscious ethnography.

# 7  Introducing the subjects

The task of introducing the reader to the young people who participated in the research project in Moscow is a difficult one, for they are a collection of individuals not a delimited sociological group or a carefully sampled cross-section of young Russians. Indeed – as one of them noted – what connected them was not even that they represented Moscow *neformaly* (non-formals), but that they were all simply *nenormaly* (abnormals).

As was argued in the previous chapter, the validity of the field work does not rest on the representativeness of the informants, nevertheless, some sociological details of those who participated in the research are compiled in the Appendix, to which the reader is referred. The aim of this chapter is to reconstruct the Moscow youth cultural world as presented by these informants, and its usefulness is restricted to indicating the main players and cultural categories assigned to them. The categories themselves – since many follow familiar Western subcultural styles – are less interesting than the processes of their cultural construction (the boundaries of inclusion and exclusion) and the grey areas between categories. An analysis of both of these will be crucial to the following chapter, which has the more ambitious aim of beginning to develop an idea of the social and cultural relations which structure the Moscow youth cultural world. This chapter confines itself to a descriptive or mapping task.

## MAPPING THE MOSCOW YOUTH CULTURAL WORLD

Figure 7.1 is a diagrammatic representation of the Moscow youth cultural world in 1991. As a taxonomic analysis the diagram is far from complete or universal. It expresses only the cultural knowledge of those Moscow *neformaly* who were interviewed by the author in the spring and summer of 1991. Its comprehensiveness is also uneven. Those whose *tusovki* had little interaction with the *stiliagi* would be unlikely to be able to distinguish between *Bravisty*, *Brigadiry* and *Twistera*. In contrast, the category of 'associations' (*ob"edineniia*) is grossly underrepresented in the diagram.

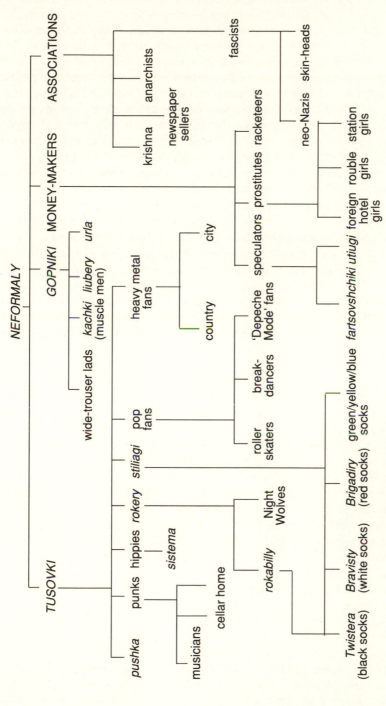

*Figure 7.1* A taxonomic analysis of Moscow *neformaly*

This is because the young people interviewed rarely came into contact with the socio-political, religious or other ideologically motivated *neformaly*.

The partiality of the taxonomy also stems from the fact that it provides a snapshot representation of the Moscow youth cultural world in 1991. In so doing it reveals certain trends in the development of the *neformaly* over the perestroika period. The very weak representation of the social and political *neformaly*, for example, indicates not only the partial view of the informants but also the gradual decline in interest in these groups as they became a norm of perestroika life, and consequently less a symbol of democratization than of political chaos. Second, the taxonomy shows the growing significance of the 'economic *neformaly*' in the everyday lives of Moscow youth. By economic *neformaly* is meant those who 'do business' (*delaiut biznes*). This constitutes a cultural category rather than a professional classification since doing business in contemporary Russia is a whole way of life not a career choice. It involves a lifestyle revolving around selling, interaction with foreigners, and protection. Again, there is no claim to comprehensiveness here – detailed studies of speculation and of prostitution would suggest many more subsets of these two groups – only those cultural categories which were spontaneously referred to by informants have been incorporated. The significance of such changes over time will be dealt with in the following chapter, the remainder of this chapter will concern itself with introducing the reader to the Moscow youth cultural world.

### Explaining the categories: grey areas

The first category in need of explanation is that of the *neformaly* itself. As is clear from the earlier discussion of the employment of this category in the youth press, the term *neformaly* was not an authentic category but had been adopted and employed by a number of agencies to signify the real, visible change wrought by perestroika. But this symbol of democratic change could only work if accompanied by 'civic responsibility' and this meant the constant need to 'guide' and 'channel' the activity of the *neformaly*. Hence, the non-formal organizations were subjected to repeated attempts to institutionalize them, as local *Komsomol* committees entrusted reliable members with the task of 'work with the *neformaly*'.

This premise was confirmed by the interviewing process. Those interviewed did not regularly employ the term *neformaly* to refer to either their own, or to other groups. Nevertheless, the term was not completely absent from youth cultural vocabulary and for this reason it was included as a category in the second round of interviewing. It was anticipated that the label '*neformaly*' would not withstand such scrutiny and would be rejected as a self-description, but it was not. Repeatedly, the term was affirmed as a general label which could be applied to all the groups being talked about *including* one's own. This was indicated by definitions of the *neformaly* such as 'all the tendencies together', '. . . all of them. Punks and *liubery* and everyone, everyone . . .', and even 'they are us'. The taxonomy therefore became one of 'kinds of *neformaly*' and the author was forced to confront the grey area between the codes of dominant cultural representation and those of youth cultural activity itself.

The acceptance of the term *neformaly* to describe all youth cultural groups need not imply the groups' acceptance of a common cause, common interest or even common activity. Nor does it necessitate a reversion to any kind of 'children of perestroika' explanation of their activity. The fact that young people adopted the label assigned is rather what Hebdige refers to as the 'reflexive circuitry of production and reproduction' (Hebdige 1979: 86). The idea that subcultural groups articulate not only '*blocked* readings' but also many of the preferred meanings of the dominant culture is the key to an understanding of the grey area between formal and non-formal worlds. Subcultural activity may be not only 'responses to' official discourses, but embodiments of it, or even plays on it (87).

This allows us to see the *neformaly* not as an explosion of pent-up frustration which burst forth as soon as the ideological barriers had been lifted, but a taking up and working through of key themes of the dominant culture. The appropriation of visibly Western styles need not be read as political resistance, but may be viewed as part of the official discourse of modernization, individualization and opening up, and of the private discourse of material self-improvement, both of which were embedded in dominant culture throughout the 1970s and early 1980s. That such different and conflicting subcultural dramatizations as the *liubery* and the punks should emerge simultaneously is not surprising given the reconstruction of dominant cultural meanings underway, as well as the breakdown of the strict division between their public and private articulation. The division between the 'formal' and the 'non-formal' spheres of activity, therefore, is important to retain not only because it is not rejected by youth cultural groups but because it is an important explanatory relation.

In the case of the *liubery* the interaction between lived socio-cultural relations and constructed texts about those relations is particularly clear (see Chapter 4). The publicity surrounding the phenomenon of the *liubery* facilitated its development and channelled its activities. According to one Soviet researcher, the *liuber* type groups acted only against adolescent and youth groupings which were actively criticized in the mass media and by official institutions (Fain 1990: 37). Thus, he argued, when breakdance sections began to be accepted and were organized in schools and houses of culture, the number of clashes declined sharply (ibid.).

A more unusual example of such a direct relationship between the media and group activity occurred following the publication of an interview with a former *stiliaga* in a local Moscow paper. The interviewee scorned the inability of the *stiliagi* lads to stand up for themselves and, displeased by this portrayal of the *stiliagi*, one of their members subjected the interviewee to physical proof to the contrary.

In other cases, the interaction between formal and non-formal worlds was more subtly enmeshed in the group's whole way of life. The *stiliagi*, for example, combined a subcultural style and activity with an active membership of their family environments. Those parents the author talked to tended to adopt a fairly pragmatic attitude to their children's style; 'better this than being a dirty hippy or revolting punk'. Members of the group themselves explained their parents' acceptance of their subcultural activity by the fact that the style reminded them of their own teenage days. Their parents often even helped them obtain 1950s' style clothes from friends and colleagues who had kept them.

With other institutions of the formal world, the *stiliagi* had more ambiguous relations. The police were seen as both aggressors (who on occasion detained them unnecessarily and with undue force) and as protectors (the police had guided them safely out of concerts after having been threatened by local yobs). Active resistance to the control of formal institutions, however, appeared to be confined to one – the army. Of the eleven male *stiliagi* old enough to do military service who were interviewed, only six had completed or were still completing it. Three managed to evade conscription (through feigning mental illness), one served six months of the two years before securing release (having again feigned mental illness), and one committed suicide whilst serving. The hostility with which the army is viewed is reflected in the group's refusal to accept this version of their friend's death which, they argued, was likely to have been a more direct result of bullying.

For other groups, interaction with the formal world was experienced as systematically oppressive. The punks' main interaction with the formal world was the experience of having been brought to order by various agencies of social control: school, *Komsomol*, parents, neighbours and the medical establishment. All the punks interviewed had been certified mentally ill and had undergone, or were undergoing, compulsory treatment for their diagnosed illness. This experience was central to the group narrative. On the one hand there was an acceptance, even pride in the certification of mental illness, which expressed itself in tales of hospital incarceration, comparisons of classifications of mental illness given (stamped in their military service record cards) and of assertions that they were 'sick people'.

The definitions imposed from outside fed the group narrative in a more material way as well. The drugs given to cure them, such as *tsiklodol*, were used to trip. Drugs prescribed to be taken once or twice a day, if taken all at once could result in two days of non-stop hallucinations. Even taken occasionally with alcohol, they could 'make you do mad things'. Another group narrative surrounded a toy machine-gun which was taken on night walks. This was a play on an incident from the past when one of the group had been accused by the local *Komsomol* committee of having a weapons store in preparation for a punk, armed revolution.

Like the *liubery*'s 'ideological mission', therefore, the mental insanity and anti-social behaviour ascribed to the punks, was taken up, absorbed and turned into part of a group narrative which helped constitute their identity. Where interaction with the formal world could be beneficial to them, on the other hand, the punks showed little hesitation in using the opportunity. One punk band agreed to record songs for a feature film because, although receiving no payment, they would be allowed access to decent recording equipment. The film, ironically, disseminated the familiar reconstructed representations of glasnost and was essentially concerned with the evils of the youth subcultural world and one father's attempt to save his daughter from it – significantly, the father was a policeman. In contrast to other groups, however, for the punks media exposure did not present a desired opportunity for social prestige or mobility, and they did not even bother to go see the film.

The significance of the interaction between constructed text and lived social and cultural relations will be discussed in the following chapter. It suffices here to note that the term *neformaly* was accepted by young people active in youth cultural groups since it allowed them to adopt a distanced position from formal institutions without blocking their space for inter-action with them. Within the non-formal sphere of activity, however, the cultural world was delineated not according to form (non-formal/formal) but content – what people *did*. It is to the cultural categories ascribed to different kinds of *neformaly* which attention is now turned.

## KINDS OF NEFORMALY

The cultural categories described were drawn from descriptions of the youth cultural world given during interviews. The classificatory categories – *tusovki*, *gopniki*, economic *neformaly* and associations – are, however, the author's, who takes full responsibility for any inaccuracies in their categorization or in the description of their basic characteristics which is undertaken below.

### Associations

From 1986 onwards the socio-political non-formal groups (referred to here as 'associations') grew, as the Russian saying goes, 'like mushrooms after the rain'. Although from the end of 1988 onwards there was a slow-down in their rate of growth as they exhausted their recruitment potential, never-theless such associations exist today in over 200 cities across the former Soviet Union and range from clubs of a dozen members to popular fronts with a mass membership. There are any number of ways of categorizing such groups, the most common being by form of organization (popular fronts/reform movements; political parties; independent publications groups; independent trade unions) and by content of activity (ecological; patriotic/national; historico-cultural; independent labour; committees for self-government; peace movements; democratic and human/civic rights groups) (Berezovskii and Krotov 1990).

Either way, it is clear from Figure 7.1 that many of the socio-political groupings were not spontaneously mentioned by interviewees. Political parties, democratic reform movements and civic rights groups are completely unrecognized as are ecological, peace and historico-cultural groups, which are more usually associated with subcultural *neformaly*. On the other hand, independent publications groups (*gazetchiki*) and patriotic/nationalist groups (*fashisty*) are mentioned and, arguably, the anarchists could be classified either as an organization of self-government, or, in their anarcho-syndicalist guise, as an independent labour organization. In addition, an important reference is made to the growing number of religious/mystical groups – represented in the diagram by the *Hare Krishna*.

Only those groups referred to spontaneously by interviewees are included in the diagram, although this in no way indicates any particular political allegiance to or interest in them by Moscow youth. The anarchists, for example, were known because of their association with the punks, while the fascists could not escape notice because of the peculiar shock effect of their ideology (given the suffering of the Soviet people during the Second World War). The newspaper sellers (*gazetchiki*) was a term used to indicate not a particular political group but all those selling their independent newspapers at central meeting places such as Pushka and the Truba in the heyday of democratization (1988–90). Subsequently these key locations were favoured by sellers of more dubious material (pornography) and their pushers were economically rather than politically motivated.

Undoubtably, the right-wing political groups (by which is meant national-chauvinist as well as market-authoritarian groups) were the best known, but it remained difficult to judge just how well organized they were among young people. There was general agreement that groups of neo-fascists existed and that skinheads (sometimes referred to as *skinkhedy* and sometimes literally translated into Russian as *britogolovie*) shared their political outlook – suggesting a clear link between the socio-political and youth subcultural groups. On other occasions, however, the term skinhead would be used more to equate people with (specifically) British football hooligans, which, although carrying an overtone of nationalism, indicated primarily aggressive, thuggish behaviour and a specific style of dress. None of the informants referred to themselves as skinheads although some expressed sympathy with what they interpreted to be their views.

### Economic neformaly

A significant role in the youth cultural world was played by the economic *neformaly*. The groups informants referred to – speculators, prostitutes and racketeers – have not generally been categorized as *neformaly*, but since they conform to the general definition used – groups of people who gather together in the public sphere but who consciously stay outside of the formal or official institutions – and, since they were seen as an important part of the youth cultural world by informants, there seems no reason to exclude them.

Their past exclusion from classification systems of informal groups appears to have two root causes. First, the *neformaly* label was a product of the glasnost/democratization discourse, which did not include economic non-formal behaviour – this remained officially regarded as a product of moral laxity stemming from the Brezhnev era of stagnation and corruption. Second, *unofficially* it was assumed that virtually all young people involved themselves in the second economy in some way in order to obtain the clothes, records or other goods they desired.[1] This universal complicity meant that it was difficult to categorize any group of *neformaly* as specifically concerned with the second economy. Since the activity in which they were involved was deemed not only socially negative but actually criminal, however, where such activity went beyond that to which a blind eye could be turned, its perpetrators were treated harshly by the law.

Interviews with informants suggested that economic *neformaly* had their own groups and meeting places just like other *neformaly*. Interviewees also clearly differentiated between those who simply used the second economy in order to get hold of deficit goods (who were 'like me') from those who used the second economy as a source of income. People who made money out of the informal economy were classified as speculators and racketeers. The racketeers used protection to cream off profit from the speculators. They were also heavily involved in the organization of prostitution – which, in a material though not a moral sense, was seen as a female variant of speculation, fulfilling the same function of providing access to foreign money and goods. In fact, of course, despite the dominant Soviet image of a prostitute as a successful young 'businesswoman' travelling from hotel to hotel in her private taxi, the reality for many young women was draughty stations, insalubrious mens' toilets, beatings from pimps and competing girls, and a 'profit' of a few roubles. Racketeers were known of and talked about, but they were not usually part of the everyday world of those interviewed. Those who they came across daily were the *fartsovshchiki* and the *utiugi*.

The *fartsovshchik* had long been part of Soviet young people's reality, and refers to someone who deals in goods in the second economy on a fairly small scale – acting as a middle-person in the trading process and earning a profit from this activity. The *utiug* is a more recent phenomenon, since she/he is involved primarily with buying from or selling to foreigners and, in Moscow, the best known location of the *utiugi* in 1991 was the Arbat. The importance of the *utiugi* in the youth cultural world is evidenced in the adoption of many of their trade words into youth slang. Such words reflect the regional-national origin of foreigners (the recognition of which is a source of pride amongst *utiugi*) and different denominations and kinds of currency (e.g. *Britisha* – 'Brits'; *grin, baksy* – 'bucks'; and *firma* – 'foreigner').

Early and frequent acquaintance with speculators of various kinds on the part of other *neformaly* led to many being attracted into their way of life, especially after they had finished school and were forced to earn a living. For many, the prospect of accepting the kind of work and pay on offer in the real world was highly unattractive and they justified their movement into the world of the economic *neformaly* through the attitude that 'they [the state] have brought it on themselves'. There were two perceived failures on the state's part: its failure to fulfil its obligation to offer them interesting, adequately paid work; and its economic liberalization which allowed them to deal illegally. Hence many normalized their chosen means of making a living by referring to it as 'doing business', whilst others, in conscious defiance of deviance-labelling, called it 'speculation'.

Despite the bravado about 'easy come, easy go' money and the uselessness of possessing roubles anyway, those who did rely on 'dealing' for the maintenance of their lifestyle, nevertheless adopted a professional attitude to it. Their life revolved around phoning contacts, arranging meetings and – regardless of other distractions – keeping those appointed meetings. Moreover, sometimes they were forced to treat the issue seriously; when deals went badly, the 'business world' revealed itself to be a tightly-knit and oppressive structure from which it was difficult to extract oneself. The system (borrowed from the criminal world and practised by territorially based gangs in the large cities) of putting debt defaulters on a meter (*shchetchik*) meant that debt increased with every day of non-payment. One consequence of this was the frequent 'disappearances' of young speculators as they went underground to escape their debts and the wrath of those to whom they were indebted. Another practice borrowed from criminal gangs was the importance of the hierarchical structuring of the world of speculation. Each location would have its own hierarchy – in Estonia this reportedly consisted of: '*dvorniazhki*', the small-fry who pestered foreigners; '*okhotniki*' who dealt in antiques, icons and hard currency; and '*kity*' who had a chain of smaller speculators under them and dealt in thousands of roubles (Teterin and Miil' 1987).

## Gopniki

'*Gopniki*' is often used interchangeably with the terms indicated as subsets in Figure 7.1: *urla, kachki, shirokoshtanniki* (wide-trouser lads) and *liubery*. It is, however, the only one of these terms which may encompass all the others and, for this reason, was adopted as the generic term.

The 'wide-trouser lads' (*shirokoshtanniki*) are associated mainly with the provincial cities, especially those situated along the river Volga. They are hostile to those from the capital and prestigious cities in the west of Russia whom they see as having an undeservedly higher standard of living. In order to rectify this state of affairs, they make 'tours' (*gastroli*) to the big cities where they beat up and steal fashionable items from the young 'trendies'. Their style (wide trousers for lads and long skirts for girls) is an indication of their adoption of a consciously provincial (neo-proletarian, anti-Moscow fashion) style and this tendency is reflected in the style of related groups such as the *fufaechniki*. This group is so called because its members adorn the padded jacket or *fufaika* generally used as work clothes by manual workers in the former Soviet Union. Another similar group are the *telagi* who adorn a similar padded coat called the *telogreika*. Neither of these groups appears in Figure 7.1 since they were not spontaneously mentioned, although they would be recognized as *liuber*-types. The attacks on youth in other cities is only one manifestation of a whole way of life in these provincial cities involving the subordination and humiliation of the individual in the name of gang rivalry (see Chapters 4 and 8).

Another associated group are the *kachki*. '*Kachat'sia*' in Russian means to 'pump iron' and this illustrates another aspect of many of these groups' activities – body-building. Being referred to as one of the *kachki* does not necessarily imply any particular group allegiance (the term can even be used playfully to describe members of very different groups who are unusually sporty or macho in their image) but it is generally associated with the *liuber* and *gopnik* types. Because of the origins of these groups in the provinces and working-class suburbs of large cities and their adoption of working-class, Soviet style, they have often been associated with a particular political strategy – that of 'neo-Stalinists' (see Chapter 4). This is particularly true of the *liubery* and the *remontniki*.[2]

From the point of view of the Moscow *tusovki*, however, what is definitive about these groups is less their political allegiance than their social origin. This is why the term *urla* – frequently used by young Muscovites but rarely referred to in academic or journalistic material – is important. The term is very difficult to translate and its origins hard to trace. It was suggested that it might have developed as a shortened form of *urodlivii* meaning 'ugly', but its sense is clearly more social than aesthetic. Perhaps the nearest translation in English would be 'yob' or 'lout' because these suggest the implied *lack of culture* of the *urla*. The culture lacked by the *urla* is a very specific one, however, it is that of *urban culture* and thus the translation informants often came up with was 'country-boy'. The scorn of young Muscovites for those from the 'country' is very much a reflection of dominant adult culture and the continued existence of a stark urban–rural social stratification in a relatively recently urbanized country. Consequently, informants tended to define the *urla* as body builders from other towns, 'country boys' or simply 'stupid people'.

## Tusovki

The word *tusovka* has been part of Russian youth slang since the 1960s but its origin is unclear. Common-sense interpretations trace it to the word *tasovka* from the verb *tasovat'* meaning 'to shuffle', as in 'to shuffle cards'. *Tasovat'* itself, according to Dal', stems from the French verb *tasser* which, in its reflexive form, means 'to huddle together'. This is close to the current, slang usage of *tusovat'sia* as 'to gather', 'to get together'. The social and cultural meanings invested in this kind of youth cultural activity will be the subject of the following chapter. Here, the reader is simply guided through the groups described as *tusovki* by those interviewed. Particular emphasis is laid on the *stiliagi* since this is the group on whom the field work was centred.

### The stiliagi

The *stiliagi* emerged in the 1950s and are generally considered to be the first youth cultural group in the Soviet Union. The essence of the *stiliagi* was style; both dress and dance style. According to Aleksei Kozlov (a rock musician and one of the original *stiliagi*) the term *stiliagi* was invented by the author of a biting newspaper article in order to indicate the negative traits of these young people. These were defined as their lack of spiritual or political interests, and their concern only with the superficial sides of life; dancing, fashion and music (Troitsky 1987: 2). But since the *stiliagi* considered an interest in new styles and trends to be positive, they chose to adopt this name (although also perhaps because it was preferable to the other name they were given in this article 'the mould') (ibid.).

The original *stiliagi* flourished in a period of social activation similar to the mid-1980s: the period of de-Stalinization, democratization and cultural renewal. The rejection by the *stiliagi* of the weighty tasks of the day thus appeared almost treacherous. But their political apathy was only one side of the coin, worse still was the fact that the styles they were adopting were Western and therefore bourgeois and ideologically reprehensible. The consequent slippage of the term *stiliaga* to denote both a particular rock 'n' roll style and 'anything Western' was recorded by Thomas Magner, writing in 1957, when he reported that he and an academic colleague 'were hailed as *stiliagi* by passing urchins who had caught sight or our "Western dress" ' (Magner 1957: 195). This association led the *stiliagi* into clashes with those upholding the ideological values of Soviet society, especially active members of the *Komsomol* who saw it as their duty to make the *stiliagi* aware of their moral decadence by direct action, taking the form of forcibly cutting off their hair or their distinctive narrow trousers. The group history of persecution remains reflected in contemporary graffiti of the *stiliagi* such as '*stiliaga – modnii no vsegda golodnii*' (a *stiliaga* is fashionable, but always hungry).

*Plate 1 Stiliagi* dancing,
February 1989.

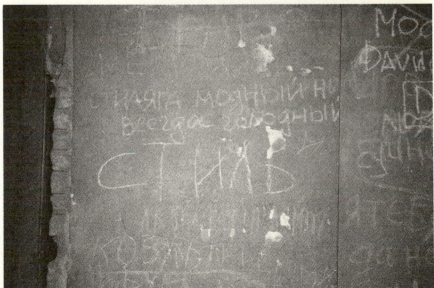

*Plate 2* Graffiti at the 'Catacombs' reads, 'A *stiliaga* is fashionable but always hungry'.

A second problem for the *stiliagi* was their association with what were considered to be a class of morally degenerate young elite known as the *zolotaia molodezh'* or 'gilded youth' whose influential parents allowed them greater access to all things Western and to expensive lifestyles in restaurants and bars. Although the gilded youth constituted only a small section of the *stiliagi*, it was their image which dominated their general perception and representation.

In the mid-1980s there was a significant revival of the group and at the height of this new wave there were an estimated 200–300 *stiliagi* active in the Moscow area. The very first *stiliagi* listened to jazz with some moving on to rock 'n' roll in the late 1950s and early 1960s. The revivalist *stiliagi* of the 1980s define themselves as lovers of rock 'n' roll music, but the bands which inspired the 1980s revival – 'Bravo' and 'Brigada S' – also had very strong jazz influences. In fact 'Brigada S' was referred to sometimes as the 'Proletarian jazz orchestra'. These two groups were forged out of the fragments of the same two amateur groups in the early 1980s – 'Postskrip-tum' and 'Gulliver' – and they continued to be closely connected. Igor' Sukachev (the lead signer of 'Brigada S') wrote the text to the 'Bravo' song *Belii Den'* and at one point was virtually a member of 'Bravo'. 'Bravo's first public performance was in December 1983. Many of the *stiliagi* thus started out as fans of 'Bravo' (*Bravisty*) or of 'Brigada S' (*Brigadiry*).

The style (*stil'*) of the *stiliagi* was a re-creation of the 1950s rock 'n' roll style, although often interpreted through the prism of 'Bravo' group members, and to a lesser extent, the 'Brigada S' group. In particular the lead singer of 'Bravo', Zhanna Aguzarova, was painstakingly followed by both girls and boys. Her style comprised black suit, white shirt, narrow tie and patent leather shoes, accompanied often by a small briefcase and umbrella, and its adoption lent the *stiliagi* their image of being clean, smart and, very importantly, of being above the general banality (*poshlost'*) of their surroundings. In this sense they carried with them some of the identity of the original *stiliagi*, but in other ways their image was radically different. Whereas in the 1950s they were the sole symbol of Western aping, in the 1980s their image was associated fondly with part of the Soviet past and thus their dress was often a source of amusement and pleasurable nostalgia rather than outrage to the older generation.

## Punks

In some ways Soviet punk is one of the clearest examples of 'imitation' of Western subcultural forms – there can after all be no social base for a movement subverting consumerist lifestyles in a society where a safety pin or a dustbin bag is an article of deficit not abundance. Nevertheless, Soviet punks do choose to live in a way which resists the chief indicators of respectability – primarily avoiding work, military service and settling down. It could also be argued that there is a rejection among Soviet punks of the obsession with material goods which is a product of a deficit economy and it is certainly true that they do not hanker for the imported (*firmennie*) clothes which are the object of desire for many Soviet teenagers (although a 'Sex Pistols' T-shirt remains a valued commodity). Their style is generally taken from Western punks – the multicoloured mohicans tend to be worn by younger punks, while older punks are more likely to adopt short spiky haircuts which can be more easily adapted into respectable forms.

There is a greater sense among punks than among other *tusovki* of being outsiders in mainstream society and many punks spend much of their time, or even live, in disused basements of blocks of flats. These punks were referred to as 'cellar' or 'garage' punks by the punks interviewed in Moscow, in contrast to themselves who were 'home' (*domashnie*) punks since they continued to live at home, although adapting their rooms to suit their lifestyle. There is evidence of a hierarchical differentiation between older and younger punks and between 'authentic' punks and those who simply adopt the outward manifestation of the punk lifestyle (Zapesotskii and Fain 1990: 168). The latter are referred to as *lokhi* (the wider cultural context of this term is discussed below).

One of the factors limiting the spread of punk appears to be the disempowerment of punk music since, unlike in the West, it could not break through from the underground to smash the established norms of rock music but has always had to share that underground with more mainstream musical forms. A number of purist punk bands have attained success (most notably 'Chiudo-Iudo' and 'NII Kosmetiki') whilst others with punk roots have achieved greater fame after developing distinct post-punk identities (e.g. 'Va-Bank', 'Alisa', 'DK' and 'Zvuki Mu'). There is a manifest lack of political identity among Moscow punks, despite odd indications of punk activism such as a reported demonstration 'against shortages' ('Panki golosuiut za El'tsina' 1990). The shortages which were being protested were of condoms, hairspray and cigarettes which prevented the punks living the kind of lifestyle they wished to and they reportedly left chanting 'Down with the trousers' (*doloi shtany*) referring to the *gopnik* types from the Moscow suburbs and Russian provincial cities (ibid.). Hence the reporter's reading of the event as being a demonstration in support of Yeltsin seems somewhat of an overstatement.

Anarchy is expressed by most punks as their ideal, but it appears to consist of little more than a dislike for the *Komsomol*, school and the lack of freely available alcohol. In this sense Soviet punk disrupts not the norms of bourgeois society, but the norms of the collective society by declaring the right to 'let the side down', to be at 'the bottom of the pile'. This sense of defending the right to be 'the dregs of society' seems to have been reinforced by the decline of punk in the West. The favourite saying of the Moscow punks interviewed, and the most frequently encountered punk graffiti, was 'punk's not dead', which is intended to hold up a warning to society that those on the bottom of the pile will continue to rot there until the stench eventually rises to irritate even those at the very top.

## Hippies

The hippies emerged in the mid-1960s and were the first significant subcultural group after the *stiliagi*. They became the core of many of the youth cultures that followed, especially through the development of a youth jargon, much of which is still used in today's *tusovki*. Following the crushing of the Prague Spring the hippies became more politicized and constituted a key element of the pacifist movement. After the clampdown on dissent which began in 1972, the hippies were driven onto the periphery of society, became closed to outsiders, more ritualistic in their way of life and more like their Western counterparts in their style (Meier *et al.* 1990: 26). A new wave of hippies, and the largest to date, appeared in the late 1970s, before their renewed decline in the early to mid-1980s as a plethora of youth groups emerged (Rozin 1990: 44).

Hippies may also be referred to as the *khairasti* or *volosatie*. The former term is one of a number of words adapted from the English 'hair' in hippy slang, the latter is from the Russian for 'hair', meaning 'the hairy ones'. Both are used by hippies to refer to each other, while the latter is also used in a more or less negative way by non-hippies. Another important term is *sistema* referring to the country-wide mutual help network established by the hippies to help their brethren visiting from other cities. The *sistema* emerged alongside the hippy movement in the 1960s and overlaps, although is not completely coterminous, with it since members of other *tusovki* may also be part of the *sistema*.[3] Within the *sistema* there are individual *tusovki* which have their own meeting places. The main hierarchical division among hippies is based on the length of time in the movement and thus commitment to it. New members are referred to as *pionery* ('pioneers') while the most respected are the *oldovye* ('the old ones'). Soviet researchers have suggested that this hierarchical division is evident in the hippy symbolic system; since hair grows slowly its length indicates how long someone has been in the system (Rozin 1990: 48).

## Pop fans

The pop fans (sometimes called *volnisty*) are those who listen to fashionable pop groups and in some cases practise specific dance and movement trends associated with that music. In the past breakdancers and skateboarders have enjoyed considerable popularity. In 1991 the largest such *tusovka* appeared to be the *Depesha* ('Depeche Mode' fans), although rap was gaining an increasing following (largely as a result of the popularity of the Russian rap group led by Bogdan Titomir) and roller-skating seemed to have taken over from skateboarding as the biggest movement craze. There

*Plate 3* A punk at the Moscow Rock Laboratory, summer 1991.

*Plate 4* Moscow punks in the metro, summer 1991.

was also evidence of an emergent acid house scene in St Petersburg and Moscow. Not surprisingly music and movement *tusovki* were often closely linked and by summer 1992, for example, the central *tusovki* of the roller-skaters (*rolliki*) and the *Depesha* had virtually merged, with both hanging out in the Alexander Gardens which skirt the walls of the Kremlin. None of those interviewed were current members of such groups although many had acquaintances from within their ranks or had mixed with such *tusovki* (especially the *Depesha*) in the past.

### Heavy metal fans

The classification of heavy metal fans (*metallisty*) in Figure 7.1 is non-authentic; *metallisty* would be more likely to classify themselves according to the kind of metal they listened to (i.e. by how 'heavy' the metal is) while Soviet observers focus on the division between 'Satanists', 'black' *metallisty* (who listen to anti-Soviet groups and sometimes overlap with pro-fascist groups) and speed-metal fans who adopt a militarized style of dress (Zapesotskii and Fain, 1990: 177; Fain 1990: 33).

The outward appearance of heavy metal fans is dominated by leather and metal attributes: studs, rivets, spikes, zips and belt buckles. Some metal fans also dye their hair and paint their faces, thus giving an impression of punk influence. The *metallisty* were probably at their height in the mid-1980s but now, like the football fans, to whom many observers originally compared them, they seem to be on the decline in the major cities. There has also been a sharpening of hierarchical divisions between those who are real connoisseurs of metal (primarily those who have access to prestigious records and music journals) and those, often living in small towns, who know little more than a few names of groups and songs but profess allegiance to the *metallisty*. This sharp division is reflected in the apparent dissociation of these leaders from the mass and it is this division (between 'city' and 'country' *metallisty*) which is the one the author encountered in Moscow. One informant even recounted how he had offended a heavy metal fan by asking him if he was a *metallist* – the 'real' metal fans, he was told, now refer to themselves as *metallera*.

Despite the mass popularity of heavy metal, many of the Moscow *tusovki* members remain fond of metal and consider it to be the common starting point of (male) teenagers' interest in rock music.

### Rokery

The importance of the *rokery* will be discussed at length in the next chapter. Here it is important to note only that the *rokery* combine a love of heavy rock music with a passion for night-time motorbike riding. Bikers are generally considered – alongside the heavy metal and football fans – to be of predominantly low-status backgrounds. Among their members there is reportedly a disproportionately high rate of working-class kids and PTU students (Andreeva and Novikova, 1988: 31). They model themselves on American bikers and wear black leather jackets, cowboy boots and bandannas with as much Harley Davidson insignia as can be obtained. They have a much harder image than the other *tusovki* and, in Moscow, their leader – nicknamed *Khirurg* ('Surgeon') – was the widely acknowledged 'king of the Moscow scene'. Nevertheless, according to Borisov, the bikers have never numbered more than 400–600 in Moscow (Borisov 1991: 240).

Since the emergence of the 'Night Wolves' biker gang (also under the leadership of *Khirurg* and a number of smaller splinter gangs, it could be argued that the bikers have ceased to be a *tusovka* as such and have become much more akin to the biker gang structure in the United States. Nevertheless, in summer 1992 there was still a widely known general *tusovka* site of the *rokery* outside the art gallery (Tsentral'nii Dom Khudozhnika or TsDK) on Krimskii Val.

*Pushka*

*Pushka* is the affectionate name for Pushkin Square, a central Moscow square which has been one of the key sites of subcultural activity since the 1960s. It has been the site of *tusovki* for most Moscow youth cultures at some point in their history, often simultaneously. Then as now there is a set of people who simply hang out there, rather than move with any particular *tusovka* – hence the distinct, although rapidly changing *pushka tusovka*.

**CONCLUSION**

This chapter has attempted to provide a very brief overview of the Moscow youth cultural world and the people who move in it. Extensive field work would need to be done with each of the groups in order to provide a more authentic picture and such a goal is beyond the scope of this book. Here attention has simply been drawn to some of the socio-cultural peculiarities of what might at first seem familiar subcultural styles and strategies. What emerges from this kind of analysis is no more than an alternative classificatory system based on the 'spurious authenticity' of the articulated understandings of a particular set of interviewees. The following chapter will therefore attempt a more detailed ethnographic account of a particular group of young people as well as subject that account to some of the same kind of decoding work as other constructed texts.

# 8 Doing the Moscow shuffle
## An analysis of the cultural practices of a Moscow tusovka

The roots of the *tusovka* in the youth cultural world of the 1960s and 1970s explain the very specific interpretation of its cultural meaning adopted by some commentators. Artemii Troitsky, the well-known Soviet rock critic, uses the term *tusovka* almost synonymously with both 'scene' (by which is meant formerly forbidden, unofficial art forms) and 'new wave'[1] (Troitsky 1990: 134, back cover). Indeed, the link between the *tusovki* and 'new wave' in art and music is very important to the understanding of youth cultural styles. To take the case of the *stiliagi*, it is true to say that the two bands chiefly associated with the revival of the *stiliagi* in the 1980s – 'Bravo' and 'Brigada S' – were also two of the first, and most successful, 'new wave' bands (Dugin, in Zaitsev 1990: 78–81). Furthermore, the roots of the *tusovka* in the underground music scene help explain some of the cultural practices of individual *tusovki* today. Among these could be included: the importance of personal acquaintance with rock stars, and group narratives around the forming of this acquaintance; the cult of knowledge about music and its use in the formation of hierarchies both within and between *tusovki*; and the centrality of concerts and gigs in *tusovka* life.

The *equation* of the *tusovka* with the new wave rock scene, however, carries over the high culture/low culture division of society at large to within the low culture world itself. It falsely implies that there is a single, authentic *tusovka* (a 'new wave' elite) and various groups of fans who consume the culture the rock musicians produce. The division between producers and consumers is revealed in Dugin's discussion of the contribution of 'Bravo' to the 'new wave' scene. For him, it is the band which creates the meanings (their 'light-hearted post-war optimism infecting the audiences with a carelessness of the past') while the *stiliagi* are reduced to 'New Wave fans who get a kick out of their appearance, plain retro and who adore shake' (78–9).

In contrast, a much broader definition of the *tusovka* is adopted here: it is a distinct form of youth cultural activity and *the basic unit of central Moscow youth cultural activity*.[2] Music-use (listening to, dancing to or swopping information about a preferred rock music form and experimenting with creating one's own band) is central to *tusovka* life, but does not constitute its whole activity or meaning. It is the importance attached to the human communication and interaction in *tusovka* activity rather than its ability to bring together fans of a particular kind of music that lies at the heart of this definition.

Interaction occurs not only within but also between *tusovki*. This results in significant movement between groups of very different styles and is often cited as an indication of the instability, superficiality and childishness of youth cultural activity – not least by long-standing *tusovka* members or ex-members referring to the younger generations. Far from being the result of mindless trend-following manipulated by market or media, the observations of the author suggest that the *tusovka* ('shuffle') formation, characteristic of Moscow youth culture, has meanings which cannot be deciphered in isolation from either the youth cultural world as a whole or the adult cultural world to which it refers. The Moscow 'shuffle' in fact indicates the extreme fluidity and plurality of the youth cultural sphere in the second half of the 1980s. The institutional collapse of the perestroika years led to a suspension of the old mechanisms of urban youth cultural control such as the *Komsomol* before those associated with the West (market and media) were fully formed. The result was that the space for youth cultural activity became boundless. This boundlessness was expressed not in the removal of the usual mechanisms of control applied to youth on the streets – the coercive arm of the state intervened to control their activity frequently and sometimes brutally – but in the fact that youth cultural activity was not bound by a rigidly structured youth world.

The result of these processes has been similar to that in the political sphere where a significant amount of public activity is accompanied by the absence of clearly delineated and institutionalized groups, or, more accurately, a constant process of broad alliance formation followed by fragmentation and re-alignment. This leads to a temporary suspension of the usual norms of signification. At the level of high politics, the signifier 'liberal', for example, may be used to indicate anything from reform-communism to market-authoritarianism while that of 'democratic' is not only polysemic but omni-semic. In the youth cultural world, likewise, a leather jacket, shades, skull and crossbones and American stars and stripes appear in very different assemblages of style and might signify simultaneously 'hard', 'cool' or 'out of control', 'American hero', 'French/Italian sophisticate' or 'British thug'. In more concrete terms, the lack of an institutionalized and commercialized youth culture also meant that symbolic places (for meeting, listening to music, dancing) were shared, negotiated and renegotiated, fostering a constant process of slippage between *tusovki*.

During the course of the perestroika years this plurality and diffuseness began to give way to the construction of new institutions and cultural codes. In the youth cultural world, an important factor in this was the process of the commercialization and institutionalization of rock music. At the individual level, the new social contract being offered by the reformers was founded on the principle of reward for performance not ideological compliance, and financial security and self-reliance became increasingly important. This encouraged a gradual change in priorities and attribution of prestige according to which the speculator became the young businessman and 'hero of *his* time'. In turn, this facilitated the rooting of new codes of masculinity and femininity in which the world of business became the domain of men in which women were the symbolic object of the activity,[3] whilst remaining firmly excluded from it.

This chapter explores these processes of change within the Moscow youth cultural world through an analysis of the cultural practices of a single Moscow *tusovka* – the *stiliagi* – as it is positioned within the wider youth cultural world.

## 'EMBODIED COMMUNICATION': DEFINING A FRAMEWORK FOR ANALYSIS

In order to undertake such an exploration, a more culturally rooted definition of the *tusovka* must be adopted, and the term that appears to best express the meaning of the *tusovka* for the young people who were interviewed in the Moscow field work is that of 'embodied communication'. This notion expresses the urban specificity of the *tusovka* apparent in its peculiar integration of people and space. In the quicksand of the urban environment, the *tusovka* roots a certain set of people to a defined space, at least for a short time. Hence *tusovka* indicates both the place people get together ('I have been going to the *tusovki* since I was 15 years old' – *s 15 let, ia khodila na tusovki*) and the group of people involved ('our *tusovka* was really friendly' – *u nas byla druzhnaia tusovka*).

These two meanings are knitted together in definitions of *tusovka* which focus on the act of getting together or gathering. Hence *tusovka* may be defined as 'the interaction of people of one's own milieu' (*obshchenie liudei svoei sredy*) (Leont'eva 1989) or 'an assembling or gathering of people with similar interests in a certain area' (*sborishche liudei s odinakovimi interesami v opredelennoi oblasti*), which was a definition offered by members of the *stiliagi*. The implication here is that the *tusovka* is not the site of goal-orientated activity – only once was a rationale for being part of a *tusovka* offered – it is the outwardly visible result of a process of getting and being together.

Although not imputing rationale, interviewees were conscious of what their participation in the *tusovki* meant to them. It is meaning rather than role which is important here for the concept of role disembodies the activity by positing it as a mask or identity which can be assumed – and thus also discarded – as required. In contrast, even those former members of *tusovki* who sought to distance themselves from the group by classifying their participation as being a part of 'growing up', nevertheless retained a strong sense of what they carried with them into the future. The term 'embodied communication', then, is used to indicate first, the location of *tusovka* activity in the body rather than the mind, and, second, to suggest that the meanings generated by the *tusovka* nevertheless have a social and political, not solely psychological, significance.

## Meanings of the tusovka

The meanings ascribed to *tusovka* life by interviewees fell into three broad categories:

- The quantitative and qualitative improvement of communicative inter-action (*obshchenie*). The *tusovka* brought: 'lots of new friends' (*mnogo novikh druzei*); 'interesting communication' (*interesnoe obshchenie*); 'the chance to interact with different kinds of people' (*vozmozhnost' obshchat'sia s raznimi liud'mi*); and 'an interesting life' (*interesno zhit'*).
- A growing sense of self. This meant the achievement of greater security in oneself expressed by: 'self-confidence' (*uverennost' v sebe*); 'feeling good' (*khoroshii zhiznennii tonus*); 'having no worries' (*khoroshoe nastroenie ot bezzabotnosti*); and 'life becoming easier' (*legche zhit'*). But it was also associated with feeling confident about those around you, hence the *tusovka* was seen as enabling you to: 'be with kind people' (*byt' s liud'mi dobrozhelatel'nimi*); and 'relate to people more easily' (*otnosit'sia k liudiam proshche*).
- Intellectual and physical development. Awareness of one's own intellec-tual and physical development is clearly linked to the above category (growing sense of self) but statements about this kind of development reveal a more instrumental world-view and a more consciously upward orientation. Examples of such articulations include: 'self-improvement' (*sovershenstvo sebia*); 'broadening of the mind' (*imet' bolee obshirnie vzgliady*); 'not becoming a "yob" ' (*ne stal gopnikom*); and 'amassing information' (*nakoplenie informatsii*).

The centrality of 'communication' (*obshchenie*) in *tusovka* activity is evi-dent in the first category of meanings (the quantitative and qualitative improvement of human intercourse). Strictly defined *obshchenie* means 'intercourse, relations, links' but the verb *obshchat'sia* means 'to mix or associate with' and, more informally, 'to chat, talk'. The importance of this is that the communicative process of *obshchenie* is inclusive and communa-lizing. The root of the word '*obshch*' means 'general, common, public, social' and suggests a commonality leading to communality, e.g. *my nashli obshchii iazyk* – 'we found a common language' or, more colloquially, 'we hit it off'. Hence *obshchenie* is the process of 'doing, being or making social, public or common'.

The second and third categories primarily relate to the perceived effects of this *obshchenie* – the communality created. This is apparent in the sense of security lent to the individual by the group, which allows the intellectual and physical growth of the individual within the safe environment of the *tusovka*. But in order for the security to be maintained, the communality must be preserved. Hence the *tusovka* may become exclusive once the bounds of inclusivity have been established.

But why *embodied* communication? The first reason is that it helps distinguish *tusovka* activity from other forms of communication. As is apparent from Figure 7.1, socio-political groups were excluded from the *tusovka* world even though they often shared the same *tusovka* places. The key to their exclusion lies in interviewees' understanding of the activity of the political *neformaly* as being primarily associated with the articulation and dissemination of viewpoints, symbolized by the production and selling of newspapers. Be they formally or non-formally produced (and regardless of whether the intended end product was a young Communist, a reborn Russian nationalist, or a Western-orientated democrat) words, especially printed words, remained the vehicles of ideology and were rejected in favour of more physical forms of communication.

Second, the notion of the embodied nature of communication avoids dependency on articulated meanings proffered by interviewees in the analysis of cultural meanings of *tusovka* life. Such articulations suggest a high level of consciousness by young people of the part the *tusovka* plays in siting themselves in the world beyond the family and they are central to explanations of youth culture which see it as facilitating the transition from childhood to adulthood. This kind of structural-functionalist interpretation posits the *tusovka* as a space in which different forms of 'self' are developed, allowing the better management of this transition. Hence *tusovka* activity is seen not as *embodied* but *mind-ful* and young people as engaged in the process of 'identity-formation'.

'Resistance theories' of youth cultures also rely heavily on the notion of identity formation; the difference is that they see youth cultures as allowing young people to escape and resist the suburban culture of achievement and responsibility (Brake 1985: 190). Not only does this approach tend towards a romanticization of resistance and rebellion (which often ignores the way in which subcultures act to reproduce many dominant cultural meanings) but, like structural-functionalist approaches, it also prioritizes articulated reflections over behaviour. In this way, the subculture – being an extension of the peer group – acts as an alternative development route to the construction of an integrated sense of self in society – a social identity. In Brake's view, it is precisely the knowledge that they have taken a 'side road' which allows young people to subsequently discard their subcultural lifestyle and re-enter the dominant culture, declaring their subcultural identity to be simply part of adolescence (191). Thus, despite Brake's emphasis on the subculture's ability to provide a 'free area', a space away from 'the scrutiny and demands of the adult world', the room to develop 'alternative scripts', his analysis suggests an overwhelming pull back into the fixed subject positions of the dominant culture whereby the alternative identity is eventually discarded as 'no longer them' (ibid.).

A notion of 'embodied communication', on the other hand, should help move away from this fixity by grounding the notion of subcultural activity in the individual *and* the collective body. This is expressed in Phil Cohen's understanding of youth cultures as working not only in reaction to, but also acting within the codes which structure youth experience. Working-class youth cultures, he argues, may: disrupt these codes providing new forms of practice (especially in the sexual and recreational spheres); act selectively on codes to sometimes strengthen an otherwise weak combination (such as in the racialization of the male, working-class community seen in the 'skinhead solution' or the development of independent options by young working-class women often through early pregnancy and single-parent households); or facilitate the incorporation of elements of working-class codes within middle-class ones and vice versa (through social mobility of the individual) (Cohen, P. 1986: 62–5). Cohen's attention to the bodily location of youth cultural strategies not only advances a more sophisticated approach to the interaction of class and youth than notions of working-class youth's 'status problems' or their 'symbolic resistance', it also opens up new avenues for analysis of ethnographic data. The more flexible understanding of the structure of both youth and adult worlds, as well as their shifts and restructurings, helps break down the search for identity problems and their resolutions, oppressions and resistances. In other words, it allows the possibility of confirmations *and* refutations, resistance *and* conformity, 'delinquency' *and* achievement.

But these new avenues of analysis must be informed by attention to another concept which, whilst obvious, is often underplayed in studies of youth culture. The activities of the youth cultural group, which are under observation and analysis, may constitute work to the researcher, but to the young people themselves they are essentially and primarily *pleasurable*. The analytic importance of the introduction of the concept of pleasure lies in its multiplicity of sites and forms. Here Barthes' distinction between *plaisir* and *jouissance* is useful. Whereas *plaisir* may be attributed to a conscious pleasure in self-growth through improving one's knowledge about a music form, developing new friends and widening one's social circles, *jouissance* is theorized as a moment of pleasure when the body breaks free from social and cultural control, when a single moment of pleasure induces a loss of self and of the subjectivity that controls and governs the self (Fiske 1989: 50).

This distinction facilitates the analysis of the activities of youth cultural groups not only as processes of the construction of self but of the deconstruction of socially constructed selves. It is these *jouissant* forms of youth cultural activity which are securely located in the body (loud rhythmic music, pumping iron, release through drugs and alcohol) and which 'embody' the communication of the *tusovka*. In this sense although the raw materials and forms of the activity of subcultural groups (rock music, complex drug and alcohol compounds, semiotically sophisticated dress styles) are generally seen as being a product of the fast pace and complex nature of urban lifestyles, their meanings may be intentionally simple invoking a pre-urban and communalizing space; a space in which there might be a temporary liberation from the established order which allows a communication impossible in everyday life.[4]

What follows is an analysis of this special type of communication found in one Moscow *tusovka*.

## PLEASURE AND SUBJECTIVITY: FORMS AND SITES OF 'EMBODIED COMMUNICATION'

The observations, conversations and interview responses concerning the cultural practices of Moscow *tusovki* revealed three key sites of 'embodied communication': music and dance; style; and play. Discussing each in turn, the following analysis will focus on the *tusovka* of the Moscow *stiliagi* but refer to other *tusovki* and other youth cultural forms where relevant.

### Music and dance

The accepted critical appreciation of Soviet rock of the mid-1980s is that it lays much greater weight on lyrics and text than does contemporary Western, rhythm-dominated rock music (Troitsky 1989). Members of the Soviet rock fraternity confirm this: the lead singer of 'Alisa', Kostia Kinchev, has argued that it is precisely this attention to text which clearly distinguishes Soviet rock (and implicitly *authentic*) music from the new, commercialized pop music (Gasparian 1990).

Without knowing how this weight is calculated (whether subjectively on the basis of the relative importance accorded to each by music producers, whether more objectively on the basis of content analyses of the ratio of music to text, or whether ideologically on the basis of the estimated level of social meaning in texts), it is impossible to confirm or dispute this claim. If it is true, however, the reasons for the predominance of text over music are much more complex than suggested by the attribution of ideological motivation to Soviet rock musicians on the grounds of their heritage in the 'underground'.

This is not to dismiss the ideological factor completely. Instead it is to bring to light other explanations (only tenuously linked to ideology) of why text might predominate over music in Soviet rock. These include: the traditional popularity of bard music with its mixture of poetry and song; the retained communality of the singing act kept alive in the Russian folk choir and student campfire songs; the greater scope in the West for developing interesting instrumental sections or pieces due to better and more widespread access to technical equipment; and the relatively weak development in the former Soviet Union of noise music which requires its disseminator (the ghetto blaster) and spaces free from societal noise control.

Such a questioning of the assumption that Soviet rock is inherently text-dominated arises from indications from those interviewed in Moscow that, on the contrary, music overrode text. First, new, and less well-known music producers and performers who were interviewed declared their aim to be precisely the movement away from what they referred to as 'the overemphasis of text'. This phenomenon may well be peculiar to Moscow; certainly there was a conscious attempt to define a Moscow voice through a rejection of the heavily social and political texts of the dominant Leningrad perestroika rock scene (often referred to disparagingly as 'red rock'). Alternatively, it could be read as a reaction among young rock musicians to the first wave of Soviet rock. This would confirm the claim that original Soviet rock was indeed text-based. Finally, it might also suggest that text-dominated rock had become predominant because other forms of music activity had simply never been allowed the space for development. Given that rock music did not only need to prove itself benign but of positive ideological merit (see Chapter 2), music with a heavy text-base was, ironically, at an advantage over more music-dominated forms in gaining official approval. This situation might be compared to the hostility with which empirical sociology or abstract art have been treated in the past. Where the meaning is not spelled out the audience ceases to receive a message but creates her/his own interpretation, and this is much less readily controlled and therefore more subversive.

The second reason for suspecting that there has always been at least a strong undercurrent of rhythm- and beat-orientated music is that music use among the youth cultural groups included in the research project centred around rhythm or noise dominated music forms (heavy metal, hard rock, punk rock and rock 'n' roll). Although this music use included listening to Western groups (primarily classics such as Elvis Presley, Chuck Berry, Deep Purple, the Scorpions and the Sex Pistols), this must be seen within the context of the prestige associated with knowledge and possession of such music, and the fact that the same young people also listened extensively to home-grown bands. For the *stiliagi*, the sites of music-listening – gigs, concerts, discos, around a tape-recorder on the street or in the metro, or around a live band on the Arbat – confirmed that text and words were very much subordinate to the immediate sensation of the music. Even where particular tracks did have audible lyrics, their meaning for the listeners was limited by their knowledge of English which tended to be chorus-line deep. Soviet bands followed by the *stiliagi*, on the other hand, sang predominantly in Russian and the words of their songs were often known by heart. Nevertheless, the importance of this knowledge lay not in the meanings embedded in the texts, but those which emerged out of the joint singing at concerts and in the metro on the way home from them. An associated ritual centred on dance. At each metro station where one of the group was leaving, the group would get out of the carriage and dance a farewell number on the platform around the cassette recorder before boarding the next train.

It is true that one band followed by many *stiliagi* – 'Brigada S' – did have a reputation for producing heavily sarcastic or ironic songs with a political motif (titles such as 'They', 'The Man in the Hat' and 'Stop Following Us' speak for themselves) and, as a result, they were periodically accused by the press of having fascistic tendencies. Given that Sukachev and the band were writing songs in mid-1980s Russia, it would be almost impossible not to have reflected some of the social and political turmoil going on around them. Even 'Brigada S', however, remained primarily committed to the development of style, declaring their peculiar sound to be 'new-punk-jazz'. The other Soviet band around which the revivalist *stiliagi* were centred, 'Bravo', was even more clearly style-orientated, taking up the rhythms of early American rock 'n' roll and imbuing them with the distinctive sound and look of the lead singer, Zhanna Aguzarova. The texts of 'Bravo' were light-weight, but this did not detract from their immense popularity, since music use was centred on rhythm.

The predominance of rhythm in the 'Bravo' songs echoed the displacement of melody as the dominant aspect of popular music by rhythm in 1950s' rock 'n' roll, which has been interpreted as the key to its phenomenal success (Bradley 1989: 169–70). This displacement had another important effect – music became synonymous with dancing. At discos the *stiliagi* would rush *en masse* on to the dance floor at the first beat of a rock 'n' roll number. Dancing for the *stiliagi* involved the acquisition of some basic steps (mainly twist, shake and jive) and certain members of the group were considered to be particularly good dancers. But prowess on the dance floor was not the prime denoter of respect in the group. Although later, more attention was paid to the techniques and forms of dancing (this will be discussed at greater length below), at the height of the *stil'naia tusovka*, those who treated rock'n'roll as a sport (the couples who came in trainers and loose clothing and danced paired rock 'n' roll) were derided.

The main meaning of the dancing was in the physical pleasure derived from it and the way it gave focus to the evening. At the cafe 'Moloko',[5] where weekly rock 'n' roll nights attracted *stiliagi* from all corners of Moscow, time would be passed in eager anticipation of a rock 'n' roll track (since the disc jockey interspersed them among more mainstream disco tracks) and the evening would be evaluated by how many tracks had been played. The period after the rock 'n' roll tracks had ended allowed time for a break to recover from the physical exertion and to have a smoke. The *jouissant* nature of this high energy exertion followed by relaxation need not be spelled out. In contrast to the controlled steps and sensual movements of the disco dancers, the *stiliagi* displayed frenzy: the invasion of the dance floor, the shrieks of delight with which each track was greeted, the distorted twists, wriggles and bends of the figures, the leaps and falls. But the periodization of the evening also worked to solidify the group feeling. The dance floor would be seized and controlled while rock 'n' roll was played. This was followed by a dramatic withdrawal from centre stage as soon as the beat changed. The post-dance relocation of the group and the rest period provided an opportunity for information to be swopped but also for would-be *stiliagi* to make contact with existing members of the *tusovka*.

## Style

A second aspect of embodied communication is the adornment of the body – the adoption of a distinctive or peculiar style. The importance of style has at one and the same time been overplayed and yet underestimated in explanations of Russian youth culture. It has generally been seen as meaningless *form* which is not rooted in Soviet reality but copied or imitated from images of Western subcultural styles and for this reason it is considered to be devoid of socio-cultural content. At the same time, since the groups are seen as being all form and no content their style has been taken as their defining characteristic.

The issue of style has been considered seriously in analyses of youth cultural groups only in isolated cases and even then employed only as visual evidence of the Westernizer-deviant versus neo-Stalinist-conformist dichotomy (see Chapter 4). Punks, hippies, heavy metal fans and others are seen as aiming to shock the general public with their haircuts, scruffiness and studs respectively, while the *liubery* express pride in their Soviet heritage through the sporting of a smart, clean-cut proletarian style. The relationship between style and youth cultural strategy is more complex than this and in the following section the importance of style in denoting alternative youth cultural strategies among Moscow youth will be explored, as well as the meaning of style within the *tusovka* of the *stiliagi*.

As suggested by the group's name, style (*stil'*) is central to the identity of the *stiliagi*. As was noted in the previous chapter, *stil'* is a re-creation of rock 'n' roll styles originally worn by the *stiliagi* of the 1950s but since, later, styles of the early 1960s were incorporated into the *stil'* of the *stiliagi* rather than being seen as a separate entity, *stil'* to Western eyes looks like a curious mixture between ted and mod styles – perhaps not dissimilar to the trend known as the 'stylists' who also sported a hybrid style (Hamblett and Deverson 1964: 20).

The 'gear' or dress (*prikid*) of contemporary *stiliagi* is an assemblage of items recalling the styles of the 1950s and early 1960s and their interpretations by retro-bands such as 'Bravo', and to a lesser extent 'Brigada S'. *Stil'*, therefore, was much more than 'a sort of uniform' of 'Bravo' fans as Dugin suggests (Dugin in Zaitsev 1990: 79). Certainly the style contained a number of essential or immutable parts for identification (the uniform factor), but just as important were the elements that could be experimented with, made original and which enabled one to stand out from the group. Vital elements of the *prikid* were: pointed, lace-up shoes (*shuzy*), brightly coloured socks, narrow trousers (*dudochki*) or wide black trousers for *Bravisty*, white shirt, broad, garish tie, braces and double-breasted, wide jacket. Girls sometimes wore short, pleated or full skirts instead of the *Bravisty* trousers, with black stockings. Additional items which were worn or carried included document wallets, umbrellas, small briefcases, badges or brooches and caps. Narrow black sunglasses known as *kiski* (from the affectionate word for cat) or *lisichki* were also considered good *stil'*. Hairstyles included the teddy-boy quiff (*kok*) or long greased-back fringe (copying the lead singer of 'Brigada S', Igor' Sukachev) with optional long sideburns (*baki*). Girls adopted simple, short styles or Zhanna Aguzarova-looks including long false plaits, ponytails or buns. Within the *tusovka*, individuals sometimes took up a particular distinctly 1950s or distinctly 1960s style – the former being associated with *dudochki* and wide, garish ties, the latter with wide trousers and narrow ties (*seledki*). The *seledki* though were generally associated with the group 'Sekret' which was not liked by the *stiliagi* and so few sported them.

The basic style was personalized by the 'quirks' (*fen'ki*) of particular members which became part of an individual's persona within the group. This was often reflected in nicknames given to members of the group e.g. *Kletchatii* (literally meaning 'checked', because he wore a checked jacket), *Zolotoi* (literally meaning 'golden' because he had a gold-coloured tie), *Dotsent* (literally meaning 'lecturer' because his style was particularly smart and he carried a document wallet), *Brezhnev* (after the former General Secretary of the CPSU because he was notable for the amount of brooches and badges he wore,[6] and *Kerensky* (after the leader of the Provisional Government, because of his military style of dress). Although other nicknames evolved from funny incidents (*prikoly*) which had taken place during *tusovki* or as carry-overs from school nicknames, most were associated with one's *prikid*.

But what is the meaning of this style? Firsthand reports of encounters with *stiliagi* in Russia in the 1950s suggest a simple relationship between their style and their Western orientations. One journalist, describing his meeting with a *stiliaga* in Moscow, declared that, 'The hallmark of success for a *stiliago* (*sic*) is the acquisition of genuine Western clothes' since for him, 'The [communist] present was made bearable only by acting out a charade of Westernization' (MacGregor-Hastie 1961: 71). This is a viewpoint with which the poet Voznesensky seems to agree. In a commentary on his poem 'Beatnik's monologue', he notes that:

> the *stiliaga* phenomenon was mainly focused on clothes and dance, and in most cases it was a caricature, because they simply did not have

*Plate 5*
*Stiliagi* in February 1989.

*Plate 6* The popularity of revivalist rock 'n' roll bands 'Bravo' and 'Brigada S' heavily influenced *stil'*.

enough information about Western culture . . . When the jeans came, there weren't any *stiliagis* left.

(Voznesenskii in Lauridsen and Dalgard 1990: 43–4)

The meaning of style for contemporary *stiliagi*, it is argued here, is less in reflecting any Western or American orientation than in invoking their direct forbears, the Soviet *stiliagi* of the 1950s. In its reworked form, the style loses its Westernizing nature since the symbols adopted are no longer those which signify 'West'. This becomes apparent if the style of the *stiliagi* is contrasted to that of other *tusovki* also associated with American rock 'n' roll. The *rokabilly*, for example, adopted a more recognizably American style: leather jackets, checked shirts or T-shirts, jeans, bandannas and cowboy boots (*kazaki*). The gear of the more prestigious *rokery* (bikers) is similar although more designer orientated – particularly valued are items emblazoned with Harley Davidson insignia – and, in contrast, the *stiliagi* looked old-fashioned and quaint. For the *stiliagi* then, their 'style' gave them the opportunity not to look trendy and/or Western but to 'stand out from the crowd', to 'make everyone look at you' and 'to differentiate yourself from others'. These 'others' were 'the mass of youth' who, as far as the *stiliagi* were concerned, were the ones aping Western fashions.

The adoption of *stil'* by the *stiliagi* of the 1980s is best understood, therefore, not as an indication of rebellious resistance to Soviet or adult dress codes, but as invoking an earlier time which appeared to them to be one of real 'opening up', when people and their values were more forthright and genuine. The clean, smart 1950s' style they adopted allowed them to stand out from the youth crowd and thus rise above the banality to which Soviet reality had been reduced. This 'standing out to get out' strategy is one associated in Britain with the mods as well as the teddy boys, with whom the style of the *stiliagi* is normally compared, but is also nicely captured in Elizabeth Wilson's description of the American hipster as 'a typical lower class dandy' whose outward elegance was adopted in order 'to distinguish him from the gross impulsive types that surrounded him in the ghetto' and acted as an outward expression of his aspiration to 'the finer things in life' (Wilson 1985: 200). If one substitutes *gopniki* for 'gross impulsive types' and everyday banality (*poshlost'*) for 'ghetto', then the closeness of the strategy becomes apparent. Becoming a *stiliaga* meant:

> not becoming a *gopnik* like other friends, not starting to drink and beat others up but rising above them.
>
> (S)[7]

This upward orientation is clearly expressed in the *stiliaga* style. There was no desire to shock or intimidate the general public – this was a trait the *stiliagi* attributed to the *rokery* and the punks. If a shock value is to be found, then it is in their cleanliness, tidiness and politeness, in their white and well-ironed shirts, polished shoes and civil replies to (even abusive) passers-by.

As the above quote suggests, however, the upward orientation is relational to other youth cultural strategies and is neither a direct reflection of Western orientation nor of class position. In the 1950s, the *stiliagi* were associated with an elite of mainly students and young people whose parents' position gave them access to Western goods (see Chapter 7). This heritage was recognized by revivalist *stiliagi* who noted that many of the original *stiliagi* had become well-known intelligentsia figures of today. They expressed a pride in this, but no aspiration to it. They saw the original group members as embodying the spirit of their time by taking up the new opportunities offered by the so-called cultural thaw and following the most current trends which became increasingly accessible as the Soviet Union opened up to the West.

The first wave of *stiliagi* embodied the zeitgeist not only in a spiritual but also a material sense. Consumerist mentality in the Soviet Union is generally traced to the 'little deal' of the Brezhnev period by which the population's political compliance was rewarded by a blind eye being turned to second economy activity (Millar 1985). The relation between citizenship of the first socialist state and the acquisition of material things is more complex than this, however, and has played an important role in the negotiation of social relations throughout the history of the Soviet Union. Vera Dunham, for example, talks about the 'Big Deal' struck between the Stalinist regime and the newly emergent Soviet middle class of white-collar administrators and professionals (Fitzpatrick 1988: 20). Under Stalin, the material manifestations of such 'middle-class' values were confined to the new class and, when politically convenient, could still be denounced as evidence of a bourgeois lifestyle. Under Khrushchev, however, a commitment to the lowering of differentials in income, the narrowing of the urban–rural divide and the equalizing of educational opportunities allowed these values to be extended across the Soviet population. Furthermore, Soviet citizens under Khrushchev were actually being invited to participate in the 'catching up with the West' as consumer-citizens; it was in per capita production and consumption not political correctness that Khrushchev declared the Soviet Union would surpass the United States by 1980.

In this sense, the *stiliagi* of the 1950s were not a deviant subculture but a stylish embodiment of the spirit of the times – they had already caught up with the West. Bearing this in mind, it becomes more comprehensible why one *stiliaga* in 1989 noted that the nearest contemporary equivalent to the original *stiliagi* were not their revivalists (who tried to recreate the optimistic spirit of the post-war period when the future looked bright for all) but those who were referred to as the *mazhory*[8] – for it was the latter who caught the mood of the designer-orientated 1980s in which the rich got richer and the poor poorer (E). The similarities between the original *stiliagi* and the *mazhory* is articulated by the emigre writer Vasilii Aksenov in his description of a party he attended as a student in Moscow in 1952 where he found himself among a group of high society (mainly the offspring of diplomats) dressed in *stiliaga* style. In fact, he discovered, the group did not consider themselves *stiliagi* but '*shtatniki*' and were distinguished by a love for the States which 'had gone so far that they rejected everything which was not American, even if it was French' (Aksenov 1987: 15).

The connection between privilege, access and youth cultural association was as much a feature of the 1950s as it was of the 1980s, therefore, and the orientation towards commodity culture found among Russian youth today is not born exclusively of political disillusionment in the Brezhnev period of 'stagnation' (*zastoi*) but is historically rooted in Soviet culture. Below, questions of the interaction of class position, commodity culture and Western aspirations will be considered by contrasting contemporary *stiliaga* strategy in relation to those adopted by two other youth cultural groups: the *mazhory* and the *gopniki*.

### From privilege to commodity culture: the case of the mazhory

That the Moscow *stiliagi* were often accused of having privileged backgrounds was evident from their ready refutations of any such suggestion with the claim that there were 'all sorts' of people in their *tusovka*. The limited background data collected by the author seems to be bear this out, providing that the reference group is taken to be that of Moscow and not the Russian population as a whole (see Appendix).

Further evidence to this end was that, beyond protecting themselves from accusations of elitism, the *stiliagi* interviewed showed no real signs of class identity. Of course, this might also be said of British teenagers, for example. But, although among the latter, class might not be recognized as such, its signifiers – such as accent, parents' job or car – almost certainly would. Among Moscow teenagers, on the other hand, the nearest to a consciousness of class encountered was the recognition of 'privilege'. Privilege was associated with *access* to things and the only concrete discussions of differential access within the *stiliagi* concerned the size and location of flats in which people lived (from communal flats to 3–4 bedroomed flats, and from flats located outside the Moscow boundary – or at the end of the metro lines – to those virtually in the city centre). This confirms the earlier argument that it was space rather than class as such which was the chief indicator of privilege for young people. Even this acknowledged privilege, however, was generally attributed not to socio-structural factors but to 'luck'.

There was one relation of privilege which was seen as structural by those interviewed; the access to things (commodities) as a result of the political position of one's parents. This privileged access had its youth cultural expression in the group known as the *mazhory* and the ambiguous and changing relation of the *stiliagi* to the *mazhory* is indicative of the way in which the relationship class–commodity–West–style is being reconstructed.

At the beginning of 1989, the Moscow *stiliagi* clearly saw the *mazhory* as an 'other'. At that time the term *mazhory* was used primarily to indicate those of 'highly placed parents' (*vysokopostavlennie roditeli*), a young elite who were to be scorned.[9] Style was an important site of antagonism. The chief visual attribute of the *mazhory* was that they dressed in Western, designer (*firmennie*) clothes. Reportedly, within the *mazhory* there were groups of 'pseudo Italians', 'pseudo French' and 'pseudo Americans', referring to the country of origin of their clothes and thus what particular style they were adopting (Fain 1990: 24). These subtle distinctions were not noted by those interviewed by the author; the importance of *mazhory* style to them was simply that it was Western and therefore acted as an outward manifestation of social position. Thus, if the *stiliagi* were 'standing out to get out', the *mazhory* strategy appeared to be one of 'getting out to stand out', since their ability to be different was dependent upon their foreign connections.

In contrast, the *stiliagi* did not purchase style but created it. The components of *stil'* were not bought on the black market or brought back by contacts from foreign visits, but hunted for at the Tishinskii market – a local flea-market where old clothes were sold second hand for anything from a few kopeks to a few roubles. As far as the *stiliagi* themselves were concerned this set them apart from the 'mass' of youth who were obsessed with fashionable clothes (*shmotki*) and who, in order to satisfy this obsession, had to scrounge from their parents and invest most of their time, money and energy in dealings with the speculator-controlled clothes market. To the *stiliagi*, the *mazhory* were just those who had access to what the mass of normal youth wanted – they were not *neformaly*, therefore, just privileged *formaly*.

There is evidence, however, to suggest that the relationship of class–commodity–West–style is changing. By 1991, the way in which the opening up of the economy had begun to affect perceptions of class was more than apparent. The major *tusovka* of the *mazhory* in 1991 was generally held to be the new McDonalds restaurant on Pushkin Square. Although the initial, universal attraction of the restaurant quickly declined due to the steep price rises rapidly introduced, nevertheless, its central position and its late opening hours meant it remained a key place of interaction for a variety of Moscow youth cultural groups. Consequently, there was a growing interaction between the *mazhory* and other youth cultural trends which served to weaken some of the sense of 'otherness'. Another important factor was the opening of many more shops selling foreign goods for roubles (*kommissionie*). Although prices were highly inflated, nevertheless the proliferation of these shops meant that access to the symbols of high class (foreign clothes, perfume, cigarettes and beer) became less dependent upon foreign connections than on cash.

By summer 1991, the term *mazhory* had undergone considerable slippage. It had acquired two additional, and, at a surface level, contradictory meanings. The *mazhory* were not only the children of well-connected parents but also a self-made elite, a new class of business people (*delovie liudi*) or *fartsovshchiki*. At the same time, *mazhor* had come to indicate a birthright, a class position into which one was born. The two categories cease to appear contradictory when one considers the fact that for many people economic liberalization appeared as a process of the transformation of old, intangible privilege into new, and very tangible, wealth. Thus, although interviewees continued to exclude the *mazhory* from the category of *tusovki* this was now because they were considered to constitute not a reprehensible and 'other' way of life but a social stratum or class position into which one was born or had risen through 'doing business'. It was now deemed perfectly possible to be a *mazhor* and a *stiliaga* at the same time, or more likely, to progress from the latter to the former.

Style, then, has been a very important site of Russian youth culture. At one level it has acted simply as a subcultural identifier in the contemporary urban jungle and highlights the significance of social anomie, immigration and ghettoization in former Soviet society. The lack of conscious class identification amongst young Russians reinforces this aspect of style as opposed to that suggested by British subculturalists such as Clarke *et al.* (see Chapter 1). Moreover the importance of 'the West' in Russian youth cultural strategies intervenes in the class–commodity–style relationship and disrupts the upward/downward binary of working-class youth cultural orientation. Using the above explanatory model, for example, the *stiliagi* would seem to be simultaneously adopting both an upward and a downward orientation. By setting themselves apart from the *gopniki* and adopting their peculiar style and behavioural norms, they projected an upward orientation like that of the teddy boys (in their appropriation of upper-class Edwardian dress) or the mods (who attempted to abstract themselves from their ascribed class location with a neat, hip image). In order to create this style, though, the *stiliagi* re-appropriated parts of the Soviet past, and directly built on their parent culture,[10] in a way associated in British subculturalist literature with the skinheads' celebration of working-class style.

The relationship between parent culture and youth cultural strategy then must be explored further if it is to be useful in explaining Russian subcultural activity, and this is taken up in the discussion of the different youth cultural strategies adopted by the *stiliagi* and the *gopniki* which follows. A comparison of these two strategies in relation to both parent culture and dominant culture offers an alternative explanation of the roots of youth cultural activity to those given by Soviet sociologists who, as was shown in

Chapter 4, have tended to view it as a product of widespread social disaffection and anomie.

*Centre and periphery: the legacy of Soviet modernization*

The modernization and urbanization programme undertaken in the Soviet Union at once created centripetal and centrifugal forces. The economic planning system meant that decisions were taken at the centre (be it All-Union, republican or regional) and passed down to the more peripheral units. Thus, just as had been the case in pre-revolutionary Russia, prestige and power accrued to those who were in central locations. This was underscored in the Soviet period by the ideological weight placed upon, and thus additional social prestige accorded to, the urban proletariat in the forging of a new society. Urban centres have remained better provided for in terms of housing, public services and social and cultural facilities and thus the cultural distinctions between those from 'the centre' and those from 'the provinces' remain prominent in popular consciousness. This ideology of urban superiority, though, went hand in hand with that of egalitarianism, and although the centre acted to reinforce old privileges, it also attempted to redistribute the fruits of national economic progress. The consequence is a latent sense of injustice amongst both central and peripheral residents that finds clear expression in the youth cultural sphere.

Before relations between youth cultural groups are explored, however, it is important to locate the youth cultural space itself in relation to the dominant culture. Although the press discussion of youth cultural activity might lead one to expect to find it buried in its own basements and archways or aimlessly roaming the uncontrolled streets of the city, in fact those who participated in *tusovka* life generally sited their activity in specific, open and densely peopled spaces. In Moscow, these places could be of three kinds: general *tusovochnie* places; spaces shared by a limited number of groups; and meeting places exclusive to a particular *tusovka*. Examples of the first category would be the Arbat or Pushkin Square where all manner of *tusovki* took place. Places shared by a limited number of groups included many cafes such as the 'Moloko' or 'Prospekt', the 'Catacombs' (the old trade centre behind GUM where a raised, stone, rectangular, covered walkway overlooking a courtyard provided a dry and warm hang-out for a number of groups), the metro station '*Iashka*' (*Ploshchad' Sverdlova*, now renamed *Teatral'naia*), the courtyard of Sadovaia no. 52 (originally inhabited by Bulgakov fans but which subsequently became the hang-out of young punks as well as acting as a useful, secluded but central spot for trading). Exclusive meeting places of the *stiliagi* included Tishinskii market and the bench opposite the Prague restaurant, while the cafe 'Margarita' was known to be a *rokery* hang-out and Maiakovskii Square and metro station were the haunt of the *Depesha*, before they were moved on by the police.

The culture of the basement (*podval*) is associated with those younger than average *tusovka* members and often marks a direct continuation of the *dvor* group, which takes to warmer and more sheltered spaces than the street or courtyard when winter sets in. In contrast, *tusovka* strategy seemed to be concerned not with finding alternative places for their activity, out of the way of mainstream society, but in reclaiming key urban spaces for their own play and pleasure.

This was more apparent among some *tusovki* than others. The claiming of the city streets after nightfall has long been one of the key activities of the *rokery* and is achieved through a never-ending battle for control with the traffic police (see Chapter 4). The *Komsomol* failed miserably to attract the *rokery* into its motorcycle clubs because it did not understand that to cycle within a controlled space would be to invert the central meaning of their activity – the gaining of control through the mastering of space. Other groups may have been less obviously concerned with the control of urban space, but their activity nevertheless reflected its importance. One of the rituals of the punks interviewed, for example, was a night-time roof-top wander. Again, a symbolic capturing of the city is evident – they even sometimes took a toy machine gun with them. Even among the *stiliagi*, one of the most romanticized activities was the night-time walks around Moscow, and one of the bitterest memories, the fact that the *gopniki* put a stop to these.

Claiming space then was crucial in determining relations between youth cultural groups as well as between youth groups and the 'formal' world. The battle for territory was not so much an issue between *tusovki* – who fairly amicably divided up the city centre – as between the *tusovki* and the *gopniki*.[11] In Moscow, physical altercations between *tusovki* and *gopnik* groups occurred where one or the other's space was violated: when members of *tusovki* gathered at concerts in suburban (and *gopnik* dominated) districts of the city; and when those from outside central areas were refused access to trendy discos or cafes in the centre. Of course, the theme of control of urban territory must be read in unison with other activities and strategies – in particular that of the assertion of gender identity – and the overlapping of codes of masculinity and the defence of territory are discussed at greater length below. Here, therefore, only the social background to issues of space and youth culture in the Russian context is outlined.

In order to explain the deep social divides resulting from spatial location, another aspect of the socio-economic development of Soviet society must be examined, i.e. the political. The first issue of importance is the political control of the modernization programme. The crash industrialization policy embarked upon in 1928 accorded primacy to the development of heavy industry, expanded the ranks of the urban proletariat by encouraging mass migration from the countryside into the newly-emerging industrial

*Plate 7* Lords of all they survey! Rooftop walking gives these punks a sense of control in the urban jungle.

*Plate 8* The *stiliagi* go missing from their usual haunt. The inscription reads, '*Stiliagi*! Where are you?' followed by the reply, 'We are here', dated 31 March 1991.

cities and facilitated rapid and long-range social mobility through its policy of *vydvizhenie* or worker promotion (Fitzpatrick 1978: 32). This policy was framed in an ideology of class war on the peasantry, however, and despite later attempts by both Khrushchev and Brezhnev to deal with the legacy of the impoverishment and disempowerment of the peasantry, their position remained unequal. In addition, the opportunities for upward social mobility through migration available in the early post-revolutionary period became curtailed through the introduction in 1932 of the system of internal passports. This system (which included the obligation to acquire a residence permit, *propiska*, in order to remain in a city) was used to limit migration into the most prestigious cities or so-called closed cities of the Soviet Union (Zaslavsky 1982: 137–40).[12] The political control of migration into closed cities gave them a peculiar nature, being characterized by an aging population, low birth-rate and constant labour shortage (141).

The latter factor, together with the social prestige and material benefits of living in such cities, has had two important social effects: it has facilitated a reproduction of the intelligentsia; and it has fuelled the formation of a new underclass of internal *gastarbeiter*. These are the migrant workers coming into the large cities (especially Moscow, St Petersburg and former republic capitals) in order to work and study, with the eventual aim of gaining a right to permanent residence (the granting of a *propiska*). Such migrant workers (referred to as *limitchiki* since they live and work *po limitu*, 'on the edge of the city') are despised by permanent urban dwellers who see them as depressing their own standard of living. They are accused of 'feeding off' the city by marrying or becoming pregnant in order to gain housing which should go to indigenous city-dwellers.[13] Attacks on hostels where they are housed are not uncommon. Where the migrant workers are of non-Russian ethnic origin and concentrated in a single area, however, *limitchiki* have been known to participate in conflict situations on the side of permanent residents against the non-Russian 'immigrants' (Osin 1989: 80).

The second political factor to shape spatial stratification was the attempt to foster a two-tier national identity among Soviet citizens. Soviet nationalities' policy which encouraged both the 'flowering' (*rastsvet*) of national cultures as well as their eventual 'drawing together' (*sblizhenie*) or, under Khrushchev, even 'merging' (*sliianie*) was founded on the assumption that political and cultural identities were separate ('national in form, socialist in content'). In other words, the institutions and practice of national language and culture were permissible whilst traditional, national forms of social, economic and political organization were forbidden. At the same time, the Soviet national identity which was being encouraged at the civic or political level was in fact saturated with cultural content. The failure to develop institutions of the RSFSR separate from Soviet ones, the Russification of minority languages and cultures and the glorification of the Russian people as the 'first among equals' in the Union meant that Soviet identity appeared to other ethnic groups to be synonymous with the acceptance of Russian imperialism.[14]

The centre–periphery divide, in both its urban–rural and its centre–republic/province guises, is one of the key factors determining inclusion and exclusion among Moscow *neformaly*. At a subjective level, ethnic identity was not a conscious part of *tusovka* identity; 'Russianness' was assumed. Even when directly questioned, interviewees would admit that it was obvious from physical characteristics that some people in the group were not Russian, or only partly Russian, but nevertheless insisted that ethnic origin was not an issue in inclusion or exclusion. Where the control of one's own space was less secure, however, the underlying structures of ethnic relations were exposed. Russian interviewees who had moved to Moscow after growing up in former Central Asian or Transcaucasian republics openly expressed racist views. Ironically, such views were often justified by reference to the relation between black and white people in the West. Non-Slavic peoples were often referred to as 'Soviet blacks' or 'our blacks', as if the ability to subordinate peoples of a different skin-colour was a prerequisite for entrance into the First-World club and, as such, wholly desirable.

The other key experience of ethnic difference was derived from military service. Letters from former members of the *tusovka* serving in the armed forces to the girls back in Moscow revealed how racial intolerance developed. In the army, Russian conscripts often found themselves in a minority position for the first time and, with the dominant and subordinate roles inverted, they complained bitterly of the emergence of cliques among certain ethnic groups who controlled and bullied the new 'outsiders'. In particular, there developed a hatred for Central Asians (referred to as '*uriuki*', literally meaning 'dried apricots' and a direct reference to skin colour or '*ali*', a more culturally derived term of abuse), and for Transcaucasians (called *churki*, literally meaning 'block or lump' and meant to indicate their dull-wittedness). In this environment embedded notions of who was and who was not 'like me' emerged very clearly: 'like me' were other Muscovites, failing them, other native Russians.

### Space and style: the case of the gopniki

Relations between centre and periphery did not need rooting in ethnic differences before they could be articulated. The common element between all those groups defined as *gopniki* and as such excluded from the *tusovki* by interviewees was that they were groups associated with the periphery, whether it be the periphery of European Russia (Kazan' and other Volga or Urals cities) or only of Moscow (Liubertsy and the Zhdanov district). Indeed Soviet sociologists have suggested that there is a clear link between aggressive subcultural lifestyles and the 'marginal culture' of the semi-urbanized. A marginal culture is seen to be characteristic of rural–

urban migrants as well as residents of suburban villages newly taken into city boundaries (in order to resolve labour shortage problems). It is manifested among young people in a desire to acquire and adopt the outer trappings of urban life without the concomitant spiritual values (Mialo 1988b: 40–1; Andreeva and Novikova 1988: 31–2). Without denying this, the key point here is surely not that the *tusovki* are made up of privileged, central youth who come into conflict with working-class, deprived youth from the peripheral areas but that the claiming of central urban space is a signifier of social prestige or pretension to such. In the case of the *stiliagi* the central location of the *tusovki* was part of an upwardly-orientated strategy. One *stiliaga* (from a peripheral part of Moscow similar in nature to Liubertsy) described why he became a member of a central *tusovka* thus:

> My friend and I were more outgoing [than the local lads], he is a punk, not like them and we began to become more or less well-known there, we became centralites (*tsentrovie*). He became a *stiliaga* as well and we went [into the centre] together . . .

> (S)

This interviewee came from an area just outside Moscow and one domi-nated by *gopnik* strategy. The peripheral nature of the area is experienced as a constraint. The term translated here as 'outgoing' is in fact *raskreposh-chennie*, literally meaning 'emancipated' or 'unchained' and is used in this context to suggest the bonds of the semi-urban or peripheral urban commu-nity which are escaped by venturing into the centre of the city and claiming spaces there through participation in a central *tusovka*. This did not mean that all ties with the home community were broken. Most of the female *stiliagi* retained former female friends (often from their schooldays) from whatever area of Moscow they had grown up in, while the lads often continued to hang out with their home crowd based either on school or the courtyard. One male interviewee who himself associated with the *Pushka tusovka* – the most central of the central *tusovki* – said that, in winter, when he could not be bothered to go into the centre because of the cold, he hung around the local area. It was possible, therefore to retain links with one's home crowd but at the same time to mark out a separate strategy for oneself, symbolized by its different location.

For groups which did not adopt the same kind of upward-orientation as the *stiliagi*, the centrality of their *tusovki* must be explained in different ways. The punks interviewed, for example, explained why the main punk *tusovka* was in the centre of the city thus:

> The people who gather there [in the central areas] are from those areas where there aren't any punks or so few of them that . . . they have to go into the centre because they have no-one to talk to (*obshchat'sia*).

> (L and M)

In contrast, they themselves spent little time in the centre, they said, because their district of Moscow had its own punk *tusovka*. These punks, however, were simply redrawing a centre–periphery divide. They clearly differentiated, for example, between their home area where they chose to hang out, and where the people were 'okay' and the next area to them (moving outwards from the centre) who they referred to as 'wide-trouser' types.

The grey areas between *tusovka* and *gopnik* strategies will be discussed at greater length below, here only one or two points directly related to the issues of space and youth cultural strategy will be developed. The *gopnik* strategy would appear to be most comparable to a skinhead style resistance through the reaffirmation, re-creation and reassertion of 'parent-culture'. If this is taken to be Soviet proletarian culture, then it is an analysis which has been well developed in relation to the most famous of the *gopnik* groups, the *liubery* (see Chapter 4 and especially the explanations offered by Davydov and Riordan). The thesis is that the relative deprivation in peripheral towns has left a frustrated youth, angry at the decadence of those growing up in more privileged locations. Alongside these ideologically-motivated 'have-nots' are placed the *Afgantsy*; young men who, having returned from military service in Afghanistan, were outraged by the slide into Western materialism they found among Soviet youth. These two sections of society (the latter often organizing, or leading the former) were seen as providing the social base for the activity of 'vigilante' or 'muscular socialist' groups such as the *liubery*. The ideological motivation of the *liubery* may be challenged, however, by considering their other activities, which rarely featured in press reports and which strongly suggest that *liuber* activity is just one example of a wider *gopnik* strategy.

The point of departure for an alternative analysis must be the differentiated nature of 'parent culture' (see above) and the possibility of partial reaffirmations of that culture. Like the British skinheads, the *liubery* borrowed from the parent culture by espousing the values of the proud, Soviet worker and taking onto the streets his (*sic*) defence against Western decadence. In this sense the *liubery* take up and embody elements inscribed in Soviet ideology. Like the skinheads, however, the majority of the *liubery* remained essentially apolitical and their activities and strategy were closer to the wider phenomenon of *gopnik* activity than to the politicized self-help or justice-seeking groups which emerged in the perestroika period as part of a rebirth of community-based politics. This becomes apparent if the *liubery* are compared to groups in other, more peripheral, Russian cities where their's is the dominant form of youth cultural activity. The example considered here is that of Cheboksary.

Situated on the right bank of the Volga and the capital of the Chuvash Autonomous Republic, Cheboksary has a population of over 300,000 and its major industries are textiles and electrical equipment production. The city is one of a number along the Volga which has experienced a sharp rise in youth gang fighting although most media attention has been focused on the situation in Kazan'. In contrast to the discussion in Chapter 4 of the development of the 'moral panic' about this phenomenon in the central press, the picture of life as a teenager in Cheboksary painted below draws primarily from first-hand accounts of that life contained in letters to the local youth paper, *Molodoi Kommunist*.[15]

These accounts revealed that in each district of the city gangs compete for influence, leaving the majority of Cheboksary teenagers caught up in the battle and in a state of constant terror. Lads are forced to pay into the gang central fund (*obshchak*) from the age of twelve or thirteen and newcomers into the district must pay for their '*propiska*' (residence permit), the right to which would be haggled over by competing gangs. Dues are collected weekly or monthly and those who do not pay what is owed would be put on a 'meter' which added an interest to their debt daily. Any lad refusing to join the local gang (*sbor*) would be subjected to sexual humiliation by the gang, just as would any girl who refused to sleep with one of the group leaders. Yet if a girl submitted (believing that it was better to lose her virginity than to lose both her virginity *and* her pride), the gang would spread rumours to the effect that not only had she been 'had' but that she had not been a virgin anyway (Eremin 1991a). There is considerable evidence that these gangs have strong links with the criminal underworld and that criminal subcultural practice is transmitted to a wide section of the city's youth via gang members returning from prison (Eremin 1991b; Mialo 1988a).

More important in terms of making comparisons between Moscow *liuber* and Volga city *gopnik* activities, however, is another practice known as '*obut'*' (literally meaning to 'shoe' or 'provide with shoes'). The practice of *obut'* in contemporary *gopnik* culture involves the forceful appropriation of Western-style clothes and accessories from their wearers. Analysis of *liuber* activity has suggested that these Western symbols are taken from their subcultural owners as a mark of ideological protest (Osin 1989: 78). Nevertheless, it is recognized by some observers that the objects taken are generally sold or traded on the black market, and even that the older *liubery* primarily attack and rob *fartsovshchiki* (Iakovlev 1987a: 21). This practice may not seem very different from the mugging of teenagers by their peers for their Reeboks in the West, but there is one striking difference. It would appear that the clothes and other items taken by Soviet teenagers are not worn by the perpetrators of the crime themselves.

An ideological explanation of this fact can be found in discussion of *liuber* activity; early journalistic reports noted that a smart dress-style consisting of white shirts, jackets and thin ties was adopted in order to symbolize the group's rejection of the spectacular dress-styles of 'Westernizing' subcultural groups (see Chapter 4). However, by 1988 Moscow *tusovka* members were identifying *liubery* as those dressed in (Soviet) track-suits and trainers or in widish Soviet-made trousers with jumpers tucked in at the waist and thus suggesting not their role as ideological 'cleansers' or 'menders' but nevertheless a distinctive style of dress which did not conform to Western norms.

Among the Volga city gangs the same confusion is apparent. One journalist suggested that girls involved in Cheboksary *gopnik* gangs mugged other girls in order to obtain the clothes and other fashion items that they desired and which their parents could not afford (Ivanova 1990). Other observers argued that although expensive clothes, watches, jewellery, shoes (and even stockings and underwear) would be taken from victims of their attacks, the preferred style of the gangs themselves would be the wide trousers or long skirts so derided by the Muscovites (Eremin 1991b; Kuz'mina 1991).

The different explanations are not mutually exclusive if one sees the fighting between teenage gangs and the muggings (*obut'*) as separate practices. Gang fighting is usually between people dressed in the same way, and it is a matter of honour among gang members not to steal from those left injured, while the muggings are directed against those with designer jeans who go to the special schools and who are not involved in gang fighting (Mialo 1988a: 42). The practices of the *liubery*, originally also differentiated, became merged in media representations which saw both practices as fuelled by an ideological mission. As one journalist – himself a resident of Liubertsy – noted, at first the Liubertsy district was divided between conflicting zones (village against village) and the fights were between different groups of local lads and between Muscovites and lads from Liubertsy. The confrontation between them and metallists, hippies and punks only came later and for the *liubery* they remained simply the inhabitants of another village (Epifanov 1988: 35).

If style itself is recognized as a key signifier of spatial power, however, it becomes possible to see the two practices as linked at a deeper level. The centrality of the conflict over style is visible in letters to *Molodoi Kommunist*. Some of the teenagers who wrote to the paper clearly coveted Western styles and envied those young people who could afford or had means of access to them. Some girls wrote to praise lads they had met in the city who 'were so smartly dressed that when I saw them I thought that they were foreigners' (Lenochka 1990), while others bemoaned the state of Cheboksary girls and pleaded with them to 'at least pick up a fashion magazine' (Ferida, Izaura and Karen 1990). Teenagers from Moscow and Leningrad visiting the city wrote in to tell the Cheboksary teenagers how old-fashioned they looked and to give hints on how they should be dressing. According to one, girls should wear 'light make-up, mini-skirts with leather or denim jackets' while the lads should stop 'swimming in their trousers' and wear 'grey (but not wide) trousers or jeans with a denim or leather jacket' (Serii *et al.* 1990). Another complained that:

> there are no cool lads in your city – they all have the same haircut, like

schoolboys. There are no 'Bros'-cuts and no Pyramids,[16] even though they have been in fashion for two years now. Girls look like they are 30 not 16 and there are no nice legs – they all wear *long* skirts.

(Oksana 1990: 12)

Other letters, however, showed a pride in an alternative fashion distinct from that dictated by Moscow and Leningrad, and which expressed a proudly provincial identity. One letter declared that 'the best lads and girls are ours, in Cheboksary. The best fashion is ours. The best city is Cheboksary.' (Pavlik and Serii 1990). Another more tentatively sought confirmation of this:

> surely it's true that there is nothing better than Cheboksary. Aguzarova praised our fashion. And why should we follow the example of Leningraders, Muscovites and Kievans? They come and then write that 'it's terrible here, the girls are horrible, the lads completely mad' . . . But everyone should have their own fashion. What difference does it make how wide your trousers are or how long your skirt is? We don't walk around showing off our legs.

('Sad April' 1990: 12)

The insecurity of young people in the Volga and other peripheral cities has been linked to their loss of ethnic identity (Chuvash, Tartar, Kazakh, etc.) in the process of Sovietization (Eremin 1991b). This can only ever be a partial explanation, however, since the situation is not peculiar to certain regions or ethnic groups. On the contrary, it is argued here, space is central to all Russian youth cultural strategies and it is an inherently personal and political issue since the control of space must be won over others.

In the first period of field work in Moscow (1988–9) a number of young people explained their attraction to, and movement between, *tusovki* by a desire to find 'my place' (*svoe mesto*) in society. When the later work did not reveal the same concern, this articulation of motive was attributed to learned response; it repeated many common-sense understandings of why young people chose youth cultural options and echoed the sentiments expressed in the popular film of the time *Is it Easy to be Young?* which was subtitled 'About those who seek their place in life'. In retrospect, however, the centrality of finding space in youth cultural strategies must be reasserted.

The more extensive field work with the *stiliagi* did not produce the same spontaneous reference to the need to find *svoe mesto* because this space had, temporarily, been found in the *tusovka*. In contrast, those interviewed in the first period of field work were a more varied group of young people whose *tusovka* careers were similarly chequered. A second important explanatory factor here is gender. The first period of field work was conducted almost exclusively with young men, whose spatial security was constantly threatened by imminent military conscription. Military service not only displaced young people physically and emotionally, but postponed the moment when one's place in society would be fixed. This was particulary resented by those returning from their military service who appeared embittered by the fact that, in terms of self-development (career, education and personal relations), they were two years behind those who had not served. Since, in the later work, many more girls were interviewed, this threatened disruption of the created, subcultural space did not feature as prominently. It is also true that female interviewees on the whole retained a much stronger link with the formal world and their place within it, the structural reasons for which are explained in Chapter 1.

The need to find one's place in society is not restricted to the period of adolescence and thus resolved upon full integration (socialization) into the adult world. Russian cultural history is laden with images of those who fail to find their place. This is the fate of the well known hero of Russian literature, the 'superfluous man' (*lishnii chelovek*) whose appearance in a series of works (most notably those of Turgenev and Goncharov) in the mid-nineteenth century epitomizes the demise of the Russian gentry class who became socially redundant following the ending of obligatory state service in 1762. But the superfluous man had earlier incarnations (in the works of both Pushkin and Griboedov) and elements of him are evident in Dostoevskii's 'insulted and injured' characters who experience a more urban alienation and dehumanization and whose anguish sends them into the underground from where they express their anger and bitterness.

For contemporary Russian teenagers, the problems of securing one's desired place in society has been magnified by social, economic and cultural developments of the last two decades. The slow-down of economic development together with the Brezhnevite politics of stability led to a severe stagnation of social mobility. At the same time the centrally planned education system continued to overproduce highly educated people, leaving Soviet society with a glut of 'specialists' (especially engineers) seeking employment in an increasingly outdated industrial production network. Given the state commitment to full employment this has meant their placement in menial jobs for which they are overqualified. In cities with strict controls on immigration, manual jobs could often not be filled since the educated urban population spurned them and migrant workers (*limitchiki*) were encouraged into the cities to do the jobs no one else would do. In Moscow and St Petersburg, for example, more than half the students studying at the vocational-technical colleges (PTUs) are from outside the city – the figure rising to 90 per cent or more in particularly unpopular professions such as construction, machine building and textile and food industries (Butko and Denisov 1988: 73). The sense of superfluousness today is thus reinforced by the presence of 'outsiders' whose perceived aim is precisely to take that space which is felt to be 'mine' and symbolized by the *propiska*.

The sense of social superfluity among young people has been fuelled further by attempts to lower (or rechannel) their aspirations through education reforms aimed at discouraging young people from entering higher education and encouraging them, instead, to train for skilled manual work (see Chapter 3). The reforms were, in fact, a resounding disaster and the majority of those interviewed by the author did remain at the general secondary school or enter the *tekhnikum* or *uchilishche*, which whilst vocational were nonetheless considerably more prestigious than the PTU. The attempted implementation of the reforms, accompanied by the usual gamut of exhortations and ideological slogans, nevertheless moulded the experiences of this age cohort and their successful resistance to government pressure was experienced only as a victory of superfluity over political manipulation.

One issue of superfluity and displacement which was considered at length by Soviet academics prior to perestroika was that resulting from the break-up of families. The earlier unquestioned connection made between single-parent families and juvenile delinquency is now challenged, however, and counter-evidence cited to suggest that, where a family breaks up because of problems of alcoholism or other disorder, children's behaviour actually improves after the divorce (Grigor'eva 1985: 75). It is certainly true that single-parent families are common in contemporary Russia – divorce runs at around the same rate as other industrialized countries and, by the mid-1980s, one in eight births were outside of marriage (Lane 1990: 224,126). However, the testimonies of interviewees in Moscow youth cultural groups suggested that there was nothing intrinsically destabilizing about a single-parent family. Virtually all those who had grown up in such home environments expressed sympathy for the hard life that their mothers had had to lead, although the sympathetic rather than empathetic tone of such statements may suggest some degree of judgement here.

Where the family consisted of both parents, fathers were more likely to be criticized, usually for moments of authoritarianism (refusing to let them go out where they wanted, dress how they wanted, throwing them out of the family flat). In such instances there was a tendency to use political metaphors to describe the interference. Being 'grounded' for example was referred to as the introduction of 'red terror', whilst another interviewee cited an occasion when he had been thrown out of the flat (for wearing an ear-ring) as evidence of his father's co-operation with the KGB.

Nevertheless, there was little evidence from interviewees to support the claims made in 'restructured' Soviet academic literature that informal group participation was linked to the moral vacuum with which young people had been faced as they watched the material acquisitiveness of their parents in private fly in the face of the lofty exhortations to communist ideas which the adult generation subjected them to in public. The young Muscovites interviewed did not reject the family-first values of their parents, on the contrary, criticisms of them were voiced in metaphors of the intrusion of the political sphere into the private.

The aim of this section has been to show that subcultural styles adopted by youth cultural groups in Russia are not simply imitations of their Western peers. The aspirations of young people towards Western cultural artefacts and ways of life (including subcultural ones) are only one of a complex of cultural experiences which shape the strategies they adopt. These strategies are related to their positioning within the social stratification system, but are only partially understood through the discourse of class. Crucial to the strategies of both the *tusovki* and the *gopniki* is the claiming of urban space as a symbolic assertion of their own placing in society. This is related to the importance of centre–periphery divides in determining social position as well as to overcoming the sense of social superfluity which is both an ongoing Russian cultural theme as well as an experience specific to what is often termed 'the lost generation'. Youth cultural activity does not only provide young people with a mechanism for solving these social and cultural dislocations at the individual and psychological level, however. The occupation of space and the struggle for it – often involving physical altercations – has a directly bodily form which is a source not of escape but of pleasure. It is these forms and their meanings which are discussed below.

## Play

While music use and style may have marked out both different youth cultural strategies and individual *tusovki* from each other, some activities were common to the vast majority of groups. These activities – which are referred to here as 'play' – were essentially internally-orientated and concerned directly with the abstention from fixed subject positions which distinguishes *jouissant* forms of pleasure. By this is meant that the activities take over the body and the mind in a way generally experienced by the participants as liberating. They are unconcerned with the rationalized purpose of the *tusovka* (music use, trade, roller-skating) and are almost wholly pleasure orientated. They take place in spaces already won for the group through the processes described above, whether these be fixed *tusovka* sites or spaces secured temporarily through the physical presence of the group. It is the fact that subjectivity can be displaced within such spaces which marks out the *tusovki* and *gopniki* from youth cultural strategies of a more counter-cultural kind (hippies, radical student groups, ecological groups) or socio-political associations, which depend on moulding fixed subject positions into political strategies.

The forms of play encountered have been divided into four broad areas: 'getting high'; 'going mad'; 'having a laugh'; and 'being sussed'. These categories are derived from the verbal expressions of youth slang which have emerged to express this playful activity. A fuller glossary of such slang is included at the end of the book. In the course of a *tusovka* meeting it is likely that some or all forms of play will be encountered and that the forms will overlap. The importance of these expressions lies in the sense conveyed by them as well as the fact that their articulation in slang removes them from the formal world. Nevertheless, it should not be forgotten that although articulated at a verbal level they remain fundamentally physical activities which would ordinarily be frowned upon for their social unacceptability, being classified as deviant, childish or aggressive.

### 'Getting high'

Among contemporary *stiliagi* drug use is negligible, nevertheless the language of the drug-induced high is as common as it is among other youth cultural groups. This is due in part to the incorporation into general youth slang of terminology originating amongst drug subcultures, but it is also necessitated by the fact that other activities in which the *stiliagi* involve themselves induce the same kind of 'highs' for which an expression must be found.

The most common expressions are those based on *kaif* and *baldezh* – both meaning 'high' in drug-users' slang. These expressions are mainly used by the *stiliagi* to describe their experiences at concerts, gigs or other events of the *tusovka* involving music use. Expressions such as *ia uletela* (literally 'I took off') or *my obaldeli* (literally 'we were stupefied') clearly suggest loss of self and fixity, whilst the concert itself would be described as *v kaif*. The adverb *obaldenno* is now a slang term used in much wider circles than the *tusovki* and for this reason has virtually lost its original meaning. It is important, nonetheless, to recall the comparison being made; the music or dance, the atmosphere of a crowded concert hall, and the sensation of being surrounded by your own crowd is being equated to the effects of drug taking. The difference is that the experience is a collective not an individual one. A gig (*seishn*), for example, is only considered *obaldenno* or *v kaif* if everyone is participating in the experience, if the music and dance take over the collective body. If, as was often the case at officially organized concerts, the favoured band performed only one or two numbers as part of a whole show designed to suit all tastes, then it would be considered 'rubbish' (*lazha*) and not worthy of inscription into the *tusovka* narrative.

Other drug-related phrases are used almost exclusively in conjunction with the word 'music' or a specific form of music or group. Such expressions include *(za)tashchit'sia* (from the root *taska* which is a synonym for *kaif*) and *(pri)torchat'* both meaning 'to get high'. The term *torchok* is used by drug addicts to refer to themselves (Prisiazhnii 1990). In their verbal forms both are used to mean 'to like, to gain pleasure' from such things as rock 'n' roll, 1950s memorabilia or a certain person. The sense is that the pleasure involves a very physical reaction which sends one into an ecstatic state.

The way in which music and concerts are talked about may usefully be contrasted to the terms used by *stiliagi* to describe their only form of actual drug use – drinking. Whereas a *stiliaga* would 'take off' (*uletet'*) at a concert, evenings where alcohol consumption was the prime event would simply be described as *my drinchali* (from *drinchat'* – youth slang for 'to drink') or less commonly *my bukhali* (from *bukhat'*, slightly cruder slang for the same).

Among other interviewees, drugs and alcohol were taken much more instrumentally in order to induce 'highs' or bursts of energy – to 'make things happen'. The most frequently used term by people actually taking drugs was the verb *vmazat'sia/vmazyvat'sia* meaning 'to get a hit'. The things which did happen as a result would be worked into the group narrative. In other words they would become the material for a constructed collective self, but one which could be constantly reconstructed through references to partial memory of the event, hyperbole and distorted recollections. The normal logic of events is suspended and the rules of time and space reinvented. Whether the 'high' was induced by music or drugs, then, the experience was a dual one: an individual release during which self merges with the collective body or which is relived collectively as part of the forging of a collective self.

### *'Going crazy'*

As was mentioned in the previous chapter, being labelled by society as insane was a key element of the cultural practice of the punks: it defined their place in society; drew the lines of their interaction with the state; formed the outlines of their group narratives; and to some extent provided the material existence of that madness through the abuse of drugs prescribed. Because this 'madness' was the site of official, repressive intervention into their lives, occasionally discussions of madness would include descriptions of enforced hospitalization and treatment:

> The policeman said, 'In our country it is not acceptable to go round like that.' And for that they sent me to a loony-bin (*durdom*) . . . I've been there more than once . . . The first time the treatment is forty-five days. Then, it depends on your behaviour . . . They inject you with crude drugs like *aminazin* and *sul'fazin*.[17] Then they do experiments. They test new drugs . . . They treat alcoholics, of course, all kinds of hooligans. And those whom Soviet power doesn't like, those who don't fit into its framework . . .
>
> (L)

Predominantly, however, madness was the site of the punks' own offensive; an offensive upon everyday, 'normal' rationality and motivation. Madness was a site of pleasure and fun and punk music was a perfect vehicle by which they broke through the acceptable bounds of behaviour. Hence, the idea to start up a punk band was, according to the group narrative, born of an hallucination whilst the band leader was being 'treated' in hospital. Another member discovered his talents as a drummer after falling from the third floor of a block of flats whilst under the influence of tranquillizers. What the authorities sought in 'treating' the punks was the inversion of this pleasure in madness, its transformation into a 'normal' and thus more controllable madness.

The different content of the *tusovka* of the *stiliagi* meant a more restricted role of 'madness' which took two forms. The first was 'going crazy' (*pokreizit'*) which was used to indicate 'letting off steam' or 'having a good time'. This effectively gave space for child-like activity by suggesting its functional purpose. The second was 'being mad' and was expressed by the phrases *krysha poekhala* or *sdvinut' kryshu* ('to go off your head') or adjectives such as *sumasshedshii* ('mad') or *tronutii* ('touched'). These were used to make space for normally excessive behaviour by pre-ascribing 'madness'. This labelling was used to release one another from the external bounds of sociability and could be applied long-term to a particular member of a group, or momentarily to a wider group of members.

### 'Having a laugh'

'Having a laugh' is crucial to *tusovka* life and is much more important than providing a harmless way of passing time. A key term here is that of the *fen'ka*. In original youth slang of the 1960s and 1970s *fen'ki* or *fenechki* meant 'adornments' (usually beads) worn by hippies and it is still used in this sense, as for example in describing the quirks of an individual's dress-style (*prikid*). In the use of the contemporary *stiliagi*, however, it also means 'a good joke' in phrases such as *ia v"ezhala v tvoiu fen'ku* ('I've sussed your little joke). It is only if the two meanings are seen in conjunction that the role of the *fen'ka* in group life can be understood.

*Fen'ki* are the way of showing one's individuality within the group; they are that which is closest to you, your idiosyncrasy or way of standing out. Nevertheless they are something which can be adorned, and thus discarded. They are stories or jokes which can enhance your image the first time they are told or played but quickly lose their impact.

A second important term is *prikol* (literally 'a stake') also used to mean 'a joke', 'a funny incident' or, alternatively, 'interest in' or 'participation in' something. The latter meaning is inherent particularly in the verbal form (*prikolot' (sia)*) suggesting, for example, 'I'm not into that kind of thing' (*eto menia ne prikalyvaet*) although generally, in its reflexive form, the verb simply means 'to mess around' or 'to have a laugh'. The forms this activity takes are highly physical and involve chasing, mock fighting or beatings and playing children's games.

The physical effect of 'messing around' is indicated by the cross-over term *ulet*. As was suggested above, the verb *uletet'* is used to indicate the effect of listening to music you really like. In its noun form, though, the term is used as a synonym of *prikol* and the adjective *uletnii* or adverb *uletno* suggests something 'unusual, beautiful or amazing'. Here sensual excitement, the fun in giving way to that excitement, and the physical sensation of doing so, meet.

But 'having fun' could also be at the expense of others and could be used to assert oneself over them or to determine relations within the group. Here 'the joke', and the laughter it elicited, is more associated with 'making fun *of*' or teasing. The *steb*, for example, is a kind of mocking, sarcastic laughter directed at someone or something and its aim of intimidating or putting down is seen in its other uses such as in the terms *stebat'sia* meaning 'to be frightened' or *zastebat'* ('to hassle, frighten'). In the phrase *zastebat' narod* ('to wind people up') is seen most clearly the Bakhtinian carnival laughter which 'degrades and materializes' (Bakhtin 1984: 24) as the sacred Soviet people (*sovetskii narod*), the harbingers of a new world order, are concretized and ridiculed.

The most common form of the more aggressive side to 'making fun' is found in the practice of *naekhat'*. *Naekhat'* (literally meaning 'to run over') means 'to hassle', 'to give grief' and was used as a way of asserting power both vertically within a group (by older members over younger ones) or horizontally (by stronger or more prestigious groups over weaker ones). How this was actually practised will be described in more detail below.

### 'Being sussed'

'Being sussed' involved the art of pretence and deception. It could demand the adopting of a mask, most frequently that of insanity in order to acquire a certificate of mental disorder and thus avoid military conscription (*zal otkosit' ot armii*). Such deception was not shameful since it mocked those in official positions who tried to control and shape their lives. It could also demand being wise to attempts to deceive – most commonly experienced when 'doing deals'. From *fartsovshchik* slang the term *proletet'* was adopted meaning 'to lose out' or 'be gazumped' as, for example, when something you had intended to buy (on the black market) is sold to someone else first. Similarly, if you were not careful you could be 'sold something defective', or be 'taken for a ride' (*kinut'*).

This kind of deception can ruin your mood or put you in an awkward position and this experience is expressed by the term *oblomat'* whose root is the drug-users' term *oblom* meaning 'a state of being without drugs'. The verbal form (*oblomat'*) as well as the synonym *pogasit'* can also be used to mean 'to cut someone off' (whilst speaking), or more generally to let someone down, deceive someone. In principle the verb *dinamit'* has the same meaning – 'to disappoint', 'to fail to keep a promise' – but it is generally used more jokingly and does not jeopardize friendship. A common use would be *ona liubit dinamit'* meaning 'she has a habit of turning up late'. But, when the deception is more serious, and becomes outright betrayal, then it is expressed by the verbs *zalozhit'* or *nastugat'*.

*Tusovka* members feel surrounded by deception and this makes 'being sussed' very important. To *prosekat'* is 'to understand someone when they are talking ambiguously' through the double-speak of everyday life, while *dokhodit'* indicates that you 'understand what has been said'. At a deeper level, *vrubat'sia* and *v"ekhat'* mean 'to have sussed out', 'to know what you are talking about' and these are key qualities of *tusovka* members. In particular there is a distinction between those who 'are sussed' and those who are not. This is determined through one's relation to the common language of music and dance which are central to *tusovka* life not only as physical, pleasurable forms of communication (*obshchenie*) but also as the subject of that *obshchenie*.

As the common language, music acts both as unifier and differentiator. It brings people together since it is the interest they share in common, but sets people apart in revealing levels of knowledge about and access to the tools of that *obshchenie* – rock 'n' roll records, tapes, information and posters. Those who simply adopt the mask of the *tusovka* – who use the group to draw attention to themselves without knowing anything about the music or dance – are labelled *lokhi* and accused of 'not knowing anything' (*ni vo chto ne vrubaiut'sia*). The *lokh* is the lowest form of *tusovka* life because she/he not only really belongs to the other world (as does the *botanik* - the 'swot' or 'bookworm') but adopts the mask of the *tusovka* and thus tarnishes its truth.

The discussion of the cultural practices of Moscow youth cultural groups suggests that the 'second world' that they inhabit is conducive to a special type of communication impossible in everyday life – an embodied communication expressed in music and dance, style, play and speech. It is a form of communication which is, playfully, subversive of the dominant culture and its official institutions described in Part II. Nevertheless, it is neither separate nor completely opposed to this culture. For this reason, the second part of this chapter will examine the extent to which the *tusovka* and its embodied communication provide space for the negotiation of new social and cultural relations and to what extent that space is constrained by the dominant culture and its established norms of domination and subordination. What will be considered are the relations of gender within the *tusovka* of the Moscow *stiliagi*, and the centrality of gender relations themselves to the structuring of the wider youth cultural world.

## EN-GENDERING YOUTH CULTURAL ACTIVITY: CODES OF FEMININITY AND MASCULINITY IN MOSCOW TUSOVKI

That youth cultural activity is a gendered experience was recognized by the press in its depiction of a distinct female experience of sexual victimization and sexual deviance. The key to the analysis offered by the glasnost press was that the gendered nature of youth culture stemmed from the *different activities* of young men and women in youth culture. This referred to the youth cultural groups in which girls participated and to the *role* that they played within them (as either willing prostitutes or as enslaved 'girls for common use', i.e. *obshchie devushki*). In both cases the sexual 'needs' of the male group members were naturalized and seen as one component of a whole, male culture. For the girls, however, sexual activity was definitive and their 'sexual promiscuity' was used by the press to signify 'the general state of things' in a disintegrating Soviet society.

The field work conducted in Moscow did not in any way suggest that gender relations were unimportant to youth cultural activity. However, the way in which they were structured appeared to be more complex than the analysis offered in the press suggested. In order to understand their significance, an exploration not only of the kinds of sexual relations prevalent in the groups but also of the codes of femininity and masculinity employed in the cultural practice of both young women and young men is required. These codes have been constructed not in isolation from, but with reference to a dominant culture coming to terms with what became known as the 'costs of emancipation' (*izderzhki emantsipatsii*). These 'costs', according to Gorbachev, were a gamut of social problems resulting from the mistaken desire 'to make men and women equal in everything' (Gorbachev 1987c: 117).

But the youth cultural codes of masculinity and femininity are not just extreme versions of a wider rejection of the 'new Soviet man and woman', whereby men reclaim their inheritance through a cult of masculine strength and violence while girls' desperation to gain access to the cultural commodities which supposedly create femininity (perfume, expensive clothes and jewellery and candle-lit meals in restaurants) means that they are prepared to do anything, even sell their bodies. Although never escaping the norms of adult society, the youth cultural sphere provides a space where many of its codes are experimented with and disrupted. This section will explore the way in which codes of femininity and masculinity were negotiated by both young women and young men within one *tusovka* – the *stiliagi* – and how these codes structured relations between different youth cultural strategies.

### 'The main thing was that I didn't become a gopnik': Subcultures as explorations of masculine identity

The notion of the youth world being divided into warring factions of young males is not an innovation born of glasnost, but follows a pattern of youth cultural studies elsewhere – a tendency perhaps most succinctly expressed by Mike Brake's claim that subcultures can only ever be explorations of masculine identity (Brake 1985: ix). In discussions of Soviet youth, gender has been seen to play a role invariably only *within* individual groups or strategies and has been discussed in terms of the degree of abuse of girls by boys. Although the existence of this kind of abuse cannot be denied, the example of the *stiliagi* revealed that traditional hierarchies of masculine strength and female subordination may be most clearly reinforced on the inter-group level. In this sense, gender identity is inextricably linked with the centre–periphery divide in the structuring of hierarchies within the Moscow youth cultural world.

For the male *stiliaga*, becoming part of a *tusovka* means rising above the 'mass' by rejecting the banality or vulgarity (*poshlost'*) of the everyday world. This is symbolized by his physical removal from that world as he begins to go into the city centre to meet up with the *tusovka* at discos, cafés or squares where its members gather. The journey to *tusovki* propels the *stiliaga* out of the banality he confronts at home and into a new world which broadens his horizons and offers new opportunities. This is summed up by one former *stiliaga* thus:

> The central *stil'naia tusovka* gave me a lot, because . . . it brought me to the centre . . . i.e. it taught me the ABC of *tusovka* life.
>
> (P)

Joining a *tusovka* also means adopting a style of dress and behaviour which sets you apart from those around you. The distance travelled each day to the central *tusovka* sites marks a ritual severing of one's life-strategy from the narrow world of the *gopnik*, or in Moscow, the *liuber*-types (*tipa liubera*) since, in the capital city, the term *liuber* is used by *neformaly* as a shorthand to describe almost any working-class, provincial young male. As a key reference group, therefore, a thorough understanding of *liuber* strategy is essential for analysing the structure of the Moscow youth cultural scene as a whole.

The favoured political or ideological understanding of *liuber* strategy, however, remains deeply problematic since it rests on the linking of key parts of *liuber* activity with statements and interpretations which suggest its ideological motivation. The first problem concerns the overlap between formal and non-formal (dominant and subcultural) worlds which makes it difficult to draw lines between labelling and self-labelling as the *liubery* quickly learned the publicity value of declaring ideological intentions (this is analysed in Chapter 4). The second problem is the assumption that the two *liuber* practices of body-building and fighting in Moscow with other youth cultural groups are instrumentally connected. Third there is the problem of the partial examination of the activities of the *liubery* and the failure to account for those activities which do not lend themselves to an ideological reading. Bearing these points in mind, *liuber* activity is reconsidered below.

### Men with a mission? Rereading liuber body-politics

A central tenet of the ideological interpretation is the *liuber* obsession with muscular strength and the creation of secret body-building dens (*kachalki*). The dominant reading of this aspect of their activity is that the dens were used to train for planned raids into Moscow where they would beat up *neformaly* considered to be Westernizing infidels. This reading relies heavily on the articulated claims of some *liubery* that they have an ideological mission to clear the streets of Moscow of punks, hippies and the like (see Chapter 4). In so doing it fails to confirm these statements by reference to the actual behaviour of the *liubery*. How, for example, can these statements be squared with evidence that the *kachalki* themselves are papered with posters of *Western* body-building and martial arts heroes and that the training programmes of the *liubery* are often taken from heroes such as Arnold Schwarzenegger?

This kind of instrumentalism also ignores other ways in which the body might be a key site of youth cultural practice without it being used directly in battle. The struggle for the proletarian body has its roots in the post-revolutionary era and the clash between the Russian and the Marxist revolutionary spirit over the forging of the new Soviet person (see Chapter 2). Kollontai, for example, considered the sphere of sexual relations to be more than a superstructure which could be added after the economic base of society had been changed and thus argued for the active construction of a *proletarian* sexual morality as part of the revolutionary strategy (Kollontai 1977: 249). Lunacharsky also saw the power of the liberated body and encouraged the adoption of traditions of carnival – with its colour, abandon and pleasures – in forging a new communist culture (Stites 1989: 98). Despite their efforts, however, in post-revolutionary Russia bodily pleasures were increasingly harnessed to the machines which would construct the new society. As part of this process leisure time came to be seen as time for physical recuperation for the next working day and Lenin's 'festival of the expressed and exploited' (97) increasingly became an orchestrated march towards communism. The need to keep the body fit and prepared (for defence of the motherland), the desire to keep leisure organized, controlled and off the street, and, later, the drive to show the superiority of the 'Soviet way of life' forged a physical culture designed to make the proletarian body fit for the proletarian conscience. In its most extreme form this culture of work and sport did not only embody the proletarian spirit but harnessed it through its sublimation of the anarchic, sexual tendencies of the proletarian body, epitomized by Zalkind's 'Twelve principles of sexual behaviour' (Zalkind 1925: 76). According to Zalkind, sexual relations should be infrequent, monogamous, free of 'perversions', entered into only after marriage and never purely on the basis of physical attraction. Whilst claiming that this conformed to women's natural desire, in fact, it seems, what he feared above all were sexual relations which were anarchic, multi-sited and conducted not in order to reproduce – in other words, the sexually liberated female body. It is not surprising then that he attacked Kollontai for portraying as a revolutionary hero in one of her works a woman 'who changes partners at will' and is 'interested only in the physical side of relationships' (84).

Also in the 1920s the belief was established that physical culture and sport could be used in the forging of a new society to combat socially and politically undesirable phenomena (Riordan 1978: 22). Whilst at first sight it might appear that the *liubery* took up this instrumental use of physical culture in their claims to use their *kachalki* to train for ideological raids into the capital, in fact their practices are also subversive of it. They subvert it, first, by the form of activity adopted – body-building – which was one of the sports (along with martial arts) linked to Eastern religions and traditionally frowned upon for its cultivation of 'egoism' and 'narcissism' typical of bourgeois culture. Second, the use of the physical development of the body in order to stake out territory subverts at a fundamental level the original intention to use sport to bring people of different social milieu together and to forge a collective spirit whether it be at the level of school, town or country. Sport was intended to break down the barriers of uneven development not reinforce old rivalries between villages and between town and village. Finally, the assertion by the *liubery* of an exclusively male proletarian body and an oppressive masculinism subverts the 'rational' use of sport to encourage the liberation of women especially from the oppressive, 'irrational' dress and behaviourial codes of Islam (ibid.). This connection between physical strength, territorial invasions and the subordination of women is explored further below.

But what empirical evidence is there to refute the apparently rational or instrumental relationship between 'pumping iron' and attacks on Moscow subcultural groups? Central to this must be an exploration of the circumstances in which fights begin:

> It would usually happen like this: some lad who was nicely or smartly (*tsivil'no*) dressed would be walking along and they would just start having a go at him (*naekhat' na nego*). But usually they [the *liubery*] descended on the *tusovki* of the hippy or *stiliagi*. Why? Because they are weaker. The majority are women, girls. It is easier to pick on them, insult them. They can't stand up for themselves.
>
> (X)

This recollection was supported by a second argument used to explain the vulnerability of the *stiliagi* lads:

> There was also an age factor. These lads were older after all, and the *stiliagi* were younger. A few years at that age can make a big difference.
>
> (X)

The girls suggested that the reason for the *stiliagi* being picked on was less to do with the girls' than the lads' inability to stand up for themselves:

> When the *gopniki* or *liubery* picked on us, and we went to defend our lads, they [the *liubery*] said, "We are letting your lads go only because of you girls. If there were more girls like you, it would be wonderful."
>
> (F)

Regardless of whose version is nearer the truth, the implication is clear: the *stiliagi* were picked on because in the eyes of those adopting a *gopnik* strategy, they were less *manly*. The evidence of this was: their age, the fact that they went around with girls, and that they could not, or chose not to, fight back. This was voiced directly by one of the male *stiliagi,* talking about how other students at his technical college reacted to the *stiliagi*:

> It was associated with being feminine somehow. If you were a *stiliaga*, it meant you were weak, you could be easily insulted.
>
> (W)

As far as the *stiliagi* were concerned, therefore, they were a target for the *liubery* not because of any deviant ideological stance but because they displayed a deviant gender identity – they appeared to disrupt the dominant code of masculinity. This is evident from the linking of these accusations of femininity to style. A typical situation would be that the *liubery* would approach a group of *stiliagi* or punks and ask:

> "Why are you so dressed up?" . . . "Why are you so good that you can look like that and I can't? Take it off!"
>
> (X)

Although the *stiliagi* dressed in second-hand, 1950s-style suits and did not reject traditional norms of smart dressing like the punks and hippies, nevertheless their suits, ties, shiny shoes, umbrellas and attaché cases appeared 'fancy' and did not meet with the approval of the *liubery*. For other groups, it was hairstyles – especially the long hair of the heavy metal fans and hippies, their leather jackets and jewellery which evoked the anger of the *liubery*. But it was specifically the combination of these styles with a strategy of not 'standing up for yourself' which was so despised. This kind of attitude is summed up by one lad talking about the Depeche Mode fans whom he drove away from their meeting place at Maiakovskii Square:

> Just two of you can go up to all thirty of them and say quietly and calmly, "Lads, you are not going to hang out (*tusovat'sia*) here any more, get lost!", and they will go and won't come back again. They won't stand up for their views . . . You could call them hippies.
>
> (Q)

The speaker quoted above did not adopt a specifically *gopnik* strategy, but he did adhere to a strong masculine identity typical of them, and the label 'hippy' is used by him as a generic term for all groups adopting a 'soft' masculine identity. The hippies appear universally despised by *gopniki* and *tusovki* alike. While the former may cut off the hair of their 'enemies', the latter labelled them 'dirty' and thus 'untouchables'. The three themes of hippyism, feminine weakness and revulsion are woven together in a statement made by teenagers from Lytkarino interviewed in the youth literary journal *Iunost'* about the spread of *'liuber*ism'. Replying to a journalist's question as to what they, as *liuber* followers were fighting for, one teenager replied:

> We are against all these long-haired people (*volosatiki*), punks – they go round like old women (*baby*). It's disgusting.
>
> (cited in Osin 1989: 79)

But why was it so important for the *liubery* to crush these alternative masculine styles? The answer, it is argued here, is that the lack of assertiveness of the hippies is seen as pernicious, for it whittles away the basis of masculine rule – the apportioning of women. The subversive nature of this 'free love' is summed up by Rozin (a Soviet psychologist researching youth culture) when he describes it in words which a *liuber* himself would have been proud of:

> A hippy boy proves incapable of living with one girl; so he calls it following the principle of free love. Hippyism is therefore a special cultural niche where people condemned to be failures in society may acquire high self-esteem and the recognition of others.
>
> (Rozin 1990: 69)

A second practice of the *liubery*, which is rarely addressed since it fails to confirm the ideological interpretation of their activity, is 'snatching girls' (*snimat' devochki*). According to the *stiliagi* this practice was often the cause of fights with the *liubery*:

> They might say: "Oh, look at those girls! Come with us!" And all hell would let loose.
>
> (X)

Although the *stiliagi* claimed that the snatching of girls was commonplace, it is hardly ever discussed as a central component of *liuber* activity. Three of the *stiliagi* girls recounted how a girl they knew had been 'snatched', taken back to Liubertsy, beaten up and raped. She only narrowly escaped being drowned in a nearby, small lake after the attack. The snatching of Moscow girls from discos and cafes meant that for young women, the *liubery* were not an anti-Western subculture but predatory males who must be got rid of using the usual armoury of devices.[18]

If this part of *liuber* activity is brought back into the equation, then the 'raids' into Moscow by the *liubery* might be seen as targeted not only at spaces where subcultural groups were likely to be found – cafes, discos and clubs – but also where access might be gained to women. The ensuing fights may thus represent the traditional resolution of territorial invasions which constitute a deliberate violation of the norms regulating the control of access to girls.

The fact that the youth community should take this regulatory function upon itself is not surprising. In pre-revolutionary Russian society, as in other pre-industrial or industrializing European societies, youth communities were entrusted with ensuring social and moral norms were adhered to. In the Russian case the youth peer group gathered primarily at the *khorovod*, which was essentially a group for round-dancing but in fact undertook a whole complex of activities and served a crucial role of social control (Gromyko 1986: 161) and at the evening, festive *posidelki*.[19] Although at least one older married woman supervised the *posidelka* (Worobec 1991: 131), the evidence suggests that young people were allowed considerable freedom and that pre-marital sexual relations were engaged in. Kollontai cites the blind eye turned to what went on at these parties as evidence of hypocritical bourgeois morality (Kollontai 1977: 241), while Frank notes that government figures on rural illegitimacy suggest a correlation between winter festivities and incidence of birth outside marriage (Frank 1992: 720).

On the other hand, the strict rules governing the establishment of courting couples effectively constituted a secure mechanism of controlling the sexuality of women. The evening parties were the first stage in the courting process which led to marriage and, although physical intimacy in private was allowed between courting couples, there were strict rules about the limits to which this could go. Those who overstepped this mark would be subjected to community control – the girl would be publicly humiliated while the lad would be forced to marry his now discredited fiancée (Worobec 1991: 138–9). There were also controls exercised on the choosing of the courting partner governed by wealth and position, the marriage market, and peasant folklore. Although girls might be invited to festivities in neighbouring villages – especially where the size of villages made the marriage market highly competitive – they rarely went alone and they would be seated separately from local girls.

The appearance of boys at an evening party in another village, on the other hand, 'frequently led to trouble' (Frank 1992: 722). If no agreement was reached between the local lads and the 'invaders' (often through the offering of vodka as a gift in return for the right to court or dance with a local girl), then fighting would ensue. When the beaten lad returned with others from his village to seek revenge, a full-scale village against village brawl might develop (ibid.). A contemporary example of how this community control is exerted was revealed by a newspaper article which described the activities of the so-called '*striguny*' ('hair cutters') of the town of Volzhskii. Calling themselves 'fighters for morality' they cut off the hair of local girls known to be going out with Italian men working at a nearby factory (Ratvanin 1987). Without the symbol of their femininity, the girls would be forced to stay at home and thus be effectively excluded from the marriage market.

The *khorovod* also took upon itself a wider role of social levelling and public censure. If a member of the village was guilty of some anti-social behaviour, the *posidelki* might be taken out onto the street and in a shaming ritual known as *charivari*, the house of the offender would be blocked with logs, carts, harrows and sledges and the young people would laugh, sing mocking songs and call obscenities (Frank 1992: 724). Tensions and splits did not only occur between villages or between the youth community and the adult world, but also among young people themselves. Frank notes that by the 1890s it was quite common for youth evening parties to be split by social wealth and status reflected either in seating arrangements which kept poor and well-off apart, or, in the development of entirely separate forms of entertainment (718).

The centrality of space (especially centre–periphery stratification) in the formation of youth cultural activities therefore must be considered in tandem with issues of gender identity. In contemporary Russian society, where access to commodity culture has been reserved for those in central areas, the urban strategy of 'dressing up', 'standing out' and 'winning the girl' through the sporting of Western (*firmennie*) gear and styles is denied to large sections of Russian youth. On the periphery of the central areas this injustice is experienced particularly painfully and the young male community may intervene to reorder and redistribute privilege. The selling of gear taken from the 'city-slickers' serves a levelling function in that it provides the means to finance trips to Moscow, entrance to discos and taking girls out. At the same time, at the symbolic level, through shows of masculine superiority – physical attacks on both girls and lads in Moscow – the *liubery* attempt to regain centrality, normality, hegemony and push out the hippy/weak masculinity strategy to the periphery, the deviant and the abnormal.

### 'As usual, it was the girls in front and the boys behind': Subcultures as explorations of feminine identity

Subcultural activity did not only provide spaces for the exploration of masculinity, however. One of the remarkable features of the *stiliagi* of the mid-1980s was that it was virtually impossible to ignore the presence of girls in group. As one male member noted:

> In the *tusovka* there were usually more girls than boys – it was about 60–70 per cent girls. There were occasions when we went to concerts and there would be three lads and the other eight or nine would be girls.
>
> (X)

The reason for this is that many of the group's members (both male and female) came to the *stiliagi* via the *Bravisty*, i.e. fans of the Soviet rock group 'Bravo' which was led, until the end of 1988, by the dynamic female singer Zhanna Aguzarova whose distinctive style was described in the previous chapter. It was Zhanna's image which attracted many of the girls to the *stiliagi*:

> when Aguzarova started out, Z did not know because she was away at a pioneer camp somewhere. But she also dressed strangely and people started calling her 'Aguzarikha' [because she looked like Aguzarova] and so she got interested in her and became involved in it all. For Z it was above all the image.
>
> (S)

Another female *stiliaga* noted the importance of Zhanna in providing a positive role model:

> For me Zhanna was the most important thing . . . Her image led me to the *tusovka*. And all that I am now is thanks to Zhanna.
>
> (F)

The importance of the fact that it was Zhanna's style which was followed cannot be underestimated, since it is style (*stil'*) which lies at the heart of the group identity of the *stiliagi*. The creation of their own *stil'* gave the girls a space for the positive construction of their own femininity. As a *stiliaga*, the girls could stand out from the crowd by their own efforts, by buying clothes at the Tishinskii rag-market for a few roubles or scouring the wardrobes of their relatives and friends (see Plate 9). This released them from the dominant feminine code which was rooted in dependency on the income of their parents or on the expensive 'presents' of foreign perfume, cosmetics and clothes given by men.

However, the *stiliaga* image cannot be read simply as gender subversive, as replacing the almost obligatory denim or leather mini-skirt, high heels and expensive stockings with baggy trousers and oversized jacket. Over time, Zhanna's image moved a long way from its original masculine style, changed on virtually every appearance and mixed past Soviet styles and images with the latest Western fashions. For the *stiliagi* girls, however, this reinforced rather than limited Zhanna's appeal. Above all she appeared able to do that which seemed impossible in the conditions of 'Soviet reality' – she looked original. Aguzarova employed an almost punkish strategy of use and abuse of everyday items and clothes in the construction of style and it was her ability to create something unique and 'her own' out of Soviet reality which inspired the girls.

Among the *stiliagi*, therefore, it was the lads not the girls who felt insecure in their adopted style. The centrality of Zhanna in the determination of style left the lads in search of a role model. Some of them turned to the male members of 'Bravo' or to Igor' Sukachev, the leader of 'Brigada S', for inspiration while others looked to the *stiliagi* of the 1950s.

Either way, they remained subject to the scorn of their male contemporaries for the 'feminine' nature of their style. This perceived femininity was not associated with particular articles of clothing or make-up (as for example in glamrock style) but in the value laid on cleanliness, smartness and orderliness which conflicted with the torn, tattered, unkempt look of the greaser style of the *rokery* or the, sometimes, smart but determinedly styleless proletarian image of the *gopniki*. In contrast, *stiliaga* lads would never wear a white shirt twice without washing it, their clothes would always be carefully ironed and a *stiliaga* trip to a concert would be heralded by a whole row of *stiliagi* lads sitting on the tube cleaning their shoes with the shoe brushes they always carried with them.

### Reading stil': a case of gender-bending?

In a culture which defines femininity as 'modesty' and 'self-sacrifice' (Rasputin 1990), the *stiliagi* girls were creating a highly positive identity for themselves around the image of a strikingly non-traditional woman. But was this evidence of their resistance to the dominant codes of femininity? The results of interviews and observations with regard to this were ambiguous and contradictory. There was, on the one hand, some awareness of the breaking of dress norms. As one former *stiliaga* (who began as a *Brigadirka* rather than a *Bravistka*) saw it, Zhanna's adoption of the style legitimized it and made it more acceptable for them:

> At first, I was a bit afraid to wear this man's suit, because, after all, there were no women in 'Brigada S'. When I saw 'Bravo' and Zhanna Aguzarova in this suit, I realized that I could go around in this male suit as well.
>
> (E)

On the other hand, many of the girls of the second generation talked of their later realization that they should not really be dressing in male suits but in dresses:

> [the *tusovka* broke up because] we did not know what to wear . . . the girls in our *tusovka* wore male gear. When I came to the *tusovka*, Z sat down next to me and said, "girls if you want to be *stiliagi* of the 1950s and 1960s, you must wear dresses".
>
> (G)

Zhanna's style thus became an object of criticism by male members of the group; it came to signify Soviet, retro versions of rock 'n' roll as opposed to 'authentic' rock 'n' roll. Indeed Zhanna's style had come to dominate the understanding of *stil'* among the revivalist *stiliagi* – girls no longer wore the *dudochki* that they might have done earlier but only the wide, short trousers associated with Aguzarova. The implications for the development of the *tusovka* of the association of Zhanna's style with *Soviet* and retro

*Plate 9  Stiliagi* girls at the 'Moloko' cafe, February 1989.

*Plate 10* Former *stiliagi* girls and their *rokabilly* friends, 1991.

versions of rock 'n' roll are much more important than this minor change in style, however, and are discussed in more detail below.

Nevertheless, despite the criticisms, the girls continued to justify wearing the men's suits, especially in winter when it simply was not practical to wear anything else. Indeed, the practicality argument itself is an interesting deviation from dominant feminine codes stressing glamour and 'taking trouble' over comfort and convenience. Consequently their style enabled rather than disabled the girls, as is shown by one of the group narratives recounted. In the scramble to get to Zhanna's dressing room after a 'Bravo' concert, it was the lads' restrictive clothing (the narrow *dudochki*) which held them back – ripping as they climbed onto the stage – while the girls, in their wide trousers and flat shoes, stormed on ahead (G).

Another, more ambiguous, example of the way in which the girls' identity in the group inverted dominant gender codes concerns how the girls themselves viewed relations with the lads in the group. There was a conscious pride in the 'gentlemanly' behaviour of the *stiliagi* lads who were, 'a model of masculine dignity – from kissing your hand in greeting to giving up their seats for you on public transport' (T). This etiquette was mentioned approvingly by all the girls interviewed – perhaps not least because it placed the responsibility for buying drinks, ice-creams and food on the lads – and was experienced by them as an act not of conformity, but of *resistance*. This is spelled out by one female *stiliaga*:

> They make me feel like a girl, a real girl . . . our lads always get out of the bus first and offer us their hand, so that the girls can get out and through the crowd . . . it shocks everybody. It's really nice for us – we walk with a look on our faces, as if to say, "go ahead, laugh at us, at how we look, but look how we are treated, just look . . ."
>
> (E)

This suggests the way in which the girls saw their treatment by the boys as a rejection of the general disrespect accorded to women in adult society. The same member, interviewed a year later, revealed how this related to the *stiliaga* strategy as a whole:

> They [the *stiliagi* lads] were very intelligent people – in the true sense of the word, from whom you would never hear a single crude word . . . They were very attentive to the female half of the group and were simply very respectable (*poriadochnie*). In the metro they shocked everyone by their attitude to the old women who work at the barriers.[20] They shocked by their attention and intelligence . . .
>
> (E)

## Limitations of the tusovka as an exploration of femininity

The strong identity the *stiliagi* girls forged for themselves also included an apparent conformity to some familiar dominant codes of femininity. The most striking of these was the way in which the labels of 'good girls' and 'bad girls' were used in their judgements of girls in other *tusovki*. The most common claim was that girls in other groups were 'prostitutes' and that the lads 'passed them round':

> I don't like girls in the *rokery* because they are prostitutes. I will be honest. They fuck with everyone. They are very vulgar and look vulgar . . . I don't like it when girls swear in *mat*,[21] get themselves tattoos, and behave like sluts (*po-bliadski*) . . . Punk girls drive me mad because they are stupid, brainless idiots. They don't understand anything. They'll fuck with anyone. The *roker* girls are at least one stage better.
>
> (F)

Although on an earlier occasion it had been suggested that sexual relations in themselves need not be reprehensible, nevertheless, the *stiliagi* girls stressed that they themselves had always been seen as 'good girls' (D, G). The distinction here was made quite clear: there were girls who were '*obshchie*' ('common girls') and there were *stiliagi* girls, some of whom – quite naturally – were with lads (the implication being that they were in a sexual relationship) but who were never *obshchie* (D, F, G).

The importance of the 'virgin/whore' dichotomy to the girls was that it allowed them to separate themselves from these 'loose' girls and keep intact their own respectability. The dangers of failing to do this were voiced by a female member of a different *tusovka*, quoting a male friend:

> My friend said . . . "For me any girl from a *tusovka* carries a label. If a girl has been in a *tusovka*, then she is a slag (*bliad'*)".
>
> (U)

Indeed, because of the often positive image given to young female prostitutes through the association of prostitution with financial independence, access to foreign goods and high lifestyle, those who sleep with men for money are often regarded more highly than those who simply behave as the men do, and have different sexual partners or a series of short-term sexual relationships. This distinction was made clear by one non-*stiliaga* interviewee talking about a group of girls who lived locally:

> They are simply girls who haven't got a clue about anything (*ni vo chto ne vrubaiutsia*) except their lads and pop music – in short, plain nymphos (*prostie davalki*). If you fancy screwing one, you just go and talk to her . . . They're not prostitutes, like Intourist girls, . . . they're just slags.
>
> (Q)

On one occasion the *stiliagi* girls employed the censure of 'slag' within their own *tusovka* – although stressing that the case was an exception. In this instance the girls seemed to base their condemnation on the lads' accounts of the offending girl's behaviour – one lad had told them that he had 'fucked her everywhere, even on the washing machine'. This evidence was only brought forward, however, after a long tirade about the way this particular girl had terrorized the younger female members of the group, jolting them on the dance floor, making comments and spreading stories about them. It was not so much the lads' stories which were the grounds for her censure, then, as the fact that the girl herself had broken the rules of female solidarity. This was confirmed by the attitude of the *stiliagi* girls to the girl punks. What the female *stiliagi* found incomprehensible about their punk counterparts was not only that they tolerated being referred to as 'toads' (*zhaby*) by the male punks, but that they even called each other this. This kind of mutual disrespect was inconceivable to the *stiliagi* girls for whom the group were 'brothers and sisters' as well as best friends, without whom life was unimaginable. A similar conclusion was reached by Sue Lees in her study of sexuality and adolescent girls from which she concluded that the power of the naming of 'slag' is central to the behaviour of girls 'irrespective of the presence or absence of boys or whether the girls are in actual competition for particular boys' (Lees 1986: 83).

The 'good girl' image was an easy one neither to establish nor to maintain, however. It required a constant renegotiation of the mixture of femininity and daring in the girls' strategy. Although the girls often seemed quite confident about their own sexuality, any rejection of the 'modesty' version of femininity remained a high-risk strategy. An example of the conflict in their adopted strategy is in the *stiliagi* girls' relations with the *roker* lads which at one and the same time was fostered and feared. The prestige of being seen out with and considered friends of the *rokery* attracted the girls, but the relationship was also fraught with dangers for them. The *rokery* lads were generally older, and freer from parental control. They also had a different attitude to girls, which the *stiliagi* girls had openly rejected. Interaction with them meant risking the trust of their parents who would not have approved and whom therefore they were forced to deceive. It also meant risking their reputations. This was revealed in the uneasiness the girls felt about the attentions of the *roker* lads, their unsureness about how far friendly familiarity should be allowed to go (for example they would allow an arm around their shoulders or waist, but would not sit on the lads' knees) and their quickness to assert that if unwanted attention occurred, lads would be swiftly rebuked. Interaction with *rokery* lads was thus both courted (by the second-generation *stiliagi* girls) and feared; it was 'cool' to sit and have a beer and a laugh with their new *rokery* 'friends' but as the evening drew to a close they would carefully extract themselves from the company and make sure that they boarded the bus home alone.

Such uneasiness is not surprising given the continued stigmatization of young women in any incident which is seen by society to overstep the boundaries of the permissible. An extreme, but revealing example of this is evident in a letter published in a provincial newspaper which recalls fondly the peasant *charivari*. In reply to an article entitled 'Cheboksary Amazons' describing the activities of girl gangs in the city of Cheboksary, the letter relates a story told by the author's grandfather about a girl from his village who became pregnant. A village assembly (*skhod*) was called and a decision was taken to throw the girl out in shame. In addition, the girl was punished by 'harnessing her to a wood sledge like a horse and driving her all around the village . . . whipping her on the back with a stick'. The author went on to recommend similar punishment for such 'Amazons' today ('Ded Mikhail' 1990). Another report from the Kursk region also suggests that communal condemnation is much greater for girls. The article concerns the trial for rape of three young men from a small village who had been accused of unlawful intercourse with underage girls (in Russian law this is considered under the rape law and is punishable by up to three years' imprisonment). At the trial it became evident that the girls had not been unwilling partners and the lads received suspended sentences and were set free. Indeed, the accused were noted to be 'physically and mentally healthy lads who had completed army service and who were "respected" in their labour collectives' - one was even known as someone 'who always offered his seat in the bus' – and were in no way considered to be guilty by the majority of their fellow villagers. The girls, on the other hand, were severely morally condemned despite their difficult family background (both parents were alcoholics and had been deprived of parental rights over them) (Belaia and Savenkov 1990).

It would be misleading, however, to suggest that *stiliagi* girls were only in the group because it was safer for 'good girls' than the other groups. On the contrary, taking risks or 'dare-devilling' was also part of the strategy of female *stiliagi*:

> The girls in our *tusovka* were more strident (*boevii*) than the lads. The girls were always at the front (*vperedi na likhom kone*).
>
> (F)

The girls rarely backed away from confrontations with *gopniki*, on occasion they even complained that sorting out such conflicts was left to them:

> In 1988 the streets were crawling with *liubery*. The lads got beaten up before the girls' very eyes. But the girls always threw themselves in, head first. They got stuck in to defend them . . .
>
> (F)

*Stiliagi* girls adopted a feminine identity which allowed them to fully participate in the *tusovka* yet retain enough of a 'good girl' image to keep their reputations and to allow a return to the formal world. This strong femininity was not won at the expense of the male members of the group and there was no inversion of traditional relations of domination and subordination. This was seen by the girls as positive and they stressed that their lads were 'real men'. The failure of the lads, on the other hand, to subvert the dominant masculine code was to whittle away at the group identity and eventually lead to the break-up of the *tusovka*.

### Limitations of the tusovka as a subversion of masculinity

Although the *stiliagi* were perceived in the youth cultural world as a 'feminine' group, there was little conscious subversion of the dominant masculine code by *stiliagi* lads. They could not be described as retaining a 'butch image' as did the teddy boys despite their 'dandyism' (Brake 1985: 74); nevertheless, there was a considerable degree of overlap between *tusovki* and *gopnik* practices which suggests a continued conformity to dominant gender codes. The most important of these is the continued adherence to the cult of masculine strength. Even in the *tusovka* of the *stiliagi* there were members of the group who practised body-building in order to project a hard masculine image. One member of the group even had a nickname derived from the term 'body-builder'. When first asked, the informants rejected any idea that this version of masculinity was part of the group identity, but once stimulated to think about the issue, they concluded that this person was not the exception which proved the rule after all – they recalled a number of other *stiliagi* lads who body-built.

It was not only that some of the group conformed to an image associated with the *gopnik* strategy, there was also much more interaction with the local, *gopnik* lads than might be anticipated considering the open hostility between them on the streets. Just as the *liubery* did not beat up punks, metal fans or hippies from Liubertsy itself, so many of the *stiliagi* lads who came from what were referred to as '*gopnik* areas' continued to have good relations with their old crowds from home. One interviewee, who although not a *stiliaga* belonged to a central *tusovka*, noted that he could find much in common with the local lads:

> The local lads don't see themselves as *gopniki*. They sit in their entrance-ways in the new development areas and have a drink. Why shouldn't I be able to find a common language with them. I live here after all.
>
> (Q)

Indeed the source of that 'common language' is explained by a joining together to redefine and reassert the boundaries of centre and periphery:

> The *gopniki* from our area and I have been down to Kazan' station together to catch people coming in from Kazan' and . . . [give them what for]
>
> (Q)

Some practices familiar from the *gopnik* strategy were also occasionally present in the *stiliagi*, e.g. that of taking things coveted from younger members by force (*obut'*). One member talked about an incident soon after she first joined the *stiliagi* when she was forced to hand over her brooch to one of the older members who demanded it. As was outlined above, this taking of fashionable items by force is common practice among the gangs of the Volga cities and other *gopnik* groups. In one instance this behaviour actually brought new members to the *tusovka*. When the *tusovka* met at the Rizhskaia metro station regularly, they used to buy brooches from two lads from Liubertsy who had taken them from people coming out of the metro station. This interaction with 'the enemy' over a long period of time ended in the two lads becoming interested in the *stiliagi*, going along to the 'Moloko' cafe with them and eventually adopting the old suits and patent leather shoes of their style.

The 'snatching' of girls was also mentioned in connection with the *stiliagi* on a couple of occasions. One former *stiliaga*, for example, noted that there were some people in the group whose main aim was to 'pick up' girls and that for most of the lads, whether conscious of it or not:

> they joined the *stiliagi* in order to stand out from the crowd and because it was trendy . . . they thought, "It's fashionable and so girls will pay attention to me."
>
> (W)

The other reference implicated not the *stiliagi* but the *rokery* – to whom many *stiliagi* aspired – and concerned a cafe which was known to be where the *rokery* went to 'pick up' girls (*snimat' devushki*). The phrase in both cases was clearly used more to mean 'to pick up' than to 'snatch' and thus held far less serious overtones than when applied to the *liubery*. The difference is one of method and crudeness rather than intention and desire, however.

Although their differentiation from the *gopniki* remained an important attraction of the *stiliagi* for many of the lads, the image of the *tusovka* came to fit uneasily with their own developing masculine identity. In particular, there was much resentment about the tendency among the *stiliagi* lads to 'run away' rather than 'stand up and fight'. This is shown by the following argument between two former members of the *stiliagi* recalling a fight with some *gopniki* outside one of the *stiliagi* cafes

> B: They just wanted to have a go, they were drunk, they just wanted a fight. And they came up to us like, "Lads, what's all this in aid of? You're all so dressed up." And they forced us to say, "So, so great hero" . . . Those who didn't say it got a smack in the head . . .
> V: But we sorted the conflict out.
> B: Yes, we kept it under control by getting a few bruises ourselves
> V: Who was "kept under control"?

    *B*: The conflict, we kept it under control, we stopped it. We got what
        was due to us and went.
    *V*: I didn't get hit.
    *B*: Okay, only I got hit.
    *V*: In general it was Z and me who sorted things out.
    *B*: And K just sloped off to one side. And a lot of lads just sloped off as
        well. Only three of us got it then: Z, myself and you.
    *V*: I didn't get hit at all . . .

The subtext of this argument lies in an earlier incident when the two
speakers had clashed over the issue of army conscription. V had just
returned from two years army service and had been accused by B of
helping to split up the *tusovka* by not managing to evade conscription.
The accuser had himself served six months before feigning suicide and
being discharged for reasons of mental instability. At this point V had
retorted angrily that he had not 'not managed to' evade the army, he had
actually wanted to serve. Both conversations revealed an insecurity about
the group's masculine identity. This uneasiness with the soft masculine
image of the *stiliagi* took a tangible form with the emergence of a pattern of
*tusovka* progression: the movement of lads out of the *stiliagi* and into the
*rokabilly*. This movement may have resolved the crisis for the lads, but it
created a new one for the girls since it began to shut down the spaces they
had found. The process of change in the youth cultural scene which is dealt
with in the next and final section of this chapter thus has an important
gender dimension.

## THE TU-SOVKA: MARKETIZATION, GLOBALIZATION AND MOSCOW YOUTH CULTURE

This chapter so far has focused on recreating, and analysing the structure
of, the Moscow youth cultural world as it was understood by those interviewed. The result has been a static picture constructed from people's
frozen perceptions of reality. The period under consideration – 1985–91 –
however, was one of enormous social and cultural change in Russia and the
youth cultural sphere was not immune to the processes of change, but was
itself undergoing a permanent process of restructuring. The following
section will offer an analysis which aims to address three issues. First, the
development of the *stiliaga tusovka* over the period 1988–91 will be
charted. Second, this internal change will be related to wider changes on
the Moscow youth cultural scene. Finally, an understanding of why these
changes came about will be suggested.

    The analysis of recorded interviews revealed three generations of *stiliagi*.
By 'generation' is meant not cohort of entry into or exit from the group;
the generations overlapped to a considerable extent and, especially during

the height of the group, there were simultaneous *tusovki* which differed significantly in their dress and behavioural codes. What is meant is reference groups around whom specific *stil'nie* identities developed. The first of these, which has been called 'retro-style' for reasons explained below, actually incorporates two generations: the very first generation of revivalist *stiliagi* who appeared from 1985 and whose numbers began to increase rapidly during 1986 and 1987; and the second generation which emerged from the end of 1987 to the beginning of 1988 and which was associated with the growing popularity and fame of the rock groups 'Bravo' and 'Brigada S'. These two generations are merged in Table 8.1 since not enough of the first generation were interviewed in order to gain a clear idea of how its identity differed from the second, although known differences (such as in gender balance) are indicated. Table 8.1 therefore essentially summarizes the chief characteristics of the three generations of *stiliagi* in Moscow between 1988 and 1991 whilst making reference to the earlier generation where possible. The purpose of Table 8.1 is not to provide a rigid classification but to illustrate a number of trends that need to be explained. The first of these is a movement away from retro or Soviet rock 'n' roll (symbolized by 'Bravo') in favour of American rock 'n' roll of the 1950s and 1960s (column 1). This was accompanied by a movement towards paired rather than singles dancing and away from information-swopping and towards game-playing and 'having a laugh' (column 5). Second, there was a gradual reduction in the number of *stiliagi* (column 2) and an accompanying trend towards less regular and more goal-orientated meetings (at gigs and concerts), and towards meetings at places which were general *tusovochnie* places rather than places exclusive to the *stiliagi*. Third, in terms of gender composition, there was at first a rise and then a marked fall in the ratio of girls to boys in the *stiliagi* (column 3). Finally there is a change in intra-group relations (column 4) showing a movement towards a more hierarchical structure before the dissolution into small *tusovki* of friends.

These trends must be explained within the context not only of internal group dynamics but also of the whole youth cultural scene. Such a contextualization reveals two major processes shaping the group between 1988 and 1991: a drive towards authenticity within the *tusovka*; and a movement towards inclusivity rather than exclusivity in relation to other *tusovki*. These two themes help explain the dynamics of change in the youth cultural world which will be explored in some detail below.

**The drive towards authenticity**

The growing popularity of the groups 'Bravo' and 'Brigada S', as well as the greater opportunity to perform in public meant that the *stil'naia*

*Table 8.1* Generations of *stiliagi* 1988–91

| Generation | Number | Ratio of girls:lads | Internal structure | Activities | Meeting places | Meeting times |
|---|---|---|---|---|---|---|
| *Retro style* (1985–mid-1988)* | Steady growth 1986–7. Peaked in 1988 (100 at gigs) | In 1986 majority were lads but by 1988 there were more girls than lads | Code of 'brothers and sisters', although certain long-standing members were seen to be moral 'leaders' | • dancing (in groups)<br>• going for walks<br>• going to the cinema<br>• going to lectures<br>• swopping info. on rock 'n' roll<br>• going to concerts<br>• wearing *prikid* | Prospekt, Moloko cafes; Arbat; Metro 'Rizhskaia' | daily |
| *Purist style* (mid-1988–mid-1989) | 100–150 | number of girls fell at first; later outflow of boys meant that by mid-1989 only girls left | hierarchy by length of time in *tusovka* | • dancing (in groups and pairs)<br>• playing<br>• going for walks<br>• having a laugh<br>• having a drink<br>• having fun<br>• forming own band<br>• 'going crazy'<br>• wearing *prikid* | Arbat; Catacombs Prospekt cafe | at first daily, then most days |
| *Post-Bravo style* (mid-1989–autumn 1991) | about 100 in Moscow as a whole | 1:10 | no clear structure other than small groups of friends | • going to concerts<br>• listening to music at home<br>• forming your own band | Arbat | at gigs, discos, concerts |

* Although 'Bravo' made their debut in December 1983, the group disappeared after Zhanna Aguzarova was detained for having false identification and imprisoned for eight months before being sent back to her parents' home in Siberia. The group reemerged on the concert scene in the summer of 1985 after Zhanna's return to Moscow (Troitsky 1990: 51–63).

*tusovka* expanded rapidly throughout 1986 and 1987. As it did so, there emerged a fear that new members would be dedicated followers of fashion rather than of rock 'n' roll. Consequently, those who were at the centre of the group increasingly distanced themselves from the periphery through a hierarchy of respect according to the length of time members had been in *stil'* and their knowledge of the music and style of the 1950s. At first this hierarchy consisted of little more than a reserved attitude to new members and complaints that *lokhi* were destroying the *tusovka*. The term *lokh* was a general term of exclusion used to describe those who 'belong to no *tusovka*', who 'are narrow minded' or 'lacking in interests' (see above). But it was often used more specifically to describe those who hung around on the periphery of any *tusovka* but remained unaccepted into the group because they appeared to be interested in only its image and to know little or nothing about the music, dance or style it followed. In this sense the term *lokh* in its plural form (*lokhi*) was sometimes used as a negative synonym for new members.

In the *stiliagi* these hierarchical divisions were articulated verbally by the labels *pionery* ('pioneers', after the communist children's organization) and *stariki* ('old timers'). The *pionery* often mixed together in their own sub-*tusovki* but since there was no fixed period of *pioner* and *starik* status, much depended on the individual involved and the coalition of the *tusovka* at the time.

It was in the second generation period that divisions between newer and older members were most strictly kept. One former *stiliaga* noted that when he first joined the *stiliagi* (during the first generation):

> You got to know everyone. If they saw a young *stiliaga*, they wouldn't call you 'a young one' or 'a pioneer'. They didn't differentiate. In principle everyone was a pioneer.
>
> (K)

Despite the later, stricter differentiation, some members became accepted as fully-fledged members because they happened to become good friends of older members or were particularly respected for their independence of mind or for their *stil'*. In one instance this happened when a *pioner* happened to be on holiday in the same place as some of the older members of the *tusovka* and they became friends (D, F, G).

Subsequently, the hierarchy according to experience became visually symbolized in the wearing of differently coloured socks (see Figure 7.1). Although the colour-coding was not strictly adhered to (in many respects it remained more important to obtain a good pair of 'stylish' socks than socks of the right colour), it did act as a visual reminder that it was length of time spent in the group, dedication to and knowledge of rock 'n' roll which were to be respected and not flashiness, wit or physical strength. During this second generation period, the colour-coding of socks became particularly important. Prior to this the colour of socks had been an indication of

*Plate 11* One group of second generation *stiliagi*.

*Plate 12* By 1991, the *stiliagi tusovka* had degenerated into little more than groups of friends. These are a couple of third generation *stiliagi* at the 'Catacombs', spring 1991.

whether you were primarily a fan of 'Bravo' (white socks), 'Brigada S' (red socks) or 'Mister Twister' (black socks).[22] By the second and third generations the colour-coding according to style and length of time in the *tusovka* had become merged leading to differing recollections of its significance. Broadly speaking, however, the second and third generation members recalled that red socks were worn by the *pionery,* white were associated with those who had been in the *tusovka* for a year, yellow were for those who had been members even longer, while blue or green were for the oldest *stariki* (F).

The desire for purity and authenticity is well advanced in most *tusovki* and is manifest especially in a reverence for the 'classics' of whatever musical trend is followed. The punks interviewed, for example, were highly suspicious of virtually any post-Sex-Pistols punk. The striving for authenticity which characterized the second generation of *stiliagi* bore not only a Soviet but also a gendered character, however.

The importance of gender is most apparent when the *tusovka* is viewed within the wider context of the Moscow youth cultural scene, since it reveals that the threat to the *tusovka* was not only of 'swamping' due to the popularity of 'Bravo', but rooted in the image of this female-led group. An uneasiness among the male members of the group with the 'Bravo' image first became evident in explanations given by *stiliagi* as to why members had left the *tusovka*. It was generally claimed that girls were loyal to the *stiliagi* and moved away from the group only when they were drawn back into 'normal life', usually through marriage or pregnancy. Lads, on the contrary, left for two reasons: because they were called up for military service; or because they joined other *tusovki*. Although *stiliagi* lads might become 'Depeche Mode' fans or punks, by far the most common progression was into the *rokabilly*. The flow of lads from the second generation of *stiliagi* into the *rokabilly* began in the spring of 1989 and by the summer of that year, there were virtually only girls left. One of the lads who left the *stiliagi* and joined the *rokabilly* summed up the reasons for this:

> They [the *rokabilly*] were more aggressive, but they were also cooler (*bolee krutie*) . . . At that time, there were very few *stiliagi* who could respond to anything aggressively, that is many were passive and I did not like that.
>
> (P)

There are two interesting implications here. First, many of the lads felt insecure with the gender identity of the *stiliagi* in the 'Bravo' period. The *rokabilly* (a style based around the group 'Mister Twister') allowed them to retain their basic orientation towards rock 'n' roll music but with a much harder masculine identity. The *rokabilly* marked a half-way house to being a *roker*, and the *rokery* were widely acknowledged as *the* coolest *tusovka* in Moscow. The *rokery* modelled themselves on the American rockers (greasers or bikers) whose macho style was accompanied by a contempt for 'effeminate' subcultural styles and for women.

Second, and perhaps even more interesting, was the fact that this movement away from 'Bravo' and the *stiliagi* came to be associated with the gaining of authenticity. The *Bravisty* (and the *Brigadiry*) became viewed as followers of a revisionist (retro) rock 'n' roll which was a kind of Soviet imitation of the genuine early American rock 'n' roll. This was noted by one of the members of the group 'Mister Twister' when he explained how the band itself had passed from being a *stil'naia* to a *rokabilly* band:

> The *stil'naia tusovka* grew out of the group 'Bravo' and when we appeared two years later, we had the same style – Soviet teddy boys. But then . . . we changed our image and began to play more American music because I would class 'Bravo' as the Soviet stereotype of rock 'n' roll. It is an interpretation of the *stiliagi* in the Soviet Union in the 1950s, it is an understanding of America through a Soviet prism.

(O)

The peculiar relationship to 'things American' among young people in the former Soviet Union is interesting in itself. As Aksenov rightly notes there is a long-standing cultural notion that somehow Americans and Russians are 'very similar'. Thus, he argues, even at the height of the cold war there were many fans of America in the highest echelons of government whilst at the mass level pro-Americanism was based on the association of the word 'America' with the appearance of American military vehicles as well as food during the famines of the war (Aksenov 1987: 16). Although today this 'oneness' with Americans is rarely elaborated upon, concretized or documented it appears to be defined against both an anti-Europeanness (Europeans as 'complex' and 'cold') and an anti-Asiaticness (Asians as 'cunning' and 'deceitful'). In the case of the *rokery* it is associated with a shared simplicity of desires, the control of space through technology and freedom.

The association of the *stiliagi* with the Soviet past rather than with America (past or present) was not uniformly viewed negatively. Many of the *stiliagi* said their interest in the group had arisen not from listening to 'Bravo' or Elvis Presley, but from a fascination with the 1950s which was associated with a sense of a more peaceful, prosperous and less stressful period of Soviet history – a period of openings (H). One member of the group had a collection of memorabilia from the 1950s and many *stiliagi* learned about the styles and music from their parents and relatives. The memory of the struggles of the first *stiliagi* with the *Komsomol* voluntary brigades (*druzhinniki*) – who cut the *stiliagi*'s narrow trousers – and the derision of their style by the general public also conjured up a romantic image of past brushes with authority. As one of the youngest *stiliagi* put it:

It was cool (*kruto*) then – they were suppressed. And I like the spirit of it somehow.

(A)

But for others, the image of the contemporary *stiliagi* was more important – as one of the early members of the *stiliagi* explained:

It is generally accepted that *stiliagi* wear little jackets, that they are 'prissy' . . . The *rokabilly* are associated with leather, studded belts, terrible embroidered patches, motorbikes and so on, whereas the *stiliagi* are associated with umbrellas and briefcases. For this reason, if you were a *rokabilly*, then you were seen as cool (*kruto*).

(W)

The process of re-identification which accompanied a movement into the *rokabilly* thus often also included the adoption of an English-sounding nickname such as 'Maikl' or 'Dzhon', which were deemed 'cooler' (G).

It was the second generation of *stiliagi* who were most acutely aware of the split in the *tusovka* between 'Mister Twister' and 'Bravo' fans and as more and more of the lads turned to the *rokabilly*, the girls began to accept its 'natural' superiority. One of them explained the difference thus:

*rokabilly* is a harder style . . . whereas 'Bravo' have gentler little songs. In general, they ['Bravo'] are more like retro-style, the style of the 1960s whereas the Twisters have always been harder, cooler, more wild – better of course. It was only later that we began to understand that they were much better . . .

(D)

This understanding was reinforced by a barrage of derision directed at 'Bravo' and their fans by the *rokabilly*. One *stiliaga* related how members of a rokabilly group:

recounted all kinds of horrid tales about her [Zhanna Aguzarova], such as how she almost broke a bottle over their heads. And [they said] that she was virtually a prostitute and generally a nasty piece of work.

(F)

By the third (post-'Bravo') generation of *stiliagi*, therefore, 'Bravo' had come to be accepted as a fond memory and starting point, from which they should move on to the real thing, i.e. the roots of rock 'n' roll.

The 'hardness' and 'coolness' sought by the *rokabilly* was not confined to the sphere of music and style, it was also related to a rejection of the street position of the *stiliagi* lads. Defining what it meant to be a good member of the *tusovka* one of the lads who had moved from the *stiliagi* to the *rokabilly* stated:

It means not making life hard for any of the *tusovka*, being an interesting person to talk to, being valued by everyone, being able to stand up for your friend, being 'one for all and all for one'.

(P)

The overtly macho image also had its advantages – whereas the *stiliagi* lads were likely to picked upon by the *liubery* and their like, the *rokabilly* and *rokery*, it was claimed, would be left untouched (X). Unlike the *stiliagi*, whose style tended to arouse curiosity and sympathy (except amongst the *liubery*), the *rokabilly* could intimidate others and leave them in awe. This was an important motivating factor in leaving the *stiliagi* since many lads were fed up with the 'unwanted attentions' of the *liubery*.

The masculinist style of the *rokabilly* was not attractive or 'cool' in the eyes of all the *stiliagi*, however. The *rokabilly* style was also associated with crudeness, drunkeness, disrespect for girls and general hooliganism. One of the lads of the third generation associated the *rokabilly* with a downward progression from the *stiliagi*:

> There were some lads from Medvedkovo [a district of Moscow] . . . they were part of our *tusovka* for about six months. At first everything was fine. We phoned each other, went to the 'Moloko' together, but then only two remained in *stil'* and the rest became *rokabilly* types – of a *gopnik* ilk. They would come to concerts to get drunk and that kind of stuff.
>
> (S)

An earlier member of the *stiliagi* also associated the *rokabilly* with an antisocial image and claimed that although at that time the *rokabilly* and the *stiliagi* were part of the same *tusovka*, in their dress and behaviour, the *rokabilly* were closer to the punks than the *stiliagi* (K). The influence of the more macho image of some of the other *tusovki* on the current *stiliagi* was particularly evident to this former *stiliaga* since he had been away on military service for eighteen months. He summed it up thus:

> They [the *stiliagi*] were so sweet (*laskovie*) then, not like now, when they thump you on the shoulder and say, "*stiliaga*, come with us!" Then they simply hugged each other.
>
> (K)

This influence is also evident in the kinds of activities in which the second generation was involved; a number of the lads noted that they would 'be boisterous', 'lark about', 'be a bit of a hooligan'. Although much of this was bravado, no such claims were made by the first generation *stiliagi*.

What is perhaps most interesting is that what was and was not considered cool (*kruto*) was defined by such an exclusively male strategy. Many of the first generation *stiliagi* had never seen the *rokabilly* as a natural progression from the *stiliagi*. The *rokabilly* were associated with drinking and swearing which were consciously excluded from the *stiliagi* image and could not be easily incorporated into a positive feminine identity. By the second generation, however, the girls had come to agree without hesitation that the coolest *tusovka* in Moscow was the *rokery* – although none would have wanted to join it, they claimed. One female *stiliaga*, who overlapped the first and second generations, explained why this was so:

> It is more terrifying, more difficult for a girl to become a *rokabilly*. It is easier for lads to find and wear ripped leather jackets and boots. We girls, could not imagine how we would look.

(E)

By the time the field work was completed at the end of August 1991, this position seemed to be more or less shared by some of the girls of the second generation. Following a concert where some of the best-known and most prestigious *rokery* had been present, two of the girls described how they had been horrified at their scruffy appearance, the poor repair of their bikes and compared them unfavourably to the *rokery* in Talinn who, they had heard, looked after themselves and behaved like real gentlemen (D). In contrast, the stories told about the Moscow *rokery* were far less savoury – including incidences of violence towards girls and the 'selling' of access to girls in order to gain acceptance into the group.

But by this time, the *stiliaga* family of 'brothers and sisters' had virtually disappeared. At a 'Mister Twister' concert in July 1991 (the memorial concert to band member Vadim Dorokhov who had died earlier that summer), there was a notable absence of girls dancing rock 'n' roll as they had done at 'Bravo' and 'Brigada S' concerts. Male versions of sexuality prevailed as, on stage, the bass player of the group fondled the back of his double bass which was decorated with a painting of a naked woman while on the dance floor, only two lads wore identifiable *stil'* and they danced rock 'n' roll together in a sexually aggressive way.

The drive for authenticity among the *stiliagi* thus indicates more than a growing sophistication in their consumption of Western music, information and artefacts. It included the move towards a more hierarchically differentiated *tusovka* in which the ritual of introducing new members to the group became increasingly important in order to prevent the swamping of the group by *lokhi*. The gaining of authenticity was also framed in the forging of a harder masculine identity. This was expressed in a move away from Soviet style rock 'n' roll to a harder American variant. The clean and respectable *stiliagi* image was rejected in favour of the harder image of the *rokery* and achieved via an adoption of some traits of the *rokabilly*, with some lads actually leaving the *stiliagi* for this group. The *rokery* strategy was not one that allowed *stiliagi* girls space to create their own positive feminine identity and this, combined with the loss of Zhanna Aguzarova from 'Bravo', left the *stiliagi* girls stranded.

*Plate 13* 'Mister, Twister' in concert, spring 1991. The *rokabilly* style offered a harder, masculine image for male *stiliagi*.

*Plate 14* At an Elvis Presley memorial concert, 1992; *roker* style now dominates the former *stiliagi* scene.

## The trend towards inclusivity

To explain the tendency to include rather than exclude people from the *stiliagi* members of the group used largely subjective factors. According to them, the *stiliagi* were a 'friendly' (*druzhnaia*) *tusovka* and as a result many other *tusovki* (including *mazhory*, *rokery* and *Depesha*) would approach them where they hung out (on the Arbat or at the metro station Ploshchad' Revoliutsii), or would come along to their nights at the 'Prospekt' cafe (D). This may be so, but other factors must also be taken into account.

First, although the drive towards authenticity might appear to be diametrically opposed to a trend towards inclusivity, in fact the two were closely linked. As the group expanded, the core strengthened itself and became more exclusive thereby distancing itself from the periphery and giving rise to greater drifting in and out of different *tusovki*. In other words, the process of increased differentiation within the group led to less differentiation between groups. This is evident in explanations of how the first generation of *stiliagi* disintegrated:

> Our own group split up because the leader got married and moved away to another city to live with his wife . . . This meant we needed a new leader, a man . . . Z could have fitted the bill . . . but by then he did not like the fact that a lot of lads who were no good had appeared in our *tusovka*. He did not want to have anything to do with them.
>
> (E)

Second, inclusivity was fostered by a gradual movement in the location of the *stil'nie tusovki*. In the early period of glasnost there were concerts, gigs or rock 'n' roll discos virtually every night. A number of factors combined to change this. First of all, the prime, and still most fondly remembered *tusovka* site, the 'Prospekt' cafe, was closed on 13 December 1988. Although the rock 'n' roll nights were moved to the 'Moloko' cafe, this was much further out of town and was consequently soon colonized by local *gopniki* and, later, 'Depeche Mode' fans. The 'Moloko' never attracted the popularity that the 'Prospekt' had, where about 150 people (mainly *stiliagi* and 'Depeche Mode' fans) had gathered every night. The 'Moloko' also periodically shut its doors, as its future was debated by the local council following complaints by local residents about the alleged noise, fights and drug taking, and while local officials worked out how best to maximize profit from the cafe in the transition to self-financing and anticipated privatization.

In addition to this, the splits in the group 'Bravo' and the departure of Zhanna Aguzarova for a solo career ruptured the key *stiliaga* band. Although the leader of the group, Zhenia Khavtan, remained with the group and a new lead singer – Zhenia Osin – appeared in the spring of 1989, the group remained unstable and dependent upon retro style in a way that it had never been with the input of Aguzarova. Finally, the opening up of opportunities to tour both within the Soviet Union and abroad as well as the increasing financial pressures on bands meant that they played less often in Moscow. By 1988, advertised concerts and gigs were being can-celled at the last minute, not due to official prohibition as might earlier have been the case, but because the band had not returned from tour. The effect on the *tusovka* was that there was a gradual shift of the main site of its activity to the Arbat. The importance of this is that the Arbat was not an exclusively *stiliagi* venue, but a common stamping ground for Moscow *neformaly*. Interaction was increased and so was peripheral drift between *tusovki*.

The third pull towards inclusivity lay with the presence and role of the girls in the group. First, as a *tusovka*, the *stiliagi* were generally of low prestige and for this reason outsiders felt no fear of mixing with them. There was no threat of being spurned by the group or being accused of trying to gain access to the group. Moreover, there were positive benefits of being in their company. Wherever the *stiliagi* were you could guarantee a predominance of girls – an important consideration when a group of lads is looking for a 'good night out'. Second, the role of the girls in the group considerably fostered inclusivity. Despite the general agreement that a male leader would have helped the group stay together, in fact there is some evidence to suggest that the girls played a key role in keeping the group together. In a practical sense, it was often the girls who organized big get-togethers by keeping the phone numbers of *tusovka* members and informing them of major events. Two of the female members' nicknames were earned as a result of this role – *Matushka* ('Mother') and *Kultorg* ('Ents-officer'). A comparison might be drawn here to the role of unmar-ried girls in organizing the *posidelki* in pre-revolutionary Russia since it was they who were responsible for renting a house for the evening festivi-ties. In a very physical sense, the *stiliagi* girls kept the *tusovka* alive when its ranks were depleted by conscription or disappearance into the *rokabilly*.

The fact that the girls stayed in the *stiliagi* or went back into 'normal life', then, is less due to 'loyalty' as was suggested above by one of the *stiliagi* lads, than that they had nowhere else to go, since the groups to which the lads went presented no real space for *stiliagi* girls. The girls who had witnessed the disintegration of their own *tusovka*, and were too old to become part of the younger generation but too young to want to withdraw altogether, began to create a new *tusovka* along less sectarian lines – i.e. more a group of *neformaly* friends than a *tusovka* in the strict sense.

This strategy was one of the decisive factors in the movement towards inclusivity. The girls' strategy was aimed at the creation of their own mixed *tusovka* which, at one and the same time, was not sexually threatening (as they perceived the *rokery* and to a lesser extent the *rokabilly* to be) but which was also exciting. As one former *stiliaga* girl put it:

My *tusovka* now consists of various people, not only *stiliagi*, but those from other tendencies. Among my *tusovka* are punks and just 'abnormal' people (*nenormaly*) who find it interesting to hang around (*tusovat'sia*) with different kinds of people.

(F)

The shifts between groups also changed the environment of the male *stiliagi*. In particular, they had increased contact with the economic *neformaly*, partly because of the need to acquire the youth cultural artefacts befitting their new crowd, but also because they increasingly felt the pressure to earn money. A number of former male *stiliagi* had gone into second economy dealing more or less full-time, a couple had ended up in jail for minor offenses and one had had to disappear to another city to escape the forcible extraction of debts incurred from this activity. One member of the *tusovka* had died during non-combat military service, while another had feigned suicide attempts in order to be released early. None, the girls said on reflection, had got on in life (*vyshli v liudi*) (D, F, G).

The girls appeared to find it easier to slip back into normal life, or, as one *stiliaga* put it, 'become domesticated' (*domashnimi*) (E). One reason for this was that they had no other subcultural space to go to when the lads disappeared, and if this coincided with beginning a new job, course of study or long-term romantic relationship, the girls quickly slipped off the youth cultural scene. A second reason was that the girls seemed better able to combine the responsibilities of adult or 'formal' life with a 'non-formal' leisure time. In part this was because the *stiliagi* strategy was perfectly compatible with most 'formal' (*tsivil'nie*) values unlike the punks, for example, who consciously rejected the values of work and family. When, in their new *tusovka*, some of the second generation girls began to mix with more 'long-term' *neformaly*, they bemoaned the aimlessness of the lives of their new found friends who spent their days sleeping, drinking or riding motorbikes. In contrast they saw themselves as having a purpose, primarily a 'chosen profession', which meant that they would always be able to find a good job and do alright for themselves (D, F, G). This was an important part of their self-worth which did not necessarily contradict their subcultural past, or present.

Despite their new lives, however, the ex-*stiliagi* girls remained nostalgic for their *tusovka* days and explaining the collapse of the group by the conscription of the lads helped shift the blame for this onto 'them' (the authorities). In fact whether or not the lads had been dragged off to the army, it is likely that the old *tusovka* about which the girls reminisced would have disintegrated. There were indications that many of the second generation lads were beginning to find *tusovka* for the sake of *tusovka* meaningless. They were already experimenting with setting up their own musical bands or dealing in records and other youth cultural currencies, while the girls began to learn paired dancing and make their own 1950s dresses. This would have wrought significant changes in the *tusovka* way: less time would have been spent just being together; partners would have had to be found for discos and gigs; there would have been increasing interaction with the *tusovki* of more established musicians and *fartsovsh-chiki*. As a result, the *tusovka* would have changed of its own accord; the lads would have taken up their new interests with increasing seriousness and the girls would probably have ended up with the same nostalgia for the old days.

## CONCLUSION

The trend towards peripheral overlap, inclusivity and realignment on the Moscow youth cultural scene is deceptive in its apparent suggestion of a growing plurality and counter-cultural cohesion. As has also been shown, the breakup of the *stiliaga tusovka* was accompanied and encouraged by increased hierarchical strictness and an adoption of the more restrictive gender codes of the dominant culture. The second period of field work conducted in Moscow in 1991 showed that the genuinely subversive poly-vocality of the 'Moscow shuffle' was already in decline, and it was to re-emerge for a final send-off only once more – on the steps of the 'White House' in August 1991 (see concluding chapter). The *tusovka* was already beginning to give way to youth cultural formations which were more hierarchically organized, more exclusive and less genuinely subversive of the dominant culture. The *tusovka* had become the *tu-sovka*;[23] a part of the peculiar Soviet existence and baggage to be left behind in the process of entrance into the new global community and market.

The ascendent youth cultural forms, however, appeared characterized less by global sophistication than by crude expressions of power and prestige. In particular, the 'gang' (*banda*) formation was favoured – prob-ably inspired by the example of the extremely prestigious 'Night Wolves' (see Chapter 7). They earned this position partly simply through age – they were a good ten years older than the average *tusovka* – but also through their image which consisted of bikes, jackets, Harley Davidson accessories, girls and media attention. The link they had with the 'formal' world added to their prestige. By the summer of 1991, *Khirurg* himself was more often to be seen on youth television programmes, video clips and in the papers, than at his former notorious hang-outs. Indeed, by that time the 'Night Wolves' appeared to have taken up a direct role of social control of their peers. At a series of open-air concerts, the Night Wolves took on the role of maintaining security at concerts. Although the Night Wolves are only one, highly prestigious group, the gang form of youth cultural activity has much in common with the *gopnik* strategy of territor-ial defence and attack as well as the masculinism of the Moscow *rokery*. Not surprisingly, then, there was evidence that the gang was attractive to Moscow lads. When asked to describe his ideal *tusovka*, one 18 year old male interviewee replied:

*Plate 15* All dressed up with nowhere to go . . . These are former *stiliagi* girls with their new crowd, summer 1991.

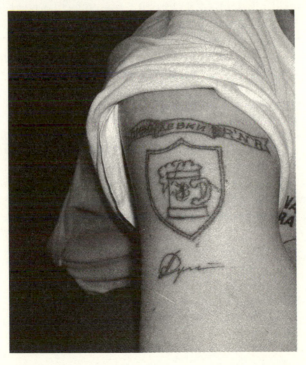

*Plate 16* One of this new crowd sports a tattoo reading, 'beer, girls and rock 'n' roll'.

I would like to have my own gang (*banda*), in fact everyone wants to have their own gang – so that everything would not depend on what kind of music you listen to. We would hang out (*tusovat'sia*) in a certain place and, when necessary, be hooligans. Naturally, [the group would consist of] lads, so that they could defend themselves against anyone.

(Q)

As might be expected from the discussion of the *gopnik* strategy, one of the key elements of such a gang is some kind of mobility. The 'Night Wolves' had their motorbikes and other existing gangs used skateboards, roller-skates or push-bikes. Having transport was crucial because: it allowed you to get to your 'business' locations better; it helped you get to and out of situations more quickly; it made the city appear controllable; and it avoided complicity with 'them' by eliminating the need to use that symbol of Soviet power, the Moscow metro.

The dynamics of the *stil'naia tusovka* and the Moscow youth cultural scene are suggestive of wider social processes. Industrial society, so rapidly constructed in the Soviet Union, was unevenly developed and heavily reliant upon key central organizations. This inhibited and, finally, prevented the transition to a post-industrial state in which the urban citizen-consumer created and satisfied her/his needs as an individual/family member. Instead relations of reciprocity and collective need-satisfaction were fuelled by the second economy and the multiple sites of interaction and identification which this fostered became a key part of Soviet social development. The *neformaly*, therefore, were not a product of a first flush of civic initiative following the lifting of the lid on a totalitarian society, but a phenomenon already part of Soviet reality. Like other *neformaly*, the *tusovki* certainly bloomed in the perestroika period but less because they finally had a political aim to which to dedicate their energies than because this was precisely a time of multiple voices. As the new economic and political structures began to speak in a single voice again, however, the *tusovka* was increasingly buried under Euro-pop and McDonalds empties. The heteroglossia of the 'Moscow shuffle' was gradually silenced by the shoring up of the dominant cultural codes – although not without one last celebration.

# Conclusion
## Partying at the barricades

Russian youth culture is shaped and reshaped continually and by the time this book goes to publication most of those young people who have contributed to its writing will be long gone from the scene and, for those who have taken their places, the practices described will appear as ancient history. Rather than summarize the preceding chapters, therefore, this final space will be used to address more directly two issues raised by both the theoretical and empirical study of Moscow youth culture: the political significance of Russian youth cultural activity; and the impact the study of Russian youth cultures might have on the theorization of youth culture world-wide.

It has been argued already that youth cultural activity in Russia has not been politically motivated either in a conscious way (a manifest desire for change) or an unconscious way (through passive resistance to politicization). This does not deny the fact that youth cultural activity has political significance, however, although the nature of this significance is open to interpretation. Below, this will be considered in the light of youth participation in the major political event to occur during the research period of this book: the attempted coup of August 1991.

### The coup as carnival

On the eve of the attempted coup one Moscow *roker* summed up his hopes and fears for the future thus:

> [all that I would like] is money and to be sure that tomorrow they won't start shooting people for wearing a leather jacket . . . this could happen because everything that happened in the past could repeat itself. Maybe soon you might be shot for having a motorbike, a leather jacket or a skull and crossbones.
>
> (Interview with Moscow *roker*, 18 August 1991)

At the time, the emphasis placed by the interviewee on the political significance of visible elements of non-conformity was interpreted by the author as registering, in fact, the value attached to them by him personally (especially since he was an aspiring rather than fully accepted *roker*). A completely different meaning was assigned to his words only on the morning following the interview, when Russia awoke to the announcement that Gorbachev's 'physical incapacity' to run the country had led to his replacement by a 'State Emergency Committee' (GKChP). From the rest of the announcement, however, it was clear that it was the President's political rather than physical deficiency which had constituted the 'emergency' for those who sought to replace him; the talk was not of the need for rest or medical help, but of the 'threat to the fatherland', of the drift into anarchy, of the need to restore order and preserve the political body (the Union) at all costs.[1] Rallying to the call of the Russian President, Boris Yeltsin, to resist the self-declared Committee there began the famous defense of the White House, and barricades were constructed around the Russian parliament building to prevent its seizure by the putschists. Information dwindled to a trickle of GKChP announcements while the real news – speculation about Gorbachev's whereabouts and possible involvement, and the state of play at the White House – circulated quickly by word of mouth. By the evening of the 21 August, however, for those defending the Russian parliament, the celebrations had already begun as it became known that the coup leaders had fled the Kremlin.

In reality, therefore, the attempted coup had not meant the return to hyper-conformity but, in the words of one participant, had provided, 'the biggest *tusovka* of the whole summer'. As the partying at the barricades came to an end, the post-party inquisition began and everywhere the first question on meeting was: 'Were you there?'. Stories were swopped of who had been where, for how long, and what they had seen. The punks professed aloofness; they had surveyed the scene from the back seat of a taxi. The *rokery* had used their motorbikes to deliver photocopies of Yeltsin's decrees and communiques. The *rokabilly* had taken their gear down to the barricades and played impromptu concerts. Former *stiliagi* confessed they 'would have gone', if they had had someone to go with. It might appear – as it did to many journalists covering the events in Moscow – that youth, and especially subcultural youth, was on the front line of perestroika after all. The central arenas of high politics had been invaded by the brightly coloured bodies of youth.

But it was not that the coup finally gave young people a chance to find their political voice and to stand up for democratic values which made the defence of the White House the event of the year. It was rather that, whilst the attempted coup should have marked the supremacy of high politics – the ultimate power of the generals – in fact it appeared as a festival in which politics had ceased to be the controlled exchange of rhetoric from which the majority was excluded. Words were replaced by bodies: that of Yeltsin as he scrambled onto a tank to denounce the attempted coup; those of children as they played on the tanks and their parents milled around Manezh Square in an atmosphere of public holiday (*narodnaia gulianiia*);

those of independent political groups as the RSFSR flag – with hammer and sickle cut out – was paraded through Moscow; those of soldiers as a group of crack troops, highly trained in blind obedience, refused to march to the tune of their officers; and those of the generals themselves, as Rutskoi and his posse raced the failed putschists to the Crimea in a 'follow that plane' finale. What happened in those cold, wet August days was that the boundaries between governing and governed, between leaders and led, insiders and outsiders were dissolved, their meanings dissipated. The punks were left to observe the spectacle instead of constituting the spectacle observed.

The reversals were momentary, but politically significant. They were so not because the people had 'stood up' – for Gorbachev, for Yeltsin, or even 'for themselves' – but because this national 'happening' marked a turning point in Russian politics. The first to feel the sea-change was Gorbachev himself who, returning from the Crimea, attempted to continue the politics of words and found that, disembodied as they were, his words froze on the air waves. Despite the apparent ground-swell of popular support for Yeltsin, even his hitherto successful politics of 'leaders and masses' was dealt a blow. Behind the outward authority, carefully won at the expense of Gorbachev, his call for collective action – for a general strike and civil disobedience – sank without trace, just as in October 1993 it was to do so again as attempts were made to muster popular support against the parliamentarians in an even more violent battle for the White House.

The importance of the attempted coup was thus ambiguous. On the one hand, its carnivalesque nature unmasked the generals and reconnected the body to its politic. Consequently, not only was the dominant meaning of politics (whether it be labelled communist or democrat) challenged but the very form of meaning (peopleless politics) was disrupted. This is not to suggest that 'the people' was reinstated to a (mythical) former glory, but that the re-embodiment of politics will release a host of *bodily politics* based on nationalisms, regionalisms and chauvinisms, as well as the politics of pleasure which challenge the old moral and social control boundaries of *rhetoric-driven politics*.

On the other hand, although carnival in its ideal type may completely disrupt established divisions and hierarchies, in contemporary Russian reality, the 'folk body' does not exist in pure isolation from the dominant order. As became apparent during the discussion of the youth cultural world in Part III of this book, embodied cultural practice remains premised upon on social divisions and zones of inclusion and exclusion (of centre–periphery, gender and race). Whilst resisting the pseudo-subjectivities of 'constructors-of-communism', therefore, youth cultural practices which bring back the body are only the starting points for the creation of other subjectivities which generally build on existing, and often oppressive, social divisions. Youth cultural activity in the perestroika era was the natural by-product neither of the lessening of political repression nor of the 'objective forces' of social and economic development. It was neither wholly incorporated into state structures nor locked away in its subcultural bunkers and wholly resistant to the dominant culture.

Its ambiguous position between culture and counter-culture need not necessarily disempower it, of course, and might indeed add a new dimension previously obscured in Western youth cultural studies. The formal/non-formal distinction helps locate the social site of the contestation of meanings and subjectivities. The delineation of the non-formal sphere in the Soviet context helps identify sites of human action where it had previously been assumed that meanings were not only fixed, but rigidly so. It remaps the social world in a 'depthless' way which suggests the horizontal rather vertical processes of cultural interaction and which envisages no simple dichotomy between state and society, culture and subculture, conformity and resistance.

At the same time, the very distinction between the realms of the formal and non-formal serves to highlight the slippage between them; the articulation of the formal/non-formal dichotomy during perestroika in fact represented not their growing apart but the dissolution of their boundaries. This period of exaggerated social slippage heralded a time of intense creative activity during which apparently rigid discourses were not only challenged but wrought asunder. This process reached its climax on the steps of the 'White House' when the excluded and the carnivalesque were brought into the official realm and the concept of public discourse was altered. This is 'the power of carnival' to which Bakhtin referred (Wills 1989: 132).

The reordering of public discourse taking place in the context of post-August 1991 political and economic reforms is likely to reinforce the social divisions referred to above, however. One effect of this has been the circumscription of the space for youth cultural forms, whose future currently appears to lie in increasingly extreme manifestations of bodily escape from social control – especially through experience-enhancing drugs. If this is the case, the carnival may well have served to strengthen the social order rather than fundamentally disrupt it.

The internal political significance of Russian youth culture in the perestroika years notwithstanding, its study confirms the importance of some current trends in the development of youth studies in the West, and suggests some new directions. The results of the study undertaken in this book support the need to construct a model of multiply divided subjects in a multiply divided society (Cohen, P. 1986: 52), whilst the peculiar experiences of class, gender and ethnic identity in former Soviet society would complicate, but refine such a model based on Western societies. In this context, the structures of social space – centre/periphery, placement/displacement – may have resonance beyond the disunited Soviet Union and especially in the 'new', but torn Europe. Furthermore, the findings confirm the need for the study of *pleasure* alongside *resistance* as a crucial site of youth activity. In particular the distinction between *plaisir* (channelled pleasure) and *jouissance* (libratory pleasure) is central to youth activity and this may be usefully developed especially in relation to current debates on 'active consumption' in contemporary cultural studies. Recognition of the 'embodied communication' of the *stiliagi* and others reveals the much greater reliance on *jouissance* than traditional Soviet classificationary analyses (based on means–end understandings of informal organizations) or Western sociological approaches (often starting out with a 'socio-economic problem: cultural solution' model) would lead one to believe.

Finally, the study of Russian youth cultures supports the movement away from the division between culture and subculture in favour of envisaging multiple incursions and separations between dominant and subordinate cultures. The distinction between formal and non-formal social spheres may aid this process by focusing attention precisely on slippage and the constant constitution and reconstitution of the boundaries between the two spheres. In this sense young people remain Russia's constructors and constructed.

# Appendix

This appendix gives some background data on the participants in the research project. In all, thirty-six young people participated in the research. Twenty-four of them took part in more or less formally structured interviews which were mainly conducted in the spring–summer 1991 period. Nine young people gave multiple interviews, the others gave only one formal interview although were met on numerous occasions. The remainder of those classed as 'participants' were young people with whom the author had a significant amount of contact, and were aware of her purpose, but who did not give recorded interviews. Table A.1 (at the end of this appendix) provides a broad social profile of each interviewee cited in the text (the 'age' and 'group affiliation' given is that at the time of interview in 1991 and level of education and/or current occupation is given where known).

## A social portrait of interviewees

The sociological data presented here are partial and cover only those twenty-four people who gave recorded interviews. The data are therefore not worthy of extensive analysis, but since, in certain instances, reference to personal background is used by group members to explain their own adoption of strategies, such a picture can illustrate important perceived differences in the membership of various groups. In order to protect the privacy of participants, the data is presented not in life-history form but by sociological category.

## Age

The average age of those interviewed was 19 (the oldest interviewees being 30 and the youngest 16). This average is higher than one might expect and reflects the author's interest in interviewing both present and past members of the groups.

## Gender

The gender breakdown showed a male dominance of 2:1 (sixteen male and eight female interviewees). However, proportionally more female informants gave multiple interviews (five male and five female) and in the main group of interest (the *stiliagi*), the imbalance was not so great (ten male and six female members were interviewed).

## Regional/ethnic background

The majority of informants (thirteen) had been born or had grown up in Moscow. Three others had grown up in the Moscow region (*oblast'*) and two had grown up in other cities. Of those who had grown up in Moscow, only two came from families which had moved into the city from outside (i.e. had parents who were not Muscovites). One of these was half Georgian, the others were apparently Russian, although interviewees noted that past members of the group had been of non-Russian or of mixed ethnic background (Latvian, Tartar, Ukrainian, Jewish).

## Education

Four of the informants had complete or incomplete further education at universities or institutes and five had completed, or were in the process of completing, ten classes (the equivalent of sixth-form in the UK) at school. Seven informants had completed eight classes at school before going on to college (*tekhnikum* or *uchilishche*), four of these at nursing college, and one had taken this route after ten classes at school.[1] Two interviewees had completed eight classes before going on to vocational-technical college (PTU) and another two went on to secondary vocational-technical college (SPTU).

The educational background of the twenty-one interviewees for whom data was available deviates somewhat from the average for the country, but less from the average for Moscow. The only significant discrepancy was the above average proportion attending or having attended specialized secondary institutions – 38 per cent as opposed to an average of around 10 per cent (Muckle 1988: 21; Krillov 1990). This may be accounted for by the greater choice of such institutions in the capital city together with the tendency for upward mobility in the already prestigious cities of Russia to be achieved through education rather than spatial mobility (migration). It should also be remembered that half of these students studied at nursing college which is of low prestige and, it is argued, is often chosen because entering the medical professions gives access to drugs and spirit.

## Employment

Despite the relatively high level of education of the interviewees, half were neither studying nor working at the time of interview. In the case of three of them, this was because they had either just returned from, were about to leave for, or trying to evade military service. Two were on disability pensions (being diagnosed mentally ill), two were happy to make their living through speculating (or 'doing business'), one was on leave to look after a small child, and one was in prison. Three gave no reasons for not working or studying. Although the growing difficulties for young people in finding places of work or study after school is giving cause for concern at the moment, the 4 per cent of school-leavers found to be in this position in 1989 (Kirillov 1990: 58) is considerably less than the proportion found among interviewees.

*Table A.1* A social profile of cited interviewees*

| Interviewee* | Age | Sex | Group affiliation | Education | Occupation |
|---|---|---|---|---|---|
| A | 17 | M | *stiliaga* | SPTU | studying |
| B | 16 | M | *rokabilly* | GSS (11) | studying |
| C | 16 | F | *stiliaga* | GSS (10) | studying |
| D | 20 | F | *stiliaga* | higher | student |
| E | 22 | F | *ex-stiliaga* | tekhnikum | n/e |
| F | 19 | F | *stiliaga* | higher | student |
| G | 19 | F | *stiliaga* | tekhnikum | typist |
| H | 19 | M | *ex-stiliaga* | n/k | n/e |
| I | 20 | M | *ex-stiliaga* | n/k | working |
| J | 16 | M | *stiliaga* | n/k | studying |
| K | 19 | M | *ex-Depesha* | SPTU | m/s |
| L | n/k | M | *punk* | PTU | n/e |
| M | 18 | M | *punk* | PTU | n/e |
| N | 25 | M | *rokabilly* | higher | engineer |
| O | 30 | M | *rokabilly* | military institute | musician |
| P | 18 | M | *roker* | tekhnikum | n/e |
| Q | 17 | M | n/a | n/k | studying |
| R | 18 | M | n/a | n/k | n/e |
| S | 18 | M | *stiliaga* | GSS | n/e |
| T | 18 | F | *stiliaga* | n/k | nurse |
| U | 20 | F | n/a | college (incomp) | n/e |
| V | 19 | F | ex-hippy | college | n/e |
| W | 21 | M | *ex-stiliaga* | tekhnikum | n/e |
| X | 19 | M | n/a | n/k | n/e |

\* Interviewees have been allocated arbitrary letter symbols in place of their names in order to protect privacy.

**Key**

| | |
|---|---|
| **GSS** | General Secondary School (if still at school, class is given in brackets) |
| **PTU** | Vocational-Technical College |
| **SPTU** | Secondary Vocational-Technical College |
| **(incomp)** | course was not completed |
| **m/s** | military service |
| **n/a** | no affiliation |
| **n/e** | not employed |
| **n/k** | not known |

# Glossary of youth culture slang

The glossary of youth slang includes only those words actually used by the young people interviewed in Moscow and which are relevant to the analysis of their cultural practice outlined in Chapter 8.[1] It is not intended to be a comprehensive dictionary of contemporary youth slang, which is rapidly changing and regionally differentiated. Some words and phrases are widely used in general *tusovka* slang and some are more specific to certain subcultural groups. The latter are indicated by the following abbreviations: S – *stiliagi*; P – punk; H – hippy. Where relevant, adjectival (adj.), adverbial (adv.), verbal (verb.), plural (pl.), diminutive (dimin.), masculine (masc.) or feminine (fem.) forms are given as well as the literal translation (lit.) before the use-meaning in youth slang. Words are listed alphabetically (in transliteration) together with any related forms.[2]

| | |
|---|---|
| *babki* | money |
| *baksy* | hard currency, 'bucks' |
| *baky* (S) | sideburns |
| *(o)baldet'* | to enjoy yourself, to go crazy |
| *obaldenno* (adv.) | fantastic, brilliant, awesome |
| *botanik* | (lit. botanist) person who studies hard, 'swot' |
| *chirik* | ten roubles |
| *chuvikha* (S) | girl (female *stiliaga*) |
| *chuvak* (S) | lad (male *stiliaga*) |
| *der'mo* | 'shit' |
| *fen'ka, fen'ki* (pl.) | |
| *fenechki* (dimin.) | adornments (usually beads) worn by hippies, funny story, joke[3] |
| *firmennii* | designer, foreign, imported (e.g. clothes) |
| *gerla* | girl |
| *gopnik* | thug, yob, provincial hooligan |
| *govno* | 'shit', rubbish |
| *griny* | dollars |
| *kachki* | bodybuilders |
| *kasha* | (active) *Komsomol* member |

| | |
|---|---|
| *katia* | a hundred roubles |
| *klassnii* | good-looking, 'cool', great |
| *klevii* | like *klassnii* but in both appearance and intellect e.g. *klevii chuvak* |
| *kok* (S) | 'quiff', teddyboy hairstyle |
| *(za/ot)kosit'* | to deceive, feign (usually mental illness in order to avoid army or prison sentence |
| *kosukha* | leather jacket, biker's jacket |
| *kosaia kurtka* | as above |
| *kosiachok* | dope, draw |
| *krezi-khaus* | psychiatric institution |
| *(po)krezit'* | to have fun, have a laugh |
| *krutoi* (adj.) *kruto* (adv.) | (lit. 'steep') stylish, 'cool', 'hard' |
| *krysha* | (lit. 'roof') head |
| *krysha poekhala* | gone mad |
| *sdvinut' kryshu* | to drive mad |
| *kusok* | a thousand roubles |
| *lazha* *lazhovii* (adj.) | rubbish!, bad, useless, pathetic |
| *lokh* (masc.) *lokhina* (fem.) *lokhovskii* (adj.) | provincial or country person, *limitchik*,[4] someone who does not belong to any *tusovka*, 'dork' |
| *lom* | low, downer (used as opposite of *kaif*, e.g. *v lom tuda idti* – 'I can't be bothered to go') |
| *mazhory* (pl.) | (lit. 'major') a group of elite youth who dress in Western, designer gear to which they have access due to the prestigious jobs of their parents |
| *men* | lad, man. Used of hippy men, or by other groups to indicate somebody male but not of their *tusovka* |
| *menty* (pl) | police |
| *mochalka* | tastelessly dressed or 'dolled up' girl, also suggests girl of 'easy virtue' |
| *mutnii* | boring, uninteresting |
| *naekhat'* (verb.) | to intimidate, hassle, give grief |
| *naezd* | (lit. 'raid') hassle, pestering |
| *nishtiak!* | brilliant!, wicked! |
| *pal'ba* or *palenka* | goods (usually clothes and accessories) produced in the USSR but made to look like Western, designer items |
| *passazhir* | friend, or person who wants something, e.g *u menia est' passazhiry na tvoi dzhinsy* – 'I have buyers for your jeans' |
| *pionery* (pl) | new members of a *tusovka* |

| | |
|---|---|
| *pont* | bluff, pretence |
| *prikid* | dress, costume, 'gear' |
| *priznat'* | to understand, accept (into the group) |
| *proletet'* (verb.) or *byt' v prolete* | to be gazumped on a deal |
| *prosekat'* | to understand someone when she/he is talking ambiguously |
| *psikh* | mad person |
| *psikhushka* | psychiatric hospital |
| *razdalbai* | person who does not pay attention to his/her *prikid*, someone who doesn't stick with their interests |
| *repa* | head, face |
| *roker* | biker, heavy rock fan |
| *samopal* | synonym for *pal'ba*. |
| *seishn* | gig, get-together with live music |
| *sovok* | (lit. 'shovel') USSR (the country) or Soviet citizen |
| *sovkovii* (adj.) | used to describe an attitude or mentality seen as typical of Soviet people or reality |
| *sovdep* | Soviet Union (taken from *Sovdepia* used by the |
| *sovdepskii* (adj.) | Whites during the civil war to describe land under Bolshevik control) |
| *sponsor* | someone who has money e.g *byt' sponsorom* means 'to pay for someone', 'treat someone' |
| *stariki* (pl) | longstanding members of a *tusovka* |
| *steb* | mocking, teasing, joke, sarcasm |
| *zastebat'* (verb.) | to alarm, tease, frighten |
| *stiliaga* | 1950s teddy boy or revivalist |
| *stiliagi* (pl) | rock 'n' roll fan |
| *stil'*, *stilnii* (adj.) | (lit. 'style'), style worn by *stiliagi* |
| *streliat'* | (lit. 'to shoot') to cadge (e.g. cigarette from passer-by) |
| *stremat'sia* | to be afraid, |
| *(za)stremat'* | to frighten |
| *stvol* | pistol, weapon |
| *tachka* | (lit. 'wheelbarrow') 'wheels' usually used of motorbike, but also of car |
| *tusovka* | a group or gathering of people sharing a particular interest |
| *tusovochnii* (adj.) *tusovat'sia* (verb.) | to go to *tusovki*, to hang out with a certain crowd |
| *urel, urla* (pl) | provincial, working-class youths |
| *utiug* | (lit. 'iron') speculator, someone who deals in the |
| *utiuzhit'* (verb.) | second economy, usually buying from and selling to foreigners |

| | |
|---|---|
| *v"ekhat'* | to understand, 'get', 'suss' |
| *zafenit'* | to like, to enjoy, synonym of *zatashchit'sia* |
| *zhaba* (P) | (lit. 'toad') girl, female punk |

# Notes

## 1 ON THE ROAD TO NOWHERE: UNDERSTANDING YOUTH CULTURE IN THE WEST

1 During the course of this chapter key texts in the study of youth culture and subculture will be noted and, where space permits, discussed. The best over-views of the whole debate are to be found in Cohen 1986, Brake 1985, Frith 1984 and Hebdige 1988.

2 The enclosure of agricultural lands in order to consolidate farm plots and divide communal lands took place in England during the fifteenth and sixteenth centuries (when landowners increased pasture land by enclosing land which had previously been held as 'common land') and in the eighteenth and nineteenth centuries as part of the drive towards improving agricultural efficiency.

3 Pearson notes that the precise origin of the term 'hooligan' remains unclear. The press of the time attributed various roots, the one which gained widest acceptance being that it was a corruption of 'Hooly's gang'. Hooly was a well-known swindler of the time and the source of much press attention and popular jokes. However, Pearson sees the hooligans as not just a local gang, but a whole youth culture and their name probably originated in the popular culture of working-class London, having been adopted by youths in a number of localities to describe and identify themselves (Pearson 1983: 74, 255–6).

4 Abrams quotes survey statistics suggesting that 60 per cent of teenagers visited the cinema at least once a week, whereas amongst the rest of population the figure was 13 per cent, and 49 per cent never went to the cinema (Abrams 1959: 14).

5 The particularly bleak portrayal painted by Hoggart of post-war youth in his *Uses of Literacy* is noted by Bradley (Bradley 1989: 223).

6 The successful reproduction of social relations through the guided consumption of mass media forms by subordinated groups has not only been applied to the working class or to the post-war period. One explanation given for the Los Angeles riots of April 1992 – by a member of the local black community – was that the low morality of everyday life emanating from the soap-operas, maga-zines and other media forms of mass consumption facilitated the reproduction of the subordinate position of black Americans by further weakening a commu-nity already devastated by the breakdown of the family, drugs and alcohol abuse and the poverty of the one-parent family.

7 This should not be understood as a crude manipulation of working-class kids into working-class jobs, since the acceptance of a working-class future is often the unintended by-product of progressive intentions in education aimed at achieving precisely the opposite cultural effect (Willis 1977: 178). Nevertheless, Willis has been criticized for a functionalist tendency in his privileging of the

synchronic (the system of positions or places) over the diachronic (the 'shifters' which articulate the life-historical process) (Cohen 1986: 25–7).

8 For a much more thorough examination of the origins and development of this pioneering work, see Turner 1990 and Bennett *et al.* (eds) 1981.

9 This refers to British Prime Minister Harold Macmillan's speech of July 1957 in which he articulated the self-congratulatory tone of the times through his declaration that 'our people have never had it so good'.

## 2 BUILDING THE ROAD TO NOWHERE: YOUTH IN THE SOVIET-RUSSIAN TRADITION

1 For the early part of Soviet history it would in fact be more correct to term this paradigm 'victims-of-*bourgeois*-influence', and the origins of the shift are explained below. For the sake of consistency, however, the paradigm will be referred to as 'victims-of-*Western*-influence' throughout this chapter.

2 Translations are taken here from Worobec 1991: 223. Although the focus of this section is the ways of life of Russian peasant youth, similar formations were found in other Slavic regions such as the *parubotski* and *gromady* in Belarus and Ukraine.

3 The youth labour protection promises made before the revolution were fulfilled alongside the enfranchisement of 18–19 year old workers and their granting of free entry into the universities (Baum 1987: 12). However, the degree to which the actual implementation of new legislation was possible in the period following the revolution remains an important question for debate.

4 '*Lichnost'*' is defined as 'an individual possessing such qualities as to allow him to live in society and, co-operating with other people, to produce objects satisfying his personal and social needs' (Demin 1988: 17).

5 The New Economic Policy (NEP) was introduced in March 1921 after a period of tight economic and political control during the civil war. It restored market relations in the countryside and allowed a plurality of forms of ownership (state, co-operative and private). Some saw it as no more than a temporary 'retreat' from socialism necessary in order to stabilize the economy and society after the civil war, while others saw it as an alternative, and less painful, route to communism.

6 Esenin was a contemporary poet whose suicide in 1925 inspired a movement of the disillusioned in the NEP period.

7 One such song was:

> *Komsomol* noodles
> Sold God for roubles:
> With the money they made
> They bought a mangy man* instead
> > (Bocharov 1959: 50)
> * meaning Lenin

8 This quote is taken from answers to questions put to Lenin at the Third All-Russian Congress of the RKSM on 2 October 1920 (where he delivered the famous 'Tasks of the youth leagues' speech). The full transcript of the questions and answers had just been retrieved from the Central Party Archive.

9 *Otkhodniki* were peasants who left their villages in search of seasonal work in the towns. For a more detailed discussion of the social and cultural implications of the *otkhod* in the NEP period see Weiner 1991.

10 This society grew from a membership of two million to twelve million by the end of the First Five Year Plan and acted simultaneously as a militia, home guard,

and civil defence. It was renamed DOSAAF (Volunteer Society to Aid the Army, Air Force and Naval Fleet) after the Second World War (Baum 1987: 22).

11  Particularly famous were Aleksei Stakhanov (whose records in industrial production spawned the Stakhanovite movement of socialist competition), Konstantin Borin, Pasha Angelina (the foremost woman tractor driver and as a young, peasant woman a symbol of the most 'backward elements' coming to master machinery) and Maria Demchenko (who was given the order of Lenin in 1935 for her record beetroot harvest) (Serebriannikov 1967: 98–9).

12  The construction of the 'youth city' of Komsomol' sk-na-Amure (begun in 1930 but which continued throughout the 1930s) was perhaps the greatest feat of *Komsomol* labour as well as being a self-constructing symbol of the link between youth and the future.

13  The survey of collective farm workers was conducted in the winter months when the seasonal work-load was low, and thus the figure is higher than might be expected.

14  One group of *besprizorniki* in Petersburg in the 1920s was apparently called the *gopa* and from this is derived the contemporary slang *gopnik* meaning any kind of provincial wastrel with delinquent tendencies. See Chapters 7 and 8 for a discussion of the contemporary *gopniki*. I am grateful to Alla Gracheva for making this connection during discussion of a paper presented by the author in Helsinki, 1992.

15  A similar confusion of space and people is inherent in the current youth cultural word *tusovka* meaning both where people hang out as well as a particular set of people (see Chapter 8).

16  Of the two leading characters in Shishkov's short story about the lives of the *besprizorniki*, one had been made homeless after his parents died of typhoid while the other's father had been killed in the civil war leaving his mother unable to feed her child (Shishkov 1933: 5–6).

17  Of course, campaigns against 'vestiges of the past' continued, and in some cases were intensified as in the case of the struggle against religious and 'feudal' (a code-word for Central Asian) traditions. A particularly noteworthy article from this period complained that in one region the traditional peasant *posidelki* were continuing under the guise of local *Komsomol* cells (Dudankov 1953).

18  The 'all-round developed *lichnost'*' is the antithesis of the alienated and the one-sided *lichnost'* attributed by Marx and Lenin to capitalist society (Seilerova 1988: 44).

19  The term 'sociologists' is perhaps not strictly accurate since it was not until the late 1960s that one could talk of such a trained specialist group. Nevertheless from the late 1950s onwards there emerged a group of academics from various fields who involved themselves in sociological aspects of their primary disciplines and who were subsequently to come to define the distinct area of Soviet sociology.

20  The discussion here confines itself to that work which deals directly with the culture or 'way of life' of youth. For those interested in the wider picture, Blinov's classification of the full extent of the sociology of youth in the pre-perestroika period is divided into two areas:

*Problems specific to young people*
- the nature of youth as a social group and its place and role in the class structure;
- the criteria for setting age limits and the needs, and interests of the younger generation;
- the socialization of young men and women, their socio-occupational orien-

tation and adaptation to the collective and their ideological and moral preparation for work;
* the social aspects of the *Komsomol*'s activity as a youth organization.

*Problems of general sociology concerned particularly with young people*
* questions of education, family and marriage;
* the training of young people for communism and its effectiveness;
* public opinion among various groups of young people and the effect on them of scientific-technological progress, the information technology revolution, urbanization and migration;
* the participation of young people in socialist competition;
* the development of social activism among young people

(Blinov 1983: 5–6).

21 A typical example of how this was manifested in the study of urban youth culture is provided by Naumenko. The author's 'thesis' was that the study of youth culture confirmed the fact that Soviet society had entered the period of 'mature socialism' based on evidence of the improvements which had taken place in the daily life of youth during the 1960s and 1970s (Naumenko 1979: 65). In order to prove this the author highlighted the purposeful nature of youth activity in study and self-education, sport, artistic clubs, socially-useful activity, participation in socialist competition, shock *Komsomol* construction work and student work brigades (48–50). Although 'negative tendencies' were mentioned they were confined to a brief discussion of so-called 'passive' leisure pursuits, i.e. meeting friends, watching films and television or dancing instead of more socially constructive activities (73–8). Finally the book spelled out why the cultural practices of youth were important to the development of Soviet society as a whole. This was because the formation of norms of everyday life allowed for the organic absorbtion of the best, progressive characteristics and traditions of the past and thus facilitated the continuity of generations without the ruptures of generational conflict experienced in the West.
22 Hence juveniles would be admitted to theatres, clubs and cinemas without adults only if the events being held there ended no later than this.

## INTRODUCTION and 3 YOUTH UNDER THE SPOTLIGHT OF GLASNOST, 1985–6

1 These figures are drawn from a survey conducted by Frants Sheregi and Boris Nikiforov of the Institute of Youth based on a questionnaire published in the magazine itself to which 5,321 replies were received.
2 The 'youth press' as a system of papers and journals was formed in the period 1922–5 following the reorganization of the flagging revolutionary press. The new brief of the youth press was educational rather than agitational and it was to remain under the general control of the regional committees of the party (Ganichev 1976: 56–71). By the advent of glasnost the VLKSM was publishing 247 newspapers and journals with a combined circulation of over eighty million.
3 The first use of the word glasnost by Lenin is considered to be in his work *What is to be done?* in 1902 when he noted the need for glasnost in party affairs (McNair 1991: 28).
4 Of course glasnost was not the only principle of the revolutionary and post-revolutionary press, and it is the other key principles of 'propagandizing', 'organizing', 'partiality' (*partiinost'*) and 'objectivity', which are generally seen as defining (McNair 1991: 22).
5 See *Moskovskii Komsomolets* 22 September 1985, p. 1.

6 The country's first young people's housing complex began in Kaliningrad (Moscow Province) in 1974 and the second, in Sverdlovsk, began receiving tenants in 1982. In order to qualify for participation in the MZhK young workers had to undergo a rigorous selection process taking the form of a series of labour competitions at their enterprises. The winners were formed into *Komsomol* youth brigades and took leave from their regular jobs to build the housing complex, thereby earning the right to live there (Vlasov 1984; Belkin 1986).

7 Of the six virtues of the MZhK cited by Vlasov, for example, only one concerned the direct contribution they made to the housing programme, the other five were associated with 'moral strengthening' of families (Vlasov 1984).

8 Arguably, the expansion of the MZhK sector was seen as a means of solving not only the youth housing issue, but the problem in general. It was demanded that half of the housing space created by the Moscow MZhK, for example, should be given over to the city since otherwise the social role of the MZhK would be reduced to the material interest of those young people involved (see *Moskovskii Komsomolets* 18 July 1986, p. 1).

9 In *Moskovskii Komsomolets* these issues were dealt with right up until January 1990 in rubrics called 'School period' (for school pupils), and 'Working clothes' (for young workers or PTU students). Any general problems were dealt with in the rubric 'Peer' but this dealt generally with questions of a moral nature.

10 There were notable exceptions to this rule, one being a 'Twelfth Floor' television programme broadcast on 22 May 1986 in which the Deputy Minister of Education, representatives of the teacher training establishment and the *Komsomol* were subjected to harsh criticism by young people (Mickiewicz 1988: 175).

11 BAM had always been a key symbol of youth self-sacrifice although less 'enthusiastic' labour – including that of political and criminal prisoners as well as army construction units – had also been employed (Ostrovskii 1989a; Gerasimov 1990). During the war construction stopped and rails were even taken up and sent to the western front (Ostrovskii 1989b). Work began again in the mid-1970s but by the end of the decade economic stagnation meant there was little money and few materials available for its completion (Solov'ev 1987). In 1985 BAM was incorporated into the development programme for the whole Far East region to be completed by the beginning of the twenty-first century. This effectively downgraded the importance of the project and caused disillusionment amongst those working on it (Utekhin 1987a).

12 The gendered nature of glasnost's construction of the youthful consumer is discussed in greater length in H. Pilkington, 'Young women and subcultural lifestyles: A case of "irrational needs"?', unpublished conference paper, Bath, April 1993.

13 See, for example, a series of articles in *Moskovskii Komsomolets*: 14 June 1985, p. 4, 9 July 1985, p. 2 and 11 September 1985, p. 4.

14 The extent of participation in informal groups in the early perestroika period is difficult to estimate, but in February 1986 300 informal or independent associations were reported to exist in Moscow and by July of the same year, there were an estimated 1,300 such groups in Leningrad (see *Moskovskii Komsomolets* 26 July 1986).

15 See *Moskovskii Komsomlets* 12 November 1986.

## 4 THE POLITICIZATION OF THE YOUTH DEBATE, 1987–9: THE NEFORMALY

1 In fact, from 1987 four terms for such groupings were in common use: informal associations or groups (*neformal'nie ob"edineniia* or *gruppy*); amateur associ-

ations (*liubitel'skie ob"edineniia*); independent associations (*samodeiatel'nie ob"edineniia*); and youth initiatives (*molodezhnie initsiativy*). Where the battles over naming become relevant I will refer specifically to which term is being employed. The term *neformaly* (non- or informals), however, was used in this period as shorthand for all of these phenomena and is thus that which is adopted here.

2 In contrast, questionnaires compiled by the Institute of Sociological Research (under the Academy of Sciences) focused more on general socio-demographic data and background and included in their sample more traditional street groups such as *gopniki* and *kachki* (see Chapter 7).

3 This dual purpose is evident from the speech of the First Secretary – Mironenko – to the Congress. Commitment to perestroika essentially meant the continued central role of the *Komsomol* in implementing the party's tasks and consisted of the following elements:

- participation in the struggle for the acceleration of socio-economic development;
- the facilitation of the acceleration of scientific-technical progress;
- active participation in the implementation of the social policy of the party;
- participation in the drive for social and ideological purity.

At the same time, the *Komsomol* was to recognize its own failings and to implement a thorough perestroika of itself. This entailed:

- the rejection of excessive centralization;
- strict adherence to Marxist-Leninist teaching, party guidance and discipline;
- the rejection of 'bureaucratic centralism' in favour of democratic centralism (especially by enhancing the role of the primary organization);
- increased control of cadres 'from below' (Mironenko 1988a: 31–44).

4 *Obshchina* (meaning 'community' or 'commune') was established in March 1987 by a group of students of the History Faculty of the Pedagogical Institute in Moscow as a Marxist theoretical discussion group. This group spawned a number of other political projects including the 'Democratic Faction' of the *Komsomol* and formed the core of the 'Federation of Anarcho-Syndicalists' which emerged in May 1989 (Mitrokhin 1992: 37).

5 See *Moskovskii Komsomolets* 5 June 1987, p. 1.

6 See articles under the leisure rubric in *Moskovskii Komsomolets* on 11 July 1987, p. 1, 12 August 1987, p. 2 and 21 November 1987, p. 1.

7 See *Moskovskii Komsomolets* 15 August 1987, p. 1. The theatre was particularly appealing to many of these *neformaly* since the world of theatre was prestigious yet also part of an alternative set of values and provided an opportunity for young people to use the skills they had – especially operating sound and lighting systems and constructing scenery. Having visited this theatre a number of times I think it is true to say that it did not so much alter the way of life of the people who took part in its work as become, for a shorter or longer time, part of that lifestyle. It provided somewhere warm and private for them to gather in the evenings and, in this sense, was successful in its mission to take them off the streets.

8 In fact, these young people were mainly unintended participants in a wider debate on the 'limits of pluralism'. In the absence of a law on public associations, which would guarantee their rights and stipulate the scope of their legal action, independent political groups were controlled by the arbitrary actions of the local administration. In the summer of 1987 'Temporary laws on the conducting of meetings, gatherings, demonstrations and other measures' were

adopted in twenty major cities across the USSR requiring that written notice be given to the relevant council executive committee at least seven days prior to any proposed meeting. These laws, and later a special police division responsible for the maintenance of public order, were also used to control the non-political youth groups who gathered in city centres.

9 See *Moskovskii Komsomolets* 15 October 1988, p.4.

10 This element of the glasnost agenda invokes a familiar post-revolutionary theme, see Stites 1989: 85.

11 L'vov is not usually among the cities cited as suffering from the territorial gang problem. However, its position near the Polish border means that it has been a centre of illegal trade and speculation and, more recently, of arms dealing and thus a common meeting place of mafias and gang leaders (A.F. 1991).

12 See *Moskovskii Komsomolets* 15 October 1988, p. 4.

## 5 YOUTH AS OBJECT OF SOCIAL POLICY, 1990–1

1 In December of 1989, the same process occurred in the Lithuanian Communist Party, when it decided to break away from the CPSU, effectively creating two communist parties in the republic.

2 By spring 1990, the only nation-wide unified socialist socio-political youth organizations to have been preserved were in Albania, Vietnam, Cuba, China, North Korea and Laos (Obukhov 1990).

3 One minor concession was that the organization was to be described in its statutes as a 'Federation of Communist Unions of Youth, uniting young people of communist *and socialist* orientations' (Arifdzhanov, Bykov and Dmukhovskii 1990).

4 A 'critical audience', it was found, was more likely to write letters to editors, consume information from various sources, lead informal contact groups and show greater interest in issues of perestroika.

5 In a separate article Shchepanskaia also considered the gendered nature of the symbolic system of the *sistema*. Here she argued that, whereas for the group as a whole there was a high level of semiotic content in everyday behaviour and appearance, for women in the *sistema* prestige was associated with a *lowered* level of semiotic content. In other words, in stark contrast to the encouragement of the use of the group's symbols by male members, for women a classical style of dress and mannerisms was advocated in order to emphasize the rejection of the use of the *sistema* symbolism and thereby to confirm femininity (Shchepanskaia 1991b: 18–19).

6 An additional problem faced by young people was the system of channelling distribution through social consumption funds to the extent that up to two-thirds of the individual's consumption came from this rather than from wages. Since access to the social consumption fund was directly related to one's length of time in the productive sphere, young people were significantly disadvantaged in comparison to their older colleagues.

## 6 STUDYING RUSSIA: FROM MASOCHISM TO METHODOLOGY

1 The use of the terms 'girls' and 'lads' to refer to female and male members of groups has no specific motivation beyond being the nearest translation to the terms used by interviewees to refer to each other.

2 The only exception to this was during a first interview with two punks. They asked what my 'interest' was in talking to them and when I replied that I was a sociologist, they recalled that 'there had been one of those in the psychiatric hospital'.

# 7 INTRODUCING THE SUBJECTS

1 According to a survey conducted among 17 year olds in Moscow, Leningrad, Erevan and Ashkhabad more than a third of the respondents acquired brand-name items from speculators or bought them privately from someone who had been abroad (Shchekochikhin 1988b: 11). Given that this survey was first published in 1987, it is likely that the real proportion was much higher.

2 The *remontniki* are not included in Figure 7.1 because they were not mentioned by interviewees. Nevertheless, there is evidence to suggest that such groups existed, taking it upon themselves to 'mend' (from *remont* meaning 'repairs') the ways of 'deviant' elements of Soviet youth such as punks, hippies and heavy metal fans (Shchekochikhin 1987a: 238).

3 Shchepanskaia, for example, sees the *sistema* as being a 'conglomerate' of groups and even an association 'above' trends (Shchepanskaia 1991a: 3).

# 8 DOING THE MOSCOW SHUFFLE: AN ANALYSIS OF THE CULTURAL PRACTICES OF A MOSCOW TUSOVKA

1 'New wave' in the Soviet context itself is a contested term, but is generally used to describe the distinct blend of rock music that emerged from the beginning of the 1980s in the USSR as a result of the rapid incorporation and fusion of Western musical trends of the previous two decades (Zaitsev 1990: 75).

2 This is as far as it is possible to generalize about *tusovka* culture since it remains largely restricted to urban centres, attracting those from the outskirts but not establishing itself as the dominant form of activity there. In rural areas, there is little evidence of this kind of youth cultural activity, while in provincial urban centres the basic unit of youth cultural activity is often more likely to be the local gang (*sbor*, *kontora*, *motalka* or *banda*) than the *tusovka*.

3 Culturally, this reorientation can be seen in the association of masculinity with the male wage ('a "real" man must have enough money to treat a girl properly', 'a man must be able to support his wife'), but also the blame apportioned to women when men failed to achieve their aim ('girls are only interested in men with money').

4 This kind of space is what Bakhtin refers to as the 'second world' or 'world inside out' (Bakhtin 1984: 10–11).

5 The official name of the cafe was 'U Fontana' (Fountain Cafe) but it was nicknamed the 'Moloko' (meaning 'milk', apparently because of its former life as a milk and dairy products shop) by the *stiliagi* who transferred their main gatherings there after the closing of the more centrally located 'Prospekt' cafe.

6 Many of the jokes about Brezhnev are associated with his tendency in later life to repeatedly award himself medals for 'outstanding' military and public service.

7 In order to protect the privacy of those who took part in the research project, interviewees are referenced by a letter code and a brief profile of each interviewee cited in the text is given in the Appendix. Where individuals not listed in the profile are referred to, the letter 'Z' is used.

8 The *mazhory* are not included in Figure 7.1 because interviewees insisted that they did not form a *tusovka* as such but were a 'class stratum' rather than a youth cultural group (see below).

9 The 'DDT' song 'The *mazhory* lads' (*malchiki mazhory*) immortalized the *mazhory* as the 'sons' of the political and cultural intelligentsia who could 'worm their way in anywhere without visas'.

10 The difference between 'parent culture' and 'culture of one's parents' is explained in Chapter 1.

11 Stanley Cohen found a similar pattern in his study of mods and rockers in Britain. The seafront battles, he said, were not primarily ones of music and style and the original fights were not between mods and rockers at all but between those down from London and the locals (Cohen, S. 1987: 34).

12 For former Soviet citizens a 'closed city' was one to which it was impossible to move because of the controls on residence not ones where there were strategic military bases or industrial complexes and were thus 'closed' to foreigners.

13 In addition to these *gastarbeiter*, many young people stay illegally in the major cities, hoping to find better opportunities. For them, the daily humiliation to which they are subjected by permanent residents may be even worse than the dangers of being discovered by the police. Zhanna Aguzarova, the lead singer of 'Bravo', for example, said that she forged personal documents to hide her Siberian background primarily because she hated being called a *limitchitsa* when she admitted having come to Moscow in the hope of finding work as an actress (Troitsky 1990: 54).

14 Even without this perceived imperial power, however, it is possible that Soviet nationalities policy would have encouraged ethnic tensions. The irony of this policy is that whilst attempting to defuse the political claims of national groups by providing a federal structure, it in fact fostered the development of national identity by (often arbitrarily) assigning ethnic groups territories around which to build nationalist claims and cultural institutions through which to articulate them.

15 During the period from September to December 1990, local teenagers were using the paper to denounce the state of violence in the city and to call for an end to the attacks and rapes, as well as to issue cryptic warnings to those to whom 'justice' was about to be meted out. Unfortunately it proved impossible to follow developments in the city into 1991 because, as a result of a dispute over payments, the central Moscow newspaper archive and other central libraries were no longer receiving the paper.

16 'Pyramids' are jeans imported from Turkey with an emblem of a camel on the back pocket.

17 *Aminazin* is a drug used as a sedative in the treatment of mental illness similar to chlorpromazine, thorazine, chloractil or largactil. *Sul'fazin* (sulphazin) is also used to treat mental illness, allegedly as a punishment. It consists of a 1 per cent solution of purified sulphur in peach oil and induces fever, weight loss and exhaustion (Marder 1987: 10, 12).

18 This was the only non-elicited, first-hand experience I myself have had of the *liuber* strategy and the way in which the young Russian woman who was with me at the time dealt with the situation could only be described as bizarre if premised on the assumption that the *liubery* are essentially ideologically motivated. Although the *liuber* had assumed I was a Soviet citizen from one of the Baltic republics, my friend played up the fact that I was a Westerner and that, if they tried to abduct us, there would be an enormous scandal. The result was not that we were beaten up or otherwise attacked for spreading bourgeois ideas among Soviet youth, but a kind of disbelieving retreat on the part of the *liuber*, just in case the story was true.

19 There were also labour-orientated *posidelki*, see Chapter 2.

20 The escalators and barriers at metro stations are often attended by pensioners, working to supplement their paltry pensions. They are made fun of because they epitomize the 'little despot' – having virtually no real power in their own lives they exert as much as they can in their official positions, frequently shouting at passengers, especially young people, for not obeying strictly the 'rules of the Moscow underground'.

21 *Mat* is a form of swearing whose level of obscenity goes beyond anything known

in the English language. It is considered unacceptable to use *mat* in the company of women.

22 This was the case among the first generation *tusovka* although members of the second generation associated red socks with 'Bravo' fans. This is probably explained by the fact that in this *tusovka* red socks were worn by the new members (*pionery*) who were generally 'Bravo' fans.

23 *Sovok* (*sovka* in the genitive case) is youth slang meaning 'Soviet Union' or 'Soviet citizen' and is used in a derisive fashion to indicate the 'deformed' nature of social reality and mentalité in the former Soviet Union.

## CONCLUSION

1 Although the social and political roots of the attempted coup go much deeper, the issue which sparked the attempt to seize power was the impending signing (on 20 August) of a new Union treaty which would have granted *de facto* recognition of the secession of six republics and stripped central government of nearly all its powers.

## APPENDIX

1 College education is considered to be 'specialist secondary' education and trains people for professional or semi-professional positions (Muckle 1988: 21).

## GLOSSARY

1 The glossary was generated from transcribed interviews and words were subsequently tested for confirmation or refutation among interviewees from various groups. However, I would like to thank Terence Wade for his initial help in tracing published literature on Russian youth slang and Mikhail Kochurenkov for allowing me to consult his bank of youth slang terms.

2 Here, and thereafter, the transliteration scheme employed is that of the Library of Congress. Russian speakers should note that this scheme does not distinguish between hard and soft adjective endings or between a soft 'e' ('ye') a stressed 'e' ('yo'and a hard 'e' ('e'). An excellent reference book which includes many of these words (as well as their stress) is S. Marder, *A Supplementary Russian–English Dictionary* (Columbus: Slavica, 1992).

3 "Po-feni" was used by **stiliagi** in the 1950s to mean "in **stiliagi** slang" e.g. **botaesh po-feni?** means "do you speak **stiliagi** slang?" (Magner 1957). Contemporary **stiliagi** use **fen′ka** to indicate a distinctive item of clothing, joke or habit of members of the **tusovka**.

4 **Limitehiki** are migrant workers from rural or provincial areas who work on the edges of major cities in return for the right to a residence permit for the city after a given period of time.

# Bibliography

**ENGLISH LANGUAGE SOURCES**

Abrams, M. (1959) *The Teenage Consumer*, London: London Press Exchange.
Allen, S. (1968) 'Some theoretical problems in the study of youth', *Sociological Review* 16, 3: 319–31.
Althusser, L. (1970) *Reading Capital*, London: New Left Books.
—— (1971) *Lenin and Philosophy and Other Essays*, New York: Monthly Review Press.
Avtorkhanov, A. (1959) 'A brief history of the Komsomol', in N. Novak-Deker (ed.) *Soviet Youth: Twelve Komsomol Histories*, Munich: Institute for the Study of the USSR.
Bakhtin, M. (1984) *Rabelais and his world*, Bloomington: Indiana University Press.
Balaian, Z. (1984) 'A "dry law" for children', *Current Digest of the Soviet Press* 36, 20: 7.
Balkarei, B. and Zhavoronkov, G. (1984) 'Adults, teenagers and the street', *Current Digest of the Soviet Press* 36, 5: 1–4.
Barthes, R. (1989) *Mythologies*, London: Paladin.
Baum, A. (1987) *Komsomol Participation in the Soviet First Five-year Plan*, London: Macmillan.
Bekhtereva, N. (1988) 'I like dance music', *Moscow News* 10.
Belkin, A. (1986) 'Youth housing complexes (organisational and legal questions)', *Soviet Law and Government* 25, 4: 69–80.
Bennett, T., Martin, G., Mercer, C. and Woollacott, J. (eds) (1981) *Culture, Ideology and Social Process*, London: Open University Press.
'Between lectures' (1985) *Current Digest of the Soviet Press* 37, 3: 4.
Biggart, J. (1987) 'Bukharin and the origins of the 'proletarian culture' debate', *Soviet Studies* 39, 2: 229–46.
Blanch, M. (1979) 'Imperialism, nationalism and organized youth', in J. Clarke, C. Critcher and R. Johnson (eds) *Working Class Culture*, London: Hutchinson.
Blinov, N. (1983) 'The sociology of youth: achievements and problems', *Soviet Sociology* 21, 4: 3–19.
Bocharov, N. (1959) 'Off the beaten track' in N. Novak-Deker, (ed.) *Soviet Youth: Twelve Komsomol Histories*, Munich: Institute for the Study of the USSR.
Bondarev, Iu., Belov, V. and Rasputin, V. (1988) 'Young people: discarding flattery and demagogy', *Moscow News* 6: 5–6.
Borisov, I. (1991) 'Critical situations (crises) and their management in informal youth associations', *Soviet Education* 33, 10: 35–53.
Bosewitz, R. (1988) *Waifdom in the Soviet Union*, Frankfurt: Verlag Peter Lang.
Boyne, R. and Rattansi, A. (eds) (1990) *Postmodernism and Society*, London: Macmillan.

Bradley, R. (1989) 'From Rock 'n' Roll to Beat in Britain, an Exploration in the Cultural Study of Music', PhD Thesis, University of Birmingham.
—— (1992) *Understanding Rock 'n' Roll: Popular Music in Britain 1955–1964*, London: Open University Press.
Brake, M. (1985) *Comparative Youth Culture*, London: Routledge & Kegan Paul.
Buckley, M. (ed.) *Perestroika and Soviet Women*, Cambridge: Cambridge University Press.
Carter, E. (1984) 'Alice in the Consumer Wonderland', in A. McRobbie and M. Nava (eds) *Gender and Generation*, London: Macmillan Education.
Cixous, H. (1981) 'The laugh of the medusa', in E. Marks and I. De Courtivron (eds) *New French Feminisms*, Brighton: Harvester Press.
Clarke, J. (1973) 'The Skinheads and the study of youth culture', *CCCS Stencilled Occasional Paper* 23.
—— (1976) 'Style', in S. Hall and Jefferson, T. (eds) *Resistance through Rituals. Youth Subcultures in Post-War Britain*, London: Hutchinson.
Clarke, J. (1991) *New Times and Old Enemies: Essays on Cultural Studies and America*, London: Harper Collins Academic.
Clarke, J., Critcher, C. and Johnson, R. (eds) (1979) *Working Class Culture*, London: Hutchinson.
Clarke, J. and Jefferson, T. (1976) 'Working class youth cultures', in G. Mungham and G. Pearson (eds) *Working Class Youth Culture*, London: Routledge & Kegan Paul.
Clarke, J., Hall, S., Jefferson, T. and Roberts, B. (1976) 'Subcultures, cultures and class – a theoretical overview' in S. Hall and T. Jefferson (eds) *Resistance through Rituals. Youth Subcultures in Post-War Britain*, London: Hutchinson.
Cloward, R. and Ohlin, L. (1960) *Delinquency and Opportunity. A Theory of Delinquent Gangs*, New York: The Free Press.
Cohen, A. (1955) *Delinquent Boys: The Culture of the Gang*, New York: The Free Press.
Cohen, P. (1972) 'Subcultural conflict and working class community', *Working Papers in Cultural Studies* 2.
—— (1986) *Rethinking The Youth Question*, London: Post 16 Education Centre, Institute of Education.
Cohen, S. (1987) *Folk Devils and Moral Panics. The Creation of the Mods and Rockers*, Oxford: Basil Blackwell.
'Communist Party Programme and Party Statutes' (1986) *Current Digest of the Soviet Press* 38, 52: 33–4.
'Concerning the family, the school and children's upbringing' (1954) *Current Digest of the Soviet Press* 6, 15: 3–4.
Coward, R. and Ellis, J. (1977) *Language and Materialism*, London: Routledge & Kegan Paul.
Craib, I. (1984) *Modern Social Theory*, Brighton: Wheatsheaf.
Detraz, M-P. (1992) 'The Attrition of Dogma in the Legal Press Under Brezhnev', PhD Thesis, University of Birmingham.
Downes, D. (1966) *The Delinquent Solution. A Study in Subcultural Theory*, London: Routledge & Kegan Paul.
Druzenko, A. and Ezhelev, A. (1984) 'A shortage stemming from a surplus', *Current Digest of the Soviet Press* 36, 35: 7–8.
Dudankov, N. (1953) 'About spinning bees', *Current Digest of the Soviet Press* 5, 9: 27–8.
Dunstan, J. (1985) 'Soviet education beyond 1984', *Compare* 15, 2: 161–87.
Eisenstadt, S. (1956) *From Generation to Generation*, New York: Glencoe.
Elster, J. (ed.) (1986) *Karl Marx: A Reader*, Cambridge: Cambridge University Press.

Fain, A. (1990) 'Specific features of informal youth associations in large cities', *Soviet Sociology* 29, 1: 20–42.

Fedosov, V. (1985) 'Rear political fighters, internationlists and impassioned propagandists of the Soviet way of life', *Current Digest of the Soviet Press* 37, 46: 8–9.

Filinov, Iu. (1984) 'Barbarossa Rock 'N' Roll', *Current Digest of the Soviet Press* 36, 37: 4.

Fischer, C. (1975) 'Toward a subcultural theory of urbanism', *American Journal of Sociology* 80: 1319–41.

Fisher, R. (1959) *Pattern For Soviet Youth*, New York: Columbia University Press.

Fiske, J. (1989) *Understanding Popular Culture*, Boston: Unwin Hyman.

Fitzpatrick, S. (ed.) (1978) *Cultural Revolution in Russia, 1928–31*, Bloomington: Indiana University Press.

—— (1988) ''Middle-class values' and Soviet life in the 1930s', in T. Thompson and R. Sheldon (eds) *Soviet Society and Culture*, Boulder: Westview Press Inc.

Fitzpatrick, S., Rabinowitch, A. and Stites, R. (eds) (1991) *Russia in the Era of NEP: Explorations in Soviet Society and Culture*, Bloomington: Indiana University Press.

Fleron, F. and Hoffmann, E. (1991) 'Sovietology and perestroika: methodology and lessons from the past', *The Harriman Institute Forum* 5, 1: 1–12.

Frank, S. (1992) 'Simple folk, savage customs? Youth, sociability, and the dynamics of culture in rural Russia, 1856–1914', *Journal of Social History* 25, 4: 711–36.

Frith, S. (1983) *Sound Effects. Youth, Leisure, and the Politics of Rock 'n' Roll*, London: Constable.

—— (1984) *The Sociology of Youth*, Ormskirk: Causeway Press.

Fyvel, T. (1961) *The Insecure Offenders*, London: Chatto & Windus.

Galinskii, Ia. (1991) 'Illusions are not a way out: the crime scene in Russia', *Current Politics and Economics of Russia* 2, 3: 269–72.

Geiko, Iu. (1984) 'Yes, you can argue about tastes!', *Current Digest of the Soviet Press* 36, 40: 10.

Giddens, A. (1979) *Central Problems in Social Theory*, London: Macmillan.

Gillis, J. (1974) *Youth and History*, London: Academic Press.

Gilroy, P. (1987) *There Ain't No Black in the Union Jack*, London: Hutchinson.

Gindikin, V. (1985) 'Don't fill the teenager's wineglass', *Current Digest of the Soviet Press* 37, 21: 11–12.

Girnius, S. (1989) 'The Lithuanian Komsomol Congress', *Radio Liberty Report on USSR* 1, 34: 21–3.

Gleason, A., Kenez, P. and Stites, R. (eds) (1985) *Bolshevik Culture*, Bloomington: Indiana University Press.

Gorbachev, M. (1987c) *Perestroika*, London: Collins.

Gramsci, A. (1971) 'Wave of materialism' and 'Crisis of authority', in Q. Hoare and G. Nowell Smith (eds) *Selections from the Prison Notebooks of Antonio Gramsci*, London: Lawrence & Wishart.

Gross, N. (1990) 'Youth and the army in the USSR in the 1980s', *Soviet Studies* 42, 3: 481–98.

Gurko, T., Matsovskii, M. and Solodnikov, V. (1987) 'A new kind of assistance to the young family', *Soviet Sociology* 26, 1: 21–3.

Hall, S. and Jefferson, T. (eds) (1976) *Resistance Through Rituals. Youth Subcultures in Post-War Britain*, London: Hutchinson.

Hamblett, C. and Deverson, J. (1964) *Generation X*, London: Library 33.

Hebdige, D. (1979) *Subculture. The Meaning of Style*, London: Methuen

—— (1988) *Hiding in the Light*, London: Comedia.

Held, D. (1980) *Introduction to Critical Theory. Horkheimer to Habermas*, Berkeley: University of California Press.

Hill, D. (1989) *'Out of his Skin'. The John Barnes Phenomenon*, London: Faber & Faber.

Hirschkop, K., and Shepherd, D. (eds) (1979) *Bakhtin and Cultural Theory*, Manchester: Manchester University Press.

Hoare, Q. and Nowell Smith, G. (eds) (1971) *Selections from the Prison Notebooks of Antonio Gramsai*, London: Lawrence & Wishart.

Hoggart, R. (1957) *The Uses of Literacy*, London: Chatto & Windus.

Hollway, W. (1989) *Subjectivity and Method in Psychology*, London: Sage.

Hryshko, W. (1959) 'An interloper in the Komsomol', in N. Novak-Deker (ed.) *Soviet Youth: Twelve Komsomol Histories*, Munich: Institute for the Study of the USSR.

Hudson, B. (1984) 'Femininity and adolescence', in A. McRobbie and M. Nava (eds) *Gender and Generation*, London: Macmillan Education.

Iliin, V. (1984) 'Watch out – children', *Current Digest of the Soviet Press* 36, 20: 6–7

'In the CPSU Central Committee' (1986) *Current Digest of the Soviet Press* 38, 17: 9.

Ivanov, G. (1954) 'Bad taste', *Current Digest of the Soviet Press* 6, 39: 10–11.

Jefferson, T. (1973) 'The Teds – a political resurrection', *CCCS Stencilled Occasional Paper* 22.

Juviler, P. (1985) 'Contradictions of revolution: juvenile crime and rehabilitation', in A. Gleason, P. Kenez and R. Stites (eds) *Bolshevik Culture*, Bloomington: Indiana University Press.

Karelova, G. (1987) 'The house is already built', *Soviet Sociology* 26, 1: 8–16.

Karpinsky, L., Mokeev, V. and Pisigin, V. (1988) 'Don't fritter away your time', *Moscow News* 41: 8.

Kassoff, A. (1965) *The Soviet Youth Program: Regimentation and Rebellion*, Cambridge: Harvard University Press.

Kollontai, A. (1977) *Selected Writings*, London: Allison & Busby.

Kondakov, I. (1989) 'Spiritual culture: Old and new thinking', *Social Sciences* 1: 75–89.

Konovalov, V. and Serdiukov, M. (1984) 'Foreign-made mirage', *Current Digest of the Soviet Press* 37, 5: 7–8.

Korsakova, T. (1986) 'A choice for a lifetime', *Current Digest of the Soviet Press* 38, 12: 21,39.

Kravchenko, A. (1985) 'Young people's high rises: yesterday, today, tomorrow', *Current Digest of the Soviet Press* 37, 12: 12–13.

Krivoruchenko, V. (ed.) (1976) *Youth and the Party: Documents*, Moscow: Progress Publishers.

Kruzhkov, N. (1957) 'The mitrofans of modern times', *Current Digest of the Soviet Press* 9, 6: 32.

Kuniaev, S. (1984) 'What songs are being sung to you?', *Current Digest of the Soviet Press* 36, 42: 14–15.

Lane, D. (1990) *Soviet Society Under Perestroika*, London: Unwin Hyman.

Lauridsen, I. and Dalgard, P. (1990) *The Beat Generation and the Russian New Wave*, Ann Arbor: Ardis.

Lavrova, K. (1985b) 'Choice', *Current Digest of the Soviet Press* 37, 18: 6–7.

Lebedev, Iu. (1991) 'The final and decisive congress of the All-union Leninist Young Communist League', *Current Digest of the Soviet Press* 43, 39: 16–17.

Lees, S. (1986) *Losing Out: Sexuality and Adolescent Girls*, London: Hutchinson.

Leitch, D. (1993) 'Independent social organisations in the city of Voronezh, Central Russia, November 1992', M.Soc.Sc. dissertation, University of Birmingham.

Lenin, V. (1976) *The Tasks of the Youth Leagues: Speech Delivered at the Third*

*All-Russia Congress of the Russian Young Communist League October 2 1920*, Moscow: Progress Publishers.

—— (1977) *On Youth*, Moscow: Progress.

Lesoto, E. (1985) 'Some thoughts about a trial', *Current Digest of the Soviet Press* 37, 38: 13–14.

Lewin, M. (1978) 'Society, state and ideology during the first five-year plan', in S. Fitzpatrick (ed.) *Cultural Revolution in Russia 1928–31*, Bloomington: Indiana University Press.

Logachev, Iu. (1984) 'Jeans, T-shirts and athletics shoes', *Current Digest of the Soviet Press* 36, 35: 17–18.

Lunev, N. (1959) 'Blind faith in a bright future', in N.Novak-Deker (ed.) *Soviet Youth: Twelve Komsomol Histories*, Munich: Institute for the Study of the USSR.

MacGregor-Hastie, R. (1961) *Don't Send Me To Omsk!*, London: MacDonald.

McLellan, D. (ed.) (1977) *Karl Marx: Selected Writings*, Oxford: Oxford University Press.

McNair, B. (1991) *Glasnost', Perestroika and the Soviet Media*, London: Routledge.

McRobbie, A. (1980) 'Settling accounts with subcultures – a feminist critique', *Screen Education* 34: 37–49.

—— (1991) *Feminism and Youth Culture: From 'Jackie' to 'Just Seventeen'*, Basingstoke: Macmillan.

McRobbie, A. and Garber, J. (1976) 'Girls and subcultures – an exploration', in S. Hall and T. Jefferson (eds) *Resistance through Rituals. Youth Subcultures in Post-War Britain*, London: Hutchinson.

McRobbie, A. and Nava, M. (eds) (1984) *Gender and Generation*, London: Macmillan.

Magner, T. (1957) 'The stiliaga and his language', *Slavic and East European Journal* 15, 1: 192–5.

Mally, L. (1990) *Culture of the Future: The Proletkult Movement in Revolutionary Russia*, Berkeley: University of California Press.

Manaev, O. (1991) 'A dissenting audience', *Soviet Sociology* 30, 3: 23–40.

Mannheim, K. (1927) 'The Problem of Generations', in K. Mannheim, *Essays on the Sociology of Knowledge* (1952) London: Routledge & Kegan Paul.

Marder, S. (1987) 'More Russian drug terminology', *No Uncertain Terms* 2, 4: 10–13.

Marder, S. (1992) *A Supplementary Russian–English Dictionary*, Columbus: Slavica.

Marks, E. and De Courtivron, I. (eds) *New French Feminisms*, Brighton: Harvester Press.

Marx, K. (1977) 'The German ideology', in D. McLellan (ed.) *Karl Marx: Selected Writings*, Oxford: Oxford University Press.

Matza, D. and Sykes, G. (1957) 'Techniques of neutralization', *American Sociological Review* 22: 664–70.

Mazurova, A. and Rozin, V. (1991) 'Family conflicts of countercultural youth in the USSR and possible psychotherapeutic approaches', *The American Journal of Family Therapy* 19, 1: 47–53.

Mead, M. (1972) *Culture and Commitment. A Study of the Generation Gap*, London: Panther.

'Meeting seeks revival of Moscow *Komsomol* organization' (1992) *BBC World Summary*, 6 February: B/11.

Mickiewicz, E. (1981) *Media and the Russian Public*, New York: Praeger.

—— (1988) *Split Signals: Television and Politics in the Soviet Union*, Oxford: Oxford University Press.

Mikhailov, M. (1984) 'He hasn't come of age', *Current Digest of the Soviet Press* 36, 5: 6,12.

Millar, J. (1985) 'The little deal: Brezhnev's contribution to acquisitive socialism', *Slavic Review* 44, 4: 694–706.

'Minor abuse' (1990) *Arguments and Facts International* 1, 3: 7.

Mochalina, N. (1992) 'A lost generation', *Current Digest of the Post-Soviet Press* 44, 3: 29.

Mogliat, A. and Khlystun, V. (1984) 'Youth affairs committees operate in both chambers of the USSR Supreme Soviet', *Current Digest of the Soviet Press* 36, 8: 19.

Muckle, J. (1988) 'The educational experience of the Soviet young person', in J. Riordan (ed.) *Soviet Education: The Gifted and the Handicapped*, London: Routledge.

Mungham, G. and Pearson, G. (eds) (1976), *Working Class Youth Culture*, London: Routledge & Kegan Paul.

Novak-Deker, N. (ed.) (1959) *Soviet Youth: Twelve Komsomol Histories*, Munich: Institute for the Study of the USSR 1, 51: 7–23.

Nozhin, E. (1984) 'They won't accept a word on faith', *Current Digest of the Soviet Press* 36, 37: 1–3.

'On extending the rights and possibilities of the Komsomol in tackling socio-economic tasks' (1990) *Current Politics of the Soviet Union* 1, 2: 129–32.

'On the construction of housing for young people' (1985) *Current Digest of the Soviet Press* 37, 33: 17–18.

Ordzhonikidze, I. (1985) 'YCL shock construction projects', *Current Digest of the Soviet Press* 37, 25: 14.

Parsons, T. (1942) 'Age and sex in the social structure of the United States', in T. Parsons (1954) *Essays in Sociological Theory*, Glencoe: The Free Press.

Patton, F. (1980) 'Expressive means in Russian youth slang', *Slavic and East European Journal* 24, 3: 270–82.

Pavlov, S. (1959) 'Youth accomplishes new feats', *Current Digest of the Soviet Press* 11, 45: 26–7.

Pavlov, A. (1984) 'What's being peddled in the 'clearing'?', *Current Digest of the Soviet Press* 36, 14: 19–20.

Pearson, G. (1983) *Hooligan. A History of Respectable Fears*, London: Macmillan.

Pilkington, H. (1992) ''Going out in style': girls in youth cultural activity', in M. Buckley (ed.) *Perestroika and Soviet Women*, Cambridge: Cambridge University Press.

—— (1993) ''Good girls in trousers'. Codes of masculinity and femininity in Moscow youth culture', in M. Liljeström, E. Mäntyssari and A. Rosenholm (eds) *Gender Restructuring in Russian Studies*, Tampere: University of Tampere.

Pochivalov, L. (1958) 'How wide should trouser legs be cut?', *Current Digest of the Soviet Press* 10, 44: 12–13.

Pristupko, V. and Elkind,V. (1985) 'Deviation', *Current Digest of the Soviet Press* 37, 3: 5,19.

Radov, A. (1986) 'Detochkin's children', *Current Digest of the Soviet Press* 38, 42: 8–10.

Radyshevsky, D. (1989) ''"Guest Performers"'', *Moscow News* 7: 12.

Radzikhovskii, L. (1988b) 'Problems of the psychological investigation of informal youth associations', *Soviet Sociology* 29, 1: 12–18.

Reshetov, P. and Skurlatov, V. (1977) *Soviet Youth – A Socio-political Outline*, Moscow: Progress Publishers.

Riordan, J. (ed.) (1978) *Sport Under Communism*, London: C.Hurst & Company.

—— (1988) 'Soviet youth: pioneers of change', *Soviet Studies* 40, 4: 556–72.

—— (ed.) (1989) *Soviet Youth Culture*, Basingstoke: Macmillan.

Roberts, R. (1971) *The Classic Slum. Salford Life in the First Quarter of the Century*, Manchester: Manchester University Press.

Roman, L. (1988) 'Intimacy, labor, and class: ideologies of feminine sexuality in the punk slam dance', in L. Roman and L. Christian-Smith (eds) *Becoming Feminine: The Politics of Popular Culture*, London: The Falmer Press.

Roman, L. and Christian-Smith, L. (eds) (1988) *Becoming Feminine: The Politics of Popular Culture*, London: The Falmer Press.

Romaniuk, V. (1984) 'Love, love me, do!', *Current Digest of the Soviet Press* 36, 31: 22–3.

Rozin, M. (1990) 'The psychology of Moscow's hippies', *Soviet Sociology* 29, 1: 44–72.

—— (1991) 'Psychological consequences of participation in the informal movement', *Soviet Education* 33, 10: 54–85.

Ryback, T. (1990) *Rock Around The Bloc. A History of Rock Music in Eastern Europe and the Soviet Union*, Oxford: Oxford University Press.

Rymashevskaia, A. and Rubetskaia, N. (1959) 'Our debates', *Current Digest of the Soviet Press* 11, 6–7: 30–1.

Sakharov, A. (1974) 'Appeal for Gradual Democratization', in G. Saunders (ed.) *Samizdat: Voices of the Soviet Opposition*, New York: Pathfinder.

Shatunovsky, I. (1959) 'Pitiful chewing-gum knights', *Current Digest of the Soviet Press* 11, 10: 37–8.

Shchekochikhin, Iu. (1987b) 'About the *"liubery"* and more', *Current Digest of the Soviet Press* 39, 10: 6.

—— (1988b) 'Before the mirror', *Soviet Sociology* 26, 4: 6–17.

Shchepanskaia, T. (1991a) 'The symbols of the youth subculture', *Soviet Education* 33, 10: 3–16.

Shlapentokh, V. (1987) *The Politics of Sociology in the Soviet Union*, Boulder: Westview Press.

Smirnov, V. (1985) 'Impudent, incomprehensible boys', *Current Digest of the Soviet Press* 37, 6: 14.

Solnick, S. (1990) 'Does the Komsomol have a future?', *Radio Liberty Report on the USSR* 2, 38: 9–13.

Spradley, J. (1979) *The Ethnographic Interview*, New York: Holt, Rinehart and Winston.

'Spring conscription threatened by lack of recruits' (1992) *BBC World Summary* 29 April: C2/3.

Starr, S. (1983) *Red and Hot.The Fate of Jazz in the Soviet Union*, New York: Oxford University Press.

Stites, R. (1989) *Revolutionary Dreams*, New York: Oxford University Press.

—— (1992) *Russian Popular Culture, Entertainment and Society Since 1900*, Cambridge: Cambridge University Press.

Stolee, M. (1988) 'Homeless children in the USSR, 1917–57', *Soviet Studies* 40, 1: 64–83.

Sturrock, J. (ed.) (1979) *Structuralism and Since*, Oxford: Oxford University Press.

Tempest, R. (1984) 'Youth Soviet style', *Problems of Communism* 33, 3: 60–4.

Thompson, E.P. (1968) *The Making of the English Working Class*, Harmondsworth: Penguin.

Thompson, J. (1981) *Critical Hermeneutics*, Cambridge: Cambridge University Press.

Thompson, T. and Sheldon, R. (eds) (1988) *Soviet Society and Culture*, Boulder: Westview Press.

Thrasher, F. (1963) *The Gang*, Chicago: University of Chicago Press.

Tirado, I. (1988) *Young Guard! The Communist Youth League Petrograd 1917–1920*, Connecticut: Greenwood Press.

Troitsky, A. (1987) *Back in the USSR: The True Story of Rock in Russia*, London: Omnibus Press.

—— (1989) 'What is Soviet rock music?', *New Beginnings – Symposium on Rock in the Soviet Union*, Strathclyde University, 2 December.

—— (1990) *Tusovka: Who's Who in the New Soviet Rock Culture*, London: Omnibus Press.

Turner, G. (1990) *British Cultural Studies*, London: Unwin Hyman.

Urban, M. (1992) 'Boris El'tsin, Democratic Russia and the campaign for the Russian presidency', *Soviet Studies* 44, 2: 187–207.

Vasil'ev, A. and Zhavoronkov, G. (1988) 'No written law for them so far', *Moscow News* 3: 12.

Viarich, A. (1959) 'Youth it was that led us', in N. Novak-Deker (ed.) *Soviet Youth: Twelve Komsomol Histories*, Munich: Institute for the Study of the USSR.

Vinitskaia, G. (1992) 'Komsomol revives itself with aim of restoring USSR', *BBC World Summary*, 23 April: B/1.

Vlasov, S. (1984) 'Apartment building and collective', *Current Digest of the Soviet Press* 37, 12: 10–11.

Voloshinov, V. (1973) *Marxism and the Philosophy of the Language*, New York: Seminar Press.

Waters, E. (1989) 'Restructuring the "woman question"', *Feminist Review* 33: 3–19.

Wedgwood Benn, D. (1992) '*Glasnost'* and the media' in S. White, A. Pravda and Z. Gitelman (eds) *Developments in Soviet and Post-Soviet Politics*, London: Macmillan.

Weedon, C. (1989) *Feminist Practice and Poststructuralist Theory*, Oxford: Basil Blackwell.

Weiner, D. (1991) '"Razmychka?" Urban unemployment and peasant in-migration as sources of social conflict', in S. Fitzpatrick, A. Rabinowitch and R. Stites (eds) *Russia in the Era of NEP: Explorations in Soviet Society and Culture*, Bloomington: Indiana University Press.

White, S., Pravda, A. and Z. Gitelman (eds) (1992) *Developments in Soviet and Post-Soviet Politics*, London: Macmillan.

White, H. (1979) 'Michel Foucault', in J. Sturrock (ed.) *Structuralism and Since*, Oxford: Oxford University Press.

Whyte, W.F. (1955) *Street Corner Society. The Social Structure of an Italian Slum*, London: University of Chicago Press.

Williams, R. (1981) *Culture*, London: Fontana.

—— (1988) *Keywords. A Vocabulary of Culture and Society*, London: Fontana.

Williamson, J. (1986) 'The problems of being popular', *New Socialist* September 1986: 14–15.

Willis, P. (1977) *Learning to Labour*, Farnborough: Saxon House.

—— (1978) *Profane Culture*, London: Routledge & Kegan Paul.

—— (1990) *Common Culture*, Milton Keynes: Open University Press.

Wills, C. (1989) 'Upsetting the public: carnival, hysteria and women's texts', in K. Hirschkop and D. Shepherd (eds) *Bakhtin and Cultural Theory*, Manchester: Manchester University Press.

Wilson, E. (1985) *Adorned in Dreams. Fashion and Modernity*, London: Virago.

—— (1990) 'These new components of the spectacle: Fashion and postmodernism', in R. Boyne and A. Rattansi (eds) *Postmodernism and Society*, London: Macmillan.

Wittgenstein, L. (1969) *The Blue and Brown Books*, Oxford: Basil Blackwell.

Worobec, C. (1991) *Peasant Russia*, Princeton: Princeton University Press.

'Young Communist League Cultural Campaign' (1958) *Current Digest of the Soviet Press* 10, 9: 25–6.

Zaitsev, I. (ed.) (1990) *Soviet Rock*, Moscow: Progress Publishers.

Zakharov, R. (1954) 'On true against sham beauty in dance', *Current Digest of the Soviet Press* 6, 39: 11–12.

Zaslavsky, V. (1982) *The Neo-Stalinist State: Class Ethnicity and Consensus in Soviet Society*, Brighton: Harvester Press.

## RUSSIAN LANGUAGE SOURCES

A.F. (1991) 'V voinu igraiut ne tol'ko politiki', *Komsomol'skaia Pravda* 12 March: 2.

Aksenov, V. (1987) *V Poiskakh Grustnogo Bebi*, New York: Liberty Publishing House.

Aleinikov, A. and Chepurin, V. (1991) 'VLKSM: Chto zhe s nami proiskhodit?', *Perspektivy* 9: 20–6.

Alekseevich, S. (1987) 'Stroili sebia, stroili stranu', *Komsomol'skaia Pravda* 18 August: 1.

Alekseeva, V. (1977) 'Neformal'nie gruppy podrostkov v usloviiakh goroda', *Sotsiologicheskie Issledovaniia* 3: 60–70.

Alpatov, V. (1986) 'Bor'ba za "p'edestal pocheta"', *Moskovskii Komsomolets* 6 August: 2.

Andreeva, I. and Novikova, L. (1988) 'Subkul'turnie dominanty netraditsionnikh form povedeniia molodezhi', in V. Semenova (ed.) *Neformal'nie Ob"edineniia Molodezhi, vchera, segodnia . . . a zavtra?*, Moskva: VKSh pri TsK VLKSM.

Andreeva, I., Golubkova, N. and Novikova, L. (1989) 'Molodezhnaia subkul'tura: normy i sistema tsennostei', *Sotsiologicheskie Issledovaniia* 4: 48–56.

Anokhin, S. (1991) In interview with the author, 9 January.

Antonova, Iu. (1990) 'K voprosu o neformal'nikh ob"edineniiakh molodezhi', in A. Bystritskii and M. Roshchin (eds) *Molodezhnii Renessans*, Moskva: Nauka.

Apresian, Z., Gusev, P. and Bazhenov, V. (1988) 'Kakoi Komsomol nam nuzhen?', *Molodoi Kommunist* 10: 31–7.

Arifdzhanov, R. (1990), 'Pod znakom ryby', *Sobesednik* 6: 5.

Arifdzhanov, R., Bykov, D. and Dmukhovskii, M. (1990) 'Sindrom obshchei sud'by', *Sobesednik* 17: 2,4–5.

Arshavskii, A. and Vilks, A. (1990) 'Antiobshchestvennie proiavleniia v molodezhnoi srede: opyt regional'nogo prognoza', *Sotsiologicheskie Issledovaniia* 4: 57–65.

Askin, Ia. (1988) 'Funktsii kul'tury i problemy vremeni molodezhi', in V. Iarskaia (ed.) *Aktual'nie Voprosy Kul'tury Molodezhi v Svete Reshenii XXVII S"ezda KPSS*, Saratov: Saratovskii Universitet.

Astaf'ev, Ia. (1989) 'Eshche raz o molodezhnom stile: dannie prikladnoi sotsiologii', *Tekhnicheskaia Estetika* 8: 5–7.

Avdeev, S., Korchagin, M., Larin, V., Trushkin, A. and Chudakov, A. (1987) 'Porazhenie na Arbate', *Komsomol'skaia Pravda* 27 November: 2.

Avilov, V. (1987) 'Rok ili urok?', *Komsomol'skaia Pravda* 12 March: 2.

Baal', E. (1991) 'V konflikte s zakonom', in K. Igoshev and G. Min'kovskii (eds) *Po Nepisanim Zakonam Ulitsy*, Moskva: Iuridicheskaia Literatura.

Baikov, A., Dudarenko, V., Kiselev, A., Loktionov, S. and Putrin, V. (1988) 'Komsomol i perestroika', *Pravda* 29 October: 3.

Batku, I. (1984) 'Sotsial'nie faktory preodoleniia anti-obshchestvennogo povedeniia sredi podrostkov', Dissertation for degree of Kandidat Nauk, Kishniev.

Batygin, G. (1987) 'Rok: muzyka? Subkul'tura? Stil' zhizni?', *Sotsiologicheskie Issledovaniia* 6: 29–51.

Bek, A. (1990) 'Chto zadumali MGK VLKSM i G Pavlov?', *Moskovksii Komsomolets* 4 September: 1.

Bek, A., Graivoronskii, V. and Romanov, P. (1990), 'Inaia tochka zreniia', *Komsomol'skaia Pravda* 3 April: 2–3.

Belaia, T. (1987) 'Rebiata s nashego dvora', *Komsomol'skaia Pravda* 24 October: 4.

Belaia, R. and Savenkov, V. (1990) 'Seks po-derevenski?', *Komsomol'skaia Pravda* 4 November: 2.

Beliaev, D. (1983) 'Stiliaga', in M. Semenov (ed.) *Krokodilu–60 Let*, Moskva: Pravda.

Beliaeva, N. (1988) 'Svoi sredi svoikh', *Kul'turno-Prosvetitel'naia Rabota* 9: 13–16.

Berezovskii, V. and Krotov, N. (1990) *Neformal'naia Rossiia*, Moskva: Molodaia Gvardiia.

Beslov, A. (1987) 'My sosedy', *Moskovskii Komsomolets* 28th February: 3.

Bestuzhev-Lada, I. (1987a) 'Iabloki ot iabloni', *Komsomol'skaia Pravda* 20 June: 2.

— (1987b) 'Neformaly – kto, otkuda?', *Sem'ia i Shkola* 12: 28–30.

Blinkov, I. (1989) 'Kuda ukhodiat den'gi?', *Moskovskii Komsomolets* 10 January: 1.

Blinov, N. (1985) 'V bor'be s vliianiem chuzhdoi ideologii i morali', *Slovo Lektora* 1: 50–2.

— (1987) 'Ideino-politicheskoe stanovlenie molodezhi: opyt, problemy', *Sotsiologicheskie Issledovaniia* 2: 22–33.

Bogatyreva, T. (1990) 'O vliianii urbanizatsii na stanovlenie lichnosti molodogo cheloveka' in *NTR, Kollektiv, Molodezh'*, rukopis' dep v INION, no. 42172: 51–73.

Boriaz, V. (1973) *Molodezh': Metodologicheskie Problemy Issledovaniia*, Leningrad: Nauka.

Borisov, I. (1988) ' "Gedonisticheskii risk" v neformal'nikh molodezhnikh ob"edineniiakh' in D. Fel'dshtein and L. Radzikhovskii (eds) *Psikhologicheskie Problemy Izucheniia Neformal'nikh Molodezhnikh Ob"edinenii*, Moskva: APN USSR.

— (1991) 'Koe-chto o rokerakh' in K. Igoshev and G. Min'kovskii (eds) *Po Nepisanim Zakonam Ulitsy*, Moskva: Iuridicheskaia Literatura.

Bortsov, A. (1985) 'Tebe, rodina – nash trud i vdokhnovenie', *Moskovskii Komsomolets* 13 January: 1–2.

Bratus, B. (1987) 'Dom bez menia', *Moskovskii Komsomolets* 10 January: 2.

Bronshtein, B. (1993) 'Kuda ushli ' "Kazanskie bandy" ', *Izvestiia*, 20 February: 4.

Bukharin, N. (1988) 'O kommunisticheskom vospitannii molodezhi v usloviiakh NEPa', *Komsomol'skaia Pravda* 13 October: 2.

Bunakov, L. (1990) 'Vystupleniia v preniiakh na XXI S"ezde VLKSM', *Komsomol'skaia Pravda* 14 April: 2.

Buro TsK VLKSM (1986) 'Formirovat' interesy molodezhi', *Komsomol'skaia Pravda* 14 February: 1.

Butakhin, O. (1987) 'Kto takie rokery . . .', *Argumenty i Fakty* 44.

Butko, E. and Denisov, N. (1988) 'Inogorodniaia molodezh' v proftekhuchilishchakh Moskvy i Leningrada', *Sotsiologicheskie Issledovaniia* 4: 73–4.

Bychkova, O. (1989a) 'Andrei Isaev: "Byl obrugan otdel'nimi tovarishchami . . ." ', *Moskovskii Komsomolets* 31 January: 2.

— (1989b) 'Litovskii eksperiment', *Moskovskii Komsomolets* 24 June: 1.

— (1990a) 'Trudnosti s parlamentom', *Moskovskii Komsomolets* 13 April: 1.

— (1990b) ' "Rabota takaia krutaia . . ." ', *Moskovskii Komsomolets* 6 June: 1.

Bystritskii, A. and Roshchin, M. (eds) (1990) *Molodezhnii Renessans*, Moskva: Nauka.

Chepurin, V. (1987) 'Strategiia nashikh deistvii', *Moskovskii Komsomolets* 16 June: 2.

Cherniak, I. (1987) 'Ofitsial'naia dolzhnost'', *Sobesednik* 2: 4.

Chirkin, A. (1988) 'Podrostok, sem'ia i rok-muzyka', *Nash Sovremennik* 10: 141–8.

Chistiakov, V. and Sanachev, I. (1988) 'Troianskii Kon'', *Nash Sovremennik* 10: 126–41.

Churbanov, V. and Neliubin, A. (1988) 'Neformal'nie ob"edinieniia: Priroda, problemy, prognozy', *Politicheskoe Obrazovanie* 12: 58–64.

Davydov, Iu. (1977) 'Kontrkul'tura i krizis sotsializatsii molodezhi v usloviiakh "obshchestva potrebleniia" ', *Sotsiologicheskie Issledovaniia* 3: 78–87.

'Ded Mikhail' (1990) *Molodoi Kommunist* 27 December: 2.

Demin, M. (1988) 'Lichnost' kak sistema sotsial'nikh kachestv' in M. Demin and L. Ganzel (eds) *Lichnost' v Sotsialisticheskom Obshchestve*, Moskva: Mysl'.

Demin, M. and Ganzel, L. (eds) (1988) *Lichnost' v Sotsialisticheskom Obshchestve*, Moskva: Mysl'.

Deriugin, Iu. (1990) ' "Dedovshchina": sotsial'no-psikhologicheskii analiz iavleniia', *Psikhologicheskii Zhurnal* 11, 1: 109–16.

Desiaterik, V. (1988) 'Lenin otvechaet na voprosy', *Komsomol'skaia Pravda* 2 October: 2.

'Diagnoz postavlen. Trebuetsia lechenie' (1989) *Sobesednik* 32: 2.

Dmukhovskii, M. (1989) 'Ocherednoi skandal?', *Sobesednik* 49: 5.

Dolgodvorov, V. (1988) 'Tikhii vecher v Dzerzhinske', *Trud* 2 November.

Dolgov, V. (1989) 'Pryzhok bez razgona: strakh pered neformalami v istoricheskom kontekste', *Moskovskii Komsomolets* 14 July: 2.

Dudukina, I. (1988) 'Komsomol i kommertsiia', *Moskovskii Komsomolets* 7 October: 2.

'Ei, Komsomol, ty eshche zhiv?' (1991) *Moskovskii Komsomolets* 27 March: 2.

Epifanov, I. (1988) 'Igra v "liubery" ', *Zhurnalist* 5: 35–7.

Eremin, V. (1987a) 'Budem na "ty"!', *Molodoi Kommunist* 10: 73–83.

—— (1987b) 'Krushenie "Grinabelia" ', *Komsomol'skaia Pravda* 12 August: 2.

—— (1988) 'Sovsem ne detskie igry', *Vozhatii* 3: 39–42.

—— (1991a) 'Vorovskoi orden', *Nedelia* 13: 16–17.

—— (1991b) In conversation with the author, 28 May.

'Eshche raz o 'dele KPM" (1989) *Komsomol'skaia Pravda* 1 March: 1.

Ezhelev, A. (1987a) 'Komu urok?', *Izvestiia* 27 March: 6.

—— (1987b) 'Urok ne vprek', *Izvestiia* 9 April: 6.

—— (1987c) 'V odnoi lodke', *Izvestiia* 1 August: 3.

Fadeev, V. (1990) 'Perestroika s tochki zreniia sotsializatsii', in A. Bystritskii and M. Roshchin (eds) *Molodezhnii Renessans*, Moskva: Nauka.

Fel'dshtein, D. (1987) 'Psikhologo-pedagogicheskie aspekty izucheniia neformal'nikh molodezhnikh ob"edinenii', *Sovetskaia Pedagogika* 6: 42–7.

—— (1988) 'Psikhologo-pedagogicheskie aspekty izucheniia neformal'nikh molodezhnikh ob"edinenii', in D. Fel'dshtein and L. Radzikhovskii (eds) *Psikhologicheskie Problemy Izucheniia Neformal'nikh Molodezhnikh Ob"edinenii*, Moskva: APN SSSR.

—— (1989) 'Formalizm v vospitanii i neformaly', *Voprosy Psikhologii* 4: 24–31.

Fel'dshtein, D. and Radzikhovskii, L. (eds) (1988) *Psikhologicheskie Problemy Izucheniia Neformal'nikh Molodezhnikh Ob"edinenii*, Moskva: APN SSSR.

Ferida, Izaura and Karen, (1990) *Molodoi Kommunist* 18 October: 11.

Filatov, A. (1988a) 'S kem rabotaet Komsomol?', *Molodezhnii Ekspress* 40: 4.

—— (1988b), 'Interbrigady podnimaiutsia v razvedku', *Komsomol'skaia Pravda* 28 November: 2.

Filinov, Iu. (1986) 'Na konverte pishite "ABV"', *Komsomol'skaia Pravda* 15 January: 4.

Galgan, A. (1987) 'Ne staraias' ugodit', *Komsomol'skaia Pravda*, 22 December: 1.
Ganichev, V. (1976) *Molodezhnaia Pechat': Istoriia, Teoriia, Praktika*, Moskva: Mysl'.
Gapochka, I. (1986) 'Ubiistva po vole roka', *Sobesednik* 41: 6.
Gasparian, A. (1990) ' "Ia takoi kak prezhde" ', *Moskovskii Komsomolets* 21 October: 3.
Gatov, V. (1988) '"Usobshcha"', *Nedelia* 12: 6–7.
Gerasimov, K. (1990) 'Eshche raz o BAMe', *Moskovskii Komsomolets* 4 January: 2.
Gorbachev, M. (1986) *Otvety na voprosy gazety 'Iumanite'*, Moskva: Politizdat.
—— (1987a) *Molodezh' – Tvorcheskaia Sila Revoliutsionnogo Obnovleniia*, Moskva: Izdatel'stvo Politicheskoi Literatury.
—— (1987b) 'Vystuplenie na S"ezde VLKSM', *Moskovskii Komsomolets* 17 April: 1.
—— (1988) 'Perestroika i molodezh': vremia deistvii', *Trud* 1 November: 1–2.
Gorin, I. (1985) 'I vnov' prodolzhaetsia BAM', *Sobesednik* 20: 8–9.
Graivoronskii, V. (1990) 'Kuda letiat milliony', *Moskovskii Komsomolets* 24 April: 1.
Grigor'eva, I. (1985) 'Sotsializatsiia molodezhi v usloviiakh sovremennogo sotsialisticheskogo goroda', Dissertation submitted for degree of Kandidat Nauk, Leningrad.
Grishin, V. (1989) 'Subkul'tura. Ee proiavleniia v molodezhnoi srede', in *Problemy Ispolneniia Nakazaniia v Vospitatel'no-trudovikh Koloniiakh i Preduprezhdeniia Prestupnosti Molodezhi*, Moskva: VNII MVD SSSR.
Grishina, E. (1988) 'Religiozny li my?', *Molodezhnii Ekspress* 49: 14–20.
Gromyko, M. (1986) *Traditsionnie Normy Povedeniia i Formy Obshcheniia Russkikh Krest'ian XIX Veka*, Moskva: Nauka.
Gubenko, V. and Piskarev, N. (1988) 'Samozvantsy i "samodel'shchiki"', *Komsomol'skaia Pravda* 31 January: 2.
Gun'ko, B. (1988) 'Dve estetiki', *Nash Sovremennik* 10: 121–5.
Gusev, P. (1991) In interview with author, June 1991.
Gutiontov, P. (1987) 'Sotvorili mif o "liuberakh" ', *Sovetskaia Rossiia* 4 March: 6.
'I eto vse o nas' (1990) *Sobesednik* 35: 4–5.
'Ia ne broshu tebia v bede' (1986) *Sobesednik* 51: 11.
Iakovlev, V. (1987a) 'Kontora "Liuberov" ', *Ogonek* 5: 21–2.
—— (1987b) 'Proshchanie s Bazarovim', *Ogonek* 36: 4–5.
Iakovleva, E. (1988) 'Bor'ba i pobeda', *Komsomol'skaia Pravda* 31 August: 2.
Iakovleva, E. and Muratov, D. (1988) 'Vtoraia popytka', *Komsomol'skaia Pravda* 25 October: 4.
Ianovskii, R. (ed.) *Chelovek i Nravstvennost' v Usloviiakh Perestroiki*, Minsk: Belarus'.
Iarskaia, V. (ed.) (1988) *Aktual'nie Voprosy Kul'tury Molodezhi v Svete Reshenii XXVII S"ezda KPSS*, Saratov: Saratovskii Universitet.
'Ideino-politicheskoe stanovlenie molodezhi: opyt, problemy' (1987) *Sotsiologicheskie Issledovaniia* 2: 22–33.
Igoshev, K. and Min'kovskii, G. (eds) (1991) *Po Nepisanim Zakonam Ulitsy*, Moskva: Iuridicheskaia Literatura.
Ikonnikova, S. (1974) *Molodezh': Sotsiologicheskii i sotsial'no-psikhologicheskii Analiz*, Leningrad: Leningradskii Gosudarstvenii Universitet.
—— (1976) *Kritika Burzhuaznikh Kontseptsii 'Molodezhnoi Kul'tury'*, Moskva: Obshchestvo 'Znanie' RSFSR.
Ikonnikova, S. and Kon, I. (1970) *Molodezh' kak sotsial'naia kategoriia*, Moskva.
Il'inskii, I. (1985) 'Issledovaniia problem molodezhi v SSSR', *Obshchestvennie Nauki* 4: 28–41.

—— (1987a) 'Problemy formirovaniia obraza zhizni sovetskoi molodezhi v usloviiakh perestroiki', in *Sotsialisticheskii Obraz Zhizni Molodezhi v Usloviiakh
Uskoreniia Sotsial'no-ekonomicheskogo Razvitiia*, Moskva: VLKSM VKSh pri
TsK VLKSM.
—— (1987b) 'Razvitie sotsializma i molodezh'', *Kommunist* 6: 20–7.
—— (1988a) 'Molodezh': stereotipy i realnost'', *Agitator* 7: 8–10.
—— (1988b) 'Imeem pravo!', *Komsomol'skaia Pravda* 22 January: 2.
'Informatsionnoe Soobshchenie' (1990) *Komsomol'skaia Pravda* 27 October: 1.
I.S. (1986) 'Ia nashel v sebe sily', *Sobesednik* 42: 13.
Iudanov, B. (1987) 'Po kom zvenit "metall" ', *Sovetskaia Kul'tura* 8 August: 6.
Iushenkov,S. (ed.) (1990) *Neformaly: Sotsial'nie Initsiativy*, Moskva: Moskovskii
Rabochii.
Ivanova, V. (1990) 'Cheboksarskie amazonki', *Sovetskaia Chuvashiia*, 24
November: 2–3.
Kadulin, V. and Kolesnikov, S. (1987) 'Leningrad v oktiabre', *Kommunist* 17:
41–53.
'Kak zakaliaetsia mysl'' (1988) *Komsomol'skaia Pravda* 16 October: 1.
Kalinin, A. (1987) 'Na sviaz' vyzyvaiutsia', *Komsomol'skaia Pravda* 4 October: 1.
Kaplinskii, Ia. (1988) 'O proiavleniiakh fashizma', *Raduga* 7: 75–81.
Karpets, I. (1990) ' "Zhestokost' porozhdaet tol'ko zhestokost' . . ." ', *Sobesednik*
9: 10.
Kartavaia, E. (1988) 'Kul'tura i ideologiia', in *Problemy Sotsial'nogo i
Dukhovnogo Razvitiia Sotsialisticheskogo Obshchestva v Usloviiakh Perestroiki*,
Vladivostok: Ministry of Culture of the RSFSR, Far Eastern Pedagogical
Institute of Arts.
Kashelkin, A. and Ovchinskii, V. (1991) 'Po nepisanim zakonam ulitsy . . .', in K.
Igoshev and G. Min'kovskii (eds) *Po Nepisanim Zakonam Ulitsy*, Moskva:
Iuridicheskaia Literatura.
Kataev, S. (1986) 'Muzykal'nie vkusy molodezhi', *Sotsiologicheskie Issledovaniia*
1: 105–8.
Katoza, T. and Skvortsov, V. (1987) 'Po brachnomu svidetel'stvu',
*Komsomol'skaia Pravda* 22 September: 2.
Khaitina, Iu. (1986) 'Za slovom delo', *Moskovskii Komsomolets* 8 August: 2.
—— (1990a) 'Umirat' poka rano!', *Moskovskii Komsomolets* 31 January: 1.
—— (1990b), 'Oppozitsiia igraet va-bank', *Moskovskii Komsomolets* 3 April: 2.
—— (1990c) 'Dobrovol'tsy', *Moskovskii Komsomolets* 10 April: 1.
—— (1990d) ' "Priniat' k svedeniiu" ', *Moskovskii Komsomolets* 5 June: 1.
—— (1990e) 'V poiskakh "zolotoi serediny" ', *Moskovksii Komsomolets* 22 August:
1.
—— (1990f) 'Eshche odna popytka', *Moskovskii Komsomolets* 4 November: 1.
—— (1991) 'Aleksandry pervie, kotorie ni o chem ne zhaleiut', *Moskovskii
Komsomolets* 27 March: 2.
Khaitina, Iu. and Bychkova, O. (1990) 'Kuda plyvet korabl'?', *Moskovskii
Komsomolets* 26 January: 1.
Khudaverdian, V. (1977) 'O nekotorikh novikh tendentsiiakh v sovremennoi burz-
huaznoi sotsiologii molodezhi (kriticheskii analiz)', *Sotsiologicheskie Issledo-
vaniia* 3: 71–7.
—— (1986) *Sovremennie Al'ternativnie Dvizheniia (Molodezh' Zapada i "Novii
Irratsionalizm")*, Moskva: Mysl'.
Kirillov, I. (1990) 'O zaniatosti molodezhi, okonchivshei predniuiu shkolu', *Vestnik
Statistiki* 10: 58–60.
Kirillovy, O. and V. (1990) ' "Zhrits liubvi" – na sluzhbu gosudarstvu?',
*Moskovksii Komsomolets* 20 October: 2.

Kirin, A. (1988), 'Tsirkuliarov ne budet', *Komsomol'skaia Pravda* 15 December: 2.

Kokliagina, L. (1992) 'Istoki marginal'nosti rossiiskoi molodezhi', in M. Malysheva (ed.) *Molodezh' Rossii Na Rubezhe 90-kh Godov*, Moskva: RAN Institut Sotsiologii.

Kolkov, M. (1990) 'Chto zadumali MGK VLKSM i G. Pavlov?', *Moskovksii Komsomolets* 15 September: 1.

Komarov, A. (1986) 'Na chto zhaluetsia gramplastinka', *Sobesednik* 39: 12.

Komarova, E. (1989) 'Problemy vozniknoveniia i razvitiia neformal'nikh obrazova-nii molodezhi v usloviiakh sotsializma', Dissertation submitted for degree of Kandidat Nauk, Moscow.

Komissarenko, S. (1988) 'Ob"ekt stanovit'sia sub"ektom, ili "eto my ne prokho-dili" ', *Kul'turno-Prosvetitel'naia Rabota* 9: 16–17.

Kononov, V. (1989) 'Razvitie sotsial'noi initsiativy molodezhi v usloviiakh sover-shenstvovaniia sotsializma, Doctoral dissertation, Moscow.

Koroleva, K. (1991) ' "K starosti ponimaesh', chto bit' mordy glupo" ', *Komsomol'skaia Pravda* 12 March 1991: 2.

Korsakova, T. *et al.* (1987) 'Ne ukhodiat v otstavku soldaty', *Komsomol'skaia Pravda* 18 November: 1.

Kosarev, A. and Kraval', I. (eds) (1936) *Molodezh SSSR*, Moscow: TsUNKhU Gosplan SSSR.

Koshelkin, A. (1991) 'O vrede perestroiki v prestupnom mire', *Komsomol'skaia Pravda* 12 March: 2.

Kostenko, N. (1990) 'Molodezhnaia pechat': interesy i tsennosti', *Filosofskaia i Sotsiologicheskaia Mysl'* 1: 82–7.

Koveshnikov, Iu. and Cherniak, I. (1988) 'V dolgu pered derzhavoi', *Sobesednik* 31: 4–5.

Kozheurov, S., Nekrasov, V., Pankratov, A. and Khantsevich, A. (1989) 'ChP soiuznogo masshtaba', *Komsomol'skaia Pravda* 31 January: 2.

Kozin, V. (1987a) ' "Kaskad" speshit na pomoshch'', *Komsomol'skaia Pravda* 20 February: 2.

—— (1987b) 'Front bez tyla', *Komsomol'skaia Pravda* 20 December: 1.

—— (1988) 'Staia: V chem prichiny poiavleniia gruppirovok podrostkov v Kazani?', *Komsomol'skaia Pravda* 29 April: 2.

Kozlov, A. and Lisovskii, A. (1986) *Molodoi Chelovek: Stanovlenie Obraza Zhizni*, Moskva: Politicheskaia Literatura.

Kozlova, N. (1990) 'Lovushki istorii – molodezh' i revoliutsionnii avangardizm' in V. Levicheva (ed.) *Neformal'naia Volna*, Moskva: NITs pri VKSh.

Kozyrev, S. (1987) 'Vy pisali v 1987 godu', *Komsomol'skaia Pravda* 30 December: 1.

Kravchenko, V. (1988) 'Rol' rabochei molodezhi v ukreplenii material'nikh i dukhovnikh osnov sotsialisticheskogo obraza zhizni' in V. Iarskaia (ed.) *Aktual'nie Voprosy Kul'tury Molodezhi v Svete Reshenii XXVII S"ezda KPSS*, Saratov: Saratovskii Universitet.

Kruglov, M. (1988) 'Draka v stile "disko" ', *Komsomol'skaia Pravda* 10 August: 2.

Kuchmaeva, I. (ed.) (1987) *Subkul'turnie Ob"edineniia Molodezhi: Kriticheskii Analiz*, Moskva.

—— (1987) 'Molodezhnie subkul'turnie ob"edineniia kak faktor dinamiki kul'tury', in I. Kuchmaeva (ed.) *Subkul'turnie Ob"edineniia Molodezhi: Kriticheskii Analiz*, Moskva.

Kuchmaeva, I. and Matveeva, S. (eds) (1989) *Problemy Kul'turnogo Nasledovaniia v Filosofskoi Teorii i Praktike Sovremennogo Zapada*, Moskva: Institut Filosofii AN SSSR.

## 340  Bibliography

'Kuda idut nashi den'gi' (1989) *Komsomol'skaia Pravda* 1 February: 1–2.
Kukeva, I. and Mikhailov, K. (1986) 'Lefortovo v kol'tse', *Sobesednik* 34: 5.
Kukhtevich, T. and Dobrynin, V. (1990) 'Molodezhnaia kul'tura: problemy i perspektivy razvitiia' in *Aktual'nie Problemy Sovremennoi Molodezhnoi Kul'tury*, Gorkii: Gorkii Gosuniversitet.
Kulikov, V. (1986a), 'Konets kvartiry 50?', *Komsomol'skaia Pravda* 30 August: 4.
—— (1986b) ' "Krutie parni" ', *Komsomol'skaia Pravda* 26 October: 4.
Kupriianov, A. (1985) 'Dvoiniki', *Komsomol'skaia Pravda* 20 January: 4.
—— (1986) 'Vechernii siuzhet dlia gorkoma', *Komsomol'skaia Pravda* 9 April: 4.
—— (1987) 'Liubertsy – pri svete fonarei, ili pasynki stolitsy', *Sobesednik* 7: 10–15.
Kupriianov, A. and Iakovlev, V. (1986) 'Nochnoi mototsiklist', *Sobesednik* 41: 12–13.
Kurbanova, A. (1985) 'Fenomen "subkul'tur" i ideologicheskaia bor'ba', in *Problemy Kul'tury v Sovremennom Kapitalisticheskom Obshchestve (Tsennostnie Aspekty)*, Moskva.
—— (1986) 'Protsess samorealizatsii lichnosti v molodezhnikh subkul'turakh' in *Kul'tura i Lichnost' v Kapitalisticheskom Obshchestve*, Moskva.
Kushnerev, S. (1987) ' "A vy kto takie?" ', *Pravda* 30 March: 4.
—— (1988) 'Prishel'tsy?', *Komsomol'skaia Pravda* 22 May: 4.
Kuz'min, S. (1990) *Komsomol'skaia Pravda* 30 October: 2.
Kuz'mina, V. (1991) In conversation with the author, 23 August.
Kuznetsov, V., Nikiforov, V. and Krasner, L. (1990) 'Maket korablia v natural'nuiu velichinu', *Moskovskii Komsomolets* 14 February: 1.
Ladatko, A. (1990) 'V soiuze s neformalami', *Vospitanie Shol'nikov* 3: 48–9.
Lapin, A. (1987) 'Nochnoi eksport', *Moskovskii Komsomolets* 15 November: 2–3.
Lavrova, K. (1985a), 'Vecherom, u pod"ezda', *Komsomol'skaia Pravda*, 12 January: 2.
—— (1985c) 'Chudaki iz kvartala "V": neformal'nie ob"edineniia molodezhi trebuiut vnimaniia', *Komsomol'skaia Pravda* 12 December: 4.
—— (1986) 'Otvet zhdu s neterpeniem', *Komsomol'skaia Pravda* 20 March: 2.
—— (1987) ' "Za etu liubov' ia otdam vse" ', *Komsomol'skaia Pravda* 13 September: 2.
Lenin, V. (1987) *O Proletarskoi Kul'ture*, Moskva: Politizdat.
Lenochka (1990) *Molodoi Kommunist* 11 October: 11.
Leont'eva, A. (1989) 'My i oni', *Sobesednik* 43: 14.
Levanov, E. (1987a) 'Samodeiatel'nie Ob"edineniia Molodezhi', in *Sotsialisticheskii Obraz Zhizni Molodezhi v Usloviiakh Uskoreniia Sotsial'no-ekonomicheskogo Razvitiia*, Moskva: VKSh pri TsK VLKSM.
—— (1987b) 'Uchenii idet k "neformalam" ', *Komsomol'skaia Pravda* 11 December: 4.
Levanov, E. and Levicheva, V. (1988) 'Eti mnogolikie "neformaly" ', *Orientiry* 12: 20–4.
Levanov, E., Levicheva, V., and Rubanova, N. (1989) 'Samodeiatel'nie ob"edineniia molodezhi kak obshchestvennoe iavlenie', *Aktual'nie Problemy Ideino-politicheskogo Vospitaniia Molodezhi*, Moskva: VKSh pri TsK VLKSM.
Levicheva, V. (1988) 'Politicheskaia kul'tura molodezhi kak produkt sotsialisticheskogo dukhovnogo proizvodstva', in *Komsomol i Formirovanie Politicheskoi Kul'tury Molodezhi*, Moskva: NITs VKSh pri TsK VLKSM.
—— (ed.) (1990) *Neformal'naia Volna*, Moskva: NITs pri VKSh.
—— (1991) 'Samodeiatel'noe dvizhenie molodezhi v rusle grazhdanskogo dialoga', in K. Igoshev and G. Min'kovskii (eds) *Po Nepisanim Za Konam Ulitsy*, Moskva: Iuridich-eskaia Literatura.
Likhachev, D. (1987) 'Im neobkhodimo doverie', *Literaturnaia Gazeta* 21: 13.
Likhanov, D. (1988) ' "Driannie" mal'chishki', *Ogonek* 29: 20–2.

Liuboshchits, S. (1986) 'Sotsial'nomu pereustroistvu sela – Komsomol'skoe shefstvo', *Moskovskii Komsomolets* 5 August: 1.

Loshkarev, Iu. (1989) 'Molodezhnaia pechat' v formirovanii novogo myshleniia' in E. Volodinae *et al.* (eds) *Molodezh'–89: Obshchestvennoe Pobzhenie Molodzeh' i Voprosy Molodezhnoi Politiki v SSR*, Moskva: VKSh pri Tsk VLKSM.

Lugovaia, L. (1986) ' "Bum!" No.4', *Sobesednik* 29: 6.

Luk'ianova, I. (1986) 'Kritika sovremennikh idealisticheskikh kontseptsii molodezhnoi kul'tury', in *Kritika Burzhuaznikh Filosofskikh i Sotsiologicheskikh Kontseptsii Kul'tury*, Leningrad: LGIK imeni N.K. Krupskoi.

Lukov, V. (1988) 'Est' mneniia', *Komsomol'skaia Pravda* 21 May: 2.

Malysheva, M. (ed.) (1992) *Molodezh' Rossii Na Rubezhe 90–kh Godov*, Moskva: RAN Institut Sotsiologii.

Markarian, K. (1990) 'Latvia: Komsomol ostaetsia', *Komsomol'skaia Pravda* 3 February: 1.

Marsov, V. (1988) 'Vsesilie zla ili bespomoshchnost' vlasti?', *Moskovskie Novosti* 3: 11.

Matveeva, S. (1987) 'Subkul'tura v dinamike kul'tury', in I. Kuchmaeva (ed.) *Subkul'turnie Ob"edineniia Molodezhi: Kriticheskii Analiz*, Moskva.

Matvienko, A. (1989) 'O tekushchem momente', *Komsomol'skaia Pravda* 31 October: 3.

Medvedev, V. (1987) 'Pisarev za vse otvetit', *Komsomol'skaia Pravda* 3 September: 1.

Meier, M., Filippova, E. and Shchepanskaia, T. (1990) 'Veshchi ne v sebe', *Dekorativnoe Iskusstvo SSSR* 5: 21–8.

Meinert, N. (1987) 'Po vole roka', *Sotsiologicheskie Issledovaniia* 4: 88–93.

Meshcherkin, A. and Meshcherkina, E. (1992) 'Avtoportret rossiiskoi provintsial'noi molodezhi na dosuge', in M. Malysheva (ed.) *Molodezh' Rossii Na Rubezhe 90–kh Godov*, Moskva: RAN Institut Sotsiologii.

Mialo, K. (1988a) 'Kazanskii fenomen', *Novoe Vremia* 33: 41–4.

— (1988b) 'Kazanskii fenomen', *Novoe Vremia* 34: 40–2.

— (1991) *Vremia Vybora*, Moskva: Izdatel''tvo Politicheskoi Literatury.

Mikeladze, N. and Mursaliev, A. (1990), 'Poslednii s"ezd?', *Komsomol'skaia Pravda* 27 March: 4.

Mikhailov, K. (1986) 'Razrushenie po planu?', *Sobesednik* 50: 13.

Mironenko, V. (1988a) 'Otchet TsK VLKSM i zadachi Komsomola po dal'neishemu usileniiu kommunisticheskogo vospitaniia molodezhi v svete ustanovok XXVII S"ezda KPSS', in *Dokumenty i Materialy XX S"ezda Vsesoiuznogo Leninskogo Kommunisticheskogo Soiuza Molodezhi (15–18 April 1987)*, Moskva: Molodaia Gvardiia.

— (1988b) 'Rech' deputata V.I. Mironenko', *Pravda* 30 November: 6.

— (1988c) *Moskovskii Komsomolets* 27 October: 1.

— (1989a) 'O polozhenii v VLKSM', *Komsomol'skaia Pravda* 1 August: 1.

— (1989b) 'O tekushchem momente', *Komsomol'skaia Pravda* 31 October: 1–2.

— (1990a) 'Otchet TsK VLKSM XXI S"ezdu Komsomola', *Komsomol'skaia Pravda* 30 March: 1–2.

— (1990b) 'Doklad pervogo sekretaria TsK VLKSM V. Mironenko', *Komsomol'skaia Pravda* 13 April: 1–2.

— (1990c) 'Vystupleniia v preniiakh na XXI S"ezde VLKSM', *Komsomol'skaia Pravda* 19 April: 2.

Mironova, G. (1987) 'Kapitany bez komandy', *Komsomol'skaia Pravda* 23 June: 1.

Misiuchenko, V. (1986) ' "Shalynishki" i predatel'stvo', *Sobesednik* 21: 6.

Mitrokhin, S. (1992) 'Molodezh' i politika v epokhu pereotsenki tsennostei', in M. Malysheva (ed.) *Molodezh' Rossii Na Rubezhe 90–kh Godov*, Moskva: RAN Institut Sotsiologii.

'Molodezh' v sovremennom mire' (1990) *Voprosy Filosofii* 5: 12–33.

*Molodezh' SSSR – Statisticheskii Sbornik* (1990) Moskva: Finansy i Statistiki.

Morozov, I. (1987) 'Poniat' Bogacheva', *Komsomol'skaia Pravda* 23 December: 1.

Morozov, N. (1988) 'Vo vlasti ulitsy', *Pravda* 12 October: 3.

'My ne proshchaemsia rebiata' (1987) *Komsomol'skaia Pravda* 19 November: 1.

'My vmeste' (1988) *Komsomol'skaia Pravda* 9 December 1988: 1.

Naloev, A. (1986) 'D'iavoly ″metallisticheskogo roka', *Sobesednik* 38: 7.

'Nashi plany i nadezhdy' (1986) *Moskovskii Komsomolets* 11 September: 1.

Nastichenko, V. (1988) 'Ne dorosli ili nedorosli?', *Sovetskaia Kul'tura* 4 October: 3.

Naumenko, G. (1979) *Molodezh' Sotsialisticheskogo Goroda: Byt, Traditsii, Obriady*, Kiev: Naukova Dumka.

Nazarov, L. (1988) 'Rabota komitetov Komsomola Novosibirskoi oblasti s samodeiatel'nimi ob″edineniiami: Opyt i problemy', *Orientiry* 6: 15.

Nevar, S. (1989) 'Demokratizatsiia sovetskogo obshchestva i samodeiatel'nie ob″edineniia molodezhi″', in *Obshchestvennoe Soznanie i Molodezh'*, Moskva: VKSh pri TsK VLKSM.

Nikolaev, A. (1986) 'Khochu byt' pervym', *Moskovskii Komsomolets* 10 August: 1.

—— (1987) 'Vozvrashchenie domoi', *Moskovskii Komsomolets* 23 August: 2.

'Nuzhna li molodezhi naiania?' (1990) *Moskovksii Komsomolets*, 5 September: 1.

'O problemakh, zadachakh i perspektivakh molodezhnogo dosuga', *Moskovskii Komsomolets* 7 July: 1.

'Ob obshchikh nachalakh gosudarstvennoi molodezhnoi politiki v SSSR' (1991) *Izvestiia* 2 May: 2.

Obukhov, S. (1990) 'My shli vmeste', *Sobesednik* 15: 11.

Oganian, S. (1987) 'Molodezh' 2000 goda', *Komsomol'skaia Pravda* 13 September: 1.

Oizerman, T. (1983) 'Problemy kul'tury v filosofii marksizma', *Voprosy Filosofii* 7: 72–86.

Oksana (1990) *Molodoi Kommunist* 6 September: 12.

Orlov, A. (1989) 'Geroi asfal'ta', *Komsomol'skaia Pravda* 17 October: 1.

—— (1990) ' "Sku-u-chno, patsany . . ." ', *Komsomol'skaia Pravda* 21 March: 2.

Orlova, E. (1987) 'Subkul'tury v strukture sovremennogo obshchestva', in I. Kuchmaeva (ed.) *Subkul'turnie Ob″edineniia Molodezhi: Kriticheskii Analiz*, Moskva.

Osin, A. (1989) 'Obrechena na ischeznovenie', *Daugava* 2: 73–81.

—— (1991) 'Poslednii shans', *Perspektivy* 3: 27–31.

Ostrovskii, A. (1989a) 'Rokossovskogo – po etapu . . . vel etot chelovek v kontse tridtsatikh', *Moskovskii Komsomolets* 4 July: 2.

—— (1989b) 'Zapomni vse', *Moskovskii Komsomolets* 12 December: 2.

Os'kin, A. (1990) 'Ia protiv zakona o molodezhi', *Moskovksii Komsomolets* 23 November: 2.

'Otchetnii doklad' (1987) *Moskovskii Komsomolets* 8 March: 2.

Ovchinskii, V. (1988) 'Netraditsionnie gruppy molodezhi: otkloniaiushcheesia povedenie i ego profilaktika', in D. Fel'dshtein and L. Radzikhovskii (eds) *Psikologicheskie Problemy Izucheniia Neformal'nikh Molodezhnikh Ob″edinenii*, Moskva: APN SSSR.

—— (1989) 'Neformal v zakone', *Sotsiologicheskie Issledovaniia* 2: 63–70.

—— (1991) ' "Mama, ia liubera liubliu . . ." ', in K. Igoshev and G. Min'kovskii (eds) *Po Nepisanim Zakonam Ulitsy*, Moskva: Iuridicheskaia Literatura.

Pal'tsev, N. (1989) 'O Komsomole Litvy', *Komsomol'skaia Pravda* 22 August: 1.

'Panki golosuiut za El'tsina' (1990) *Moskovskii Komsomolets* 8 August 1990: 1.

Pankratov, A. (1987) 'Podtusovka', *Komsomol'skaia Pravda* 16 July: 2.

—— (1990) 'Kazan'-nostra', *Komsomol'skaia Pravda* 17 January: 3.

Pavlik and Serii (1990) *Molodoi Kommunist* 20 September: 13.

Pel'man, G. (1987) 'Prover' v sebia!' *Sobesednik* 26: 11.

Petrov, A. (1986) 'Osnovy sotsial'nogo eksperimenta', *Moskovskii Komsomolets* 6 August: 2.

Pishchulin, N. (1985) *Moskovskii Komsomolets*, 11 January: 2.

Plaksii, I. (1983) 'Kakie potrebnosti razumni?', *Kul'turno-prosvetlitel'naia Rabota* 2: 34–7.

—— (1985) *Otkloneniia Ot Norm Sotsialistcheskogo Obraza Zhizni v Molodezhnoi Srede: Sushchnost' i Puti Preodoleniia*, Moskva: Molodaia Gvardia.

—— (1988a) ' "Neformaly" – synov'ia ili pasynki?', *Politicheskoe Samoobrazovanie* April: 84–90.

—— (1988b) *Molodezhnie Gruppy i Ob"edineniia: Prichiny Vozniknoveniia i Osobennosti Deiatel'nosti*, Moskva: Znanie.

—— (1989) 'Molodezh' v period utverzhdeniia novoi ekonomicheskoi situatsii: nekotorie tendentsii i protivorechiia', in E. Volodina *et al.* (eds) *Molodezh'–89: Obshchestvennoe Polozhenie Molodezh' i Voprosy Molodezhnoi Politiki v SSSR*, Moskva: VKSh pri TsK VLKSM.

Platonov, A. (1987) 'Energeticheskaia podzariadka ili podelki pod rok?', *Komsomol'skaia Zhizn'* 5: 29–30.

Podol'skii, V. and Zhukov, S. (1989) ' "Motalki" ', *Komsomol'skaia Pravda* 24 December: 4.

Poliakov, A. (1987) 'Nuzhno li borot'sia s molodezh'iu?', *Moskovskii Komsomolets* 31 March: 3.

Ponomarev, V. (1987) ' "Novodvorskoe veche . . ." ', *Sobesednik* 44: 12–13.

'Postanovlenie IV Plenuma TsK VLKSM, "O dal'neishei demokratizatsii zhizni Komsomola" ', (1988) *Komsomol'skaia Pravda* 21 November: 1–2.

Potekhin, A. (1990) 'Konets vechnosti', *Sobesednik* 5: 2.

Potekhina, I. (1990) 'Komsomol sleva', *Komsomol'skaia Pravda* 14 August: 1.

Prisiazhnii, S. (1990) 'Spetsial'naia terminologiia, primeniaemaia narkomanami' in A. Bystritskii and M. Roshchin (eds.) *Molodezhnii Renessans*, Moskva: Nauka.

'Programma VLKSM: Vozmozhny varianty' (1989) *Sobesednik* 37: 3 and 41: 3.

Radzikhovskii, L. (1988a) 'Neformal'nie molodezhnie b"edineniia: problemy psikhologicheskogo analiza', *Sovetskaia Pedagogika* 9: 75–9.

Ragozin, Iu. (1990) 'Seichas v Komsomole kar'eru ne delaiut', *Komsomol'skaia Pravda* 31 July: 1–2.

Rakovskaia, O. (1992) 'Perekhod k rynku i molodezh'' in M. Malysheva (ed.) *Molodezh' Rossii Na Rubezhe 90-Kh Godov*, Moskva: RAN Institut Sotsiologii.

Rasputin, V. (1990) 'Cherchez la femme', *Nash Sovremennik* 3: 171–2.

Ratvanin, F. (1987) 'Vorota-degtem', *Sobesednik* 50: 10.

Revin, V. (1991) 'Neformaly i militsiia: protivoborstvo ili sotrudnichestvo?', in K. Igoshev and G. Min'kovskii (eds) *Po Nepisanim Zakonam Ulitsy*, Moskva: Iuridicheskaia Literatura.

Rogozhuk, S. (1987) ' "Kach" bol'she ne v mode', *Komsomol'skaia Zhizn'* 5: 26–8.

Rozin, M. (1988) 'Dramaturgiia ili koldovstvo?', *Znanie-Sila* 12: 26–33.

Rozova, T. (1988) 'Formirovanie sotsial'noi otvetstvennosti molodezhi v protsesse preemstvennosti sotsialisticheskikh pokolenii', Dissertation for degree of Kandidat Nauk, Odessa.

Rubanova, N. (1987) 'Nekotorie problemy formirovaniia politicheskoi kul'tury molodezhi', in *Politicheskaia Kul'tura Molodezhi: Sostoianie, Problemy Formirovaniia*, Moskva: VKSh pri TsK VLKSM.

—— (1988) 'Samodeiatel'nie ob"edineniia kak forma realizatsii interesov molodezhi', Unpublished paper, NITs VKSh pri TsK VLKSM.

Rudenko, L. and Osadchii, G. (1988) ' Molodezh' sela i kul'tura', in V. Iarskaia (ed.) *Aktual'nie Voprosy Kul'tury Molodezhi v Svete Reshenii XXVII S"ezda KPSS*, Saratov: Saratovskii Universitet.

Ryleva, S. (1987) 'Ogranichennost' sotsiologo-kul'turologicheskikh interpretatsii molodezhnikh subkul'tur', in I. Kuchmaeva (ed.) *Subkul'turnie Ob"edinenaiia Molodezhi: Kriticheskii Analiz*, Moskva.

'S "metallom" v golose' (1986) *Komsomol'skaia Pravda* 2 November.

'Sad April' (1990) *Molodoi Kommunist* 8 November: 12.

Samofalov, N. (1988) 'Komsomol i politicheskaia kul'tura molodezhi', in R. Ianovskii (ed.) *Chelovek i Nravstvennost' v Usloviiakh Perestroiki*, Minsk: Belarus'.

Samoilova, E. (1990) 'I vse razoshlis' samoopredeliat'sia', *Moskovksii Komsomolets* 24 October: 1.

Sarkitov, N. (1987) 'Ot "khard-roka" k "khevi-metallu": effekt oglupleniia', *Sotsiologicheskie Issledovaniia* 4: 93–4.

Seilerova, B. (1988) 'Vsestoronne razvitaia lichnost'' – vysshii ideal kommunizma', in M. Demin and L. Ganzel (eds) *Lichnost' v Sotsialisticheskom Obshchestve*, Moskva: Mysl'.

Semenov, M. (ed.) (1983) *Krokodilu – 60 Let*, Moskva: Pravda.

Semenov, V. (1990) 'Sotsial'no-istoricheskie aspekty problemy neformal'nikh ob"edinenii molodezhi', in V. Levicheva (ed.) *Neformal'naia Volna*, Moskva: NITs pri VKSh.

Serebriannikov, P. (1967) *Istoriia VLKSM 1929–45*, Moscow: Molodaia Gvardiia.

Serii, Lekhin, Sashka, 'Chernii', Vovchik and Serii (1990) *Molodoi Kommunist* 4 October: 12.

Shabanov, A. (1991) 'Eshche odna federatsiia', *Moskovskii Komsomolets* 27 March: 2.

Shchekochikhin, Iu. (1987a) '*Allo My Vas Slyshim'*, Moskva: Molodaia Gvardiia.

—— (1988a) 'Ekstremal'naia Model'', *Literaturnaia Gazeta* 41: 13.

Shchepanskaia, T. (1991b) 'Zhenshchina, gruppa, simvol (na materialakh molodezhnoi subkul'tury)', *Etnicheskie Stereotipy Muzhskogo i Zhenskogo Povedeniia*, Sankt-Peterburg: Nauka.

Shein, A. (1990) 'Kul'turologicheskie predposylki formirovaniia i razvitiia neformal'nikh dvizhenii', in A. Bystritskii and M. Roshchin (eds) *Molodezhnii Renessans*, Moskva: Nauka,

Sheregi, F. (1989) 'Raspredelitel'nie otnosheniia v zerkale obshchestvennogo mneniia molodezhi', in E. Volodina *et al.* (eds) *Molodezh' – 89: Obshchestvennoe Polozhenie Molodezh' i Voprosy Molodezhnoi Politiki v SSSR*, Moskva: VKSh pri TsK VLKSM.

Shibaeva, M. (1987) 'Molodezhnii dosug kak fakt kul'turnoi zhizni', in I. Kuchmaeva (ed.) *Subkul'turnie Ob"edineniia Molodezhi: Kriticheskii Analiz*, Moskva.

Shishkov, V. (1933) *Fil'ka i Amel'ka*, Paris: Illiustrirovannoi Rossii.

Sibirev, N. (1988) 'Nuzhny li v Komosmole fraktsii?', *Sobesednik* 47: 4–5.

—— (1989a) 'Krutoi perelom', *Sobesednik* 32: 12–13.

—— (1989b) 'I vnov' nadezhdy na aprel'', *Sobesednik* 45: 2.

—— (1989c), 'Vykhod iz VLKSM', *Sobesednik* 48: 1.

Sidorov, V. and Krasner, L. (1990) 'Zdravstvui, plemia molodoe . . . predprinimatelei', *Moskovskii Komsomolets* 31 January: 1.

Smirnov, S. (1985) 'Vystuplenie na plenume MGK VLKSM', *Moskovskii Komsomolets* 25 June: 1–2.

—— (1986) 'Vystuplenie na plenume MGK VLKSM', *Moskovskii Komsomolets* 29 April: 2.

Snegirev, V. (1986) 'Rovesniki, naden'te ordena', *Komsomol'skaia Pravda* 13 August: 1.

Sokolov, V. (1986) 'Vechnii dvigatel', *Moskovskii Komsomolets* 15th August: 2.

Solomkin, A. (1986) 'Na povestke dnia – vnedrenie', *Moskovskii Komsomolets* 13 August: 1.

Solntsev, V. (1988) 'Metallisty, rokery – kto oni?', *Detskaia Literatura* 4: 2–4.

Solov'ev, V. (1987) 'Net zatis'iu', *Komsomol'skaia Pravda* 25 August: 1.

Sotnikov, M. (1990) 'Vystupleniia v preniiakh na XXI S"ezde VLKSM', *Komsomol'skaia Pravda* 18 April: 2.

Strokanov, A. and Zinov'ev, A. (1988) ' "Molodezh' . . . chast' revoliutsii" ', *Pravda* 24 October: 2.

Strynin, A. (1987) 'Gonka za liderom', *Komsomol'skaia Pravda* 27 September: 2.

Sundiev, I. (1987) 'Neformal'nie molodezhnie ob"edineniia: Opyt ekspozitsii', *Sotsiologicheskie Issledovaniia* 5: 56–62.

—— (1989) 'Samodeiatel'nie ob"edineniia molodezhi', *Sotsiologicheskie Issledovaniia* 2: 56–62.

—— (1990) 'Nashestvie marsian? . . .', in S. Iushenkov (ed.) *Neformaly: Sotsial'nie Initsiativy*, Moskva: Moskovskii Rabochii.

Sungorkin, V. (1988) 'Tainy tonnelia veka', *Sobesednik* 23: 12–13.

Svetlova, E. (1986) 'Svet v kontse tonnelia', *Moskovskii Komsomolets* 30 August: 2.

TASS (1988) 'Samostoiatel'no – znachit otvetstvenno', *Komsomol'skaia Pravda* 30 January: 1.

Teletaip TsK VLKSM (1991a) *Komsomol'skaia Pravda* 20 March: 1.

Teletaip TsK VLKSM (1991b) *Komsomol'skaia Pravda* 3 April: 2.

Tepliuk, A. and Chudakov, A. (1988) 'Razvedka politboem', *Komsomol'skaia Pravda* 18 October: 1–2.

Teterin, I. (1988) 'Chrezvychainii plenum', *Komsomol'skaia Pravda* 23 November: 2.

Teterin, I. and Miil', O. (1987) 'Teni na tom beregu', *Komsomol'skaia Pravda*, 6 May: 4 and *Komsomol'skaia Pravda*, 7 May: 4.

Tishchenko, T. (1989) 'Svobodnoe vremia kak faktor povysheniia urovnia politicheskogo soznaniia molodezhi v usloviiakh obnovlennia sotsializma', Dissertation submitted for degree of Kandidat Nauk, L'vov.

Topalov, M. (1988) 'Rol' neformal'nikh molodezhnikh ob"edineniiakh v razvitii sotsial'noi aktivnosti molodezhi', in *Molodezh': Aktual'nie Problemy Sotsial'nogo Razvitiia – Sbornik Nauchnikh Trudov Sovetskikh i Chekhoslovatskikh Sotsiologov*, Moskva: AN SSSR (IS)/Chekh. AN.

Trubin, N. (1990) 'Prestupnost' nesovershennoletnikh i problemy ee preduprezhdeniia', *Sovetskaia Iustitsiia* 10: 2–3.

Tskhvaradze, M. (1990) 'Vystupleniia v preniiakh na XXI S"ezde VLKSM', *Komsomol'skaia Pravda* 18 April: 3.

Tsotsuev, A. (1990) 'Levoi, levoi, levoi . . .', *Komsomol'skaia Pravda* 19 August: 2.

Tsukerman, A. (1990) 'Chto proiskhodit v Kazani?', *Sem'ia i Shkola* 4: 29–31.

Tsybukh, V. (1990) 'Zavtra budet pozdno', *Pravda* 9 April: 2.

'Ty nuzhen, ty mozhesh" (1986), *Komsomol'skaia Pravda* 4 July: 3.

Ul'ianov, V. (1990) 'Komu nuzhen razvod?', *Komsomol'skaia Pravda* 12 April: 3.

Utekhin, B. (1987a) 'Na BAMe posle buma', *Komsomol'skaia Pravda* 12 August: 1–2.

—— (1987b) 'Khochu stat' nachal'nikom', *Komsomol'skaia Pravda* 17 October: 1.

—— (1987c) 'Na dal'nikh stantsiiakh', *Komsomol'skaia Pravda* 1 November: 1.

Utrenkov, E. (1987) 'Kto, esli ne my?', *Komsomol'skaia Pravda* 30 October: 4.

'Utverzhdat' novie podkhody v rabote s molodezh'iu' (1988) *Partiinaia Zhizn'* 8: 62–7.

'Vasha Pozitsiia?' (1989) *Komsomol'skaia Pravda* 7 September: 3.

Vasilov, A., Kupriianov, A., and Cherniak, I. (1986) 'Muzyku zakazyvaet raikom', *Sobesednik* 20: 8–10.

Vasil'ev, V., Kulagin, A. and Chuprov, V. (1967) *Vashe Mnenie? Prikladnie Sotsiologicheskie Issledovaniia Po Problemam Molodezhi*, Moskva: Sovetskaia Rossiia.

Virabov, I. (1987) 'Neliubitie liubiteli', *Komsomol'skaia Pravda*, 19 September: 2.

Vishnevskii, B., and Utekhin, B. (1987a) 'A kar'eroi . . . na kur'erskoi', *Komsomol'skaia Pravda* 28 October: 1.

—— (1987b) 'BAM sdelaet vybor', *Komsomol'skaia Pravda*, 24 November: 1–2.

—— (1987c) 'BAM pered vyborom', *Komsomol'skaia Pravda*, 2 September: 1.

Volkov, V. (1989) 'Normy sotsialisticheskoi kul'tury', Dissertation for degree of Kandidat Nauk, Sverdlovsk.

Volkova, L. (1985) 'Dolg', *Moskovskii Komsomolets* 19 November: 2.

Volodina, E. *et al.* (eds) (1989) *Molodezh' – 89: Obshchestvennoe Polozhenie Molodezh' i Voprosy Molodezhnoi Politiki v SSSR*, Moskva: VKSh pri TsK VLKSM.

'Vopros, kotorogo byt' ne dolzhno' (1987) *Moskovskii Komsomolets* 2 April: 1.

Voronkov, P. (1987) 'Da zdravstvuet klub!', *Moskovskii Komsomolets* 25 July: 1.

'Vozhdiu narodov, uchiteliu i drugu sovetskoi molodezhi – tovarishchu Stalinu' (1949) *Izvestiia*, 10 April: 1.

Zakharov, S. (1987) 'Kak borot'sia s "tusovkoi"?', *Molodoi Kommunist* 7: 80–2.

Zalkind, A. (1925) 'Revoliutsionnie normy polovogo povedeniia i molodezh'', in *Revoliutsiia i Molodezh'*, Moskva: Komun-t im. Sverdlova.

Zapesotskii, A. and Fain, A. (1990) *Eta Neponiatnaia Molodezh': Problemy Neformal'nikh Molodezhnikh Ob"edinenii*, Moskva: Profizdat.

Zaripov, R. (1990) 'Uiti ot izdivenchestva', *Moskovskii Komsomolets* 10 April: 1.

Zborovskii, G. (1989) 'Legko li izuchat' molodikh?, *Molodoi Kommunist* 9: 101–4.

Zhitenev, V. (1978) 'Issledovanie problem molodezhi: sostoianie i zadachi', *Sotsiologicheskie Issledovaniia* 2: 12–20.

Zhuganov, A. (1988) 'Demokratiia, samoupravlenie, molodezh'', *Nauchnii Kommunizm* 9: 25–33.

Ziukin, V. (1990a) 'Modeli i "model'ery" ', *Komsomol'skaia Pravda* 10 February: 3.

—— (1990b) 'Doklad Sekretaria TsK VLKSM V. Ziukina', *Komsomol'skaia Pravda* 13 April: 3–4.

# Index